THE
DECLASSIFICATION
ENGINE

THE
DECLASSIFICATION
ENGINE

**WHAT HISTORY REVEALS ABOUT
AMERICA'S TOP SECRETS**

MATTHEW CONNELLY

PANTHEON BOOKS NEW YORK

Pantheon Books and colophon are registered
trademarks of Penguin Random House LLC.

Library of Congress Cataloging-in-Publication Data

Name: Connelly, Matthew James, author.
Title: The declassification engine : what history reveals
about America's top secrets / Matthew Connelly.
Description: First Edition. New York : Pantheon Books, 2023.
Includes bibliographical references and index.
Identifiers: LCCN 2022019182 (print). LCCN 2022019183 (ebook).
ISBN 9781101871577 (hardcover). ISBN 9781101871584 (ebook).
Subjects: LCSH: Transparency in government—United States.
Government information—Access control—United States. Public
administration—United States. United States—Politics and government.
Classification: LCC JK468.S4 C656 2023 (print) | LCC JK468.S4 (ebook) |
DDC 352.3/790973—dc23/eng/20220803
LC record available at https://lccn.loc.gov/2022019182
LC ebook record available at https://lccn.loc.gov/2022019183

www.pantheonbooks.com

Jacket design by Tyler Comrie

Printed in the United States of America
1st Printing

For Sarah,
who sees right through me,
keeps my secrets,
and solves my mysteries.

Contents

There I was, sitting at a massive conference table inside a multibillion-dollar foundation, staring at the wood-paneled walls. I was facing a battery of high-powered attorneys, including the former general counsel to the National Security Agency, and another who had been chief of the Major Crimes Unit at the U.S. Attorney's Office in the Southern District of New York. The foundation was paying each of them about a thousand dollars an hour to determine whether I could be prosecuted under the Espionage Act.

I am a history professor, and my only offense had been to apply for a research grant. I proposed to team up with data scientists at Columbia University to investigate the exponential growth in government secrecy. Earlier that year, in 2013, officials reported that they had classified information more than ninety-five million times over the preceding twelve months, or three times every second. Every time one of these officials decided that some transcript, or e-mail, or PowerPoint presentation was "confidential," "secret," or "top secret," it became subject to elaborate protocols to ensure safe handling. No one without a security clearance would see these records until, decades from now, other government officials decided disclosure no longer endangered national security. The cost of keeping all these secrets was growing year by year, covering everything from retinal scanners to barbed-wire fencing to personnel training programs, and already totaled well over eleven billion dollars. But so, too, were the number and size of data breaches and leaks. At the same time, archivists were overwhelmed by the challenge of managing just the first generation of classified electronic records, dating to the 1970s. Charged with identifying and preserving the subset of public records with enduring historical significance but with no increase in staff or any new technology, they were recommending the deletion of hundreds of thousands of State Department cables, memoranda, and reports, sight unseen. The costs in terms of democratic accountability were incalculable and included the loss of public confidence in political institutions, the proliferation of conspiracy theories, and the increasing difficulty historians would have in reconstructing what our leaders do under the cloak of secrecy.

We wanted to assemble a database of declassified documents and use algorithms to reveal patterns and anomalies in the way bureaucrats decide what information must be kept secret and what information can be released. To what extent were these decisions balanced and rule-based, as official spokesmen have long claimed? Were they consistent with federal laws and executive orders requiring the preservation of public records, and prompt disclosure when possible? Were the exceptions so numerous as to prove the existence of unwritten rules that really served the interests of a "deep state"? Or was the whole system so dysfunctional as to be random and inexplicable, as other critics insist?

We were trying to determine whether we could reverse-engineer these processes, and develop technology that could help identify truly sensitive information. If we assembled millions of documents in databases, and harnessed the power of high-performance computing clusters, it might be possible to train algorithms to look for sensitive records requiring the closest scrutiny and accelerate the release of everything else. The promise was to make the crucial but dysfunctional declassification process more equitable and far more efficient. We had begun to call it a "declassification engine," and if someone did not start building and testing prototypes, the exponential increase in government secrets—more and more of them consisting of data rather than paper documents—might make it impossible for public officials to meet their own legal responsibilities to maximize transparency. Even if we failed to get the government to adopt this kind of technology, testing these tools and techniques would reveal gaps and distortions in the public record, whether from official secrecy or archival destruction.

The lawyers in front of me started to discuss the worst-case scenarios, and the officers of the foundation grew visibly uncomfortable. What if my team was able to reveal the identity of covert operatives? What if we uncovered information that would help someone build a nuclear weapon? If the foundation gave us the money, their lawyers warned that the foundation staff might be prosecuted for aiding and abetting a criminal conspiracy. Why, the most senior program officer asked, should they help us build "a tool that is purpose-built to break the law"?

The only one who did not seem nervous was the former ACLU lawyer whom Columbia had hired to represent us. He had argued cases before the Supreme Court. He had defended people who published schematics of nuclear weapons—and won. He had shown how any successful prosecution required proving that someone had possession of actual classified information. How could the government go after scholars doing research on *declassified* documents?

The ex–government lawyers pointed out that we were not just academics making educated guesses about state secrets—not when we were using high-performance computers and sophisticated algorithms. True, no journalist, no historian, can absorb hundreds of thousands of documents, analyze all of the words in them, instantly recall every one, and rank each according to one or multiple criteria. But scientists and engineers can turn millions of documents into billions of data points and use machine learning—or teaching a computer to teach itself—to detect patterns and make predictions. We agree with these predictions every time we watch a movie Netflix recommends, or buy a book that Amazon suggests. If we threw enough data at the problem of parsing redacted documents—the ones in which government officials have covered up the parts they do not want us to see—couldn't these techniques "recommend" the words most likely to be hiding behind the black boxes, which presumably were hidden for good reason?

We tried to explain that this was beyond the scope of our project. This kind of research is really difficult. It can take years just to aggregate and "clean" messy data, and there is nothing more disorganized than millions of government documents spread across multiple archives and online databases. So, even if we were to stray into classified realms, there would be plenty of time to ponder the results and pull the plug before any super-computer started revealing state secrets. Lawyers, however, are paid to dream up other people's nightmares, and these former prosecutors had succeeded in spooking the foundation's program officers.

Then one of the program officers—the youngest one—asked a simple question, the most important question of all: why did we even want to do this research? He reminded me of one of my seminar students, and for a moment it felt like I was back in the classroom. I realized he had handed me an opportunity to remind everyone why we were there—why, that is, professors do research, why foundations try to help them, and why we need a government that protects all of us from people who would take away this kind of freedom—the freedom to seek out the truth, wherever it takes us.

We were—and are—trying to better understand state secrecy because it is a matter of enormous and growing public importance. A whole series of intensely polarizing incidents have made the American people ever more skeptical of whether they can trust government officials—from WikiLeaks and Iraq war crimes to Edward Snowden's revelation of NSA "exploits," from Hillary Clinton's private e-mail server to the FBI's surveillance of the Trump campaign and search for classified documents at Mar-a-Lago. Suspicion that a secretive "deep state" is unaccountable even to presidential power fuels conspiracy theories that are sapping the strength of our democracy.

Now, with computational methods, we might not only help to restore confidence that citizens can hold government officials accountable for past actions, but also learn from those actions so the government could make better decisions in the first place. We could start doing advanced research to better inform public policy on a whole range of vital topics, whether international trade, early warning of wars and revolutions, or the spread of weapons of mass destruction. For decades, scholars have struggled to piece together scraps of archival evidence in order to probe the inner workings of what we call "the official mind." Now, with data science and enormous collections of declassified documents, we can carry out the functional equivalent of CT scans and magnetic resonance imaging to examine the body politic. Should the risks to national security of forgoing these insights, and forgetting the lessons of the past, not also weigh in the balance?

Even in terms of the more narrow concern about information security, the government's current policies and practices are increasingly ineffective. China has exfiltrated tens of millions of records revealing personal information about people who worked for the U.S. government, and Russia has infiltrated hundreds of government and corporate networks. A whole series of government committees and commissions have identified the same fundamental problem: officials have not clearly and consistently specified what information actually requires safekeeping, making it impossible to prioritize what is truly sensitive. They will painstakingly study forty-year-old military-service records page by page because of the infinitesimal risk that a nuclear-bomb design might slip through. Meanwhile, sniper manuals and recipe books for high explosives—documents that could easily kill people—are accidentally released and left on the open shelves of the National Archives.

Unless someone is allowed to systematically analyze what kind of information is classified, and why, we cannot begin to develop practical techniques required for a more rational, risk-management approach to releasing nonsensitive records. Without such techniques, the CIA was telling us that the whole system for declassification would shut down. It was simply impossible to review and redact billions of classified e-mails, text messages, and PowerPoint presentations manually. If instead these records were withheld indefinitely, or destroyed, it would be impossible to reconstruct what officials did under the cloak of secrecy. And if, at the end of the day, our government is not even accountable in the court of history, it truly is accountable to no one.

I looked around the room, and it seemed that some of the tension had lifted. My main collaborator, David Madigan, was chair of Columbia's statistics department, and would shortly be named dean of the Faculty of Arts and Sciences. He has a fine Irish wit, and the two of us had some fun with the idea that we might run amok. If we did uncover anything we thought posed a potential risk to national security, we assured them we could first show it to people with the knowledge and the responsibility to act, much as newspaper editors have done for decades. Even the ex–NSA lawyer admitted we had a very strong defense against any overreaching prosecutor: the First Amendment to the U.S. Constitution. As Chief Justice Earl Warren wrote in 1957, "Scholarship cannot flourish in an atmosphere of suspicion and distrust. Teachers and students must always remain free to inquire, to study and to evaluate, to gain new maturity and understanding; otherwise our civilization will stagnate and die."

In the end, there were handshakes all around, and the most senior program officer took me aside to discuss next steps. He confided that the foundation president himself had said he did not understand why the project had been subject to this kind of scrutiny. He would support the grant and send it to their board of trustees, though with some conditions to be specified later. Soon after, the board gave its approval, subject to final legal review. In the meantime, we received provisional approval for a much bigger grant from the MacArthur Foundation. It seemed we were on our way.

We were astonished when, three months later, the foundation told us what conditions they planned to impose through an intellectual-property agreement: all the members of our team would have to sign nondisclosure agreements that would bar us from discussing the work with anyone else. Even student volunteers could not talk about the project with their professors. A steering committee of national-security experts would first have to approve any such communication. And although the grant was only for one year, this confidentiality agreement would apply forever. A project tackling the problem of excessive secrecy would itself be the subject of extraordinary secrecy.

We were told that all the conditions were nonnegotiable. The program officer seemed very blunt about his aim: "The point in this case is to control the use of the resource that we are funding and to put mechanisms in place to do so." It would be a poison pill, because no one would want to participate in the project if they could never even talk about it. But if we lost this funding we might lose everything. How could we expect the MacArthur Foundation to move ahead when another foundation, with more time to consider the risks, had already backed out? With no funds to hire engineers or software developers, our "declassification engine" would be shut down before it even started.

But in that moment I understood better than ever before why it was essential that we persevere. I could now see with my own eyes that official secrecy had grown completely out of control. It has created fear far outside the confines of government offices, defense contractors, and newsrooms. Even in the halls of academia, and inside elite foundations, people have come to fear prosecution just for doing research on state secrecy. I have seen this fear—seen, for instance, an eminent computer scientist break down in tears, explaining that colleagues had warned him to withdraw immediately from the project or risk deportation. I've seen graduate students told by their professors that they dare not present this research in public. My own students regularly joke—nervously—about whether we might all be under surveillance. Many data scientists depend on contracts from the Pentagon and the intelligence community, so even the perception of official displeasure can be enough to drive them away from this kind of work.

But in the end, our university stood by us, and the MacArthur Foundation was undeterred. Columbia's president, Lee Bollinger, is a scholar of the First Amendment, and he would go on to make the danger of exponential growth in official secrecy a keynote in his 2014 commencement address. Robert Gallucci, MacArthur's leader at the time, personally approved the project.

As a former diplomat, one who previously led nuclear-weapons negotiations with North Korea, Gallucci was not the kind of person to be intimidated by high-priced lawyers preaching about national security.

With the MacArthur grant, I created History Lab, a team of data scientists and social scientists dedicated to exploring the past in order to discover lessons for the present and the future. I still get warnings from people with security clearances that some government officials think I could be prosecuted under the Espionage Act. There are risks in data-mining declassified documents, and this book will take some risks in revealing what is possible. But the technology for surveilling government secrecy, machine learning, is technology the government itself began to develop decades ago in order to surveil *us*. It starts with aggregating all the data we can gather, much as the NSA assembles communications and personal information in databases. When we can't access the content of those communications, such as when they are still classified, we analyze the metadata, just as the data scientists do at Fort Meade. And, like them, we use all the tools in our toolbox to sift and sort through the information to generate insights. It ranges from traffic analysis, which can reveal "bursts" of communications corresponding to unusual events, to anomaly detection, which uncovers documents that have been misclassified or inconsistently redacted, to predictive analytics, which can identify what kind of information government reviewers seemed particularly intent on concealing. Rather than a simple machine, *the declassification engine* described in this book is best understood as a platform that combines big data, high-performance computing, and sophisticated algorithms to reveal what the government did not want us to know, and why they did not want us to know it.

Obviously, we don't have the resources of the NSA. But over the last eight years, we have built the world's largest database of declassified documents. The data scientists I have been privileged to work with in academia are at least as good as those working for the government. And though university-based, high-performance computing clusters are not as fast as those employed by the government, they are much more powerful than anything available to the NSA when it was creating these secrets decades ago.

It may still seem like a story of David versus Goliath. But the goal is not to vanquish government secrecy. It is to demonstrate how we can and must take a more balanced approach to protecting truly sensitive information. We need to distinguish the kind of information that really does require safeguarding from the information that citizens urgently need in order to hold their leaders to account. This is the only way to uphold *both* national security *and* democratic accountability. There is nothing more dangerous—both to itself, and to others—than a nuclear-armed superpower that is not even answerable to its own people.

As citizens, we have been on the losing end of struggles over state secrecy for far too long. We have to use every legal means at our disposal to reclaim our right to know what leaders do in our name. That does not necessarily mean we need to know the details of particular secrets, or specific things the government still has good reason to keep classified. It means we need to know the *kinds* of things officials guard most closely. Most important, we need to understand *why* they insisted on keeping those secrets for so long.

As I write this, the government can no longer even estimate how many secrets it creates each year, or how much it is spending to try to protect them all. The National Archives cannot cope with the impossibly large task of reviewing all the government's classified records, and as of 2023 will not even accept any more paper documents, in part because it has no place to put them. Meanwhile, potentially dangerous information is continuing to slip out. And historically vital information is being destroyed, or buried under a mountain of useless data, making it impossible for future historians to render judgment, or for future generations to learn what they have lost.

To save America's old and honorable tradition of open government—and to save history itself—we must arm ourselves with the power that knowledge gives, including the power of artificial intelligence. If we do, we can turn the weapons of state surveillance into tools to rebuild our republic.

THE
DECLASSIFICATION
ENGINE

THE RADICAL TRANSPARENCY OF THE AMERICAN REPUBLIC

A REINTRODUCTION

In July 1945, as the Second World War was coming to a close, the director of the U.S. Office of Scientific Research and Development, Vannevar Bush, published an article in *The Atlantic Monthly* that became an overnight sensation. "As We May Think" described how a "growing mountain of research" was making it difficult for even the most brilliant scientists to keep up with the rapid accumulation of ideas and information. At the same time, armies of typists and clerks were filling government offices and warehouses with unprecedented amounts of official records. Bush warned that they were already "bogged down," and vital information would "become lost in the mass of the inconsequential."

Bush's proposed solution was something he called the "Memex," for memory extender. "Consider a future device for individual use . . . a device in which an individual stores all his books, records, and communications, and which is mechanized so that it may be consulted with exceeding speed and flexibility." Users would share their data with one another, and program machines to analyze the accumulating information, revealing unexpected connections. This would add up to something more than the sum total of human intelligence: it would become a kind of artificial intelligence.

Without actually using the words, or knowing quite how all this would work, Bush was envisioning networked personal computers, machine-learning algorithms, and what would come to be known as the information revolution. The words he *did* use to describe someone using the Memex, "trail blazer," conveyed the idea that information technology would empower individuals. When he presented a use case, Bush pictured a scholar studying the history of technology, in the pure pursuit of knowledge, and freely sharing his discoveries. He was certain many others would find new uses for the Memex, whether in science, law, or medicine. "There will always be plenty of things to compute in the detailed affairs of millions of people doing complicated things."

"As We May Think" has been celebrated as a remarkable example of future forecasting. But it is also a reflection of U.S. history up to this point, the end of World War II, the moment of America's greatest triumph. A free people had shown they could defeat militaristic dictatorships even in a military competition. Whereas the Axis powers allowed dubious theories of race hygiene to dictate disastrous policies, America's victory had been won because all segments of society shared their ideas, industry, and inventions. In a public report to President Truman published the same month, Bush proposed building on these achievements by broadening opportunities for all citizens to contribute. He argued for tens of thousands of need-based scholarships to recruit talented men and women to science and engineering. He also called for greatly reducing the secrecy that had temporarily surrounded wartime research: "A broad dissemination of scientific information upon which further advances can readily be made furnishes a sounder foundation for our national security than a policy of restriction which would impede our own progress."

Long-standing American custom allowed little place in peacetime for secretive agencies, or for large standing armies and armaments industries. In keeping with this tradition, Truman soon abolished America's only centralized intelligence agency, the Office of Strategic Services. At the same time, the military began a headlong demobilization, going from 12 million servicemen to 1.5 million. Truman also abolished the office responsible for keeping classified information out of the media. Before he cleared out his desk, the government's director of wartime censorship, Byron Price, produced a report summarizing his experience. Price worried that, if he did not record the lessons learned about how to keep government secrets, they would soon be forgotten, as had occurred after previous conflicts. Bush himself, however, seemed to suggest in his report to Truman that giving free rein to research and affording citizens maximum access to information had been the real secret of America's success.

But there was another side to Vannevar Bush. Capital insiders knew him as an obsessive and tough-minded manager of classified military research. He oversaw the work of tens of thousands of engineers and scientists designing radar, proximity fuses, and the atomic bomb. His own work on programmable computers focused not on "memory extenders" for scholars, but on machines that could decipher intercepted military and diplomatic communications and match fingerprints for the FBI. Bush's article helped persuade the public to support continued government funding for science. But, according to his vision, the new National Science Foundation would not just support civilian research. It would also sponsor science the Pentagon could exploit to build advanced weaponry.

By 1948, a full reversal was under way, as the Truman administration engaged in a concerted effort to reimpose wartime secrecy. Bush told the American Society of Newspaper Editors that if they did not go along, they would "put into a potential enemy's hands information which will help him to kill our young men, devastate our cities, and overthrow our nation." This information was not limited to weapons systems and intelligence techniques: "We have constantly to bear in mind that the art of the spy is to put a half-dozen seemingly innocent facts together and from them to draw conclusions which may be fatal to our interests." Bush agreed editors had freedom to publish, but he said it was no less important that they exercise their "freedom not to publish."

Bush's bait-and-switch seems to have worked. Nowadays, much of the government-funded scientific research for which Bush advocated goes to the military—more than half, according to the most recent figures. The eighty-one billion dollars spent for military research and development is more than ten times the entire budget of the National Science Foundation. Bush's advocacy for expansive secrecy also became reality. More money goes to intelligence agencies than to all scientific research together—although the actual amount is classified. Scientists and engineers build supercomputers to decrypt communications and develop sensors to gather data, from the depths of the oceans to outer space. At the same time, they develop techniques to aggregate and analyze all this information for domestic surveillance and international espionage, much of it taken from the "memory extenders" we keep on our desks or carry in our pockets.

Ever since Bush prophesied the information revolution, our government has been accumulating more and more secret information. Even after Barack Obama promised the most transparent administration in history, he presided over exponential growth in classified information. During his term, more people who shared what they knew with journalists were prosecuted under the Espionage Act than in all previous administrations combined.

It is a mistake to imagine that some "deep state" has been doing all this in defiance of our elected leaders. This book will show how the desire to work in the shadows and evade accountability goes all the way to the top. Seeking sovereign power, or the kind of power that is not subject to the will of another, presidents above all have resisted any congressional oversight or judicial review in deciding what is secret and what can be revealed. They have been remarkably successful for more than eighty years, defying even the court of history, since few historians have even tried to explain this explosion of secrecy.

The result is best described as a dark state, dark because so much of it is not visible to outside observers, and because state secrecy has covered up some of the worst chapters in American history. But by fortifying it against all external challenges, presidents made the dark state impossible to control. Some 1.3 million Americans now have top-secret security clearances, almost double the number of people who live in the District of Columbia. But rather than making state secrets more secure, Washington has been shattered by security breaches and inundated with leaks.

In recent years, even the most senior government officials, from Hillary Clinton to James Comey to Jared Kushner, have avoided using government systems designed to keep communications secure and preserve them as public records. In Clinton's case, she was hauled before Congress and ordered to surrender every surviving e-mail—even those she had insisted were personal—under threat of prosecution. But, as we shall see, many others have hidden or destroyed public records with no consequences whatsoever. Donald Trump railed against the deep state and all its secrets, but also made a habit of tearing up presidential papers into tiny little pieces—and then fired the records managers who tried to piece them together.

Politicians like to say that they will let future historians judge. But what can future historians possibly say about leaders who will not even keep a record of what they did in our name? What good are "memory extenders" if our collective memories are being wiped clean? These manifold problems pose a manifest threat to both democracy and national security, which must be the first and main focus of this book. But over the longer run, the stakes include the future of history itself. Bush was not wrong to think that information technology would revolutionize the research scholars can do, and we will see how data-mining millions of documents yields insights that can serve humankind. Still, if even the U.S. government cannot preserve and protect what it has identified as the most sensitive and important information of all, this portends a more general crisis in how humanity preserves a record of its past.

One thing is clear: Whether under Democratic or Republican administrations, the accumulation of secret information—and the leaking, loss, or destruction of so much of this information—is becoming so relentless and so massive that what was once hidden is starting to come into view, even if we need algorithms and computer vision to see it. What we can now see is that secrecy was never just about national security. It served the interests of people who wanted to avoid democratic accountability. But the dark state always contained the seeds of its own destruction. At long last, its insular and uncontrollable nature is proving impossible to sustain. While the dark state may stagger on, its intellectual decline is now obvious, and only an outside intervention can prevent a collapse that would pose unpredictable dangers for the nation and the world.

This book is a story of rise and fall, starting in World War II and culminating in the Global War on Terror. But to see how the future might be different, and *must* be different, we first have to know how we got here. As implausible as it may now seem, America initially rose in power and reputation through radical transparency, drawing energy from an information revolution and a boundless appetite for new knowledge.

We don't usually see America this way, because for too long agencies expert in deception, like the CIA and the NSA, have succeeded in making us think that secrecy and spying have always been an honorable part of the American political tradition. In their official histories, they claim to be carrying on the work of the Founders. True, George Washington did indeed run an extremely effective espionage network during the Revolutionary War. Benjamin Franklin masterfully outmaneuvered British diplomats in Paris by disseminating incendiary propaganda. After an awkward start under the Articles of Confederation, our government as it now exists was literally conceived in secrecy. The Constitutional Convention agreed on the first day to keep its proceedings confidential, and it met in a chamber guarded by sentries and did not record its debates. Afterward, Washington's former chief of counterintelligence, John Jay, joined with Alexander Hamilton in arguing—anonymously—that the new president would sometimes need to act with "secrecy and despatch."

But the actual gestation and birth of the United States required very public debate during thirteen different state conventions. The Constitution they ratified contains not a single word that authorizes the president to keep secrets. Only Congress is accorded that power. And Congress itself had traditionally been quite open in its deliberations, publishing its own proceedings starting in 1777. Thomas Jefferson called its refusal to conceal setbacks and defeats during the Revolution "an example to the world." So, too, was the new government's determination to aggregate, preserve, and share information. Even in 1778, just weeks after the British ended their occupation of Philadelphia, and Washington's army re-emerged from Valley Forge, the Continental Congress appropriated precious funds to collect state papers. As the country's first official historian argued in making this proposal, preserving a record would demonstrate that members of Congress were both "friends of science" and "guardians of our liberties." The resulting history could show their "advances from persecution to comparative liberty, and from thence to independent empire."

After the new Constitution came into effect, the Founders also created precedents so Congress could keep presidents accountable. In 1791, during Washington's first administration, the Western Indian Confederacy annihilated virtually the entire American field army in Ohio at the Battle of the Wabash. The new Congress launched an investigation—its first ever. After consulting his Cabinet, the president agreed to produce copies of every document they asked for. Washington understood the risk. He had learned from personal experience that "intelligence becomes interesting" when seemingly unimportant facts were connected and put into context. But he realized that the new republic would face even greater dangers if it kept everything secret and failed to learn from its mistakes.

And it did indeed make mistakes, for example, concerning citizens' right to be free of state surveillance. In 1798, President John Adams and a Federalist-dominated Congress joined in spying on citizens for the first time with the Alien and Sedition Acts. But the Federalists were so badly punished at the polls that they never recovered. These former revolutionaries therefore learned, the hard way, not to try institutionalizing secrecy and surveillance. They developed a policy of protecting only the most sensitive information, such as espionage and ongoing diplomatic negotiations.

Total Number of Lines Encoded in Communications
from U.S. Legations in Europe to Washington

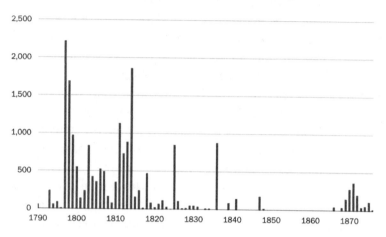

American diplomats abroad stopped encoding their communications,
even though it was common knowledge that European powers routinely
intercepted and read diplomatic dispatches to gather intelligence about
their rivals.

In fact, in the decades that followed, even diplomats stopped
shielding their work from external scrutiny. They did not change
their increasingly vulnerable codes and encrypted fewer and
fewer communications. In his spare time, Jefferson created a
device that would have made it all but impossible for foreign
powers to intercept and decipher these messages. But the government did not adopt his invention. Instead, the United States
began to conduct an ever-more-radical experiment in open
government.

After the War of 1812, when there was no longer any serious
risk of foreign invasion, the federal government all but stopped
creating new secrets. True, some presidents covertly dispatched
spies and explorers. But, unlike European states, the U.S. government had no foreign-intelligence or domestic-security
agencies, and no "black chamber" to intercept and decrypt the
communications of foreign diplomats or political subversives.
Since the original Postal Service Act of 1792, stealing mail was a
crime punishable by death.

Similarly, although there were proposals to build military
capacity—mobilization in 1812 had been a fiasco—proponents

could not overcome popular opposition to any large standing army in peacetime. The U.S. military of the early nineteenth century was an order of magnitude smaller than its European counterparts. Wars led to rapid buildups, but Congress cut the army and navy down again as soon as peace returned. To be sure, the U.S. Army always loomed large in the borderlands, and its ruthlessness and superior firepower enabled it to terrorize Indian men, women, and children. But even in the American West, it spent much of its time on projects to improve communications, such as through the construction of roads, rails, and canals.

It was not just that the government had less and less secrecy, few soldiers, and virtually no spies. The American people themselves demanded the knowledge they needed to keep their government small and open to inspection. James Madison offered a famous argument for this founding principle in 1822: "A popular Government, without popular information, or the means of acquiring it, is but a Prologue to a Farce or a Tragedy; or, perhaps both. Knowledge will forever govern ignorance: And a people who mean to be their own Governors, must arm themselves with the power which knowledge gives."

The public demand for knowledge also extended to education and a free press, which were already powerful American traditions. Literacy rates were higher than almost anywhere in Europe. The early republic also fostered a culture of information sharing by delivering newspapers at long distances at little cost through an ever-expanding network of post offices, where they were often displayed for public consumption. American post offices were far more numerous per capita than in the U.K. or France. "Where the press is free, and every man able to read," Jefferson concluded, "all is safe."

Of course, many of these men—and they were all men— who preached about freedom and self-government lived off the enslaved labor of Black families. They feared what might happen if *every* person were able to connect and share information with everyone else. These liberties were all the more prized because, at this point, only a privileged minority were able to exercise them fully. Jefferson's postmaster, Gideon Granger, spelled out the limits of his vision in a secret 1802 message to a Georgia senator warning against allowing Black men to become post riders:

By travelling from day to day, and hourly mixing with people, they must, they will acquire information. They will learn that a man's rights do not depend on his color. They will, in time, become teachers to their brethren. They become acquainted with each other on the line. Whenever the body, or a portion of them, wish to act, they are an organized corps, circulating our intelligence *openly*, their own privately.

Their travelling creates no suspicion; excites no alarm. One able man among them, perceiving the value of this machine, might lay a plan which would be communicated by your post riders from town to town, and produce a general and united operation against you.

Jefferson therefore signed legislation that made certain that only white men could operate this information-circulating "machine." Black Americans also found their own mail was sometimes opened or destroyed, even though mail-tampering was a federal crime. Southern states went even further, making it illegal for Black people to learn to read or write. Many schools excluded women, and women also risked harassment whenever they entered a post office.

But in the nineteenth century, literacy among women rose even more rapidly than among men, and Black people risked whipping, or their lives, to teach themselves in secret. Abolitionists still found ways to use the postal service to publicize their cause, such as by mass mailings of antislavery publications to Southern states. One enslaved man, Henry "Box" Brown, even managed to have himself delivered by parcel post from Virginia to Philadelphia, and to freedom. Those denied the right to participate in their own government, more than anyone, understood why they had to "arm themselves with the power which knowledge gives."

When American ideals like open access to information and the freedom to communicate without state surveillance were violated, such as when a Charleston mob broke into a post office to prevent the delivery of antislavery newspapers, it was a national story that underscored the depth of division engendered by slavery. But, more typically, these liberties elicited support from all parties, albeit for different reasons. Federalists saw supporting the press as extending governmental authority, for instance, while National Republicans viewed subsidizing public information as a check on governmental power. Both proved to be true. Writing just before the original Post Office Act was passed in 1792, the English political theorist Jeremy Bentham observed that leaders who told citizens what they were doing, and why, could do more, because obtaining the consent of the governed would make them ever more powerful.

When Andrew Jackson became president in 1828, in the first election in which nearly all white males—and not just property owners—were able to vote, he took it as a mandate to drive Native American tribes like the Choctaw and the Cherokee out of rich Southern farming land. Under the Indian Removal Act, they could choose to stay, become citizens, and receive title to a plot of land, but only on condition that a federal agent record their names in an official register book.

The Choctaws well understood the stakes, and used their own time-honored method of creating a record, carefully bundling long and short sticks representing the number of adults and children, family by family. But when they presented themselves before the federal agent, he refused to record their names, and threw the sticks aside. He hurled the register book about the office until pages fell out, and left it outside to absorb rain and sleet. It was lost and never seen again. Perhaps no one was more cognizant of the coercive power of a government that could count on popular support, and the importance of preserving records to make that government accountable, than those people who had been entirely excluded from the rights of citizenship.

Not satisfied, Jackson also sought the forcible expulsion of the entire Cherokee nation. This was in violation of a whole series of treaties, which their duly elected leaders had carefully preserved and presented as evidence. To raise awareness and rally support, the Cherokee Council established the country's first Native American newspaper, the *Cherokee Phoenix*. Soon enough, its publisher, Samuel Worcester, became a target for expulsion, but he argued his case all the way to the Supreme Court. "Our cause is your own," Principal Chief John Ross declared. "It is the cause of liberty and justice."

But Jackson just ignored the Supreme Court ruling. Like many of his countrymen, he preferred that the Choctaw and the Cherokee disappear, either dying off or being completely assimilated through the forced re-education of their children. But they were intent on preserving records and telling their own story. Cherokee women, in particular, proved so determined that they inspired white women to join their cause in the first national activist campaign spearheaded by women.

Archived records have been vital in understanding this history and revealing what powerful motives lay behind the expulsion of Native Americans—not least the profit motive. Earlier, Jackson had personally traded on inside information to enrich himself in a real-estate bubble resulting from the seizure of their lands. The men who ran the early republic could be secretive about their own property interests, and engage in shady deals. For instance, we can now see how, all the way back in 1792, Hamilton, along with the rest of Washington's Cabinet, wanted to make sure that the congressional investigation of the Battle of the Wabash would not probe "secrets of a very mischievous nature"—i.e., whether "persons in the government had been dabbling in stocks, banks &c"—secrets that historians would find essential to explain their policies.

But Jackson knew that he had at least to pay lip service to the idea that elected leaders should have nothing to hide. In 1836, his private secretary warned him that one of his Black servants, who had been targeted by a white mob, posed a security risk. He witnessed Cabinet meetings, could read and write, and might share what he knew with the president's political enemies. Jackson professed not to care:

> They are welcome, sir, said he, to anything they can get out of my papers. They will find there, among other things, false grammar and bad spelling; but they are welcome to it all, grammar and spelling included. Let them make the most of it. Our government, sir, is founded upon the intelligence of the people; it has no other basis. . . .

In fact, most voters accepted at least temporary secrecy provided they, too, could profit. When he became president, Jefferson had worried about overstepping his authority by engaging in secret negotiations for the Louisiana Purchase. But he was rewarded at the polls, since it effectively doubled the country's real estate. Cities like New York and Boston had been hotbeds of protest against Jackson's policy of exchanging the land he confiscated from the Choctaw and the Cherokee for some of the new territory beyond the Mississippi. But once the process was under way, northern bankers were eager to profit from financing the expansion of slave plantations. James K. Polk had no qualms when he engaged in secret machinations to annex Texas and maneuver Mexico into war. He claimed that what was good for America was good for the world, "opening to them new and ever-increasing markets for their products."

This, too, was very much a part of the American tradition. Political accountability meant that presidents had to prove profitability. It constituted transparency of a different kind: what some might call naked greed, scarcely concealed by the bunkum of "Manifest Destiny."

Yet Americans had good reason to believe that there was a public ledger that could be opened for inspection to reveal all these dealings. Accountability could come in many forms, including congressional investigations, elections, popular uprisings, or from history, the ultimate court of appeals. Congress delivered a steady stream of free publications to constituents, such as hundreds of thousands of pages of state papers, including the formerly secret papers of the Revolution and the early republic. They were described as "monuments of the past, beacons to the future." The decennial census was an enormous source of free public information. By 1850, it added up to over 1,150 pages of tables. Congress gave away a hundred thousand copies of the 160-page statistical abstract.

The importance of public documents seemed so great that in 1853 it became a felony for any official to destroy even a single federal record. Every department had to preserve its papers forever. This might seem like mindless hoarding, but it was extremely farsighted, and not just for purposes of keeping public officials accountable. Americans were relentlessly accumulating and storing data, because data could become valuable in ways that contemporaries might not anticipate. And they did mean *data*, even when it came to cultural production, and especially when it was produced by communities that contemporaries dismissed as having no history and no future. As the editors of the *Repository*, one of the many journals Black Americans founded in this period, declared, their goal was both to "develop the talents of our young people" and to "furnish data for future comparisons." In 1877, a presidential commission agreed. It reaffirmed that all government records had to be preserved, "however unimportant they may appear," because they "may be of value at some future time, either in a historical, biographical or pecuniary way, to the citizen, or the nation."

Preserving all records would, however, make it harder to identify and protect the most important papers, a problem that would grow in time. In 1882, a young scholar would be astonished to discover the original copy of the Constitution itself in a wholly unexpected place. It was folded up and forgotten in a small tin box at the bottom of a closet at the State Department.

America's national tradition, however, was not hiding, or spying, or cover-ups. It was not inclusive or equitable, but it *was* radically transparent, accumulating, aggregating, and giving away vast amounts of information. Once there was no longer any external threat to the nation, the United States abandoned espionage, stopped encrypting communications, and outlawed mail tampering. Instead of a domestic-intelligence agency, it had a decennial census. Instead of a powerful standing army, it had the best postal service in the world, which would soon be linked with an unrivaled network of railways and telegraph lines. And though Americans had a deep and abiding passion for history, which would be evidenced by a growing number of women-led volunteer organizations dedicated to building monuments and museums, they preferred their democratic accountability in real time. There was ultimately only one guarantee of both individual liberty and national security, and it came directly from the people—from their desire for knowledge, their insistence on their right to know, and their determination to punish anyone who tried to spy on them or limit their freedoms.

Perhaps the best example was when the new country was put to the ultimate test, a civil war to determine whether all men could be their own governors regardless of race. The passage of the Fugitive Slave Act in 1850, under which federally appointed commissioners hunted down Black people, had already started a "war before the war." Even Jefferson Davis worried that it gave the government too much power. It forced Northerners to witness the full brutality of slavery first-hand and face their own complicity.

When Abraham Lincoln was elected after he promised to stop the further expansion of slavery, and Southern states seceded, the new president decided that more people both at home and overseas would support the Union if he was open in his dealings with other countries. One hundred and fifty years before WikiLeaks, the State Department began to publish volumes of normally secret letters sent and received through embassies abroad just months after they were written. When the minister to England, Charles Francis Adams, complained that it would upset other governments, Secretary of State William Seward reminded this son and grandson of presidents of the same founding principle: they could not expect support from Congress or the people if they did not keep them informed and create a record for history.

To be sure, Lincoln did limit many domestic freedoms during wartime, in part by suspending *habeas corpus* and using military tribunals to protect sensitive information. But Congress directed the government to begin compiling a complete historical record of wartime decision making even while the war still raged. It was published starting fifteen years later, and eventually totaled hundreds of thousands of pages. The published record enabled scholars to debate Lincoln's actions in the broader context of this existential struggle—a struggle that ultimately established birthright citizenship, equal protection under the law, and the right to vote regardless of race. Moreover, the Union's improvised security apparatus was quickly dismantled after the war, in keeping with the national tradition. The withdrawal of federal troops from the defeated Confederate states was so swift, alas, that most Black Southerners found it impossible to exercise these hard-won rights.

Other governments were building up their military capacity. By the 1870s, it was not just Sweden, Italy, and Japan that all had more men in arms. The U.S. Army was also outgunned by Portugal, Belgium, and the Netherlands. Several European states passed laws to protect official secrets, which could be used to imprison anyone—including journalists—who did not have permission to possess classified information. They also built national archives to preserve their most important secrets and destroyed everything else. And they intensified domestic surveillance so as to identify and track political subversives worldwide. With no such capacity, the United States allowed foreign agents to track fugitives on American soil.

In this period, the U.S. government was so out of step with other countries that it focused more on contraception than counterterrorism. In 1873, Congress authorized the inspection of the mail to intercept "obscene" materials—especially anything that might help women avoid childbirth. But five years later, the Supreme Court affirmed that "No law of Congress can place in the hands of officials connected with the postal service any authority to invade the secrecy of letters." Religious zealots in the postal service continued their crusade against birth control by entrapping victims. But juries often refused to convict them, and many others were let go with light sentences. All the while, fertility rates steadily fell. These together were signs of a growing sentiment that all people, including women, should be free from government surveillance.

Absent any anxiety about a foreign security threat, the closest American equivalent to a permanent secret police was the Secret Service. But it was part of the Treasury Department, and in the nineteenth century focused almost exclusively on catching counterfeiters and smugglers. The United States did not create its first permanent intelligence agency until 1881, the Office of Naval Intelligence. But along with their army counterparts—and unlike European agent runners and code breakers—American navy officers mainly collected published information from overseas and catalogued it in a library.

As for diplomacy, European powers were represented by a small and self-replicating elite—all the better to keep their negotiations secret. The nineteenth century American diplomatic service, on the other hand, was wide open to drunks, criminals, and incompetents—almost any men, it seemed, as long as they were white and politically connected. One frustrated office-seeker even shot President James Garfield in the back, disappointed at not having been appointed consul in Paris. For months thereafter, a succession of doctors poked around inside the stricken president's open wound, looking for the bullet. Not only was the U.S. government uniquely transparent in this period; political patronage made it highly permeable.

With the advent of competitive civil-service exams, it became harder to deny opportunities to any candidate qualified to help process the accumulating mass of government files—at least until the Wilson administration made photographs mandatory in job applications. Women filled many of the new clerical positions, and by 1893 constituted nearly half of executive-branch employees in Washington.

Compared with those of other countries, the U.S. government was still tiny. Just twenty-five thousand people worked in the federal departments in Washington at the turn of the century. Relative to the size of their economies, European governments were three to seven times larger. But despite its comparatively small state apparatus, America had grown to become a world power, and this because of its ideas, industry, infrastructure, and labor—both visible and invisible—which together produced more wealth than the next four largest economies combined. With the important exception of immigration restrictions—which began at the federal level with the Chinese Exclusion Act of 1882—Americans were wide open to the world. They were also quite open about their manifest desire to dominate large parts of the Western Hemisphere, and were already casting eyes on markets across the Pacific. But their government still had virtually no domestic or foreign intelligence apparatus, or any system for classifying secrets, or any law to punish those who divulged sensitive government information. The exception that proved the rule was the U.S. census: enumerators had to swear an oath of confidentiality to protect the information provided by citizens, and could be jailed if they broke it.

All of that changed when, in the midst of World War I, U.S. officials faced a campaign of sabotage, as a network of German spies tried to stop American manufacturers from supplying munitions to the Allies. When he had campaigned for the presidency in 1912, Woodrow Wilson exemplified a typically American faith in transparency. He actually argued, "There ought to be no place where anything can be done that everybody does not know about." But in 1916, as German saboteurs began to set fires and plant bombs, the United States organized not one but several domestic-security agencies, vastly expanded military intelligence, and borrowed the British system for classifying the information they gathered. The 1917 Espionage Act outlawed not only the disclosure of any of these secrets to foreign governments, but also "false statements" that might cause insubordination. The Post Office rifled through private mail, the Census Bureau shared personal information with draft boards, and the Justice Department's new Bureau of Investigation rounded up thousands for alleged subversion—continuing prosecutions and deportations even after the war had ended. Tellingly, the targets were not so much actual spies, saboteurs, or armed revolutionaries, but nonconformists, labor organizers, or anyone—especially immigrants—deemed un-American.

But following what was now a time-honored tradition, this system of secrecy and surveillance was rapidly dismantled after the fighting ended. Wilson had to promise a new era of "open covenants of peace, openly arrived at." He failed to follow through at Versailles, but two years later American diplomats defied diplomatic convention by presenting their proposal to scrap dozens of warships to the entire international press corps at the Washington Naval Conference. Even before the war had ended, some judges were already insisting that state censorship violated American ideals. The most important convert was Supreme Court Justice Oliver Wendell Holmes, one of many judges who had previously given the First Amendment little force or effect. Now he rediscovered its revolutionary power and invoked the lessons of history: the passage of time "has upset many fighting faiths," he said, and only a "free trade in ideas" could ensure that the best ideas would eventually prevail.

One such idea was civil rights. Arrested for speaking out against the war, a Black newspaper editor named A. Philip Randolph went on to organize the Brotherhood of Sleeping Car Porters, the first major Black-led labor union. Just as Jefferson's postmaster had feared, this "organized corps," which traveled day and night, were able to share intelligence and extend their network, becoming the vanguard in the fight for full racial equality.

Congress joined the courts in reining in the Espionage Act, and also cut funding for intelligence gathering. One exception was the new Bureau of Investigation and its deputy director, J. Edgar Hoover. He managed to escape blame for the mass roundups, and assumed the top job in 1924 after promising, in what would become a terrible irony, to stick to law enforcement and stop political investigations. In fact, Hoover, a former librarian, held on to an already huge collection of surveillance files and invented a new classification—"Official and Confidential"—to keep them under his personal control. He continued efforts to infiltrate organizations like the ACLU and the NAACP. But Hoover—who did not travel outside the United States even once in his life—failed to develop the Bureau's basic competence in counterespionage, not least because of the agents' notorious lack of diversity. When Roosevelt later tasked Hoover with uncovering the Nazi spy network in Latin America, his agents floundered because they had neither tradecraft nor language skills.

Even code breaking—the one area in which Americans had briefly become competitive during World War I—was all but abandoned. Secretary of State Henry Stimson insisted, "Gentlemen do not read each other's mail," and shuttered the department's Cipher Bureau. Under the Communications Act of 1934, the government was barred from intercepting messages, whether by wire or radio—not even messages from foreign governments to their embassies in Washington. A small code-breaking team continued work for the army, but all of Army Intelligence amounted to just sixty-six men in 1936. The United States showed so little interest in signals intelligence in this period that the top American cryptologist, Herbert Yardley, left the country and sold his expertise to China. Once again, foreign agents found it easy to re-establish networks in New York and Washington.

At this point, most War Department records, even sensitive army counterintelligence files, were moldering in piles in a Washington garage near vats of oil and a gasoline pump. The United States still lacked a national archive with the authority to prioritize and preserve important papers and protect state secrets. Each department was responsible for maintaining its own records, and had to ask Congress for permission to destroy even one ancient receipt. When workers finally began to inventory federal records in the 1930s, they found them scattered across over sixty-five hundred different depositories, more than half showing signs of infestation by insects or vermin.

The U.S. government was a hoarder, filling a Washington garage with secret papers from the War Department.

A new era began when Congress finally accepted the need to join the many other countries that had long-established institutions to organize and maintain government records. It would prove to be a crucial step in the preservation of the most important historical documents, but a turning point also for access to and control over those documents. In 1931, ground was broken for a national archive, and three years later Roosevelt appointed Robert D. W. Connor to be the first archivist of the United States. Some departments and agencies, including the War Department, refused to give Connor control of even their oldest files. Officials did not say they were keeping them to protect national security. At least in principle, the War Department allowed scholars to access them and obtain copies of the documents. But Roosevelt was told that if the new archive opened all their files to anyone who asked to see them, at least some could cause embarrassment. The War Department tried to prove this by sharing with the president a sex worker's affidavit from the Civil War. She had been arrested on suspicion of espionage after consorting with Union officers.

That might have been the end of the story, were it not for the persistence of a historian named Margaret Leech. She had been frustrated in her efforts to research women spies during the Civil War, and wrote a withering critique of the War Department's position. She showed how it had flouted its own rules in denying her meaningful access. But she also insisted on a basic principle: although individual privacy was important, it could not forever take precedence. "We have a right," Leech argued, "to a complete record of our national past."

Leech's publisher sent her letter to Roosevelt, and he was persuaded that, after enough time had elapsed, there remained no good reason to deny scholars access to once-secret files. But under the agreement he brokered, Connor was given discretion in deciding who could see sensitive state papers. He also gained broad powers in deciding what part of the national past would be preserved. Connor won FDR's trust by assuring him that even the most mundane documents from his New York gubernatorial administration should be archived, so that future historians could chronicle every aspect of his life. "When my term is up," the president said while visiting the new archive's handsome research room, "I'm coming here to work."

More typically, Connor had no patience for amateur historians, and consolidated control of the National Archives on behalf of a new class of professionally credentialed scholars. At the same time, he sought to take possession of documents and artifacts deemed to be federal property from preservation and heritage organizations. As we have seen, many such organizations were led by women, and Connor did not think women were capable of being good historians. "They care nothing for facts," he said, "unless they conform to their preconceived prejudices." Women scarcely appeared in Connor's own scholarship on his native North Carolina, excepting those depicted as "fleeing from pursuing brutes" during the years when Black people had been permitted to vote. Of the eighty-nine professional staff members Connor hired by 1937—when the National Archives was still exempt from having to fill positions through competitive civil-service exams—there was only a single woman.

White men with graduate history degrees took all the most prestigious positions at the new archive. None were more important than the examiners whom Connor personally deputized to inspect depositories and decide which records would be preserved. They prioritized papers that chronicled the decision making of the most senior policy makers over case files that recorded the experience of private citizens. While Connor was in charge, no Black person would have any say in such decisions. The only positions they were deemed qualified to fill were as laborers and truck drivers. Under the supervision of the examiners, they loaded and unloaded some 1.4 million cubic feet of records and delivered them to the new building, leaving behind an even larger number of records for eventual destruction. Connor's deputy and successor, Solon Buck, insisted they had to destroy historically insignificant materials to make room for what really mattered: "The chief reason for destroying is to save." In the case of Roosevelt's own papers, this meant building an entirely new state-of-the-art presidential library, in part so a trusted adviser to Roosevelt could control access to his papers. On the other hand, those who went to archives decades later in search of records that would recapture the experience of less powerful people and marginalized communities would find only "silences, erasures, and distortions."

The new national archive was built to look like a Greek temple, with massive bronze doors, and griffins looking down from each end of the pediment known as the "Guardians of the Secrets of the Archives." And at the same time that Roosevelt made Connor high priest—granting access to its inner sanctum, or denying it to the uninitiated—the president began to create the secrets that would fill the new archive.

Roosevelt could see war was coming, and after Hitler's army marched into the Sudetenland he signed a law prohibiting anyone from spying on military installations or equipment, and authorized Hoover's FBI to ramp up surveillance operations. He also let army and navy cryptologists ignore laws prohibiting the interception of telegrams in order to read Axis communications. In 1940, FDR became the first president to issue an executive order that began to define a hierarchy of classified information for the entire federal government, whether "secret," "confidential," or "restricted." This system served both to identify what would be withheld from the public, and to better organize militarily useful information within government depositories. A German Jewish refugee named Ernst Posner joined Solon Buck in co-teaching a course designed for the first archive staff. He told them that the Nazis were winning in no small part because they had a better filing system, and were exploiting archived information to learn from earlier defeats.

When America entered the war, Roosevelt created a new national-intelligence agency, the Office of Strategic Services, and OSS officials—many of them trained historians—cordoned off a part of the National Archives building to sift through its files for research and analysis. State Department historians used records from prior international negotiations to plan postwar agreements. And the War and Navy Departments mined its collections to find maps, photographs, and meteorological records

A convoy of military vehicles transports War Department records from Schuylkill Arsenal down Constitution Avenue for safekeeping at "Fort Archives." The National Archives building was already famous for its steel decks and layers of reinforced concrete, which concealed and protected the secret work of the OSS, the State Department, and the armed services.

for military uses. Men like Connor had taken control of what they deemed to be the most important part of what Leech called "our national past," and treated it as their patrimony. The edifice that contained it would become the cornerstone of the dark state.

State archiving and state secrecy in America thus rose together out of the same ground, during the same historical moment, and for many of the same reasons. By "weeding out useless papers," as Buck put it, archivists helped protect important secrets—above all, the president's secrets.

But at the same time, the National Archives was a very public, steel-and-concrete commitment to preserving a record of what government officials did—no matter how secret—so that these secrets could eventually be revealed, and in that way increase the collective store of knowledge of the American people. Like his predecessors, Roosevelt did not view measures to expand the government's capacity to gather classified information, build secret weapons, and carry out covert operations to be permanent. He expected that, after the war, the military establishment would be too small to occupy the Pentagon—it would move out, so the building could be repurposed to serve as an annex to the National Archives. As FDR declared in 1941, upon founding his library in Hyde Park, New York, building archives connected history with the future, and manifested the nation's enduring faith "in the capacity of its own people so to learn from the past that they can gain in judgment in creating their own future."

Alas, many Americans continued to face a brick wall when they tried to learn about their past or create their future. Those who could be depended on to produce patriotic histories of the "emergence of the United States of America as leader of the forces of light" would be given privileged access to files filled with secrets about wartime diplomacy. On the other hand, even in state and local archives, some white archivists developed a "clearance policy" to screen Black scholars.

"National security" also dictated who could be denied employment, or even denied their freedom. That is how the War Department justified the incarceration of Japanese Americans, and how the State Department denied visas to Jewish refugees who were trying to flee the Nazis. It was the insecurity of native-born white Americans, rather than any real threat, that kept the U.S. military, many war industries, and much of Washington itself segregated by race. When surveyed, only 40 percent of white people agreed Black people should have equal employment opportunities. Just 3 percent of white soldiers favored the idea of serving in the same units as Black soldiers.

Many Americans therefore had to fight on two fronts, and work toward a double victory—over fascism and militarism abroad, and over racism and sexism at home. Black servicemen engaged in sit-ins and fought back when physically assaulted by white counterparts. But even when military bases both in the

United States and abroad were riven with racial tensions—and sometimes pitched battles involving hundreds of servicemen— Roosevelt was indifferent, and did nothing. It was only when A. Philip Randolph and the NAACP leader Walter White warned FDR that they would organize a march on Washington that the president issued an executive order that prohibited denying employment "because of race, creed, color, or national origin." The Navy finally began to integrate units by the end of the war, but not because of any commitment to equality. As Admiral Chester Nimitz, commander of the Pacific Fleet, noted: "If you put all the Negroes together they'll have a chance to share grievances and to plot among themselves, and this will damage discipline and morale. If they are distributed among other members . . . there will be less chance of trouble."

It was not until after the war, in 1948, that Truman finally committed to desegregating the rest of the military. A Japanese American unit had won more medals for bravery than any other in the entire U.S. Army, and Jewish scientists fleeing Nazi and Italian Fascist race laws played a decisive role in giving America the atomic bomb. But Truman only took this stand against racism because Randolph warned that Black men would otherwise refuse to be drafted, and he realized that their votes were crucial to his reelection. In the span of that decade, Benjamin O. Davis became America's first Black general—more than forty years after he first fought in uniform—and Eugenie Anderson became its first woman ambassador.

But just as the majority of American citizens reached the point where their work, and organizing, and bravery, and brilliance had begun to win them a more equal place in public life, senior government officials walled themselves inside a state within a state, and shielded it from outside scrutiny. Americans were told never to forget Pearl Harbor, but to let future historians determine what brought it on. This created a morbid fear of surprise attack, and a mandate for a permanent intelligence establishment with broad powers to carry out espionage and surveillance at home and abroad. After the destruction of Hiroshima and Nagasaki, Americans were assured that secret weapons—weapons so colossal that they could only be built with a massive mobilization of private industry—could deter or defeat any enemy. What turned out to be a highly exaggerated Soviet threat combined with more covert concerns about the advance of antiracism worldwide helped institutionalize a culture of secrecy. The most senior policy-making positions and millions of defense-related jobs were open only to those who could obtain a security clearance. We will see how, in time, this culture of secrecy became a cult, in which inductees were "indoctrinated," took oaths swearing their loyalty, and recognized one another through shared rituals and special badges.

Within this dark state, discriminatory practices could continue without external oversight or any hope of appeal. Anything insiders decided was secret would remain secret unless and until they decided otherwise. And anyone judged to be a security risk could be denied employment without ever being told the reason, which sometimes was nothing more than participation in a civil-rights organization. Even some kinds of nonconformity that had been tolerated until this point, provided they were carefully hidden, were now investigated as a national security threat. Those judged to be sexually "deviant" were driven out of government service on the grounds that they might be blackmailed to give up state secrets. In the years that followed, when more gay people were able to fill sensitive positions, nonwhite people were still disproportionately likely to be denied security clearances.

Without knowing the earlier history, one might think that government secrecy is inevitable, like death and taxes. The German sociologist Max Weber famously postulated, "Every bureaucracy seeks to increase the superiority of the professionally informed by keeping their knowledge and intentions secret." For the first century and a half of U.S. history, that had not been the American experience. In fact, many departments and agencies of the U.S. government are now more transparent than ever, even as the Pentagon, the State Department, and the intelligence agencies invest more and more resources to protect secrets that are twenty-five, fifty, or even a hundred years old. The people who first witnessed the rise of the dark state were astonished at how completely it broke from national traditions, and how little thought was given to the long-term consequences. As then Senator Hubert Humphrey observed in 1955:

> Our present security system is a phenomenon of only the past decade. We have enacted espionage laws and tightened existing laws; we have required investigation and clearance of millions of our citizens; we have classified information and locked it in safes behind locked doors, in locked and guarded buildings, within fenced and heavily guarded reservations. . . . We have not paused in our necessary, though frantic, quest for security to ask ourselves: What are we trying to protect, and against what?

In this book, we will see how those who did ask this question and were allowed to look inside the dark state were troubled by what they saw. What was being protected was not only "national security" but also, and especially, the security of particular people who were jealous of their privileges. One reason we know this is that, from the outset, the system did not work even on its own terms. In 1956, a Defense Department study already found that "overclassification has reached serious proportions." By 1961, the National Archives had taken custody of almost a hundred thousand cubic feet of classified records. Over the years, a series of high-level reviews all came to the same conclusion: the cult of secrecy bred cynicism among government officials and private contractors, stoked distrust in the broader public, and made it harder to prioritize the protection of truly sensitive information.

Now there are over twenty-eight million cubic feet of government files locked up in records centers all across the country. This is equivalent in volume to twenty-six Washington Monuments. And in this era of "big data," the volume of classified information in digital form is already orders of magnitude greater, stored in server farms and black sites and who knows where else. What we do know is that, in 2012, just one (unnamed) intelligence agency was already producing a petabyte of classified data every eighteen months. If these were paper records, and lined up in file cabinets, this row of secret dossiers would circle the equator.

Altogether, the United States spent $18.4 billion in 2017 trying to keep its secrets. That was close to double what it had been spending five years previously. If there were a Department of Secrets, it would now have a budget almost double that of the Department of Commerce, and almost 50 percent bigger than that of the Treasury Department.

The government is nevertheless overwhelmed by the task of protecting all this secret information, as shown by its inability to stop increasingly massive leaks. Though these leaks can shed light on what is happening within the dark state, many are actually planted to further the hidden agendas of senior officials. The wholesale release of secrets, whether planted or not, can risk the privacy or even the safety of innocent victims. At the same time, it brings down the wrath of federal prosecutors, striking fear among other would-be whistle-blowers. But the very size of this dark state—the rows upon rows of blinking servers, serviced by battalions of systems administrators—has become its own security risk. And it keeps getting bigger, from the ninety-one thousand Afghan War logs anonymously given to WikiLeaks in 2010, to the 250,000 State Department cables added by Chelsea Manning later that year, to the estimated 1.7 million intelligence files downloaded by Edward Snowden in 2013, to the more than twenty million personnel records that were reportedly taken by China two years later.

Of all Snowden's revelations, one of the most telling was a simple budgetary spreadsheet. It showed that, in 2013, the National Security Agency was already spending almost fifty million dollars a year just for basic research on "coping with information overload." To be sure, information of every kind is increasing exponentially. But at least in principle, classified information concerns intrinsically dangerous things, including everything from covert operations to nuclear weapons. Moreover, when big data is secret data, it endangers our democracy, since it allows officials to evade accountability. To manage these risks, there are laws both to protect secrets and to preserve them, so classified information can one day be safely revealed. But this presents another critical difference. Under the secrecy system started by Roosevelt, and codified by Harry Truman, every Pentagon PowerPoint, every State Department e-mail—and there are two billion of these e-mails a year—will have to be reviewed page by page before declassification, even decades after they were first created. And any department or agency that can claim it has some say in the matter can indefinitely delay the release of any record.

That is why "big data" has become an insurmountable problem for official secrecy, and even more of a problem for popular democracy. The government estimates it would need two million people to review the petabyte of data produced by that one intelligence agency to decide what could be declassified. But at the largest National Archives facility, in College Park, Maryland, there are only forty-one archivists to deal with over seven hundred thousand cubic feet of unprocessed records that have already been accessioned. Notwithstanding the exponential growth of classified data, the government is spending less than half as much on declassification as it was spending twenty years ago, and about a fifth as many pages are being released each year. If stacked in a pile next to those twenty-six Washington Monuments, it would amount to less than half of the pyramid at the top of just one of them.

Meanwhile, the operating budget of the National Archives was cut by nearly a quarter during the Obama administration, to $372 million in 2016. Under Trump, it was cut yet again, to less than half the cost of a single stealth bomber. Even the records nominally under the jurisdiction of the National Archives are now so numerous that some departments have decided it is impossible for archivists to appraise them. The State Department is experimenting with machine-learning algorithms to delete records automatically, without any archivist or historian ever looking at them, even though research shows this will likely destroy the most historically important records while preserving piles of dreck.

History itself, or what we can know about the past, is now in danger, because our government is grossly negligent in meeting its legal responsibility to preserve records and release them to the public. It is the end of official secrecy as we know it—or, rather, as we, the people, did *not* know it. We might have assumed that men in dark suits knew things that they could not tell us. We might have hoped that somehow, someday, they would finally reveal their secrets, if only in deathbed confessions. In fact, revelations of all kinds come along quite regularly now, whether from planted information, unauthorized leaks, or Wiki-sized data dumps. But these just point to the biggest revelation of all: that the government itself is succumbing to information overload, and would rather destroy or delete our national memory than adopt a more reasonable, risk-management strategy, one that would *both* protect truly dangerous secrets *and* give us the information we need to restore democratic accountability.

We don't have to just sit back and let all this happen. A team of social scientists and data scientists at Columbia has been building the biggest database of once-secret documents available anywhere in the world. We trained algorithms and high-performance computers to discover what is missing. Analyzing millions of State Department cables the same way the NSA treats foreign-signals intelligence, we used traffic analysis to reveal undiscovered events. We uncovered covert surveillance programs of the past precisely because they leave statistically conspicuous gaps in the public record. We revealed the words government censors had redacted, identifying the people and places that were particularly likely to be "sanitized." Then we followed up by digging even deeper, using old-school archival spadework and a close reading of key documents to track all this secrecy back to its source. Where did this cult of secrecy first start? And if all this secrecy is self-defeating, and does not actually work to protect national security, what work is it doing, and whom does it actually work for?

The immediate goal is not just to know what it is we were not supposed to know, and why they did not want us to know it. The goal is to define more clearly what kinds of information really do need to be protected closely—more closely than the current system makes possible. By using data science, we can see how this system actually works, and how often it fails to work.

Though many inside the dark state have the best of intentions, and sincerely believe they are protecting national security, they are unable to meet legal mandates to maximize transparency because of a basic failure of leadership. Presidents have consistently refused to accept reasonable limits to their power to define state secrets, because it is one of the few ways in which they can be completely unaccountable. But presidents come and go, the cult of secrecy keeps growing, and the dark state now answers to no one.

Luckily, the information revolution Vannevar Bush envisioned really can be liberating. Data mining is not just a tool for state or corporate surveillance. Instead, citizens can use data science to turn the tables and restore accountability to a system that has spun out of control. With maps, diagrams, and documents, each of the secrets described in the following chapters will provide another peek through the keyhole, revealing how the most powerful people act when they believe no one can see them. More than that, we can see how data-driven historical research is opening up frontiers of knowledge, helping to answer questions that seem to have been endlessly debated, while at the same time inspiring entirely new kinds of inquiries.

Some readers might wonder why so much of this book is about history, especially the secrets the government did not want us to know, and not just what they don't want us to know *right now*. First, it's no secret that there are legal limits on what anyone can reveal, such as the identities of covert operatives, methods for making nuclear weapons, and the details of code making and code breaking. Conversely, there are already books written in Pentagonese promising insider accounts (or at least insider acronyms), as well as Web sites where hackers have mapped black sites and CIA spy flights, and revealed technical specs for the anti-missile countermeasures on Air Force One.

But unless secrets tell a story, one that reveals an important truth, they tend to disappoint. What I have found after years of study, and after mining millions of secret documents—including the metadata of documents that are still classified—is that the most important secret is not the "what," but the "why": why is the government hiding all this information, even when the whole system is self-defeating? We cannot figure it out by cracking some code. We can only put together different secrets, some of them seemingly innocent, or even obvious, once they are pointed out, to form a mosaic revealing a larger whole. It is something every one of us needs to see before it is too late.

After putting together that mosaic, we will see what the composite holds for the future of state secrecy. But history has always been the best introduction—not only to how we arrived at our current predicament, but how we can imagine all possible futures. At least one of those futures looks more like the past than the present: it is a future in which Americans once again see their country the way it was always meant to be, as a radically transparent republic, one in which citizens—*all* citizens—are their own governors, arming themselves with the power that knowledge gives.

1

PEARL HARBOR

THE ORIGINAL SECRET

The dark state was conceived on December 7, 1941, when the Empire of Japan attacked the U.S. Pacific Fleet at Pearl Harbor. After the last of the Japanese planes returned to their carriers, having dropped bombs and torpedoes with near impunity for a full ninety minutes, President Roosevelt told Congress that this "surprise offensive" had come "suddenly." Washington had been "looking toward the maintenance of peace in the Pacific," only to discover that Tokyo had engaged in an elaborate deception. It was not until after the attack had begun that Japanese diplomats delivered a note declaring an end to negotiations. Roosevelt vowed that America would gain absolute victory and "make it very certain that this form of treachery shall never again endanger us."

The president's address was met with thunderous applause, Congress declared war, and a huge, stealthy apparatus began to emerge from the wreckage. Ever since, this dark state has conducted espionage and surveillance against both friend and foe, assembled a mighty arsenal of secret weapons, and organized covert operations with piles of cash and highly trained commandos. The animating concept was to deter, disrupt, or defeat any future attack by projecting American power far and wide. It was driven forward by presidents who insisted that they needed to be able to use secret powers with little or no oversight to ensure national security.

This chapter will explore how, in fact, the mishandling of secret intelligence and Roosevelt's efforts to deny Congress its constitutional authority to decide on war help explain why forces in Hawaii were taken by surprise. Rather than acknowledging that secrecy had been self-defeating, those in power instead created ever-more-elaborate systems to conceal information, and to package what they made available to the public. The promise was to prevent another surprise attack at all costs. Efforts to dismantle the dark state after World War II failed, and it continued to expand during the Cold War and the "Global War on Terror"—ostensibly for the same reason FDR gave in 1941: to make sure the United States is never again endangered by an enemy who appears out of a clear blue sky.

Now eighteen different spy agencies constantly monitor global communications. Troops stand guard at hundreds of bases and black sites, while special forces and covert operatives are continually carrying out clandestine missions and high-tech assassinations. Altogether, "national security" costs Americans a trillion dollars a year, more than the military budgets of the next eight countries combined. But Americans do not feel secure. Our history still feels like a series of surprises. Every time we endure another attack, we can't help recall the traumatic memory of the last, and wonder why those in charge of protecting us have been caught unaware yet again.

As we shall see, one reason for this continual sense of unease is that the original concept—gaining total knowledge about all possible enemies, foreign and domestic—is impossible to achieve, and hypervigilance is a source of insecurity in its own right. The desire to see all, to know all, and to keep that knowledge secret became a constant temptation that our leaders were unable to resist.

But there is another reason why Pearl Harbor is still a cause of unease: the lingering question of whether American conduct was really as innocent as Roosevelt claimed.

Until then, multiple opinion polls showed that the vast majority of Americans strongly opposed joining what they perceived to be another war of choice, just a generation after World War I, the last "war to end all wars." They well remembered wartime censorship and government-imposed propaganda, and how the persecution of dissenters had continued even after Germany had been defeated. Best-selling books and congressional investigations had exposed how munitions manufacturers profited by promoting conflict. Many, including the U.S. ambassador in Tokyo, Joseph C. Grew, thought it would have been possible to strike a deal to avoid war with Japan. But once America was involved, even those who believed the United States could have been safe in its own hemisphere, and were suspicious of Roosevelt, agreed that winning the war had to take priority over investigating the president's version of events. After his death in 1945, it became even more unseemly to suggest that the fallen leader somehow allowed Japan to kill more than two thousand American servicemen.

The day after Congress backed his call for war, the president explained in a fireside chat that the government would have to keep information secret if it might aid the enemy. But he was prepared to share the "full record of our past relations with Japan," and predicted, "with utmost confidence," that "no Americans today or a thousand years hence, need feel anything but pride in our patience and our efforts through all the years toward achieving a peace in the Pacific," and "no honest person, today or a thousand years hence, will be able to suppress a sense of indignation and horror at the treachery committed by the military dictators of Japan."

Just to be sure, after the war had ended, hand-picked historians with years of experience in the State Department and the Pentagon were given special access to secret files, and they rushed out accounts that aimed to preempt any criticism of U.S. policy. Herbert Feis, for instance, explained the war as resulting from a U.S. refusal to fall for a Japanese plot characterized by "ruse and cunning," "patient scheming," "persuasion and deceit." For William Langer and S. Everett Gleason, any "final judgment" as to U.S. conduct—whether indictment or vindication—"must encompass the whole American people, since every step on the road to war had been openly debated."

In fact, the American public was totally unaware of crucial facts about U.S.-Japan diplomacy during this period. Many papers were not public when the first exculpatory accounts were published, and some remained secret for decades. Only now is it possible to mine declassified documents and analyze how parts were redacted—covered up to conceal what was still deemed too sensitive—in order to support the official version of events. We can thereby derive lessons not just from the attack itself, but from how it was used to sustain the foundational myths that continue to obscure the true origins and nature of the dark state.

If there was any conspiracy to bring America into the war, Britain's prime minister, Winston Churchill, would have been one of the main beneficiaries, given his dire need for military support. For many he is a hero. Others point out his strategic blunders and dogged defense of colonialism. But would anyone call him a conspiracy theorist?

For many years, a crucial document revealing what he knew, and suspected, was deemed "top secret." It was kept at the Eisenhower Presidential Library in Abilene, Kansas, locked in a secure facility that was staffed, alarmed, and guarded at all times. In 1991, the document was finally reviewed for declassification, but only released after a large portion had been redacted. Even years later, when that redaction was finally removed, the document remained undiscovered, filed away with all the rest of Eisenhower's papers. It was only when we ran an experiment at History Lab that it finally emerged.

The experiment involved analyzing some 765,000 pages from documents declassified at all the presidential libraries since the 1970s in order to find redacted and unredacted versions of the same documents. It's harder than one might think, since redactions do not always take the form of blacked out text (sometimes the words are overlain with white or dotted paper), and two documents might be subtly different for many reasons besides.

After some months, a computer-science Ph.D. student on our team figured out a solution. He was able to train an algorithm to combine textual analysis—i.e., matching the words before and after redactions—with "computer vision," or recognizing different kinds of redactions by their appearance. This process produced more than three thousand examples of redacted and unredacted pairs, and we painstakingly checked each one.

That's when we came across this account of a White House dinner that Dwight Eisenhower hosted for Churchill in June 1954—twelve and a half years after Pearl Harbor—following a long, hot day of difficult meetings. The author was not an obscure figure. It was Henry Cabot Lodge, Jr., then the U.S. ambassador to the United Nations, who later became Richard Nixon's running mate in his 1960 race for the White House. Lodge was also a combat veteran of the European campaign, the only man since the Civil War to resign from a Senate seat so he could fight at the front. He understood the importance of what Churchill had said on that occasion about the war, and wrote up a detailed record that very evening.

Lodge recounted how the prime minister, who famously loved to drink late into the evening, "talked extremely freely" after the dinner guests left the table. They sat on a sofa together in the White House Red Room. Hard of hearing, Churchill was also speaking very loudly. He wanted to talk about what happened at another dinner, one that he had hosted at his country house on the evening of December 7, 1941. Gathered at Churchill's dinner were the American ambassador, John G. Winant, and Averell Harriman, a Wall Street banker, friend of Roosevelt's, and the president's personal envoy to Europe.

Just before 9:00 p.m.—still morning in Honolulu—the butler announced that news had come over the radio about a Japanese attack on the American fleet. "Get me the president," Churchill demanded. After connecting with Roosevelt, the prime minister handed the phone over to Ambassador Winant. Churchill must have expected the Americans to be distraught. Instead, Winant said, "That's fine, Mr. President, just fine." Then "the most extraordinary thing happened," Churchill told Lodge. "Winant and Harriman got up and embraced each other and danced around the room in delight." The American base at Pearl Harbor was awash with dead sailors and sunken battleships. But Ambassador Winant "insisted that it was a marvelous thing."

Churchill wasn't done yet. Still speaking freely, he told Lodge that he "remembered well" that General George Marshall "had taken a much longer horseback ride on that day than had usually been the case." Because the army chief of staff was cantering about Rock Creek Park in Washington, D.C., his top aide, Walter Bedell Smith, had been unable to give him a critical communication. American code breakers had intercepted and deciphered the Japanese message breaking off negotiations. Worse still, Smith had in fact already received thirteen of the fourteen parts of Tokyo's final message to Washington the night before, and was told to deliver them to Marshall immediately, but he didn't. After these inexplicable delays, the message was finally delivered to Marshall, and then to Honolulu at noon Washington time. It arrived just as the Japanese attack was beginning— the bicycle messenger who was supposed to give it to the base commander had to take cover in a ditch.

Nonetheless, Smith had steadily risen through the ranks over the course of the war and in the years that followed. Eventually, he became director of the CIA, and was actually in attendance at that 1954 White House dinner. He must have been startled when the Prime Minister summoned him from across the room and seized him by the arm. "Tell us about that telegram that you didn't deliver on Pearl Harbor Day," Churchill demanded. One can only imagine the expression on Smith's face. Lodge merely recorded his curt response: "I won't talk about that," he said, rebuffing the president's old friend.

Lodge gave his memorandum recording these events to Secretary of State John Foster Dulles, marking it both "Top Secret" and "Personal and Private." Dulles agreed that no one else should see it. He wrote "no distribution" across the top. The State Department maintained its sensitivity even fifty years after Pearl Harbor, still finding it necessary to redact this whole section before releasing the rest of the document. The pages released in full included discussion of a range of highly sensitive subjects, such as the CIA overthrow of the democratically elected government in Guatemala, Britain's shortage of weapons-grade nuclear material, and prospects for thermonuclear war. But it was just this section, an episode that was already receding into history in 1954, that remained "top secret" in 1991, when all the main players—Churchill, Smith, Lodge, Marshall, Eisenhower—were long dead.

The classification "top secret" is only supposed to apply to information "which reasonably could be expected to cause exceptionally grave damage to the national security." Why did the State Department think Churchill's war story—old even in 1954—was still so damaging?

One could argue that, in both 1954 and 1991, the State Department kept it classified simply to protect the reputation of a revered leader. Respecting the sensitivities of an ally is one of the more common reasons why officials redact or withhold old documents. Our algorithm revealed another such redaction, from a 1952 report to Eisenhower, according to which Churchill was already "old and tired," and had become "a source of embarrassment to his staff."

Churchill did not always hear what others were trying to tell him, and he was losing his willingness or ability to self-censor. But that may be precisely why he would say things—and say them loudly—that no one else would have dared utter, things that might have touched on matters that were sensitive to the State Department itself even decades later. What Churchill said after that White House dinner showed a detailed knowledge of key points in Pearl Harbor conspiracy theories. This includes the still-mysterious whereabouts of Marshall, who as army chief of staff was ultimately responsible for defending Pearl Harbor. To this day, many wonder why officials in Washington did not make certain all American bases in the Pacific were on high alert. U.S. B-17 Flying Fortresses, America's newest heavy bomber equipped with the high-tech Norden bombsight, had already been forward-deployed to the Philippines, and Marshall had told reporters that, if it came to war, they would be "dispatched immediately to set the paper cities of Japan on fire." Instead, hours after Japanese forces first sank the Pacific battle fleet, they caught and destroyed half these bombers before they could even leave the ground.

Churchill was connecting these dots with things only he could know. He knew that this story was potentially explosive, and never spoke of it publicly. In 1949, when he was writing his history of World War II, he initially included an account of how the Americans were delighted upon hearing of the attack, but then thought better of it and toned down this section. He also pared back other details that might have corroborated the conspiracy theories, such as his confirmation that Roosevelt and his advisers "had long burned to take part in the war against Hitler."

Many already suspected this was the case. For months leading up to the attack, FDR had not been able to persuade Congress or the American public to join the European war despite a series of violent encounters between U.S. and German ships in the Atlantic. A surprise attack in the Pacific by Hitler's Axis ally finally provided an indisputable *casus belli*. Matters became even simpler when, four days later, Hitler himself declared war on the United States.

It was only much later that Churchill learned that the United States had been decrypting Japanese communications, like the message Smith did not deliver in time on that fateful morning. In the weeks leading up to Pearl Harbor, the prime minister had struggled to understand Roosevelt's actions toward Japan, which to Churchill seemed unnecessarily provocative. Already besieged in the North Atlantic and the Mediterranean, Churchill wanted desperately to avoid having to divert forces to fight on another front in Asia, the soft white underbelly of the British Empire. To the prime minister, the more prudent course was to deter further aggression. At a time in which German cruisers still menaced Atlantic convoys, he insisted—against the advice of his admirals—on sending to Singapore two of the Royal Navy's best capital ships, HMS *Prince of Wales* and HMS *Repulse*. His intent was to warn the Japanese against attacking Britain's Asian colonies. Instead, the ships were chased down and sunk three days after the Pearl Harbor attack. Churchill called it his biggest shock of the war. The two ships took almost a thousand British sailors down with them, including Admiral Sir Tom Phillips, a personal friend of the prime minister. Churchill may have benefited from America's joining the fight against the Axis powers, but the cost of these attacks was to him considerable.

For Churchill in 1954, what had happened at Pearl Harbor was not just history, as personal and painful as those memories must have been for him. It was a vision of the future. The main subject of discussion during his 1954 visit to Washington was the danger of nuclear war with Moscow. For a British leader mulling the prospect, Pearl Harbor could be seen as a precedent, and a premonition. As soon as he let go of Smith's arm, Churchill started talking about the even greater strategic threat from a surprise attack with thermonuclear weapons.

Just ten days earlier, Churchill had decided that Britain would have to build its own hydrogen bombs, whose destructive force was potentially thousands of times greater than the atomic bomb dropped on Hiroshima. In one blow, he observed, an attack with H-bombs could level the playing field even when one side started with a ten-to-one advantage. In 1954, this ten-to-one ratio approximated the advantage the United States then had against the USSR in numbers of nuclear weapons.

What Churchill did not say—he did not need to—was where Britain would figure in Soviet war plans. Even in an age of jet aircraft and ballistic missiles, forward bases still played a central role. In 1954, both the United States and the Soviet Union were struggling to deploy weapons of sufficient range to strike each other directly. The medium-range bombers and flying tankers of the Strategic Air Command had to be deployed to bases abroad—including Britain—to bring them within striking range of the USSR, not unlike the U.S. forces that Japan had targeted in Pearl Harbor and the Philippines. But here again, forward deployment also brought these forces within striking range of a sneak attack, only this time it would be with nuclear weapons rather than bombs and torpedoes. U.S. strategists at the RAND Corporation had been warning that the entire U.S. strike force could be knocked back on its heels by a Soviet attack on these overseas bases—to say nothing of the millions of British men, women, and children who would then be eating and breathing the radioactive fallout. When Churchill was contemplating this kind of scenario at the White House dinner, his government was still having to ration sales of meat, nine years after the last war had ended.

Eisenhower and the Strategic Air Command had a simple answer to the danger of a Pearl Harbor–style first strike aimed at Western Europe, though one Churchill was not inclined to cosign. This time, the United States would make sure to strike the first blow. It would be so devastating that the USSR would be left with few means to strike back. But even if SAC decimated Soviet bases, such that there were too few bombers to threaten North America seriously, Moscow could still use shorter-range bombers and missiles to retaliate against America's European allies. Churchill was advised that just ten H-bombs on ten British cities would kill twelve million people, over twenty-five times more than the U.K. lost in all of World War II. One of the main reasons he decided Britain needed to build its own thermonuclear weapons was to "avoid any action which would weaken our power to influence United States policy"—especially when the United States was "tempted to undertake a forestalling war."

Eisenhower was indeed tempted. The previous year, he had strongly hinted that he was ready to go nuclear to end the conflict in Korea. Our algorithm revealed another redacted account of an Anglo-American meeting, which took place on the twelfth anniversary of Pearl Harbor. The prime minister warned that threatening the use of nuclear weapons would "cause widespread alarm and anger." Secretary of State John Foster Dulles was publicly talking about the need for "brinkmanship" in confronting Moscow and rolling back communist advances in Europe. This was not unlike the U.S. position in the months leading up to Pearl Harbor, when Roosevelt sought to roll back Japan's advance into China. In the 1950s, Washington was once more engaged in brinkmanship, with Churchill again caught in the middle, his country's fate in the balance.

So Churchill had good reasons to demand to know the real story of what happened at Pearl Harbor, but he had even more compelling reasons to maintain friendly relations with his powerful ally. To understand why this story seemed too sensitive to reveal even decades later, we need to pick up where Churchill left off, and combine computer vision with old-fashioned historical research. What do we learn by looking at those intercepted messages that Churchill was not allowed to see, and putting them together with FDR's words and deeds in the months leading up to the attack?

First, in this case like many others, it would be wrong to start with the assumption that even a leader as canny as Roosevelt can know all, and see all, and then keep that knowledge to himself. In fact, the White House itself did not always have access to decrypted Japanese diplomatic traffic. After the State Department lost an intelligence report that included Japanese intercepts, the army decided that the desk of FDR's military aide was not a sufficiently secure place to protect these secrets. Eventually, Roosevelt was able to get what he wanted from the navy, which shared responsibility for decrypting Japanese communications. But for a time, the president was unable to use the most sensitive and valuable intelligence on Japanese intentions even as he engaged in a dangerous game of brinkmanship.

The idea that Roosevelt knew Japanese carriers were targeting Pearl Harbor—much less that he conspired to allow thousands of Americans to be killed—beggars belief. The real question is whether he was pushing the Japanese into a corner so they had no choice but to fight, and doing so for the purpose of forcing the American people to fight back—and fight on every front. This is the "back door" theory of how America entered World War II: frustrated at his inability to provoke Hitler into attacking the United States, FDR found in Japan and the Pacific a way to enter the war from the other side.

Churchill knew Roosevelt was determined to join the war in Europe. At a secret meeting off Newfoundland in August 1941, FDR explained that trying to persuade Congress would be too slow and risk rejection. But Congress's exclusive power to declare war, granted by the Constitution, was not going to stop Roosevelt. He "said that he would wage war, but not declare it, and that he would become more and more provocative," as Churchill reported to his War Cabinet: "Everything was to be done to force an 'incident' . . . an 'incident' which would justify him in opening hostilities." U.S. forces escorting convoys in the Atlantic laden with American-made munitions were being ordered to pursue and attack any German U-boats, even if they were 300 miles away. But after many such incidents, Congress was still not ready to declare war.

There was, however, something less openly aggressive that could provoke a much bigger incident, and from the other side of the world, where Japan was bogged down in an unwinnable war with China. In 1940, Tokyo had entered into a pact with Berlin and Rome that ostensibly required each signatory to come to the aid of the others if any were attacked by a country not already involved in either the European or Asian conflicts. Roosevelt responded by arming Japan's enemies. In April 1941, he authorized sending U.S. warplanes and military pilots to China, the "Flying Tigers," and they were promised bounties for shooting down Japanese aircraft. American businessmen helped make it appear like a private venture so as to avoid a blatant violation of the Neutrality Act. But Washington did not necessarily have to attack anyone to provoke a global conflagration. Japan depended on the United States for 93 percent of its energy imports. Without U.S. oil, Japan's war machine would literally run out of gas. The day after Hitler invaded the USSR in June 1941, FDR's close confidant Harold Ickes advised, "There will never be so good a time to stop the shipment of oil to Japan."

Just threatening these severe economic sanctions might have dissuaded Tokyo from embarking on any new aggression. But Ickes does not seem to have been thinking of threats or deterrence. He wanted escalation: "There might develop from the embargoing of oil to Japan such a situation as would make it, not only possible but easy, to get into this war in an effective way." FDR worried that announcing an embargo might provoke a Japanese attack, when what he wanted was war with Germany. For Ickes, on the other hand, to go on trying to orchestrate events to provoke Hitler was an even greater risk: "It may be difficult to get into this war the right way, but if we do not do it now, we will be, when our turn comes, without an ally anywhere in the world."

So Roosevelt's options were to threaten Japan to deter further aggression, or to go ahead and impose an embargo in order to escalate. In July 1941, he made his decision. He had learned from intercepted Japanese cables that Tokyo was planning to demand that the French allow Japan to move into the southern part of their Indochina colony, expanding from the northern zone it already controlled, and thereby threatening the Dutch

East Indies as well as British Malaya. This was the kind of opening that Ickes had been looking for. Instead of intervening, and explicitly warning that he would embargo Japan's fuel supplies, as Ambassador Grew urged, FDR waited until the French acceded. He then announced that, in retaliation, the United States was seizing Japanese assets and rationing oil supplies. Soon it became an actual embargo. FDR knew full well that an embargo "would simply drive the Japanese down to the Dutch East Indies," as he himself had warned his Cabinet just a week before. These colonies, among the world's biggest oil-exporters, were also newly vulnerable, now that Japan's Axis ally occupied the Netherlands. When he issued that warning, Roosevelt himself still opposed this move, since "it would mean war in the Pacific," and he was not yet ready for that. But now he went ahead and did it anyway.

The announcement came as a shock to Japanese commanders, who had "no inkling" that Washington would react in this way. As Roosevelt anticipated, the inevitability of running out of fuel created a powerful incentive to break the embargo by seizing the Dutch colonies. Senior army and navy leaders understood that Japan had little chance of winning any such war if the United States joined as well. Their policy up to this point was based on a bluff, the brainchild of a foreign minister—Yosuke Matsuoka—who believed after an adolescence spent in Oregon that Americans respected only strength and would not begrudge Japan its own sphere of influence. Many Japanese now regretted the Tripartite Pact, especially after Hitler invaded the USSR with no prior notice to Tokyo. The agreement was supposed to deter war with the United States but was also intended to contain Germany. In fact, at the time of signing Matsuoka had insisted on a secret corollary that gave Japan sole discretion in deciding what it was obliged to do if the pact were ever invoked. But repudiating their new partner, as the Americans insisted, seemed equally dangerous, especially now that Germany was sweeping east toward Moscow. Hitler pledged to come to Japan's aid "at once" if it collided with America (a message that was intercepted and read in both London and Washington).

Rather than joining Germany in plotting war against the United States, Japanese army and navy leaders gave their prime minister, Prince Fumimaro Konoe, until mid-October to negotiate a solution. Konoe decided to propose traveling to meet Roosevelt face-to-face on American soil to try to settle their differences, and this initiative received the support of the army, the navy, and the emperor. The Japanese made this request repeatedly, both to Ambassador Grew and through their own ambassador in Washington. Grew judged that this request to meet the president—"hat-in-hand," on American soil—indicated that the United States could obtain full satisfaction.

But weeks passed before Roosevelt gave his answer. Finally, he said that Japan would first need to commit to a foreign policy consistent with basic principles of international law, such as respect for the territorial integrity and sovereignty of all nations—principles to which the United States "has long been committed" (notwithstanding a whole series of armed incursions in the Caribbean, Central, and South America). More than that, Japan would need to show how it would put these principles into practice. It would have to commit explicitly to a comprehensive settlement acceptable to the United States before Roosevelt would agree to any meeting.

Three days later, Prince Konoe broke precedent to talk personally with Grew and said that a ship was standing by so he could meet with Roosevelt. Konoe said he accepted the principles "conclusively and wholeheartedly" and also took personal responsibility for the deterioration in U.S.-Japan relations. He pledged that Japan would make no further move to the south from Indochina and would withdraw troops from China once it concluded peace. And if the United States entered the European war, Japan could stay out.

But Roosevelt and Secretary of State Hull continued demanding that Japan put in writing the specific concessions it would make before agreeing to meet. Grew explained that Konoe could not do this because opponents within the government would leak them to the Germans and Japanese extremists. Japanese leaders who appeared ready to abandon plans for imperial expansion risked assassination. That is precisely why the prince was desperate to meet face-to-face. Grew judged that Konoe was prepared to "accept the American terms whatever they might be," up to and including a Japanese withdrawal from China.

Hull's defenders would later insist that, "no matter what

papers come to light," it is impossible to know what the Japanese prime minister had intended when he sought this summit meeting. The papers that did come to light showed that army general staff officials expected that Konoe's mission would, because of the emperor's backing, entail "surrendering to the United States." "What idiots they are in Washington!" another senior army official exclaimed. "If they agree to meet with Konoe without any conditions, everything would go their way."

Konoe kept trying for a summit. He even tried to force the resignation of the hardline minister of war, Tōjō Hideki, with help from the emperor's uncle. But Konoe could not, in the end, persuade Roosevelt to meet with him, and he finally resigned. Interestingly, the Americans seemed to have lost interest in Japan's repudiating the Tripartite Pact. Japanese emissaries repeatedly asked what precise language would satisfy their concern and received no response. Tokyo's actions spoke louder than words: The Japanese did nothing to support Berlin as U.S. Navy ships pursued German U-boats.

But now the Americans were increasingly insistent on a different demand: Japan must evacuate all its troops from China. This would have been humiliating to any Japanese government. But even when Tōjō took Konoe's place as prime minister, he did not reject the idea. It was "unbearable" to admit that two hundred thousand Japanese soldiers had died in vain, he told a confidant, but Japan would lose many more if it went to war against the United States. "I just cannot decide." Japan's own most senior commander in China sent an emissary to Tokyo advising the acceptance of U.S. demands.

Tōjō therefore pushed back the deadline again, to November 25, and sent a special envoy with instructions to offer a partial withdrawal from China, leading up to a comprehensive settlement. Secretary of State Cordell Hull knew from another intercepted message that things would begin to happen "automatically" if there was no agreement. But rather than accelerate efforts to find a solution, he stalled. Time was working to the Americans' advantage, in terms of both Japan's oil reserves and U.S. war preparations. When he finally agreed to a meeting, he offered nothing in return for what the Japanese were offering.

Tokyo then went with Plan B, proposing a deal to de-escalate by restoring the status quo: The United States would resume oil shipments, and Japan would withdraw from southern Indochina. The envoy asked for a suspension of military supplies to China, but did so hoping that the United States would sponsor talks to bring about an armistice and peace treaty. The Japanese were offering concessions, and not ruling out further concessions.

In response, Roosevelt drew up his own proposal to trade American oil for a withdrawal from Indochina. Tokyo extended the deadline yet again. But when Hull met the Japanese representatives, he instead insisted on a "comprehensive Pacific settlement," including a complete withdrawal of Japanese forces from both China and Indochina, a free trade agreement, and Japanese acceptance that the United States would also have equal access to the China market. Even at this late hour, he presented this outline as "Tentative and Without Commitment," described it as a policy statement intended to appease Americans angry with Japan, and offered no indication as to when or even if the United States would unfreeze Japanese assets and resume oil deliveries.

Americans had long demanded an "Open Door" to Asian markets, and the Japanese had already indicated that they were ready to make economic concessions. But nothing could have been more provocative than for the United States first to entertain a proposal for a modus vivendi, prepare a counteroffer, but instead present what even the most sympathetic historians describe as "maximum demands," including a withdrawal of the Japanese from China so they could be replaced by U.S. investors and exporters. Provocation was the whole point: After a meeting of what FDR already called his "War Council" the day before, Secretary of War Henry Stimson recorded, "The question was how we should maneuver them into the position of firing the first shot without allowing too much danger to ourselves."

The words "without allowing too much danger" constitute a crucial caveat, one that should be obvious: there is a lot of evidence that the attack on Pearl Harbor was the consequence of a U.S. strategy to keep pushing Japan up against the wall so as to push through to the other side, provoking this war in the Pacific to start a world war against Germany—Roosevelt's ultimate goal.

But though FDR was deliberately provoking Tokyo, this does not mean that he expected, much less wanted, Japan to destroy the Pacific battle fleet. This was "too much danger." If Roosevelt knew the attack would target Pearl Harbor, why would he not make sure the American defenders were ready to repel the marauders? This would have worked just as well—perhaps even better—for his larger purpose of bringing America into the war, which would have begun with a victory. Instead, the attack killed thousands.

Afterward, the War Council immediately agreed on the need to censor sensitive information, starting with the extent of the damage. So the first secret of the war was the embarrassing fact that Japan had succeeded in crippling American naval power in the Pacific. Nevertheless, the perceived nature of the attack, which the president portrayed as unprovoked, made it much harder to focus on defeating Germany, which FDR rightly understood was the main threat.

Roosevelt's most influential critics, like the publisher of the *Chicago Tribune*, "Colonel" Robert R. McCormick, had long accused him of using unconstitutional methods to maneuver the United States into the war in Europe. Now they would insist on sending forces to defeat Japan. Ironically, while Roosevelt's top aides were relieved or celebratory on hearing the news from Pearl Harbor, the original architect of Tokyo's policy of hitching its destiny to Germany, Yosuke Matsuoka, cried bitter tears of regret: "I am now painfully aware that the signing of the Tripartite Pact was the biggest mistake of my lifetime. . . . When I think of this, it will bother me even after I die."

The keynote of all subsequent portrayals of the Japanese was "treacherous." Americans had grossly underestimated the Japanese, considering them racial inferiors, and even some senior officials assumed they could be defeated in six months to a year. They believed that Tokyo had started a race war, and responded in kind, starting with the incarceration of over one hundred thousand men, women, and children of Japanese ancestry. The admiral who took command of the ships that escaped the attack on Pearl Harbor, William "Bull" Halsey, ordered his men to "kill Japs, kill Japs, kill more Japs." Americans were now hell-bent on revenge, with a rage that the president could scarcely contain or control.

It is even more implausible to think that George Marshall, the man in charge of building an arsenal for the coming war, planned all this in advance. Like FDR, he wanted to stop Hitler from further consolidating his gains and—with the Wehrmacht just 20 miles from Moscow in December 1941—potentially knocking the USSR out of the war. For that very reason, he did not want to start a war with Japan unless and until it was absolutely necessary. Being forced to fight a two-front war without some of America's most powerful weapons was a searing experience that changed how top military commanders operated in the postwar period.

How, then, can we explain why American forces in Pearl Harbor were so completely surprised? In her classic study, the historian Roberta Wohlstetter showed that it was hardly out of the blue. Roosevelt and his top advisers knew an attack was coming. They just did not know the precise form it would take. In his foreword, Thomas Schelling summarized Wohlstetter's key insight: it "is not true that we were caught napping at the time of Pearl Harbor. Rarely has a government been more expectant." The problem was, "We just expected wrong."

Using secret information to interpret an enemy's intentions and capabilities is a tricky business. Intelligence analysts have a haystack of information to process, and relevant and reliable signals of an impending threat can be rare and hard to recognize. The reports they write for more senior officials are often contradictory, incomplete, and hedged with reservations. "Hindsight bias" leads us to think warning signs must have been obvious. In fact, those signs are often buried under a mountain of captured communications.

But before Pearl Harbor there were all too many mistakes in a more elementary task—that is, simply sharing the information. The secrecy itself hamstrung U.S. diplomacy and war preparations. We have seen how even Roosevelt sometimes did not have access to the intercepted Japanese communications. Nor were they shared with the commander of the U.S. Pacific Fleet, Admiral Husband Edward Kimmel, or the general in charge of

defending Pearl Harbor, Walter Campbell Short. These communications would have shown the two men how the Japanese were
setting a deadline for negotiations, and how thereafter actions
would proceed "automatically." The decrypts would also have
indicated Japan's increasing interest in the precise locations of
ships in Pearl Harbor. But out of an exaggerated sense of operational security—one resulting from mistakes in Washington,
rather than Hawaii—Admiral Kimmel and General Short were
kept in the dark in the four months leading up to the Japanese
attack. In postwar inquiries, no one would take responsibility for
the decision. It was literally inexcusable.

Marshall did write to General Short once he knew talks were
breaking down, warning that "hostile action [is] possible at any
moment." But Short misread this as a warning against attack
by local Japanese saboteurs, not an attack from air and sea. So,
rather than dispersing his aircraft and readying them for takeoff,
Short lined them up wingtip to wingtip, to guard them more easily against ground attack.

When the message that Japan was breaking off negotiations
arrived in Washington, Smith himself did not know exactly what
message he was delivering to Marshall. It was locked inside a
pouch, and even Smith, the secretary of the War Department
General Staff, did not have clearance to open it. One is forced
to wonder whether he would have delivered the intercepted
Japanese messages as soon as they arrived had he understood
exactly what was inside the pouch, and whether Marshall might
then have made certain American bases were fully prepared.
Ironically, this extraordinary secrecy surrounding the Japanese
decrypts may not have even been necessary. When the *Chicago
Tribune* ran a front-page story strongly hinting that the United
States was reading Japanese naval communications, Tokyo did
not address the problem, and American code breakers continued
their exploits.

The United States had secret weapons that might also have
averted disaster, or at least delivered an immediate riposte. The
army operated a radar that detected the attacking Japanese force
forty-five minutes before it reached Pearl Harbor. But inad-
equately trained operators did not know what they were see-

ing, and army-navy political games had hindered the creation of an interservice information center that could have received and acted on the warning. Even after Japanese carrier aircraft pulverized the conveniently assembled targets in Hawaii, the American commander in the Philippines, General Douglas MacArthur, was still not prepared for an aerial attack. Precious hours passed before he finally ordered a recon mission to locate Japanese bases. That is why half the B-17 bombers deployed at Clark Field were destroyed on the ground.

Officials had allowed excessive secrecy to undermine national security and failed to prepare their forces despite knowing an attack was imminent. But when government officials realize they have been incompetent, they treat the potential revelation of that fact as a grave danger to national security. Officials apparently prefer that other people—even close allies like Prime Minister Churchill—suspect them of a criminal conspiracy rather than admit that they screwed up.

This is the first of three major lessons from Pearl Harbor. Secrets are often kept to hide incompetence, and this short-sighted mistake has been repeated so many times it should no longer seem very original. But after more than eighty years, it can still take people by surprise.

The second major lesson of Pearl Harbor is that catastrophic attacks almost never come out of nowhere. There is invariably a period of tension, threats, indicators, and warnings. Sometimes, as in August 2001, there are even attention-getting intelligence reports, with unsubtle titles like "Bin Ladin Determined to Strike in US." But leaders prefer to pretend they had no warning. In fact, claiming that an attack is completely unexpected can help legitimate more espionage, domestic surveillance, and military spending. In response to the Pearl Harbor attack, for instance, Congress earnestly debated authorizing government wiretaps to ensure national security. Hoover and Roosevelt endorsed the need for new legislation, without acknowledging that both had already been ignoring a Supreme Court–ordered wiretap ban for a year and a half before the attack. It made people think that it was a lack of secret information, rather than a lack of real *intelligence*, that explained why their leaders were taken by surprise.

At the same time, it gave a veneer of democratic legitimacy to unprecedented surveillance powers that would continue long after 1945 and eventually go far, far beyond the pursuit of spies and saboteurs.

After the war, the military insisted on the need to spend heavily on complex, redundant, and highly classified systems that would supposedly make any new surprise attack impossible. Thus, the same month Japan was finally defeated, the Joint Chiefs issued a long list of requirements that were unprecedented in peacetime: dramatically expanding the military's own intelligence-gathering powers, funding an expensive weapons R&D program, building a vast overseas base system, and deploying mobile striking forces capable of pre-empting any threatened attack. The Pentagon also used Pearl Harbor in arguing for designating a single com-mander for each region. These generals and admirals became the most powerful representatives of America abroad, posing a perennial challenge for civilian control of the armed forces.

The dark state that arose out of the smoke of Pearl Harbor was assembled cumulatively and relentlessly. The ensuing Cold War gave us the CIA, the NSA, the Strategic Air Command, and the North American Aerospace Defense Command. After 9/11, the dark state continued growing, with the Department of Homeland Security, the Office of the Director of National Intelligence, and three more intelligence agencies. After 2017 new layers were added with Cyber Command, the Space Force and—why not?—Space Force Intelligence.

Over the course of this book, we shall see how the tightly interconnected nature of these systems, hair-trigger alerts, con-stant drilling, and imperviousness to external oversight created multiple war-scares. In some cases, the U.S. military itself has prepared to launch nuclear weapons based on false warnings. We still live in fear of surprise attacks, as shown by the panic created in Hawaii in 2018 after an alarm indicated an imminent missile strike. We should actually be more alarmed by the very real risk that all our preparations for war will result in the United States' provoking just such an attack, or accidentally launching one of our own. Together, these fears constitute the very opposite of national security.

The third major lesson of Pearl Harbor, the original secret at the root of all the others, is that our leaders think we can't handle the truth and wouldn't support their plans if we knew what they were. In the years that followed, historians who were also former officials helped package the Pearl Harbor story for the public. They dismissed dissenting scholars as "isolationists." Thomas A. Bailey, author of the popular textbook *The American Pageant*, claimed that Charles A. Beard had "prostituted" history by questioning the precedents Roosevelt set in expanding state secrecy and presidential war powers. Despite Beard's lifetime of distinguished scholarship, the historical profession treated him as a pariah. But in a moment of rare candor, Bailey admitted Beard's thesis was basically correct: "Because the masses are notoriously shortsighted and generally cannot see danger until it is at their throats, our statesmen are forced to deceive them into an awareness of their own long-run interests. This is clearly what Roosevelt had to do, and who shall say that posterity will not thank him for it?" As for his own work, Bailey told his publisher to expect big sales, because *America Faces Russia* could be "widely used in the armed services for indoctrination purposes."

For that date in infamy, we know the truth. Roosevelt wanted a war. He wanted Japan to attack. And he was relieved when they did. But when he faced Congress and the people, he called it an "unprovoked and dastardly attack" bespeaking Japanese "treachery." Churchill knew better, of course, but he also knew how to keep a secret.

We may now all know, but it is only because—unlike many of our leaders today—Roosevelt honored the American tradition of preserving a record of his decisions. Even if he did not think his contemporaries could handle the truth, he trusted that his countrymen would eventually learn from the records he left behind, and use that wisdom to make their own future.

Looking back, we can now see how the story of Pearl Harbor contained in embryo form all the top secrets of the rapidly growing dark state: projecting American military bases and high-tech weapons around the world to guarantee security, only to create tempting targets for a surprise attack; surrounding code making and code breaking with extraordinary secrecy, to the point that the secrecy becomes self-defeating; using the perception of surprise and insecurity to expand surveillance powers, even when surveillance had already expanded far outside the law; international trade and investment as both a motivator for overseas engagement and a tool for coercion and covert operations; and—above all—presidential spin to conceal all these secrets, even while pretending to be open and transparent.

Of course, Roosevelt had a war to win, and the eventual victory was a triumph for all Americans and indeed the cause of democracy itself. Unfortunately, as we shall see, in the course of that war he presided over the birth of what would become a permanent system that produced many more secrets, justified by a certain conceit about how it started. With the building of the atomic bomb, the stakes of a surprise attack became incomparably greater. The dark state was born from the union of secret intelligence and secret weapons, and it became unstoppable.

And what of Churchill's war story? Why was it still sensitive in 1991, fifty years after Pearl Harbor? That very month when the document was redacted, the United States, Britain, and a coalition of other countries were marshaling forces to respond to what they insisted on calling Saddam Hussein's "surprise attack" on Kuwait. According to George H. W. Bush, it had been "without provocation or warning." But the Iraqi government later released transcripts from Saddam's prewar meeting with U.S. Ambassador April Glaspie, showing how Saddam had made a number of veiled threats. According to the Iraqi transcript, Glaspie professed "no opinion" on the dispute, and in so doing, gave Saddam the green light to invade. Congressmen and senators described the meeting as a date in "infamy." But the war also gave the United States a way to get what the Pentagon had long wanted: permanent forward bases in the Middle East— bases that, in 2001, would provoke another surprise attack.

We still don't know the whole story of the Gulf War, and perhaps we never will. For years the Bush administration asserted in court that it had no responsibility to preserve the e-mails of his National Security Council or any other electronic records. The government finally lost in court, and the National Archives took possession. But in the years that followed, the Archives have been so neglected and underfunded that staff no longer have the technical capacity to recover the e-mails of our forty-first president. So we can't handle the truth, quite literally, because the government is losing its capacity to hand over historical records. The loss or destruction of archives is the ultimate secret; it renders history unknowable by any living being.

But long ago, Pearl Harbor showed that secrecy can be self-defeating, and a failure to confront this history can still endanger national security. Covering up incompetence makes people believe that our leaders engage in criminal conspiracies. Failing to realize how they can also be ruthless practitioners of Realpolitik can lead others to think they are stupid or naïve. Trying to devise systems that reduce the risk of a surprise attack to zero increases the risk of needlessly starting new wars, whether by accident or by design. And all this squanders the opportunities that come from sharing credible intelligence with the American people when a real threat emerges, and trusting them to be intelligent enough to form reasonable conclusions and support a proportionate response.

The reasonable conclusion to draw from the Pearl Harbor debacle is that naïve people rarely rise to the top of the U.S. political system. Our leaders are sometimes conspiratorial, but they also screw up. If we can't handle these truths, and we treat attacks—even the ones we provoke—as complete surprises, we will never learn from the past or gain in judgment in creating our own future. Too many of us will refuse to live in a world that seems so utterly unpredictable, and will instead choose leaders who promise to reveal conspiracies that control events, prevent all future attacks, but then go on to pursue nothing more—and nothing less—than unaccountable power.

2

THE BOMB

BORN SECRET

If you began to work out a schematic for a nuclear weapon on the back of a paper napkin, and it was a design that might actually work, that napkin would—in a miracle of modern secrecy—immediately become classified. As a private citizen, you would not even have the right to look at it. If you passed the napkin to anyone else lacking the proper clearance, you would be liable for prosecution. If you did this "with intent to secure an advantage to any foreign nation"—even an ally—you could be sent to prison for the rest of your natural life.

Normally, government secrets must originate with some government official. If an official passes along this information, the person receiving it bears no risk of prosecution, even if they publish it on the front page of *The New York Times*. But starting with the Atomic Energy Act of 1946, any information that could be useful in creating nuclear weapons—what the government calls "restricted data" (RD)—is always restricted no matter where it comes from. The same goes for information about how to *use* nuclear weapons, which the government confusingly calls "formerly restricted data." FRD is no less sensitive than RD, but it is the category for nuclear secrets that the civilians who built the bombs agreed could be shared among the warriors who would do the bombing. RD and FRD are not just secrets the government guards very closely. They are "born secret." The moment this kind of information passes from someone's brain into the material world, it is immediately subject to the full power and authority of the United States government.

Nuclear secrets are top secrets not just in how they become classified, but also in the precautions the government takes in making sure they are not inadvertently declassified. In 1998, another layer of legal protections was added, which requires that every single document that might conceivably have RD or FRD be reviewed page by page during declassification. The Department of Energy (DOE) is so determined to prevent any unauthorized release that it double-checks what has been cleared by other departments and agencies. If a single offending document is found among thousands of others, every other record has to be reviewed again, one page at a time.

The same law gives the DOE the power to go into National Archives records centers and presidential libraries, rifle through the open files, and pull out anything that it decides should not have been released to the public. In the first eight years of the program, DOE staff had surveyed some two hundred million pages and withdrew 6,640 of them. The estimated cost incurred for this program worked out to $4,236 per page—only a bit less than the cost-per-page of a Gutenberg Bible. Only the DOE decides if, and when, these nuclear secrets will ever see the light of day.

It usually takes a long, long time for nuclear secrets to be declassified. How do we know? Because with big (declassified) data it is now possible to predict when secrets will no longer be secret. A computer scientist named Hanna Wallach found this out by using a technique called "topic modeling" to analyze all the words in all the documents researchers have managed to get declassified at presidential libraries. A topic-modeling algorithm rank-orders the words that are most or least likely to occur together—in this case, identifying words like "strike," "kill," "energy," and "bomb"—at the top of a long list of words that one is most likely to find in documents about the topic of nuclear weapons. These words appear near the bottom of the list for other topics, like international aid and trade. The algorithm also rank-orders the documents themselves according to whether they are more or less likely to include the top words characteristic of each topic compared with all the other words they contain. This technique is remarkably effective in sorting documents according to whether they concern this or that topic. In the case of the "strike," "kill," "energy" topic, all the highest ranking documents relate to nuclear weapons, from a paper describing how the Atomic Energy Commission (AEC) and the Pentagon would divide up responsibilities for building and deploying nuclear weapons, to a study of how the president would actually order a nuclear first-strike, to a memo in which nuclear physicists caution against developing hydrogen bombs.

Wallach's topic-modeling algorithm also clustered documents related to unidentified flying objects, which many have long assumed to be the ultimate government secret. She then calculated the average time elapsed between when the nuclear documents and UFO documents were first produced and when they were made available at the presidential libraries. It turns out that it takes an average of fifty-seven years for the nuclear documents to be released, and just fourteen years for the ones about UFOs.

In an exception that proves the rule for how to rank-order top secrets, it took the air force fifty-five years to declassify documents related to its own failed effort to build a flying saucer with a Canadian defense contractor. But it was not to fight aliens. Scientists believed that a saucer would be the optimal shape for a stealth aircraft, ideal for conducting aerial reconnaissance or delivering nuclear weapons against the USSR. When researchers at History Lab analyzed thousands of examples of previously redacted text, we found many more references to things like stealth aircraft, satellite reconnaissance, and electromagnetic-pulse weapons. But there was not even one little green man.

Tools to predict the half-life of state secrets also help us to look back and see the history of these secrets in a new light. This history will show that there were sometimes legitimate reasons to conceal what was happening—or not happening—in places like Roswell, New Mexico, but the reasons were rooted in U.S. nuclear strategy. It will also reveal how, for decades, the same cloak of secrecy allowed the government to cover up genuinely bizarre facts, like how nuclear scientists—not space aliens—were experimenting on hapless citizens. And perhaps most terrifying of all, officials also lied about and otherwise concealed how often there have been accidents involving thermonuclear weapons, and how close we have come to an accidental Armageddon.

In Hollywood movies, we are told that the government withholds information about planetary threats to avoid panic. But, as we will see in chapter 4, officials at the Pentagon have repeatedly tried to panic the American public by leaking what turned out to be exaggerated estimates of nuclear weapons in the hands of enemy states. False alarms about the "bomber gap" and the "missile gap" were deliberate—and successful—efforts to scare up more money for ever-more-advanced weaponry, to say nothing of Iraqi WMDs and "regime change." The upshot is that government officials actually preferred that people suspected they hid UFOs in the New Mexico desert if the alternative was to provide a full accounting of weapons development and testing programs.

This chapter will show how, after the dark state was first conceived at Pearl Harbor, it was the Manhattan Project that gave it a distinct form: a self-replicating system for controlling what is now called "sensitive compartmentalized information." Probing its history reveals the first principles and original design flaws that made this system self-serving and ultimately self-defeating, starting with the failed effort to concentrate the power to create new secrets in the hands of a small number of senior officials. There would be protocols to rank-order levels of classification, to stratify levels of security clearances, and to further compartmentalize particular secrets on a "need to know" basis. The system was meant to be self-regulating, since at the end of the war these same officials established principles and procedures for identifying what information to release so as to better contain what remained sensitive. But whereas every other element of the secrecy system empowered and emboldened any official who could create new compartments and hide inside of them, this last element, declassification, was meant to serve everyone, and therefore served no one in particular.

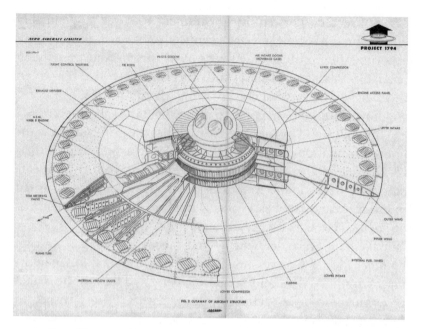

Avoid panic! An air-force attempt at building a flying saucer with alien technology—that is, Canadian technology.

As we shall see, even old secrets may still require safekeeping. Whereas many "top secrets" can be banal, countless officials have described their encounter with nuclear secrets as different, leading to a loss of innocence, and a new wariness that never goes away. Secret knowledge about the prospect that some bad actor will gain possession of the "ultimate weapon" and use it on an American city is, they say, what "keeps them up at night."

This is usually the end of the conversation, and the beginning of mistrust. Must we accept on faith that it is better we not know what officials know, especially when they tell us it is so worrisome? In fact, it is now possible to reconstruct how and why officials began to restrict information by first analyzing key historical documents, and then data-mining a mass of formerly classified text. Clearly defining what makes information dangerous is the first step in more effectively managing that risk. If there was ever an inner logic guiding this increasingly dysfunctional system, we should be able to reverse-engineer it, and then design new systems that might help bring official secrecy back under control.

This story begins in October 1941, even before Pearl Harbor, when Vannevar Bush convinced President Franklin Roosevelt that the work of British scientists justified committing resources for applied research on an atomic bomb. It started with a fifteen-hundred-dollar grant to Columbia University. But to actually produce atomic weapons required dramatically scaling up the project to amass the requisite amount of rare elements. The right kind of isotopes had to be removed atom by atom from uranium ore, a rare metal. Additionally, plutonium had to be created from uranium-238. Both processes required large and expensive plants that did not yet exist, plus an elite team of scientists and engineers to design and build the actual weapons.

Roosevelt entrusted the project to the army. Over the next few years, the Manhattan Project—named by convention for the city in which it was first located—employed hundreds of thousands of people at sites across the country. Los Alamos, New Mexico, was selected as the site for the laboratory, headed by J. Robert Oppenheimer. The Los Alamos site spanned some 45,000 acres and housed over 8,200 personnel by the end of 1945. But it was dwarfed by Oak Ridge, Tennessee, where some 75,000 people refined the uranium that would kill more than 100,000 people at Hiroshima. And in Hanford, Washington, it took 125,000 workers to produce the plutonium that destroyed Nagasaki. All housing and eating places were rigidly segregated by race, ostensibly to appease white workers who came from the South and despite organized protests by Black workers. In the case of Hanford, this required importing Jim Crow practices to the Pacific Northwest and continuing them long after Roosevelt had ordered war industries to be desegregated.

FDR wanted all this to be done in secret. He gave the Manhattan Project a secret budget funded with money siphoned away from other programs. Even the navy would be kept in the dark. As the work progressed, Roosevelt repeatedly reminded his subordinates of the need for "absolute secrecy."

Roosevelt had always been secretive, which makes reconstructing his motivation even for major decisions—including this one—highly uncertain. It might seem obvious why any president would want to keep such a program secret from the enemy. Otherwise, the massive U.S. investment might have provoked Germany and Japan to make the same effort. That was the main concern of key advisers, like Bush. Bush and George Marshall were also mindful of the power a monopoly over atomic weapons would give the United States to shape the postwar order. But while the war continued, they would need to work closely with London, which had its own systems for protecting sensitive information. That cooperation required developing methods commensurate with long-standing British standards.

The man put in charge of this effort, General Leslie Groves, shared these concerns, but later revealed still more reasons for the unprecedented secrecy of the Manhattan Project. He itemized them in a list that appeared in his postwar memoir, starting with keeping knowledge about nuclear weapons from "all other nations so that the U.S. position after the war would be as strong as possible." But he also wanted "to keep knowledge from those who would interfere directly or indirectly with the progress of the work, such as Congress and various executive branch offices," and to "limit discussion of the use of the bomb to a small group of officials."

Clearly, the secrecy surrounding the Manhattan Project was never just about winning World War II. It was about ensuring American pre-eminence over all potential rivals, and securing the power of "a small group of officials" within the U.S. government against anyone who might "interfere"—like legislators elected to represent the American people. It was reasonable to doubt the strategic vision and discretion of individual senators and representatives, as we shall see. But in time this rationale allowed any little group of bureaucrats to protect themselves from external scrutiny of any kind. Groves's last reason for upholding "absolute secrecy" was the most revealing of all: "To operate the program on a need-to-know basis by the use of compartmentalization."

So one acknowledged reason for secrecy was to be able to decide who got to know the secrets. For General Groves, the power that came with compartmentalization was an end in itself.

Groves developed new methods to safeguard these secrets. Hundreds of Manhattan Project personnel spied on their coworkers to guard against any breach in security. They impersonated electricians, painters, and exterminators—even hotel bellboys and professional gamblers. Not one person could come anywhere near these facilities without first being cleared. Even the FBI agents whose duty it was to vet project personnel were themselves required to undergo special vetting.

In the three years from the fall of 1942 to the first bomb, some four hundred thousand people were subjected to fingerprinting, citizenship verification, and close questioning about their finances, foreign countries visited, and relatives living abroad. Before being allowed to access classified information, they would all be made to read the Espionage Act and sign an oath committing themselves to absolute secrecy about every aspect of their work. It was a ritual that would be repeated countless times in the years that followed.

But background screening was just the first of five principles of the Manhattan Project security classification system. Even after they signed on the dotted line, and spent years working around the clock behind barbed-wire fences, the vast majority of these workers could not themselves create new secrets.

The second principle was therefore "original classification authority." Only certain people had the authority to classify information as an official secret. Limiting their number was supposed to limit the number of secrets, so each one could be clearly identified and closely guarded. But in practice, original classification authority mainly served to concentrate power in the hands of the most senior officials, and did little or nothing to limit secrecy overall. Because all information "derivative" of an official secret was treated as equally secret, and there was no limit to how much information—and how much paper—that might produce.

The third overarching principle was stratification. At Los Alamos, color-coded badges indicated the bearer's level of access.

The most senior scientists and officials were given white badges, which gave them access to colloquia that addressed all the most sensitive aspects of the project; other, lesser badges were given to technicians, then clerks, then warehouse employees and so on. While it was ostensibly intended only to limit access to secrets, this kind of stratification reproduced segregation. The DuPont Corporation recruited Black women to come to Hanford to be clerical workers, for instance, but somehow they ended up being reassigned to be cooks or maids and were never promoted to white-collar positions. Finding it impossible to fill all the needed clerical positions with white workers, officials still hesitated to hire Mexican Americans. Partly it was to avoid setting up a third set of segregated spaces, and partly it was because of the perception that Mexican Americans presented a security risk. Groves insisted on "careful checks as to citizenship and loyalty before these people are employed," with the result that it took three times longer to review them compared to white workers, and fewer than half were deemed acceptable.

Information was also stratified according to its level of sensitivity—restricted, confidential, secret, and top secret—with increasingly elaborate protocols for clearing people both to access such information and to handle it. In time, these different levels were defined to reflect levels of damage that might result if the secrets were revealed. Under Eisenhower, the revelation of "Confidential" information would be "prejudicial to the defense interests of the nation." Revealing "top secret" information—like Lodge's account of his conversation with Churchill—"could result in exceptionally grave damage to the Nation." The examples provided included a break in diplomatic relations, an armed attack, and the compromise of military plans or vital defense research. But here again, Groves set an example by insisting that all information related to the bomb be classified at the highest possible level.

Groves's fourth principle was compartmentalization. Even people cleared to access top-secret information would not have access to information classified at a lower level if they were not specifically "read in" to the program that produced it. Those who passed the background check were thus put into different silos, at higher or lower levels, according to which secrets they needed to know to fulfill their programmatic responsibility. Horizontal levels of classification and vertical silos for each program created a vast matrix visible only to a small elite who were both authorized to create top secrets and read into every secret program.

"Compartmentalization of knowledge to me was the very heart of security . . . ," as General Groves recalled. "Each man should know everything he needed to know to do his job and nothing else. Adherence to this rule not only provided an adequate measure of security but it greatly improved overall efficiency by making our people stick to their knitting."

In 1943, when Groves began to assemble scientists at the secret laboratory in Los Alamos to design the "gadget," some bridled at the equation of ignorance with strength. They pointed out that "ignorance equals strength" could actually be dangerous if, for instance, the engineers at Oak Ridge did not understand that $E = mc^2$. Compartmentalizing information could lead them to compartmentalize uranium, which in sufficient quantity would create a chain reaction and blow up the whole plant. Conversely, keeping smart people apart in separate compartments would hinder their ability to collaborate and innovate. After all, turning $E = mc^2$ into an efficient and reliable bomb was an unprecedented challenge. The scientists needed all the help they could get.

Additionally, the sort of absentminded professors brought to Los Alamos were not the kind of people who would always stay in their lane, or even look before crossing traffic. When the Danish physicist Niels Bohr and his son came to Los Alamos, for instance, the security officer who tailed them quickly grew exasperated:

> It was rare when either of them paid much attention to stop lights or signs, but proceeded on their way much the same as if they were walking in the woods. On one occasion, subjects proceeded across a busy intersection against the red light in a diagonal fashion, taking the longest route possible and one of greatest danger.

The agent actually had to block traffic with his vehicle to prevent the Bohrs from being run over by a truck. Father and son alike seemed oblivious to the surveillance.

Friendly, execution-avoiding advice from the Atomic Energy Commission

Other scientists, like Richard Feynman, treated secrecy strictures as a challenge, and openly mocked and defied them—whether they took the form of menacing propaganda posters, puerile government films, or censorship of their personal correspondence. Feynman, who was twenty-four at the time, had the personality of a hacker, and set about systematically testing and exploiting every hole in the system. In some cases, they were actual holes, like the one service workers had cut out of the fence around Los Alamos so as to avoid the bother of remembering their passes and waiting in line at the gated entrances. The guards never understood how Feynman seemed to go out the gate without ever coming back in. He even won a bet that security staff would not notice when he put precise information about how to locate this secret, unguarded entrance in the outgoing mail.

Feynman knew the secrets he was supposed to be guarding were quite literally explosive, and could not understand why security professionals were obsessed with orchestrating security theater while remaining oblivious to all the ways they could be hacked. Just to prove a point, he set about learning how to decode the three-digit combination of locking filing cabinets, the main way in which project personnel were supposed to protect sensitive design and engineering documents. Like most successful hackers, Feynman came to realize that the solution was not some brilliant tool or technology, but exploiting simple human weakness. This included the very human tendency to leave a file drawer unlocked, which allowed Feynman to take note of the last digit of the combination. When he came to visit a colleague and made conversation, he would play with the dial—seemingly absentmindedly—to see when the bolt moved up and down. This gave him two of the three digits, and there remained only twenty possible combinations. When the coast was clear, Feynman would come back and try each one of them until the drawers popped open—all in three minutes or less.

To Feynman, all this was great fun. He never seemed to worry about losing a top-level security clearance, not understanding that privileged access for people like himself was part of the underlying logic. Others, suspect only because of their race or ethnicity, had no hope of having this kind of security. Most of Feynman's colleagues gave little thought to the security protocols, and happily talked about their work in a spirit of open scientific inquiry. Robert Oppenheimer himself presided over weekly meetings in which senior scientists discussed all aspects of their work in detail. But the holes in the Manhattan Project system, and the security theater that represented and reinforced privilege, had extremely serious consequences, and not just in terms of who was systematically excluded. The same system failed to keep out actual spies, like Klaus Fuchs, a German-born physicist from the U.K., and David Greenglass, a machinist who worked at Oak Ridge and then Los Alamos. Neither was caught until 1950. But during the war, FBI surveillance teams twice discovered communist agents obtaining information about the Manhattan Project from American physicists. In both cases, they revoked the scientists' security clearances, drafted them into the military, and sent them to spend the rest of the war in Alaska. But since this counterespionage work was also compartmentalized, and other scientists supposedly did not "need to know," none realized that the threat was very real.

Soviet agents, for their part, knew to start cultivating physicists once research on nuclear fission stopped appearing in scientific journals. The subject's conspicuous absence made it obvious that the work was important and promising enough to be kept secret. As further proof, mentions of uranium and atomic energy all but disappeared from the popular press. As Alex Wellerstein notes in his brilliant history of nuclear secrecy, the cloak of secrecy itself could be a dead giveaway.

But the most fundamental flaw in the secrecy system was that, after having set in motion processes that produced an ever-expanding mass of classified, stratified, and compartmented information, Groves gave little thought to what they would do with it all, and how they could possibly protect all the information in those filing cabinets if the cabinets started overflowing with secret documents. He did not even begin to deal with the question of what could be disclosed until the summer of 1945. Now that Germany had surrendered, and Japan was on the brink of total defeat, some of the scientists opposed using the weapon to kill large numbers of civilians. Though they did so without violating their secrecy vows, it was clear that, once the bomb dropped, they would not keep silent, and would instead warn the world of the necessity of international control of nuclear power.

Groves handled it as a public-relations problem. As such, it would be corollary to the "need to know" principle, only now it concerned what Groves needed the public to know so as to put the Manhattan Project in the best possible light. Rather than setting in motion an actual system for declassifying all information that was no longer sensitive, Groves and his team prepared a package of press releases, authorized stories, and official reports. It would drop right after the atomic bomb dropped on Hiroshima.

"Publicity day" was a great success. With no other information available—and official notification that nothing more could be revealed about the bomb—the media and the public eagerly consumed the stories crafted by the Manhattan Project PR team. One of the main themes was how the bomb had been the war's "best kept secret," with the implication that the United States could control knowledge about the bomb to slow or stop other countries from acquiring it. Groves was so intent on pushing this particular story that he earned a reprimand from Army Intelligence for disclosing classified methods used for concealing the bomb.

So this was the fifth and final principle of Groves's security classification system: the strategic release of selected information, including classified information, if that proved necessary for favorable PR. Not all of these secrecy principles started with the Manhattan Project, but the project's reputation for success made them seem like a successful and replicable model, including security screening, original classification authority, stratification, compartmentalization, and—the flip side of official secrecy—spin.

Because the public and Congress first learned about the bomb at the same time they were told it was the ultimate weapon, it seemed both possible and necessary to create another important precedent, one that was also rather unprincipled. World War II's first "top secrets" had concerned temporarily sensitive information, like the timing and location of the D-Day landings. By classifying all information about the bomb as a "top secret," and seeking to continue this level of secrecy indefinitely, Groves was not just showing how one could game any classification system to prioritize one's own secrets. He was seeking a permanent change in how the government would handle sensitive information in peacetime.

With the creation of the AEC in 1946, officials gained formal and permanent powers over information that astonished even the government lawyers involved in drafting the law. "Is it necessary, for example, to brush aside all of the checks and balances of our form of government," Vannevar Bush's general counsel asked, ". . . constituting them as a virtual supra state?" Congress had had no input in writing the bill, and if it was passed into law even the president would have no power over the commission. But Groves was intent on overcoming growing opposition and ending congressional-committee hearings about the bomb. He finally got his way when, in February 1946, newspaper head-lines revealed the news—quite likely leaked by Groves himself—that Canada had uncovered a Soviet espionage ring. In fact, the House then insisted that the law require the FBI to conduct a full investigation of anyone accessing restricted data, and make deliberate espionage punishable by death.

It has been argued that this legislation created a parallel sys-tem for nuclear secrets, separate and apart from other secrets. But in fact, Hoover's G-men would be the gatekeepers standing in the way of countless job seekers who needed a security clear-ance as a condition of employment at many other departments and agencies. Moreover, the government would go on to obtain comparable legal powers to punish private citizens who shared information about cryptography or secret agents. The Manhat-tan Project was thus the first full prototype of a "special access program"—i.e., a program in which those special people with a "need to know" create the same kinds of protocols to prevent outsiders from knowing or saying anything about what they do. It thus started a chain reaction. The matrix of stratified and com-partmentalized knowledge, the unaccountable power that origi-nated in original classification authority, and the piles and piles of secret papers all began to grow out of control.

The different levels of secrecy, and vertical silos of compart-mentalized information, created countless spaces where unac-countable power and classified papers could accumulate long after the original rationale was lost, forgotten, or destroyed. It is well known that the things hidden in these spaces were sometimes trivial or stupid, and we will see many examples—everything from surveillance cats to psychic experiments. But we need to dig deeper if we wish to discover what secrets inspired—and seemed to require—this ever-more-unwieldy system.

More than two months after publicizing the Manhattan Project's supposed success in keeping the bomb secret, and after drafting the legislation giving the government permanent control of nuclear information, Groves finally got around to addressing a growing number of requests—even demands—from Congress and the media that the Project review and release information that no longer required safekeeping. He convened a committee of scientists to consider what process could be put in place. Declassification was, quite literally, an afterthought, and some members just stopped coming to the meetings. But Groves needed a solution. Simply destroying nonessential information was not an answer, since it was hard to predict what might later prove useful. When a shortage of plutonium forced the AEC to switch back to using one of the original wartime bomb designs, for instance, officials were dismayed to discover that all the people who made these bombs had left, and new personnel would have to reproduce this work, using whatever schematics and specifications they could find. Groves therefore realized that he could not handle information management strictly as a matter of public relations. But the more carefully he managed the downgrading and eventual release of less sensitive documents, the more control he could continue to exert over what remained. The committee would create categories that continued to define the top nuclear secrets for many years to come.

The most sensitive information was assigned to "category III," which included:

- Weapons design, e.g., details about explosive lenses, firing systems, fuses, detonators
- Bomb storage, production rates, and the size of the stockpile
- The design and operation of gaseous diffusion plants like those in Oak Ridge, including production rates, flow charts, pressure levels, and the design and capacity of pumps, filters, blowers, and motors
- Last, but not least, the potential for building a "super," or what came to be known as the Hydrogen Bomb

But even top secrets like these can greatly differ in their nature and political implications. Decades later, a Columbia law professor named David Pozen developed an analytical framework to highlight these subtler differences, distinguishing "deep" from "shallow" secrets. The first three examples of "category III" top secrets were shallow in the sense that any thoughtful observer would assume the bombs had different designs, production rates, and storage locations. These details could be devastatingly important, but they were fundamentally different from the last compartment. The H-bomb was a "deep secret" because the public did not know anything about it—and, unlike the first three secrets, no one without "special access" could even be aware that such a secret existed.

Initially, people were mainly curious about the topmost item, the design of the bomb itself. The nature of the object and its presentation—encased, self-contained, and handled with extreme care—conveyed the idea, and reality, of immense power, and of inner workings invisible to all but the initiated. It also seemed like the "absolute weapon," so the actual number of bombs did not appear nearly so important. And it was very tangible in a way that flowcharts and equations could never be. In some people—like Winston Churchill—the bomb inspired feelings that approached reverence, starting with the first press releases. "This revelation of the secrets of nature," the prime minister announced, "long mercifully withheld from man, should arouse the most solemn reflections in the mind and conscience of every human being capable of comprehension."

But other officials, with more experience managing technology and engineering projects, were skeptical about whether all the secrecy shrouding the bomb was strictly necessary. The first chairman of the Atomic Energy Commission, David Lilienthal, had previously chaired the Tennessee Valley Authority. He agreed with the scientists that too much secrecy stifled progress. After talking with them, he approached his new post with a "hunch," suspecting that "there are no secrets (that is, nothing that is not known or knowable)." Many people understood the basic physics of a nuclear chain reaction. All it took was to bring together a critical mass of enriched uranium or plutonium, such that neutrons knocking into atoms would release more neutrons. These would knock into more atoms, releasing even more neutrons, and ever more energy. The rest—i.e., how to separate the uranium isotopes, how to breed plutonium, how to mill and shape the materials—these were not solemn religious mysteries, as Churchill suggested. They were just secrets—trade secrets. The information was accessible to rival nations. All they needed was commitment, competent people, and time. In five years or so—about the same amount of time it took the United States—they could produce another "revelation," and another, and another. . . .

Even though the theoretical possibility of harnessing a chain reaction to make a bomb was widely known, until one was successfully used against another nation in wartime no one would be certain it could be engineered into a practical, deliverable weapon. That required a design that would achieve critical mass at precisely the right moment. Once the mushroom cloud appeared over Hiroshima, other nations could and would devote the necessary effort.

But when, in January 1946, Oppenheimer himself initiated Lilienthal into the story of the Manhattan Project, the new AEC chairman came away with a different feeling, finding it an "utterly bizarre and, literally, incredible business."

> There were things that have never even been hinted at that are accomplished, or virtually accomplished, facts, that change the whole thesis of our inquiry, and of the course of the world in this generation. None of this can be written down. These are the very top of the top secrets of our country; some of them are likely to remain secrets for some time to come.

Certain aspects of weaponizing a nuclear reaction would have been surprising to Lilienthal, and to anyone learning these secrets for the first time. Peering inside the Manhattan Project, Lilienthal would have seen not one absolute weapon, but two— Fat Man and Little Boy. They both solved the same basic design problem: delivering a critical mass of uranium or plutonium to the target without having the reaction start too soon or fizzle too quickly. But otherwise they were completely different.

In the "Little Boy" Hiroshima bomb, the shell casing enclosed a tube, with two masses of uranium at either end, neither big enough to go critical. Forty-four seconds after the device was released from the B-29's bomb-bay doors, an explosive charge would propel one mass down the tube to smash into the other. The chain reaction would begin as the bomber pulled safely away. The scientists in Los Alamos were so confident this "gun type" weapon would work the first time it was tried that they did not think it was even necessary to test it. The published report issued a week after it dropped acknowledged the basic design of the bomb. And if terrorists ever drive a "garage bomb" to a city near you, it will likely work much the same way.

But many of the specifics of the Hiroshima device were counterintuitive, and different design choices could have rendered the bomb a dud. For instance, decades later, an atomic hobbyist named John Coster-Mullen discovered that the common assumption about the relationship between the two masses was completely wrong. Everyone believed the projectile would be a cylindrical shell, like an artillery shell, that would be fired into a larger target. In fact, it was the other way around: the projectile had a hole in the middle, and after it was fired it enveloped a smaller cylinder.

But even when you put all this together, of the 111 pounds of uranium painstakingly collected at Oak Ridge—far more precious than gold—only 1.38 percent actually contributed to the explosion. All of it was essential to ensure maximum destruction at Hiroshima, but almost 99 percent was essentially wasted because of the crudeness of the design.

Midway through the Manhattan Project, most of the scientists switched to a different, more elegant solution to igniting a nuclear reaction, one that would use plutonium from Hanford. The idea was to create an implosion. Rather than the artillery tube in the Little Boy bomb, the internal design of "Fat Man" looked like a soccer ball, with sixty-four explosive charges arranged symmetrically around the plutonium core. If they were shaped and timed just right, the detonation of the explosives would compress the plutonium into a critical mass. Just fourteen pounds would generate energy equivalent to over forty thousand pounds of high explosive, significantly more than the bomb at Hiroshima. Stealing this secret would enable another nation—like the USSR—to focus from the outset on this more efficient design, rather than having to duplicate the effort.

But however clever, none of this information would probably have struck someone like Lilienthal—already familiar with the basic concept of engineering a chain reaction—as "bizarre," much less something that could not be written down. In fact, all of it had to be written down in great detail, as bomb-making teams struggled to devise ways to accelerate production. This struggle explains why the size of the stockpile was one of the category III "top secrets," especially as the United States and Soviet Union entered into a series of crises following the end of World War II. It is harder to explain why even President Truman himself was not briefed on the number of U.S. nuclear weapons until 1946, and possibly not until April 1947. During this period, he pressured Stalin to withdraw from a wartime occupation of northern Iran, backed Turkey against Soviet demands for naval bases on the Dardanelles, and then went to Congress seeking military aid for governments like Greece, which faced a communist insurgency. A few weeks after this congressional speech challenging the USSR, Truman was disturbed to learn that America's entire nuclear arsenal consisted of seven weapons.

One might think that even two bombs would have been enough to frighten Moscow (and Leningrad). But Stalin did not frighten easily. He had already shown in the most recent war that he was prepared to sacrifice over seventeen hundred towns, seventy thousand villages, and some twenty-five million people if that proved necessary to achieve victory. Even after the United States stockpiled more bombs—a total of fifty-six by 1948—it still added up to what some called a "hollow threat." How would American bomber crews even find their targets? Before the era of spy satellites, much of the USSR was an unmapped mystery. Many of the planes flying into the USSR would not be carrying bombs. They would be carrying cameras, just looking for (and looking like) targets.

When Curtis LeMay took over the Strategic Air Command in 1948, just one unit, the 509th Bombardment Group, was trained to drop atomic weapons, and they were still flying B-29's, the prop-driven World War II veterans. By that point, almost all the best pilots had left. In a simulated night attack on Dayton, Ohio, the few pilots who reached their target missed by more than two miles. In an actual raid on Moscow with atomic bombs, two miles would be the difference between destroying the Kremlin or just convincing everyone inside its thick walls of the need for an all-out war of revenge.

Imagine you were LeMay, and word came that the United States was going to war. At any given time, only half the nuclear-capable B-29's—perhaps two dozen—were operational. The AEC had custody of the bombs, and kept them at a different base. It would take five or six days just to bring together the bombs and the bombers and fly to forward airfields in the U.K. or Libya. The lead-acid batteries of the Fat Man bombs were only good for thirty-six hours. If you did not locate and strike a target in that window, the battery would take three days to recharge. The whole weapon had to be disassembled and reassembled with a new battery no more than ten days after the first was installed. Otherwise, the heat produced by the plutonium core would destroy the surrounding explosives. This process, too, required two to three days, and it could only be done by a special team of fifty men. There were only three such teams in the world.

After your first strike, you would therefore only have about one usable bomb every twenty-eight hours. After two weeks, the rate would slow to one bomb every fifty-six hours, accounting for the probable exhaustion of the assembly teams. The teams would also likely be under attack, both by saboteurs and Soviet bombers. And by this point, your targets might have to include Brussels, Paris, and Rome, since U.S. war plans assumed the Red Army would already have swept across Western Europe.

So when, in 1947, a rancher near the air-force base in Roswell, New Mexico, recovered strange-looking debris, and local investigators put out a press release reporting a "flying disc," more senior government officials immediately moved to quash any outside interest in what they were actually doing there. After all, Roswell was the home base of the 509th Bombardment Group, and thus two of the category III top secrets—design details of atomic bombs, and the fact that the United States lacked the capability to deliver more than a small number of them. Compounding the government's concern, the wreckage turned out to be from a top-secret research project. Scientists were deploying high-altitude balloons with sensors to detect any blasts that would signal that the Soviets had started testing their own weapons. Repurposing some of the details of the incident, they put out a cover story claiming the debris came from a weather balloon. Investigators from the Roswell base themselves did not know the full story, because the balloon project was conducted on a "need to know" basis.

So the real secret, the secret that really did appear to pose the risk of provoking an alien invasion, was not that the United States had captured a ship from outer space. It was that, even in bases hidden behind barbed-wire fences in the New Mexico desert, there was actually very little to cover up—only a very big bluff. If the Soviets had called that bluff, American officials feared the Red Army would roll over Western Europe, then mobilize its conquered resources to prepare an invasion of the Western Hemisphere. In the late 1940s, at the dawn of the Cold War, the United States was playing a very weak hand: a couple dozen prop-driven bombers, a small number of temperamental atomic bombs, and a long backlog of maintenance and supply problems.

Of course, the fact that Washington was bluffing does not mean that Moscow had a stronger hand. As we shall see in the next chapter, the Soviets were, if anything, in an even weaker position. But Lilienthal did not know that. So is this what he had in mind when he described something that was too risky to be written down or even hinted at—the puny size of the U.S. nuclear arsenal? Probably not. It was an immensely important secret, but this secret was just a number—a small number. Moreover, Lilienthal described at least part of the secret as something that had not yet been accomplished, but that would change "the course of the world."

What Lilienthal was likely talking about was not how to build an atomic bomb, or how few bombs had actually been built. Instead, he was almost certainly thinking of that deeper secret: the prospect of a far more powerful *thermonuclear* bomb. Compared with a thermonuclear weapon—also called a hydrogen bomb, or H-bomb—a Nagasaki-type atomic bomb was literally just a fuse. Even experienced strategists like Churchill and Eisenhower would confess that they found it difficult to think through how war would actually work with weapons as powerful as these. The H-bomb was indeed the kind of secret that had not yet been accomplished, that could change the world, and that had to be tightly contained.

The H-bomb really was the ultimate weapon. It would give the aggressor a huge advantage in the opening hours of an attack, as Churchill realized when he pondered a thermonuclear Pearl Harbor. But in 1947, Truman had not yet decided whether the United States should go ahead with the massive military expansion required to develop and deploy forces capable of waging thermonuclear war. If America could keep the potential for H-bombs secret, as Lilienthal probably hoped, they might continue to delay their development indefinitely. The country might not have needed to take the unprecedented step of building a peacetime military-industrial complex.

But, as would occur repeatedly in years to come, even a deep secret that was supposed to be protected at all costs did not last for long, and not just because the Soviets had so effectively penetrated the Manhattan Project. In November 1949, a grandstanding senator, Edwin C. Johnson of Colorado, told the whole world. Ironically—and stupidly—the senator was trying to make an argument for more secrecy during a televised debate, complaining that scientists had already given away too much information. The host asked why it mattered, considering the Soviets had already tested their first atomic bomb, dubbed "Joe 1." Johnson replied,

> I'm glad you asked me that question, because here's the thing that is top secret. Our scientists from the time that the bombs were detonated at Hiroshima and Nagasaki have been trying to make what is known as a superbomb. . . . Now our scientists already—already have created a bomb that has six times the effectiveness of the bomb that was dropped at Nagasaki and they're not satisfied at all; they

want one that has a thousand times the effect of that terrible bomb that was dropped at Nagasaki that snuffed out the lives of—of fifty thousand people just like that. And that's the secret, that's the big secret that the scientists in America are so anxious to divulge to the whole scientific world.

Or that *was* the big secret—the secret that Lilienthal was so determined to protect—until Senator Johnson took it upon himself to announce it on live television. Two months later, authorities discovered that Klaus Fuchs had already told the Soviets about the possibility of a thermonuclear weapon, and much else besides. With the help of Fuchs, Greenglass, and two other spies, who were not unmasked until decades later, Ted Hall and Oscar Seborer, the Soviets were able to learn the critical mass required for the implosion design, the dimensions of the key components, and the design of the initiator, tamper, and high-explosive lens. The contribution of these spies was long debated, since Russian scientists did not like to admit they had cheated on the ultimate physics exam. But it was later confirmed that the information they passed along was critically important in jump-starting the Soviet program, helping the Soviets to avoid blind alleys, and accelerating their race to completion.

Fuchs, Greenglass, and Hall acted independently and unbeknownst to one another. The vaunted secrecy system surrounding the Manhattan Project had been a failure, in no small part because all that secrecy turned out to be self-defeating. All three did it for the same reason: They did not think that one nation should monopolize the kind of power that nuclear weapons bestowed—especially when it kept the rest of the world in the dark.

As U.S. officials came to understand just how much Fuchs had given away, they despaired that there were no secrets left. Fuchs had had his hands in virtually everything. The top priority became to reveal the rest of the Soviet network and deter any other would-be spies. Greenglass's handler, Julius Rosenberg, refused to name names. So they put Rosenberg's wife, Ethel, on trial, too, in that way threatening to make orphans of their two

When viewed side by side, Fat Man and Joe 1 looked like evil twins, a dead giveaway for those already suspicious of Soviet espionage.

sons. As the testimony began to touch on technical aspects of the bomb, the judge cleared the room. But with the consent of AEC officials, he called the reporters back in again, and the prosecution introduced Exhibit 8, Greenglass's sketch "of the very atomic bomb itself."

Everyone in the courtroom was awestruck. If anything, it's

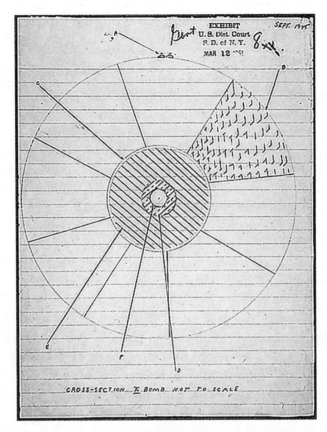

The Nagasaki implosion design for an atomic bomb

even more amazing today, now that we know how such information could be used, and not just by a superpower like the USSR. But in the early Cold War world, when the USSR seemed like the only important adversary, the moment the Soviets knew a secret it seemed to matter little if everyone else knew it, too. The overriding worry was the spread of communism as directed by Moscow, whether through subversion or invasion.

U.S. officials were not nearly as worried about the spread of nuclear weapons to other states or insurgents. When, later that same year, a top-secret intelligence estimate concluded that it would be relatively easy to smuggle a bomb into an American city on a merchant ship, the authors assumed it would be under orders from the Kremlin. Thus, convicting the Rosenbergs, and sending that message to potential spies and saboteurs for the USSR, was deemed paramount.

So little did U.S. officials worry about nuclear proliferation—much less nuclear terrorism—that they exported uranium, heavy water, and reactor designs all over the world starting in the 1950s. Under the "Atoms for Peace" policy, it was not just close allies that gained access to U.S. nuclear technology, but also India and Pakistan. What remained sensitive, even sacred, was war planning, command and control systems, and newer designs to miniaturize these devices so they could be deployed in planes and missiles.

All this began to change in the early 1960s, when the potential pace of nuclear proliferation began to dawn on U.S. officials. President John F. Kennedy warned that as many as fifteen or twenty-five countries might obtain nuclear weapons by the 1970s. In 1964, the same year China became a nuclear power, the Lawrence Livermore National Laboratory conducted "The Nth Country Experiment" to see how quickly other countries might follow. They challenged three freshly minted physics Ph.D.'s to come up with a viable design for a nuclear weapon. Even working part-time, and with no access to classified information, the team produced a workable implosion design in about two years—approximately the same length of time it had taken thousands of scientists and engineers to build the first bombs at Los Alamos. Decades later, when the report was finally released, you could *almost* see why: the team helpfully included a four-page bibliography of publicly available books and articles useful for building a bomb. Even in 2003—especially in 2003, two years after 9/11—it was thought necessary to redact every entry.

Eight years after the Nth Country Experiment, in 1972, the government began to consider the terrorist threat in deciding what information to keep secret. It was much too late. During the 1970s, college students started cribbing from publicly available information to create designs for atomic bombs, writing up their research as term papers. After newspapers reported the work of one Princeton undergrad, an official from the Pakistani Embassy reached out and tried to obtain a copy. A Harvard economics major, motivated by the prospect of making money, submitted a draft manuscript with several designs of his own to the DOE, which promptly classified and confiscated his work.

But if there had been a prize for the best student project on nuclear secrecy, it would have gone to someone who still prefers to remain anonymous. In 1970, he sent the police department of Orlando, Florida, a sketch of a thermonuclear weapon along with a ransom note demanding a million dollars. "This is no bluff," he insisted. "If you think it is ask the Atomic Energy Commission what happened to the shipments of U235 that never got to their destinations." In fact, some two hundred pounds of weapons-grade uranium had earlier gone missing in Apollo, Pennsylvania, enough for several bombs. The AEC could not rule out the possibility that this material had now turned up in Orlando, and an expert advised the FBI that it was a workable design. The authorities were getting ready to pay the ransom when the police finally apprehended the culprit: it turned out to be a fourteen-year-old boy.

Because of all the information that was made publicly available, finding a workable design is therefore not going to be the most serious challenge for a country, terrorist organization, or teenage prodigy desiring to build an atomic bomb. The hard part is to acquire a sufficient quantity of highly enriched uranium, and then work with this molten, radioactive material without inadvertently starting a fire or a chain reaction. But just to be safe, in 1986 the DOE went into the Smithsonian Museum to remove the internal components of a Little Boy shell casing.

Some would argue that no one would ever use such a museum piece as their model. Both then and now, the Little Boy design would be inefficient, and high-maintenance, and would have a short shelf-life. But the calculus would be different for a group of terrorists. They would not need a device that could fit inside the nose cone of an intercontinental ballistic missile (ICBM) and sit in the missile silo for several years. Terrorists would likely build a bomb to fit in a delivery truck and deploy it right away. Even a failed gun-type device could still start a chain reaction and produce an explosion equivalent to a hundred tons or more of TNT before it fizzled out. This nuclear dud could still wreck the White House and irradiate everything in the vicinity if deto-nated from a thousand feet away—or as far as St. John's Church, on the other side of Lafayette Square.

So it would have been better to keep that first category III compartment—schematics for bomb components—a top secret as long as possible. There was no compelling public interest in revealing the details of workable bomb designs. What remains secret and worth protecting is the security surrounding nuclear materials, and the means whereby another nation can produce them. We are talking about blueprints for the production and storage of materials, like gas centrifuges, rather than blueprints for bombs.

Since 1999, the DOE has continued reclassifying thousands of documents pertaining to nuclear weapons and withholding many more that would have been declassified at an earlier date. But the process sometimes defies reason, such as when DOE officials redacted reports on the size of the U.S. nuclear stockpile from the 1960s—figures that U.S. officials disclosed at a press conference long ago. There are also cases in which govern-ment officials—though in this case the Pentagon and the CIA—reclassified documents that had no real sensitivity. It is possible that they were trying to bury the signal in the noise, making it harder to determine what officials really wished to conceal. If so, this was a clear violation of White House executive orders, which only permit classification of truly sensitive information. And, ultimately, this reclassification program was counterpro-ductive, because watchdog groups just drew more attention to these records—still in their possession and then made available online—and thus embarrassed the CIA.

For the most part, however, it is not clever strategy that leads officials to keep too many Cold War–era documents classified. It is the original design flaw in the whole security classification system: It was one thing to set up a committee to prioritize top secrets. It was quite another to review millions of potentially sensitive records, document by document, to decide what could be released. The overall system was built to classify and com-partmentalize information with no external oversight, but with little thought given to how to limit the relentless accumulation of secret paper. From the earliest days, declassification reviewers complained that they had insufficient guidance. Even in 1954, the AEC had already accumulated sixty million classified documents, and the piles have only kept getting higher. Just training people at every declassification office to recognize restricted data is a well-nigh-impossible task. After trainees are given a quick tour of nuclear physics, they are asked to learn and remember thousands of specialized terms and "subject area indicators," from the alpha-n initiator to the atomic number for uranium. For electronic records, the DOE uses software to search automatically for these "dirty words." But that generates many, many "false positives," such as when a document with "PAL" is referring not to "permissive action links"—how the United States commands and controls nuclear weapons—but Philippine Airlines.

The stakes are extremely high. There really are dangerous secrets buried in the piles of yellowing paper, secrets that could help bad actors build or steal a bomb that could destroy an American city. Now, with electronic records, the growth of secret data is accelerating. And as more and more of the declassified records are made available online, it may become easier to ferret out useful information. The rickety system that Groves first set up some eighty years ago—made even more unwieldy by the 1998 legal requirements mandating page-by-page review—cannot possibly cope with the overwhelming accumulation of nuclear secrets in the digital age.

So is there a better way? How can we identify the really top secrets when it comes to nuclear weapons? If we can mine the data in a way that detects secrets in individual documents, we might actually be able to help the government find things that really do require safekeeping.

To do that, History Lab researchers ran a series of experiments. First, the DOE told us what software they use to scan millions of documents. They also gave us their training manual, which includes an appendix listing all of the words indicative of restricted or formerly restricted data that they feed into the system. We then replicated the DOE's process using our collection of 117,000 documents that had been declassified at presidential libraries since the 1970s. This technique produced a rank-ordered list of the documents according to which ones have the highest proportion of "dirty words" compared with all the words in the document.

Data scientists consider this approach to be relatively primitive. It's an example of first-generation computing, in which you have to decide beforehand what data and what process will produce the optimal result. In this case, the software is tasked with finding a particular set of words, counting them up, measuring how many there are relative to all the words in the document, and, finally, rank-ordering the documents from highest to lowest proportion of said words. Such brute force can be effective, as we shall see. But this method produces a lot of false positives. It's like a test for infection that identifies nearly all the people who have the virus, but also many people who do not. That means documents that are bookings with Philippine Airlines along with the ones including war plans that outline permissive action links. Inspecting all of it page by page is one of the biggest bottlenecks in the current declassification system.

We therefore experimented with a "machine learning" approach, the same approach companies like Amazon use to predict the products that you are most likely to purchase. Obviously, you can't tell a computer what words to look for when you have millions of customers and millions of products. The specific words in a customer's search query may not help much, in part because words have different meanings in different contexts. So the contextual information is key: someone who searches for "masks" after purchasing hand sanitizer is not likely to be interested in masks to wear to a Halloween party.

Data scientists develop algorithms that tirelessly try out different combinations and select for those that produce the most accurate predictions. When applied to the task of identifying documents with nuclear information, the algorithm should select for the ones with combinations of words characteristic of

RD and FRD. Ironically, in computer science this is called a classification task, and the algorithms are known as classifiers.

To start, we wanted to know which documents were created by the AEC or the DOE, the agencies most likely to deal with sensitive nuclear information. We found 95 percent of them: our algorithms only missed one target document out of twenty. But of all the documents identified as from the AEC or the DOE, fully a third were false positives—i.e., they were actually from the Pentagon, the CIA, or some other department or agency. Fortunately, machine-learning classifiers—unlike human classifiers— also rank-order the documents, making it much easier to check their work, in this case checking whether some of those documents not from the AEC or the DOE contained nuclear information. We studied the top fifty and found only one was *not* about nuclear weapons: document number 43 was a 1968 targeting list from the Joint Chiefs of Staff describing what B-52's should avoid hitting in North Vietnam. This document was a near miss. Richard Nixon would later order strikes on many of the same targets with conventional munitions, but with the same nuclear-capable B-52's, in a deliberate attempt to make people think he was the kind of madman who might actually start a nuclear war. A more typical document was number 44: a State Department memorandum that helpfully specifies the necessary barrel length for a gun-type nuclear bomb, as well as the size and weight of material needed for an implosion device.

We also found that a lot of the documents produced by the AEC itself were not about nuclear weapons per se. They were more often about personnel security, such as the investigation that eventually stripped Robert Oppenheimer of his security clearance, ostensibly because of his communist family connections. Algorithms can only be as accurate as the data with which we train them, so we needed to get more specific than just identifying documents from nuclear agencies.

So we ran a second experiment. This time we used 613 documents that actually had stamps indicating RESTRICTED DATA or FORMERLY RESTRICTED DATA to train the algorithm to find similarly categorized material. In many cases, the actual words that contained RD and FRD were redacted. We were still able to identify about 90 percent of the documents we were looking for, with 30 percent proving to be false positives. Most important, of the one hundred documents ranked highest—i.e., those the algorithms rated as most likely to have RD or FRD—all but one contained nuclear-related information.

Both experiments demonstrated how there will always be a trade-off—increase the percentage of target documents identified, and you'll inevitably increase the number of false positives, too. But with machine-learning classifiers, unlike human classifiers, we can quickly recalibrate depending on the desired goal and the available resources. The DOE would likely choose to optimize the algorithm to find the highest possible percentage of dangerous documents, as long as there are enough reviewers available to find that one true positive out of a thousand false positives. After all, one nuclear attack on an American city would be one too many.

The ideal "declassification engine" would combine brute-force and machine-learning methods to prioritize the relatively small number of records that require close scrutiny by well-trained reviewers. There would still be some risk, but that risk could be quantified, and if it seemed too high, we would know what additional resources—human resources—would be required to reduce it to an acceptable level.

We can already see how a prototype might perform by running one final experiment, comparing and combining these different methods using the same set of 117,000 documents declassified at presidential libraries, and then evaluating the results page by page to see if they succeeded in identifying highly sensitive records. If the two approaches produced totally different results, we would know that at least one of them was not working.

In fact, we found the two methods produced very similar rankings. The records that had the most similar rankings of all were the ones both methods ranked at the very top—i.e., as highly likely to have nuclear information. When we inspected them, we found that the highest-ranking records not only had nuclear secrets, they contained incredibly sensitive information about the most dangerous aspects of the nuclear-arms race.

So let's look at the top documents, the top secrets according to our prototype declassification engine. First, we will look at the document scored as most likely to have restricted data when we average results from the two methods. Second, we will examine the top document using the DOE's brute-force method. Finally, we will see which document ranked highest using machine learning.

The most sensitive document based on an average of the two methods (fifth out of 117,000 using machine learning, and third using the DOE approach) is a Joint Chiefs of Staff report from 1966. Sure enough, it's "Top Secret/Restricted Data." A cover letter from the then chairman of the Joint Chiefs, Earle Wheeler, urged special handling. Wheeler explained, "The report contains data the security aspect of which is paramount, and unauthorized disclosure of which would cause exceptionally grave danger to the nation." Therefore, it was not to be shown to any foreign nationals and was excluded from normal declassification procedures.

Anyone who obtained this 214-page report would have had a comprehensive overview of the United States' order of battle—i.e., the command structure and composition of all forces that would go to war against the communist world. It also included estimates of Soviet strategic nuclear forces, based on the most sensitive intelligence sources. It detailed critical vulnerabilities, such as how the USSR could pin down U.S. missiles by detonating a series of megaton-sized weapons in the atmosphere. Finally, it also surveyed the prospects for other countries' building their own bombs, and how they could do it.

What is significant about this report is not just its obvious sensitivity. Both the content and the extraordinary efforts to keep it secret illustrate the continuing struggle over the control of nuclear weapons and nuclear information. For the top brass, the whole point was to stop Lyndon Johnson from listening to scientists who advised negotiating a ban on testing nuclear weapons so as to stop irradiating the atmosphere. It recalled the first failed effort scientists made to prevent the use of the bomb in 1945, when General Groves successfully argued that he could keep the secret of nuclear weapons from America's enemies indefinitely. Now the generals argued the opposite: insisting that other nations would always find ways to work around any ban to build new and better weapons. As we shall see, this was the kind of united opposition to reining in military research and development that inspired people already worried about the state of civil-military relations in the nuclear era to imagine a *Seven Days in May*–type scenario, in which the military would be tempted to overthrow civilian government.

The next document is the top result using the DOE brute-force method (and number 44 out of the 117,000 ranked using machine learning). It's another top-secret study, this one dating to 1955, about how to detect whether a country has started a covert nuclear-weapons program. It details the kinds of nuclear plants the United States was exporting at the time, and how weapons-grade materials could be clandestinely diverted from them. As a study of the limitations of on-site nuclear inspections, it also serves as a how-to guide for cheaters who want to hide nuclear materials and weapons, and get away with it.

For instance, the report notes how inspections at a nuclear plant could only account for 90 percent of the materials produced—the rest could be diverted, establishing a useful benchmark for cheaters. It identifies the types of reactors that are hardest to inspect, and how lead shielding could mask any tracer additives mixed in with U.S.-supplied uranium. A covert reactor could be set up near uranium mining operations, so background radiation would hide what was happening there. Or another country could avoid the need to build a reactor altogether by using centrifuges or alternate processes for extracting materials, technology that was likely to become available in five to ten years. These were exactly the kinds of techniques Israel, India, Pakistan, South Africa, and North Korea would use over the decades that followed to build their own weapons, and provides a good example of the kind of document that merited page-by-page review before declassification.

But what if, instead of another country building more and better bombs, the real danger was that the military's obsession with preparing nuclear weapons for use against the USSR would lead them to neglect the danger of someone stealing one? The third and final document was the highest ranked using machine learning (and number 42 in terms of dirty words). It's also top-secret restricted data, and chock-full of information about the security—or lack of security—around U.S. nuclear weapons deployed at overseas bases. It dates to 1960, when a congressional committee decided to investigate whether nuclear weapons deployed abroad might be seized in the event of a coup or civil war in the countries in which the weapons were deployed. The committee found that it would take far less than they had imagined for nuclear arms to fall into the hands of bad actors, and many were already under the effective control of foreign armies. At many NATO installations, only a single American GI would stand in the way of some rogue group or individual who wanted to commandeer a tactical nuclear weapon. West German fighter-bomber pilots were flying training missions with nuclear weapons, and could easily fly off with them. This *Broken Arrow* scenario was not just a Hollywood film plot: over the years, dozens of pilots from many different nations have stolen their planes and defected. So far, none have had nuclear weapons (as far as we know).

Here again, there was good reason to guard this information closely. If it fell into the wrong hands, it would have revealed to rogue actors multiple opportunities to commandeer nuclear weapons. But it also showed how, after the AEC agreed to allow the military to take custody of these weapons, they did an extremely poor job of keeping them secure. This report would convince John F. Kennedy to insist on the installation of electro-mechanical locks to prevent unauthorized use. As we shall see, this measure elicited fierce resistance from military commanders, who created a work-around, and then kept that secret all to themselves.

The Manhattan Project, which gave birth to the bomb and the security system built to contain it, started with a small grant to Columbia University. It enabled Enrico Fermi and Leo Szilard to continue producing chain reactions with piles of uranium—one of them in a basement connected to the building where

History Lab would be born and run its first experiments some eighty years later. Both the nuclear program and the secrecy surrounding it grew dramatically over the intervening decades. But neither has actually assured national security. So it is only fitting that Columbia researchers now conduct experiments to determine how to bring this chain reaction back under control, and better protect the information that fuels nuclear proliferation.

The reason I can write about this research without worrying about the Espionage Act or the Atomic Energy Act is that we only used documents that were already declassified. We did not even have access to the most useful data: the redacted parts of those RD and FRD documents, or the ones that are withheld entirely. If the government were to scale up this research, it could use a lot of *still*-restricted data to train the algorithms, and would almost certainly get even more accurate results. The real test would be in assessing how algorithms perform compared with unassisted human reviewers—assuming these reviewers can actually agree on what information needs to be kept classified.

But government officials who only think classified thoughts in secret compartments tend only to ask the question General Groves posed some eighty years ago: what does this or that official "need to know" to accomplish their duty? We need to start asking ourselves a different question: what do we, the people, need to know to do *our* job, as citizens, to keep our government accountable? At the very least, we should know everything the latest technology and the law allow us to know, right up to that line separating the need to know from the need to not blow up the world. Using data-mining and high-performance computers, we can now see where that line is drawn, and how it has been redrawn. And we should be able to see that line. After all, we pay for this secrecy—more than eighteen billion dollars a year. We paid for nuclear weapons, more than seventy thousand of them, at a cost of more than five *trillion* dollars. And we may pay an even higher price if any of these weapons or the knowledge required to produce them ever falls into the wrong hands. To understand the true costs and risks required for more informed choices, we therefore need to know what information is out there, and what we need to be worried about, so that all of us might sleep better at night.

3

CODE MAKING AND CODE BREAKING

THE SECRET OF SECRETS

If you gathered all the secret documents you could get your hands on, and analyzed all the words contained therein, what would turn out to be the most secret words of all? How would you protect these secrets, considering that, if exposed, they could bring exceptional danger to the nation? How might someone try to hack into them? And how would you know if they had succeeded?

The very idea of identifying the government's most secret words was scarcely conceivable before the dawn of data science. After all, no one person could read more than a small fraction of the huge and growing archive of declassified documents, read around the redacted text, and recall instances where the same document might have been redacted differently. Even for someone with perfect recall and X-ray vision, calculating the odds of this or that word's being blacked out would require an inhuman amount of number crunching.

But all this became possible when my colleagues and I at History Lab began to gather millions of documents into a single database. We started by using algorithms to analyze the words that tend to appear just before and after redacted text in *The Foreign Relations of the United States*, the State Department's official record of American diplomacy. When we did that, we found, for instance, that Henry Kissinger's name appears more than twice as often as anyone else's when these documents touch on topics that are still considered sensitive. Kissinger's long-serving predecessor, Dean Rusk, is even more ubiquitous in State Department documents, but appears much less often in redacted ones. Kissinger is also more than twice as likely as Rusk to appear in top-secret documents, which at one time were judged to risk "exceptionally grave damage" to national security if publicly disclosed.

To go deeper and get at the question of who (or what) is disproportionately likely still to be secret after all these years, we ran another experiment. We calculated the odds of a word's appearing around redacted text compared with the odds of the same word's appearing anywhere else in these documents. At the top of the list were terms like CALLIGERIS, RUFUS, and ODYOKE. These are all CIA code words, and all were used in discussions of covert operations, discussions that still—even sixty years later—contain a lot of blacked-out text.

But to really get at the heart of the matter, we designed an experiment to determine what specific words are more likely not just to appear around redacted text but actually to be redacted. It took time to develop the algorithm to find redacted and unredacted versions of the same document. When we did, we turned it loose on our database, and it enabled us to identify over three thousand previously redacted passages, totaling about sixty thousand secret words altogether.

With this kind of data, we could finally identify who or what is particularly liable to be blacked out. At the top of this new list were not code words, but words *about* codes—and code making, and code breaking, and ciphers, and cryptanalysis. The words were "encrypted," "decoded," and "cryptocenter." And the people involved in these documents are not from the CIA; they are from the NSA, the National Security Agency.

It makes sense. After all, if word of how you keep a secret gets out, then all your other secrets are at risk of being exposed, whether weapons technology, war plans, or closed-door negotiations. Cryptography is therefore the secret of secrets. In this chapter, we begin to explore the making and breaking of codes to conceal crucial information. We will see how cryptography is subject to special safeguards that go even further than protections accorded nuclear weapons. We then ask whether all this secrecy actually works by investigating whether and how America's leading adversary could have hacked into the Holy of Holies: the headquarters of U.S. code making and code breaking, the National Security Agency at Fort Meade, Maryland.

———————

When the NSA was first established in 1952, wags joked that NSA stood for "No Such Agency." Its very existence was classified. It had its roots in Army and Navy Intelligence, and every single one of its directors has been either a general or an admiral. The NSA is now best known, even notorious, for its work intercepting and analyzing communications for purposes of international espionage and domestic surveillance. But it is also responsible for developing the equipment, systems, and expertise to keep other countries from doing to the United States what the United States does to them.

So, when U.S. soldiers in Korea were fought to a standstill at Heartbreak Ridge because the Chinese had tapped their lines, it was the NSA that studied the battle and trained operators in its lessons. When NASA began sending rockets into space and wished to prevent the Soviets from interfering with missile guidance systems—much as the United States has been accused of doing to North Korea—it was the NSA that developed the procedures to safeguard these launches. And when officials wanted to be sure the president could talk on a secure line to a foreign head of state, it was the NSA that developed the machines to encode and decode these voice communications so that no one else could listen in. This is why the redactions in the documents we analyzed often reveal instructions that the bearer of a "decoded copy of an encrypted message" must "CONSULT CRYPTOCENTER BEFORE DECLASSIFYING." Why? Because only the "cryptocenter"—that is, the NSA—would know if the decoded copy could be used to break an encryption system by giving an adversary access to both the unencrypted and encrypted versions of the same message.

You can find signs of these secrets—secrets about how to

keep secrets, and how to steal them—in the most important episodes in the history of the dark state. How, for instance, did the
Roosevelt White House know the Japanese were planning to
attack? How did the FBI learn that there were moles inside the
Manhattan Project? And why was the American public not told
about the actual scope of Soviet espionage in the United States?

Cryptography has always been among the most closely
guarded activities of any government. It has its origins in the
need to transmit sensitive information at a distance, such as the
dispatches of ambassadors between royal courts. It was assumed
that these messages would often be intercepted. For hundreds of
years, practically every major European power had cryptocen-
ters, or what were then called "black chambers," which engaged
in an ongoing competition to create unbreakable codes. Over
time, relatively low-tech methods like the "one-time pad,"
which randomly assigns keys to every letter in a message, were
found to be extremely effective. But as the name "one-time"
suggested, a method suited for relatively short, point-to-point
messaging could not work with the sheer volume of communication required for modern diplomacy, surveillance, and military
operations. Moreover, messages were increasingly transmitted
by telegraph and radio. Both code making and code breaking
therefore came to depend on electromechanical devices.

But as the technology of cryptography became ever more
advanced, the human factor became even more crucial in determining whether it actually contributed to national security. In
1941, for instance, a U.S. Navy listening post in Puget Sound
intercepted coded diplomatic communications sent via the air-
waves from Tokyo to San Francisco. The mechanical nature
of the Japanese encryption device—and its reverse-engineered
American replica—meant that, once the key was known, individual messages could be decrypted and delivered to the White
House in as little as a few hours. But, crucially, this couldn't happen if cryptographers refused to share what they learned with
the people who needed it the most, as occurred in the run-up
to Pearl Harbor. The secrecy of cryptography was considered
so crucial that protecting it would continue to take priority over
national policy goals during the Cold War. In the early days,

cryptologists would not share signals intelligence on the Soviet nuclear-weapons program with the intelligence section of the Manhattan Project. But the intelligence section of the Manhattan Project, for its part, refused to share information about how atomic bombs were built. As a result, Washington did not know whether the Soviets would need five or twenty years to build a bomb.

The question of which secret was *the* top secret—nuclear weapons or signals intelligence—was finally settled in a court of law, during the trial of Ethel and Julius Rosenberg. As we have seen, the government presented a diagram revealing the inner workings of the atomic bomb to prove Ethel's complicity. Why did they take this risk? It was because they did not want to give up what seemed—to them at least—like an even more precious secret: the fact that signals intelligence had succeeded in decrypting messages sent by the Rosenbergs' Soviet handlers. The Soviets had already changed the code. But the Americans apparently believed that revealing what they had achieved might make it harder to repeat.

Amazingly, it appears that even President Truman may not have been informed that this code-breaking program, code-named Venona, had proved the existence of a large network of Soviet agents. They included influential figures in the Roosevelt administration, like the State Department official Alger Hiss and the White House economist Lauchlin Currie. But the person in charge of the code breakers, General Carter Clarke, "vehemently disagreed" with the suggestion that the president be informed. Omar Bradley, army chief of staff, backed him up. Truman therefore remained skeptical of the extent of Soviet spying, and American society was consumed with bitter debate about the magnitude of the problem. This uncertainty contributed to indiscriminate accusations that huge numbers of other people were covert communists, people who were either completely innocent—like George Marshall—or completely harmless, like Hollywood screenwriters.

The way the U.S. communicates secret messages—and intercepts the communications of other states—has thus been the most closely guarded secret of all, protected at tremendous cost to the entire country. What we discovered about the most secret words in secret documents is also consistent with the special status cryptography has in the law, in presidential policy on secrecy, and in the execution of policy in everyday practice. In 1951, for instance, Congress made it a felony for anyone to reveal classified information about codes, code machines, or communications intelligence activities to any "unauthorized person." This applied not just to people the government entrusted with classified information, but to anyone who might come into possession of such information—whether a journalist, a congressman, or even a citizen of another country. This law went even further than the Espionage Act and the Atomic Energy Act: conviction did not even require demonstrating the accused knew how damaging the information could be. Presidential orders that otherwise call for "automatic" declassification specifically exempt anything that would "reveal information that would impair U.S. cryptologic systems or activities." Those who try to use the Freedom of Information Act have found that even references to code-breaking work from the 1920s are still redacted.

If cryptography constitutes the secret of secrets, sometimes too secret even for the president to know about, can we trust the code breakers and code makers to keep these secrets secure from our enemies? After all, there would have been little point in this extreme secrecy—which continues to pose huge problems for democratic accountability, especially when the code breakers surveil U.S. citizens—if others could hack into U.S. cryptologic systems. In fact, if the NSA itself was vulnerable, it would compound the inherent risks that signals intelligence and surveillance entail for civil liberties, since our enemies could then have used the NSA's information and capabilities against us and all our allies.

The question of NSA security is not just hypothetical. In 2016, an unidentified group that called itself the Shadow Brokers offered to sell a whole arsenal of hacking tools it had taken from the NSA. When no buyers came forward—perhaps unwilling to risk the Agency's wrath—the Shadow Brokers started to make their information available to everyone. These tools have now been used to infect hundreds of thousands of computers, costing governments and businesses billions of dollars. One of the hardest-hit targets was the municipal government of Baltimore, just fifteen miles from the NSA headquarters.

So how does one go about hacking into the National Security Agency? In light of the legal issues, we can—and should—approach this as a strictly historical question, from the relatively safe distance afforded by the passage of several decades. There is no doubt that the Soviets must have tried to answer this question, especially in the 1950s, when they realized that they no longer had high-level sources like Hiss and Currie who could report on U.S. intentions. They were also losing their ability to monitor U.S. communications through the NSA's development of increasingly sophisticated cryptomachines, and at the very moment U.S. military communications were becoming especially worrisome to Moscow. A military buildup that started with the Korean War completely transformed the rickety U.S. nuclear force into a massive and ruthless war machine. The United States not only had a ten-to-one advantage in the number of bombs; the Strategic Air Command (SAC) was primed like a "cocked weapon," as its commander, Curtis LeMay, liked to say. By 1954, he had some two thousand combat-capable planes, including over eight hundred bombers. Their crews now landed about half their bombs within a quarter-mile of the target. With a visual sighting it was six hundred feet, or the distance between Lenin's Tomb and the Onion Domes of St. Basil's Cathedral.

U.S. war plans from the 1950s called for unleashing virtually the entire U.S. nuclear arsenal on all communist countries simultaneously, what some RAND Corporation analysts called the "wargasm." Moscow would not even have the opportunity to surrender. This strategy would kill some sixty million people. Air-force planners wanted to patrol the skies over the USSR and make it a permanent no-fly zone, with resisters subject to renewed bombing. The surviving communist leadership would be hunted down and exterminated.

Leading figures in the U.S. national-security establishment urged using U.S. nuclear superiority before the Soviets could put together a credible deterrent. Eisenhower privately mused about whether a "duty to future generations did not require us to *initiate* war at the most propitious moment that we could designate." But he knew that, in the aftermath, the United States would face the colossal task of occupying and administering a vast wasteland stretching from East Germany to Southeast Asia. He made clear that he wanted to avoid war, in closed-door meetings with military officers. But unless Moscow bugged the White House, that desire would not have been clear to the Politburo. Instead, Soviet leaders would have seen the United States testing plans to evacuate the president and thousands of other officials from Washington to shelter in vast underground complexes. Attack drills cleared the streets of every American city, and U.S. senators were calling for initiating hostilities. The Soviet Embassy would have reported that the chief of naval operations was openly advocating this "rougher road." So-called preventive war was also the "prevailing philosophy" of the Air War College, the graduate school for the wing commanders who would lead the attack.

Fear of the Soviets' increasing nuclear capabilities is what drove Eisenhower and other U.S. officials to contemplate striking first. In 1954, a week after the first sighting of a new Soviet jet bomber, SAC sent a B-47 bomber to penetrate Soviet airspace and photograph airfields. It exchanged fire with Soviet MiG fighter jets, which continued to pursue the bomber one hundred miles into Finland. The Soviet pilots even attempted to ram the American plane. By 1956, SAC was flying dozens more such missions. The pilots were surprised to find thousands of miles of Arctic coastline virtually undefended. As many as six B-47's could parade deep into Soviet territory in broad daylight and return without a single shot fired. In a further humiliation for Moscow, the CIA sent its new U-2 spy plane directly over Leningrad, as well as the Soviet capital itself, on July 4 and 5, 1956.

From the moment that the first American reconnaissance flight escaped into Finland, the Soviets had to know that their secret was not safe. They had far fewer bombers than they claimed, and almost all were inferior copies of the American B-29. These prop-driven World War II veterans were defenseless against modern fighter-interceptors. Even the small number of new jet bombers lacked the range to strike American targets and return—Soviet crews were told they would have to bail out over Mexico. By contrast, SAC was about to deploy the jet-powered B-52 Stratofortress, which had a range of nearly nine thousand miles and a seventy-thousand-pound payload. Until the Soviets developed an early-warning system similar to what the United States had already created in Canada to cover the polar approaches, only signals intelligence—intercepted radio communications between American bombers and bases—could provide a timely and totally credible warning of an American attack.

The Soviets therefore had to worry about the development of a new generation of nearly unbreakable NSA cryptomachines. No less than the B-52, they constituted near-perfect weapons for nuclear war. The KL-7 was one such device. About the size of a portable typewriter, it was considered all but invulnerable, except that it produced radio-frequency emissions that could in theory give would-be listeners the ability to analyze the frequency and direction of communications. The NSA worked to reduce this vulnerability, and eventually developed the KW-26, a vacuum-tube-operated machine that contained no mechanical parts, meaning no radio emissions could be detected. This breakthrough quickly established the reputation of the NSA.

Early on, SAC made sure the KL-7 would work at high altitudes and in all conditions. The improved KW-26 could be used to notify forward bases of an imminent strike without creating any suspicious spike in communications traffic. The combination of a completely secure communications network, a ring of forward bases around the USSR, an arsenal of thousands of nukes, and hundreds of heavily armed jet bombers constituted a nation-killing machine. It could be set in motion at a moment's notice, strike with little to no warning, and continue the onslaught until the communist world was annihilated.

The Soviets therefore had an existential motivation to steal the secret of secrets, and do to the United States what the United States and Britain had done to Japan and Germany during World War II: intercept and decipher military communications in near real-time. Such a feat would require both detailed information about the NSA machines—if not the actual machines themselves—and some way to re-create the settings that were configured and reconfigured each day. It would have to be done quickly, considering that a surprise attack could come at any time. Hardest of all, the Soviets would have to obtain this information without tipping anyone off, since the NSA would otherwise simply change its procedures to repair the breach.

The ultimate coup would be to penetrate the NSA's own headquarters, where American scientists and engineers were developing and testing the new machines, recruiting and training personnel, and collecting and decrypting communications from around the world. The Soviets would need people on the inside. But anyone they sent to apply to work for the NSA would have to get through a multi-stage screening process. It started with intense questioning while the applicant was hooked up to a polygraph. While "lie detectors" were hardly foolproof, they could be effective—all too effective—in making even innocent subjects nervous. Investigators were then tasked with tracking down every person mentioned, including family, neighbors, teachers, banks, and previous employers, in each case verifying the applicant's claims. If it all checked out, the NSA Security Division undertook a "National Agency Check," searching the records of federal agencies that held files on criminal or subversive activity. Even if the check turned up nothing, the NSA would still launch a complete background investigation. This entailed in-person interviews with the applicant's teachers, employers, landlords, credit agencies, neighbors, acquaintances, co-workers, and police.

In a measure of the agency's growing strength, during the years 1950–59 the number of NSA personnel increased threefold. The Joint Chiefs of Staff determined that they would need a new, ultra-secure headquarters, far enough from Washington to escape destruction if the capital ever came under nuclear attack.

They approved a plan to move to Fort Knox in Kentucky, where the nation's cryptologic resources would have the same level of protection as its gold reserves. But the highly skilled civilians who worked for the NSA scuttled the plan by circulating a poll showing how many would refuse to move.

A selection committee therefore chose a big military base within commuting distance of both Washington and Baltimore, Fort Meade in Maryland. As the headquarters of the U.S. Second Army, it had many thousands of troops and armored vehicles. An additional company of marines would be deployed with the single mission of guarding the new NSA site, both during construction and after it opened. This was the only intelligence agency ever to be given its own infantry detachment.

The new NSA headquarters would be surrounded by two barbed-wire fences when it was built, with a third, electrified fence in between. The fences were to be monitored by marine guardhouses, roving patrols, and a Security Watch Office, all of them in constant contact with an alert force that could rapidly respond to any breach. The marines would also inspect the color-coded badges of anyone entering the Operational areas. When not in use, the cryptomachines and the most sensitive classified materials were to be kept in safes or file cabinets with three-position combination locks. Unlike at any other intelligence agencies at the time, marine guards at Meade would search the bags of everyone who exited the building to ensure they were not removing classified materials.

At night, state-of-the-art electronic security measures on the doors could detect unauthorized access, and watch officers patrolled inside. The marines were even equipped with oxygen tanks so that, in case of fire, they could escort firefighters. And every day, day after day, NSA personnel were surrounded with posters, signs, and even doormats warning them to be vigilant.

The new NSA building at Fort Meade would be the third-largest in the DC area and would have its own bank, drugstore, travel agency, shoe repair, dry cleaners, and a cafeteria for fourteen hundred people—all to minimize the need for any of them to leave the grounds. NSA personnel busily collected and analyzed an enormous quantity of intercepted communications from some two thousand listening posts around the world. They produced more classified paper than all other government agencies and departments combined. It added up to 104 tons monthly, of which forty tons of highly classified waste had to be burned without leaving so much as a scrap of paper behind. A two-lane driveway ran right through the building to truck all of it in and out away from prying eyes.

The NSA seemed prepared for anything—even frontal assault by Soviet commandos or home-grown communist irregulars. The marines kept enough machine guns and mortars in their barracks to quell "a major riot or uprising." Fort Meade therefore seemed like a good and secure home, and it remains the NSA headquarters to this day.

However, until the new headquarters was fully operational and the move was complete, construction workers and outside contractors continued to come and go. Many NSA personnel would have to remain at Arlington Hall—the home of the Army Security Agency—and at the Naval Security Station on Nebraska Avenue. Even as it dispersed, this workforce would continue to expand and diversify. It already included everyone from marine privates to cafeteria workers to quirky mathematicians.

The sheer scale and intensity of the U.S. cryptologic effort thus created intrinsic vulnerabilities. So, too, did the basic paradox of operational security: making it impossible for anyone to hack into NSA headquarters would also make it impossible for anyone to work there. This paradox created "a continual conflict between the objectives of operations personnel and security personnel within the Agency," as one internal study noted. The KGB could seek to exploit these conflicts and look for holes—in some cases, holes created by NSA personnel themselves. As Feynman discovered back in Los Alamos, what appeared to be formidable defense systems could create a false sense of security when, in practice, these measures were applied inconsistently, and routines turned into rituals.

The inconsistencies began with background screening. It was no secret that the NSA was moving to Fort Meade. Soviet Embassy staff could have read about it in local newspapers, because the Army Corps of Engineers needed to solicit bids

The NSA made everyone aware of potential vulnerabilities, but this poster also put a bull's-eye on any would-be infiltrator.

and announce who won construction contracts. But the government's Industrial Personnel Security Program—which was supposed to prevent security leaks among contractors—was far less stringent than that run by the NSA itself. Some of the jobs these contractors did, such as designing and building the new headquarters, could be critical for ensuring long-term operational security. Nevertheless, there were no polygraph exams even for those seeking top-secret clearances. Many contractors requiring confidential-level clearances were never even investigated. Employers only had to show that the candidate was a

U.S. citizen, with nothing in the interview or application to raise a national-security concern. Even companies that did conduct some kind of inquiry typically hired the candidates first and cleared them later. But the NSA needed its new headquarters built as quickly as possible, and competition for skilled labor in this period was intense—especially in the booming construction business in the D.C. area. The national unemployment rate in 1953 was 2.9 percent, the lowest level ever recorded.

Someone who worked on the site plan and the blueprints of the new building—or just wanted to get a look at them—would not even need a security clearance. These plans were not top secret, or secret, or even confidential. They were either "restricted"—an ambiguous category that did not require any of the normal protections for classified documents—or they were completely unclassified. At the time, the government depended on physical security systems—gates, guards, etc.—to defend sensitive information. But these defenses did not operate in the places where contractors designed the systems. Anyone entering the offices of the architects or building contractors could therefore find their designs in unlocked file cabinets, or see them strewn across drafting tables, and take them home for closer study. Blueprints and site plans would have been uniquely valuable. They would have revealed the materials and methods of construction, the location of heating and ventilation ductwork, the lighting installations that would extend into the individual work spaces, and indeed the very foundations of the structure itself.

For someone looking for vulnerabilities, the most striking fact about the new headquarters was its location on the base: it was sited on the periphery, abutting a state road. This location would make it convenient for commuters to enter and exit. But beyond that road, just two hundred feet from the southwest corner of the new building, there were thousands of acres of undeveloped land, much of it heavily wooded.

When KGB operatives became aware of where the new NSA headquarters was situated, they might have contemplated digging a tunnel underneath, since a tunnel entrance could be concealed in the forest across the road. It might seem far-fetched, but

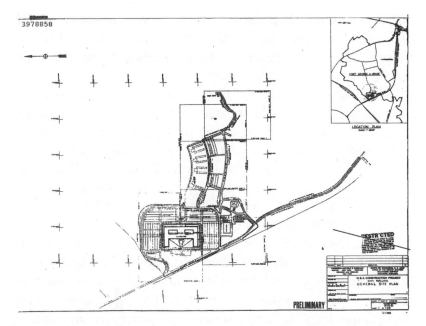

The site plan for the new NSA headquarters, showing how—in the upper-right inset—it was on the southern border of Fort Meade, alongside a state road. Most of the area beyond that road was obscured by trees.

it would have been a fitting response to the CIA's own exploits. In 1953–55, Agency operatives burrowed almost fifteen hundred feet under the streets of Berlin to tap into East German communications cables. But the CIA tunnel took more than a year to complete and required building a city-block-sized warehouse to store thousands of tons of displaced sand and dirt.

The KGB needed a surveillance plan with a shorter timeline, and less risk of immediate discovery. What they ultimately would have wanted was either to be able to record what was being discussed in the NSA or actually to listen to those conversations in real time. Such operations normally entailed a choice between two systems.

The first option required concealed microphones wired up either to recording devices or to a stationary listening post off-site. But operating a fixed listening post anywhere near the new NSA facility would pose severe risks, and the wires themselves might lead the Americans right to it. Recording devices could be concealed within the building. But someone would have to retrieve and change the tapes. The longer the delay, the less confident they could be about obtaining timely intelligence.

The second option was to wire the microphones to radio transmitters. This would leave fewer clues and allow the team to operate from a mobile listening post as far away as the signal could carry. But the stronger the signal, the more vulnerable it was to detection, and the sooner it would drain any batteries. Absent an alternative power source, the batteries would have to be changed regularly. "When the battery dies," CIA operatives liked to say, "the operation dies."

Luckily for the Soviets, in the early Cold War they had help from a genius named Leon Theremin, who was already famous for creating the first electronic musical instrument. During this period, Theremin was a prisoner of the gulag, put to work in a secret laboratory. He and his team had developed an entirely new kind of wireless surveillance system in 1945. It was not until

In May 1960, amid the controversy over the downing of a U-2 spy plane, U.S. Ambassador to the UN Henry Cabot Lodge showed how the Soviets had been spying on the U.S. Embassy in Moscow. The Great Seal in the ambassador's office was not that great for U.S. communications security.

seven years later that a CIA technician at the U.S. Embassy in Moscow discovered it. It was concealed the whole time inside a gift the youth organization Young Pioneers had presented to the ambassador: a wooden carving of the Great Seal of the United States. "The Thing" consisted of a microphone precision-tooled so the diaphragm would vibrate with the sound of human voices. It was attached to a nine-inch antenna, but had no battery and no wires. Instead, the Thing came to life when the Soviets beamed a radio signal of a specific wavelength directly at the ambassador's office, where the Great Seal hung proudly on the wall. The vocal vibrations from the microphone would modulate the signal, and the return signal revealed every spoken word. The device was undetectable when it was not in operation, and it could continue working indefinitely.

But it would be risky to depend on one technological breakthrough. A robust plan required multiple, redundant systems. The Soviets would therefore have likely used a mix of recorders, transmitters, and wireless devices, some battery-powered and others hard-wired to the building electric supply. After all, each presented its own challenges, advantages, and drawbacks. Even the Thing required a manned post nearby, where a technician would beam the radio-frequency (RF) signal and record what was returned.

The location of the listening post would be a key part of any plan. One possibility was to conceal it in the bordering woods, perhaps camouflaged to look like the trunk of a dead tree. It could be connected to a platform built into the upper branches of one of the nearby sycamores, one of the more common varieties in these parts. Some had trunks almost eight feet in diameter, and could grow to well over one hundred feet high. The topography of the area was relatively flat, so from that height an antenna would have line-of-sight radio range for miles.

An unobstructed view of the new NSA building—especially the senior-staff offices on the top floor—would also have given the KGB the opportunity to use a new Theremin invention: the infrared microphone. Theremin realized that the sound of human voices makes windowpanes vibrate. The return signal from an infrared beam pointed at the window could be read from up to sixteen hundred feet away. The beam was almost impossible to detect, and only rain or fog could interfere in its operation.

Other options required deploying a team that could plant devices within the grounds of the new NSA complex. How might they have gone about that? In the Hollywood version of the story, a Soviet submarine would infiltrate their agents and gear some moonless night. Fort Meade was just a few miles from the Severn River estuary and the Chesapeake Bay beyond. But only a midget submarine could operate in these shallow waters—as little as twenty feet deep at low tide—and it would have to sneak by a navy base and the U.S. Naval Academy at Annapolis, which straddled the mouth of the estuary.

A more practical plan would have started with having undercover Soviet agents already in place, and rafts to carry anything too heavy for a backpack. The Little Patuxent River snaked through the woods less than half a mile from the NSA site. A team could put in upriver and float components of the listening post downstream through the dense vegetation. But there was danger in these woods. For many decades, the army had used them for military maneuvers and war games. There was unexploded ordnance, and at any time an army column from Fort Meade might have stumbled upon the KGB operation. What options did that leave them?

One possibility was a center for juvenile delinquents that was just across the road from the construction site, which was becoming notorious for frequent escapes and dubious hires (including one man who passed himself off as a doctor but could produce no diplomas). Once on staff at the juvenile center, a KGB agent could move about the grounds and case the NSA site across the road without raising suspicion. Alternatively, an older agent, playing the part of a desperate parent, could bring a younger one to juvenile court and have him or her committed to the center. Visits were encouraged, so it would be good cover for parking a vehicle right across the road from the NSA. Teenage residents at this center had a lot of freedom. One might even have started an amateur radio club. Only those with a criminal background were actually locked up at night; most of the girls were not.

Of course, marines would be standing guard around the construction site across the road. But KGB operatives with the skills to install and conceal listening devices could also pass muster as electricians, carpenters, or HVAC technicians. Many of them were foreign-born, so an Eastern European accent would not be out of place.

Gaining access to the NSA construction site would have created entirely new possibilities. A KGB construction worker would be able to work with the internal wiring, which could serve both to power radio transmitters and to extend their signal. As a 1960 CIA study noted, "It is now virtually impossible to detect when a telephone is tapped by the most sophisticated methods without visually inspecting every inch of the wires and every element servicing it, down to the last screw connection." Simply dropping a transmitter into the handset of a rotary telephone could turn it into a microphone. The public-address system speakers in the new building could also be repurposed. Agents could embed microphones in wet concrete or inside the walls. Minimal shielding—even putting the bugs in bamboo— would make them undetectable in normal sweeps.

The ideal plan would be to bug the NSA Security Section offices and expand from there. These offices were in the Administrative area and were therefore given less protection than more obvious targets in the Operational area, like the cryptomachines and codebooks. Someone applying for a job could walk straight to the personnel security office, and anyone who took a polygraph exam could go to the restroom afterward, which shared a wall with the polygraph examiners' conference room. The plumbing and a pinhole through the wall might conceal both a microphone and a recording setup, which could be regularly accessed by future job applicants. Moreover, some of these KGB applicants would likely ace their interviews, and be hired to work in the building, possibly without even having to pass a background check. In this period, the NSA was under such pressure to fill staff positions that it started granting interim security clearances on the basis of a National Agency Check and a polygraph exam, and did not follow up even when this revealed derogatory information.

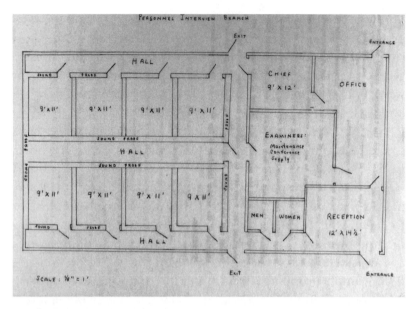

The floor plan of the Security Section that carried out lie-detector tests on NSA job applicants, showing the restrooms sharing a wall with the examiners' conference room.

A system that had elaborate procedures for screening prospective employees but did not actually investigate the information that was revealed was the very essence of security theater. In fact, this background screening itself created another vulnerability: The NSA Security Section was systematically gathering incriminating information about every NSA employee in one place—a place with the lowest level of security in the building. Similarly, the NSA personnel files, even investigation files, were not top secret, secret, or even confidential. They were merely designated "For Official Use Only," and did not therefore have to be kept in locked file cabinets.

Some of the most sensitive information would have been revealed (or not revealed) in the interview rooms themselves. Where else could the KGB listen to NSA personnel being questioned about any and every vulnerability, whether drinking, drug abuse, money problems, or what people in the 1950s called "sexual perversion"? Each of these rooms had soundproofing precisely to prevent passersby from overhearing. But the insulation meant that the sound quality from a concealed microphone would be excellent—including the sound and RF emissions from the polygraph machine itself. The information would be particularly valuable if the KGB could determine—better than the notoriously unreliable lie detector—that the subject was not being entirely truthful.

To that end, the NSA move to Fort Meade created a once-in-a-lifetime opportunity for the KGB, one that real-estate developers in Laurel, the closest town, announced for all to read about in local newspapers. There was no easy way to commute to the new site by train or bus, so thousands of NSA employees were looking for apartments nearby. A landlord would have the perfect cover story to run their own background checks. Only in this case the landlord would be a KGB agent, using them to find deadbeat applicants with bad credit and negative references who might be rejected by other landlords. Those who would normally have a hard time finding accommodation would also be most likely to lie about personal problems in their NSA polygraph exams.

For the NSA's own move, the General Services Administration would provide the movers and moving supplies. The GSA was the government's housekeeping agency, and not all of its housekeepers were trustworthy. It did fire employees who were discovered to have been members of the Communist Party. But what might have seemed like a security measure created another vulnerability: unless the GSA identified every single former party member among its twenty-eight thousand employees, the ones who remained were also vulnerable to blackmail, and they, too, could be coerced to participate in this operation.

Thus, although the security surrounding the new NSA headquarters may have looked daunting to the Soviets at first, they clearly had options. Given these vulnerabilities, especially during construction and the move between sites, how did the NSA minimize the risk of a security breach? Over many months, every division collaborated in developing a minutely detailed moving plan. Even before they broke ground, they would send in the marines. Nearly 150 would be deployed to Fort Meade in a first wave to establish a beachhead. Once the first offices were open for business, different echelons followed according to an elaborate movement-and-loading schedule. Color-coded floor plans highlighted the files and equipment to be boxed and tagged in different stages, itemized in load-manifest forms, and then inspected by supervisors. The plan also specified extra precautions for the most sensitive items. Classified material, for instance, would move in armed convoys.

But the plan itself—only classified "confidential"—would have revealed some of the most secretive parts of the NSA at the original Arlington Hall site, including the location of the Communications Center as well as the Machine Processing (MPRO) division. This is where the NSA operated enormous "Atlas" computers for code breaking. MPRO, as well as the R&D section, would not move until months after the rest of the NSA. In the meantime, the GSA movers were able to move in and out of both Fort Meade and Arlington Hall without raising suspicions.

Moreover, the simultaneous movement of NSA employees in different echelons would itself help the KGB identify who worked in each division. As an enterprising journalist, James Bamford, later discovered when doing research for his classic study of the NSA, *The Puzzle Palace*, all one needed to create an employee list was to collect license-plate numbers in the parking lot and then obtain the names and addresses from public records at the Registry of Motor Vehicles. The KGB would have been particularly interested in the very first people to move to Fort Meade after the marines. The two thousand personnel from GENS, the "General Soviet" signals-intelligence division, took up temporary residence in an older brick building adjacent to the construction site. Even this initial move proved to be extraordinarily complex and error-prone. Though rosters of who was moving and when were prepared beforehand, they had to be continually revised. Many military personnel did not even receive their moving orders.

Any individuals in uniform would therefore have had a plausible reason to be admitted to the NSA site at Fort Meade even if they lacked the proper paperwork. And if they wandered about and asked a lot of questions, they would have been acting no differently from countless others. "Elements of NSA moving to Fort Meade made major deviations from published Move Plans without proper coordination," one security official complained. These "deviations" included premature movement of classified materials without authorization. Supervisors "muddled through," leading to "many awkward situations."

It took months to install partitions in the interim building at Meade, so support personnel authorized to work in a less sensitive area would be able to see what was happening elsewhere. Moreover, the building was crowded, and NSA Security had to grant many exceptions to regulations that normally required storing sensitive signals intelligence and equipment in dial-combination safes and file cabinets. Finally, the Soviet Division had to depend on an inadequate electronic-communications system until the rest of the NSA arrived more than two years later. It could only handle the most urgent messages; the rest had to be couriered back and forth. Soviet observers could have easily spotted the couriers and targeted them for exploitation.

This situation continued for years, even after the new headquarters was completed in 1957. The brand-new building was only big enough to accommodate the NSA as it existed in 1951, when it was first planned, but the NSA's files, machines, and staff were growing by the day. A big part of the NSA—a part that was of great interest to Moscow—would have to stay behind at the Naval Security Station on Nebraska Avenue: the Communication Security operation (COMSEC). The security risks at the Nebraska Avenue site were well known and would also be known to anyone with access to the files of the Security Section. For instance, one report advised against locking the passageway doors of the Analysis and Evaluation section of COMSEC, because doing so only provided "a sense of false security." There were no fewer than three different ways to gain entry to the section, including "a large wooden pole with climbing pegs at an unlocked, screened window."

Even at the new headquarters, the NSA continued to struggle with how to maintain operational security and still get work done. The building had big open work areas, and the lack of partitions negated the "need to know" principle. There were still not enough heavy safes to lock up all the top-secret materials after hours; if there were, the floors would have collapsed beneath them. Just storing and retrieving classified materials required as much as three hours a day, which NSA management deemed impractical. Because so much classified material was left on open shelves, the security office fretted about the possibility that a foreign agent could roam about operational areas after hours. Security officers knew that badges could be forged, locks could be manipulated, and even combination safes would not long delay a skilled safecracker. At one point, they started taking names from everyone in operational areas after 5:30 p.m., but stopped when higher-ups decided this might discourage dedicated NSA staff from putting in extra hours.

Some people were specifically authorized to move about the offices at night, such as the cleaning crews, who were hired without any security clearance. Even the escorts assigned to the cleaning crews were contractors or low-level GS-4 employees of the GSA. "If they are of a caliber to be good escorts, they generally are dissatisfied to remain such," one NSA report complained, whereas "those persons who are completely satisfied to remain GS-4s are generally poor escorts."

To the extent the Soviets employed battery-powered radio transmitters and tape recorders, unescorted cleaning persons would be well positioned to replace the batteries and retrieve the tapes without being noticed. With a concealed camera, they could photograph maintenance manuals that would reveal coveted details about the NSA's prized cryptomachines, as well as operating instructions and even key lists to break the code as messages were intercepted. They might just take what they wanted. When classified materials went missing, it was supposed to be reported. But NSA officials resisted the "drudgery" of tracking down missing documents. A 1963 report found that in every case—every last one—it was decided that they must have been accidentally destroyed. No one had even been reprimanded. When the Security Section undertook a standard reinvestigation to renew employees' security clearance at five-year intervals, they might therefore have found nothing amiss even in the files of repeat offenders.

There were of course procedures for properly destroying classified materials. Security staff periodically inspected the bales of shredded paper, and only authorized vehicles were permitted to pick them up. But there was no inspection of any vehicles as they exited—whether garbage trucks, delivery vehicles, or private cars.

Though the Soviets would have been happy to obtain classified documents from NSA headquarters, the ultimate prize for the KGB would be to drive out of the building with an actual cryptomachine. Nothing was more closely guarded. Personnel trusted with the possession of a KL-7 or KW-26 were trained to prevent their loss at all costs, preferably with thermite grenades, and hammers to pulverize any leftover pieces. But even if the KGB could spend a few hours with such a machine, they would have enough time to study its design and test its vulnerabilities. They would have been particularly interested in the (nonmoving) parts of the revolutionary KW-26—the cores and vacuum-tube circuits—and the precise nature of the KL-7's radio-frequency emissions—how they might be amplified, and how they could be read.

As the same 1963 NSA report concluded, it all came down to this: "The entire physical security program is totally dependent on the integrity of personnel who have been determined to be eligible for access to NSA classified material." Rather than looking for a hole in the chain-link fences, the KGB would therefore have looked for the weakest links among the many people and organizations who were given pieces of the "Puzzle Palace," whether the architects and draftsmen, the construction workers or concession staff, the GSA movers, the cleaning crews and their escorts, or the thousands of people who were working to intercept and decipher global communications (and protect America's own).

Marines were perhaps the most critical links of all. "Their integrity must be above reproach!" as the NSA's security office insisted.

But at the NSA, military personnel were exempt from polygraph exams. This proved to be a regrettable oversight. When discharged military staff sought to continue working at the NSA as civilians, about one in five were denied employment, usually because of what was discovered during their first polygraph exams.

Twenty years earlier, the American ambassador to the USSR had had the same faith in the United States Marine Corps, and the embassy in Moscow was the world's first to be given a marine guard. That meant the Soviets now had two decades of experience in recruiting them. It had not been very hard. After all, marines were young men—as young as seventeen—who were separated from their families. Some were in the corps precisely because they had had a brush with the law, or behavioral problems, and were now forced to live on pitifully low pay. In Moscow, sometimes all it took was to supply them with a girlfriend, and nature would take its course.

So could the marines—as their battle hymn goes—keep their honor clean? If they were not fully dependable, it would provide the crucial opening to allow the entire Soviet plan to unfold. Recall the juvenile center just a few hundred feet from the new headquarters. Having juvenile delinquents on one side of the road and teenage marines on the other was already a security risk, even without a foreign power seeking to exploit it. A smitten or distracted marine guard could allow an operative to enter at night and implant listening devices in the new headquarters, where hundreds of KL-7's, KW-26's, and attached teletypewriters would soon be clattering away. In the meantime, the operative could use the chaos surrounding the move to bug the temporary quarters of the Soviet Division. If some of the personnel working there were looking for an apartment to rent in nearby Laurel, so much the better. With the KGB as their landlord, they would have no secrets. And listening devices in the personnel office could be used to identify new recruits vulnerable to blackmail. A poorly escorted cleaning person could even access their personnel files—not just to copy items, but to insert forged documents as needed. This might include a completed background check for a staff member who had come under suspicion, or for an applicant who might not otherwise survive such an investigation.

The KGB could recruit and retain someone from the Soviet Division not just with the threat of blackmail, but also with the promise of professional advancement. What better way to advance the career of a KGB mole than to guide them in the solution of one of the Soviet cryptologic systems? This kind of cover-and-deception operation could also allow them to convey whatever messages they wanted the NSA to believe, such as the existence of clandestine nuclear-weapons systems sufficient to deter any U.S. strike. And once they had an asset authorized to enter Operational areas, a friendly marine could wave them into lots of other areas as well. The rest would be history.

Could the KGB really have hacked the headquarters of the NSA? Many seemingly random facts become suspicious when viewed in the aggregate: the fake doctor discovered at the juvenile center across the street from the new headquarters building; the fact that the NSA kept on many personnel even after background checks unearthed derogatory information, with no follow-up investigation; the "many awkward situations" that occurred during the move; the climbing pole next to the unlocked window at the old headquarters; the missing documents that—in every single instance—were said to be "accidentally" destroyed. It is also suggestive that, when the CIA constructed a new headquarters building on its Langley campus in 1984, it made sure that—this time—properly cleared CIA personnel were always on site to monitor the work of tradesmen and prevent them from installing bugs.

This is not just a historical question. The NSA is once more in a period of rapid growth. Over the next decade, it is planning to demolish some of the 1950s structures and construct five new buildings. They will total 2.9 million square feet of space, double that of the original headquarters, and enough to accommodate more than thirteen thousand personnel.

The NSA itself might not know if the old buildings were bugged until they tear them down, including the building initially used for Soviet COMSEC (which later served as the marine barracks). But we already know that things like this did happen, over and over again. In 1957, a State Department report noted that, in the previous eight years, listening devices had been discovered thirty-four times in U.S. or allied embassies. Between

1953 and 1957, fully a dozen members of the staff at the Moscow embassy—including the CIA station chief—had to be sent home because of sexual blackmail. And this only counts the ones who outed themselves—not the unknown number who may have succumbed to temptation without telling anyone. In the 1980s, three marines in Moscow were charged with espionage. Though only one was convicted, senior officials believed that sexual blackmail allowed the Soviets not only to obtain blueprints of the embassy, but to roam around the cryptocenter after hours.

Beginning in the 1950s, multiple moles and defectors emerged from within the NSA itself, and without any need for blackmail. The cryptologist Joseph Petersen was arrested in 1954 after he supplied the Dutch government with years of detailed information about the NSA's success in reading allied governments' communications. In 1960, two NSA mathematicians, William Martin and Bernon Mitchell, flew to Havana and then took a trawler to the USSR. They held a press conference in Moscow to announce their defection and accuse the United States of spying on its allies and aggressively violating the airspace of other countries. In 1963, an army sergeant at the NSA named Jack Dunlap committed suicide when he came under suspicion, but not before he had provided a trove of information to his Soviet handlers. Because he was the chauffeur to the NSA chief of staff and also served as a courier, he was able to enter and exit the building without ever being searched.

Perhaps most damning of all, starting in 1967 a navy warrant officer named John Walker was giving the Soviets everything they needed to read KL-7 communications—everything except the machine itself. That came from the North Koreans, who captured a U.S. surveillance ship, the USS *Pueblo*, and confiscated examples of both the KL-7 and KW-26. "For more than seventeen years," Walker's KGB handler recalls, "Walker enabled your enemies to read your most sensitive military secrets. We knew everything. . . . We were able to read your cables!" Reading U.S. naval communications allowed the Soviets to assist their North Vietnamese allies in ambushing American aviators. In addition to giving them the secret of secrets, Walker also showed how access to personnel files could obviate practically every other security precaution. When he realized he would likely fail a reinvestigation, he stole his own file from the unlocked cabinet, filled in the reinvestigation form, and made it look official with a duplicate FBI rubber stamp.

In each case, an embarrassed NSA tried to minimize the extent of the losses, which also served to minimize the consequences for the responsible officials. And the oversights were sometimes egregious. For all the security theater, somehow they missed the fact that Petersen, Dunlap, and Walker were living well beyond their means. KGB money even enabled Dunlap to buy sports cars and speedboats.

Not for the first or last time, men who conformed to a certain version of normality appeared dependable—even men who were notorious alcoholics, like Walker, because alcoholism was common among the people with whom he worked. On the other hand, when the NSA finally tried to diversify its ranks—it was still 89 percent white in 1993—longtime employees claimed that the new Black, Hispanic, and Asian hires posed a security risk. "In its push to diversify its work force," they told *The Baltimore Sun*, "the agency is leaving sensitive national security tasks in the hands of untrained workers."

———————————

We started this investigation by data-mining a mass of declassified documents to identify the most secret words, first reading around the redactions, and then finding "cryptocenter" at the very center of the dark state. But when we dig even deeper, using classic historical methods to remove the last layers of secrecy, we again find that the core of state secrecy is not some dangerous substance, which might explode if exposed to light. Instead, we find the rot of incompetence, revealing how secrecy serves to deceive citizens when it fails to defend us from our foes.

Extreme secrecy fails in extreme ways, because it ignores the intrinsic limits of any system that ultimately depends on human beings. The rapid expansion of U.S. cryptologic capabilities itself created vulnerabilities, starting with the need to screen, hire, and house an army of new workers. Moving to a new headquarters, built from the ground up to prevent any security breach, instead created a once-in-a-lifetime opportunity to infiltrate the agency at every level. Design plans for physical security, such as fences, gates, and alarms, did not create security when the designs themselves went unprotected. Security routines became empty rituals, losing their ostensible purpose even while creating a false sense of safety. Background checks aggregated the most sensitive information of all, and conveniently filed it in alphabetical order in unlocked cabinets.

Even if extreme secrecy appears to succeed, that very success can provoke a reaction that ultimately guarantees failure. Martin and Mitchell, for instance, seem to have acted on their own, without bribes or blackmail, and no assistance from Soviet handlers. Puzzled at why they defected, the NSA closed ranks and decided—based on scant evidence—it had to be because they were in a homosexual relationship. Eisenhower himself approved a campaign to centralize lists of gay men so they would not be hired for any sensitive position anywhere in the federal government. As Bamford described it, while the Office of Security was "on full alert for limp wrists and telltale lisps," it did not notice Dunlap, a "womanizing, beer-drinking 'family man'" who earned a hundred dollars a week as an army sergeant but somehow drove both Cadillacs and Jaguars while he couriered top-secret documents in and out of the NSA parking lot.

Martin and Mitchell, on the other hand, acted on principle, and against secrecy. They tried to inform Congress that it was being lied to about how the United States was provoking clashes with Soviet aircraft, but no one seemed to care. They finally defected in order to bring attention to the danger of World War III. They believed that unrivaled American power combined with complete secrecy in its operations was a danger to the world.

Were they wrong to believe that? Would the Soviets have accepted to live in constant fear of complete annihilation, with no way to deter or detect a surprise attack? Might they not have pre-emptively launched their own attack on U.S. overseas bases? We will never know, because the United States proved incapable of protecting the secret of secrets, even without all the holes and moles at the NSA headquarters. It turns out that, after the Americans in Moscow had smashed their Great Seal and extracted the Thing, the U.S. mission was still deeply compromised. The Americans carefully monitored construction of a new embassy building, and in 1953 systematically swept for bugs before moving in. But ten years later, warnings from Soviet defectors led security staff to demolish one of the offices, whereupon they began to pull out bugs that had been deeply embedded in the walls. Forty-seven of them were active, in every important office in the building. And buried in the cement of the ceiling over the communications center, with all its otherwise invincible crypto-machines and teletypewriters clattering away with encrypted messages to and from Washington, there was a large metal grille with a wire trailing off, to who knows where.

In a postmortem, the CIA and NSA agreed that the Soviets had likely been able to read most if not all encrypted communications in and out of the U.S. Embassy in Moscow from 1953 to 1964, a period that included some of the most dangerous moments of the Cold War—from negotiations to end the Korean War to the Cuban Missile Crisis. But the report's authors found that Moscow did not use this intelligence to their own advantage, with one important exception: a 1953 cable warning that the United States was prepared to escalate in Korea if the communists did not accept the last proposal at the armistice negotiations in Panmunjom—which they promptly did. In this case, the fact that the Soviets were able to intercept and read this cable was also to the advantage of the United States, and to every living creature, considering that Eisenhower was contemplating the use of nuclear weapons if the negotiations failed.

The report's conclusion about the Soviets' decision not to act on their abundance of intelligence raises a harrowing possibility. "They always had the hope that by preserving the source, they might one day derive extremely useful operational information, namely, advance warning of an American attack. . . ." That warning would have allowed them to mobilize their own nuclear forces and carry out pre-emptive strikes on U.S. command and control systems and overseas bases. So, if American military leaders advocating "preventive" war had prevailed, we would never have known that the USSR had succeeded in bugging our embassy and perhaps the NSA headquarters itself until it was *much* too late.

Instead, between the embassy bugs from 1945 to 1952, and 1953 to 1964, and the decryption of naval communications from 1967 to 1984, the Soviets were able to rest easier at night for nearly forty years. During the Cold War, they knew that they would have timely warning of any American attack, and no need to launch a pre-emptive attack of their own. The real secret of secrets was that being radically transparent—however unwillingly, and unwittingly—was precisely what kept us safe.

4

THE MILITARY-INDUSTRIAL COMPLEX

THE DIRTY SECRET OF CIVIL-MILITARY RELATIONS

If secrecy could be summed up in a single number, it would be the numerical code required to ignite a nuclear holocaust. This code was created to prevent such a holocaust from happening by accident, or by an act of terrorism or madness. Only someone possessing it can unlock "permissive action links," the electro-mechanical devices that control nuclear weapons aboard aircraft, or the nuclear use control systems in ICBM bases. In 1962, under orders from President John F. Kennedy, the Pentagon began to install these devices. It came after that congressional inspection report—the same one our machine-learning algorithm identified as the most radioactive of all—revealed that few safeguards prevented a foreign power from seizing American nukes. Reading it late one night in the White House, Kennedy ordered his staff to "do something."

The military resisted what they saw as unwarranted interference. The U.S. commander-in-chief in Europe warned that if security was too tight, U.S. nuclear weapons might not be available when they were really needed—a warning that was redacted the first time this top-secret memorandum was reviewed for declassification. But Kennedy insisted on the safeguards, and his defense secretary, Robert McNamara, personally made sure the generals and admirals understood that these orders came directly from the president.

By design, even the president does not know the authorization code required to unlock the devices that make nuclear weapons operational. If they ever opened the nuclear "football," reports indicate that they would find targeting plans, procedures for using the emergency alert system, coordinates for safe evacuation locations, and a system to communicate with the National Military Command Center. The only code the president possesses is an identification code contained on a single card, called "the biscuit," which they would read out to establish his or her authority to command nuclear forces. It is senior military officers who, upon the president's command, issue other codes, authorization codes, to U.S. bombers and intercontinental ballistic missile bases.

These authorization codes make it impossible for some Turkish general to seize control of U.S. weapons and become a nuclear power overnight. They would also deter terrorists who might want to hijack a weapons shipment and hold Washington hostage. And they remove the danger that air-force missileers—cooped up underground in claustrophobic missile-launch control centers—will become unstable and start World War III.

But in the 1970s, a new Minuteman missile-operations officer, Bruce C. Blair, discovered something dumbfounding about this system when he first looked at the launch checklist. He knew that, if he received authorization, this series of steps would enable him and his fellow launch officer to unleash a "flight" of ten nuclear missiles, each carrying three nuclear warheads. He expected the checklist to describe the protocol for receiving and inputting the "secret unlock code." But Blair was astonished to find that he could skip this step. The authorization code was spelled out right in the checklist. It did not contain any special characters. It did not require a combination of upper- and lower-case letters. It did not even have to be changed regularly—in fact, it had not been changed in years. The checklist instructed Blair to *make sure that all the numbers in the lock were set to zero.* The secret of secrets about the ultimate weapon—the code required to start Armageddon—was simply this: 00000000.

Why did the authorization code consist of eight zeros? Because, for the Strategic Air Command, it was easy to remem-

THE MILITARY-INDUSTRIAL COMPLEX

ber, and it was an easy way to negate the president's efforts to secure the nuclear arsenal. For years, personnel at the various nuclear command and control centers, the Minuteman launch officers, both present and former—and presumably even the airmen who performed routine maintenance on the missiles—all of them knew the score. But Robert McNamara did not know. "I am shocked, absolutely shocked and outraged," McNamara responded when Blair told him about it. "Who the hell authorized that?"

To this day, we do not know. The Joint Chiefs of Staff destroyed virtually all their meeting notes, and the Pentagon continues to obstruct declassification. But it is not hard to understand why it was years before someone finally blew the whistle. Consider what happened to another air-force officer in the same period. In 1973, Major Harold L. Hering was also training to become a missile operations officer. After one of his classes at Vandenberg Air Force Base had ended, he decided to go to his instructor and ask a question: If an officer got an order to fire the missiles, how could he be sure it was a lawful order? How could he know that the order he received to launch his missiles came from the president—and that the president was sane?

Hering's question was met with silence at first. Then he was summarily dropped from the program. When he was finally reunited with his family, an air-force officer walked into the room and told Hering that he was being kicked out of the air force and would never fly again. The stated reason? In front of his wife and children, Hering was told that he was deemed to have a "defective mental attitude toward his duties."

Hering was a twenty-one-year air-force veteran, and had won a Distinguished Flying Cross in Vietnam. But his superior officers might have justified his dismissal by arguing that they were simply trying to ensure that the United States would be able to defend itself in the event the Soviets launched an attack that targeted all of the officials who could coordinate a retaliatory strike, starting with the president. If such a decapitation strike were successful, and ICBM bases did not get the codes, or if launch officers like Hering started asking too many questions, all of them might be wiped out in thirty minutes or less.

But this defense is hard to square with how the military responded to civilians who shared such concerns and wanted to streamline the nuclear chain of command. In 1971, officials high up in the Defense Department wanted to make sure that there was one person whom the president could count on to execute orders if there was insufficient time to go through the Joint Chiefs of Staff. The danger in this suggestion, as the chiefs saw it when they met to consider the question, was that the secretary of defense might give this job to a civilian. If it came to that, Admiral Elmo Zumwalt said, "Then we'd tell him 'F you.' (laughter)."

The overriding priority for the top brass was not to ensure that the United States could defend itself against a Soviet strike. Air Force General John D. Ryan pointed out that the United States "could lose two hundred million people and still have more [inhabitants] than we had at the time of the Civil War." Admiral Thomas Moorer, chairman of the Joint Chiefs, insisted in a debate with top civilians that any new system should not reduce the authority of the Joint Chiefs of Staff. Both sides agreed that executing orders to launch U.S. nuclear forces "was not the end of the world. . . ."

The main concern for the Joint Chiefs was to protect their turf against any encroachment by civilian officials appointed by the president. Moorer went so far as to have a spy in the White House steal classified, "eyes only" papers so that he and his colleagues could be a step ahead in thwarting any such plans. The navy mole at the NSC even rifled through Henry Kissinger's briefcase. But when Nixon's plumbers discovered this operation, which went on for more than a year, the president decided against trying to remove Moorer from his perch at the Pentagon. He remained chairman of the Joint Chiefs for more than two years, was feted by defense contractors at expensive weekend retreats, and retired with a full pension to serve on several corporate boards. In this capacity, he lobbied for more military spending, and against any effort to let civilians have more input in weapons-procurement decisions.

It was not until 1977 that Bruce Blair went public in warning that military efforts to subvert civilian control had left no physical impediment to an unauthorized launch of Minuteman nuclear missiles. Not only that, he showed how the silos—in remote areas of Wyoming, Montana, and the Dakotas—were many miles from help and incredibly vulnerable. In a misguided public-relations gesture, the air force had been allowing groups of visitors—as many as eight at a time—to tour launch-control centers without even bothering to do background checks. Blair pointed out that the two Minuteman officers would be no more capable of stopping such a group from taking control than flight attendants could stop a hijacking. Once attackers sealed the eight-ton steel-and-concrete blast-proof door behind them, the "capsule" was designed to make the occupants virtually invulnerable, with ample supplies and an emergency life-support system. Blair thought possession of just one launch-control center might be sufficient to unleash an entire squadron of fifty missiles, with enough warheads to destroy every Soviet city. They might even generate fake launch orders for the entire arsenal of American ICBMs, which would likely have been enough to plunge the entire planet into a nuclear winter.

After Blair published the article, the air force quickly changed the codes and upgraded security at the Minuteman silos. There was no official acknowledgment, but secrecy had clearly covered up dangerous practices. The very nature of nuclear weapons demanded tighter control of "restricted data," but it proved necessary to reveal security lapses in order to correct them. Tellingly, what had been most closely guarded in all these cases was not the secret of how to end human civilization. Instead, it was what Andrew Bacevich, a former army colonel, has called the "dirty little secret" of civil-military relations. After many years of studying the subject, he concluded that the dirty little secret is that "the commander in chief does not command the military establishment; he cajoles it, negotiates with it, and, as necessary, appeases it."

This secret protects many, many other secrets—some of them very deep—because, when the military chooses to defy civilian control, we may not even know it. Outrageous and unacceptable things can persist indefinitely when even those with a "need to know" do not actually know.

Yet, compared with nuclear and cryptologic secrets, the endless bickering and basic lack of respect between military and civil authorities do seem "dirty" and "little," like a bad marriage. Behind a public façade, we find that generals and admirals have often had self-serving and petty motivations, even when it came to decisions affecting the fate of the Earth. They did not want to give up their power to use nuclear weapons, and abused the classification system to inflate spending. They could be confident that if a president or presidential appointees actually did discover the games they were playing, they could just go work for the defense contractors that lobbied for their business. But civilians, for their part, have long tolerated this behavior, and turn a blind eye, often because of a lack of political courage or respect for their own constitutional responsibilities. They allow the military to use secrecy and leaks to subvert civilian authority because they will not risk a public confrontation that they might actually lose.

From this broader perspective, the secrets we have learned about with regard to nuclear weapons and cryptography can be seen as parts of a bigger story. Ever since Pearl Harbor, the military has established exceptional power and overweening influence under the dubious principle that their secrets keep us safe. In fact, they used secrecy when it suited them, and carved out exceptions when it did not. They employed leaks and spin no less than secrecy to protect their perquisites and push their agendas—above all, expanding military spending, defying civilian authority, and appropriating the ultimate power, deciding when the nation would go to war.

In this chapter, we will see how the secret of civil-military relations has undermined national security. That bigger story starts in the aftermath of World War II. After every war up to that point, the military receded into the background. But in the 1940s and 1950s, generals and admirals rose to new heights of power and influence. They refused to accept demobilization, and in some cases—most famously, General Douglas MacArthur— openly defied direct orders from the president. More often, insubordination happened quietly, and frequently took the form of leaking secret information. At the same time, we will see how commanders continually pressed for secret powers to plan and initiate the use of nuclear weapons. In their effort to maximize readiness to achieve victory, they created a hair-trigger system that risked thermonuclear war through miscalculation or accident. Even General Dwight Eisenhower had to "command and cajole," and continued military insubordination drove him to distraction. President Kennedy, on the other hand, tried the alternative strategy. He negotiated and appeased, until he too concluded that the military was out of control. The mutual distrust between top civilian and military leaders was a fundamental cause of America's descent into the Vietnam quagmire, and the beginning of a long crisis in civil-military relations that continues to this day.

———

Initially, in the aftermath of World War II, the United States did undertake a rapid demobilization, much as it had after previous wars. For example, in 1949 Truman canceled the first of what was supposed to be a new generation of aircraft carriers built for nuclear war. But naval officers refused to accept the decision. They were incensed about how the funds for the carrier program would be shifted to the air force. This led to what Omar Bradley called "open rebellion against the civilian control."

This "Revolt of the Admirals" might have ended quickly, but naval officers flouted rules restricting access to confidential documents to win reporters to their side. The navy's defenders admitted this was insubordination, but invoked the Nuremberg Tribunals, as if defying the president's decision to cut the navy budget was comparable to refusing to follow orders to commit war crimes. This episode showed how, at the same time senior military leaders were expanding official secrecy, they would reveal these secrets when they thought it helped their cause. Rather than forming part of a strategy for national security, secrecy was used and abused to justify spending more on weapons, which was already becoming an end in itself.

But the Revolt of the Admirals proved to be just an early skirmish in an intensifying struggle, one in which the stakes also included the power to initiate nuclear war. The outbreak of the Korean War, only one year later, was one such moment of increasing tension. A new command structure that unified the different services and divided the world into regions gave Douglas MacArthur extraordinary autonomy as the commander-in-chief in the Far East. Consolidating military authority was ostensibly intended to prevent another Pearl Harbor. But MacArthur was surprised and unprepared when the communists in North Korea invaded the South. After assuming leadership of Allied forces in the peninsula, he scorned President Truman's authority and escalated a public showdown about the strategy for the war. Above all, MacArthur wanted to bring the war to China, which would very likely have led to war with the Soviet Union. But, apparently, he was not cleared to know that the United States simply did not yet have enough nuclear weapons to win.

What almost no one knew until many years later was just how close MacArthur came to starting World War III. In April 1951, the general sabotaged a White House effort to initiate armistice negotiations, instead telling a Republican congressman that the United States should help Chiang Kai-shek's forces in Taiwan open a second front against China. On April 10, an American destroyer in the South China Sea received secret orders hand-delivered from Tokyo, where MacArthur was headquartered. It then sailed to the Chinese city of Shantou, opposite Taiwan, and upon arrival the next day parked three miles offshore. This was deep inside Communist China's territorial waters, and put the city well within the range of the destroyer's five-inch guns. The American ship was quickly surrounded by almost fifty armed Chinese junks, some of them equipped with 76mm artillery pieces. In response, American aircraft carriers launched waves of jets to fly over both the Chinese vessels and the Shantou airfield. If the Chinese tried to stop them, American cruisers and battleships were standing by to shell the coast and cover an amphibious invasion.

Just twelve years earlier, the people of Shantou saw their city attacked and occupied by Imperial Japanese invaders through a seaborne assault. Considering this history, it is remarkable that they exercised such restraint, holding their fire as American aircraft simulated dive-bombing and strafing runs. While this was happening, the White House called a press conference—at 1:00 a.m. Washington time—and announced that Truman was removing MacArthur from his command, "effective at once." The planes buzzing Shantou then withdrew, and the destroyer followed. The crew and pilots were ordered to say nothing of the incident, and the captain did not even mention it in the ship's log.

MacArthur returned to the United States and went on a publicity tour, publicly rejecting the "new and heretofore unknown and dangerous concept that the members of our armed forces owe primary allegiance and loyalty to those who temporarily exercise the authority of the executive branch of government rather than to the country and its Constitution which they are sworn to defend." According to this view, a duly elected commander-in-chief could not actually command the military, nor could the people appointed with the advice and consent of the Senate. Instead, military commanders should decide how best to defend the country, answering only to their own consciences.

To the public, MacArthur was a man who simply insisted on victory, and he had long been admired for his dogged defense of the Philippines after Pearl Harbor. But decades later, a secret came to light about what had really happened there. After MacArthur fled the Japanese invasion and took shelter in the tunnels of the island fortress of Corregidor, he told President Roosevelt that it might be advisable to withdraw U.S. forces and allow Philippine President Manuel Quezon to declare neutrality. It was Roosevelt who insisted Quezon set up a government in exile and fight on. But MacArthur refused to let Quezon leave with his wife and young daughters, who would soon have been in the hands of the Japanese. It would appear that MacArthur was waiting for Quezon to first transfer half a million dollars to the general's personal account at Chase Manhattan Bank—more than eight million in present-day dollars. Soon after this was done, the general evacuated the Philippines in a PT boat with his top advisers—whom Quezon also had to pay off—while ordering the Americans he left behind to fight to the death.

So, nine years later, when Truman relieved him of command and MacArthur returned to the United States, he was able to move into a ten-room penthouse suite at the Waldorf-Astoria Hotel in Manhattan. He toured the country excoriating Truman—at taxpayer expense—and then became chairman of the board of Remington Rand, a defense contractor, commanding a princely salary that made front-page news. This set an example for countless other generals and admirals, who began to realize they could engage in insubordination and even open revolt, and then cash in on their connections and cachet by becoming senior executives for defense contractors. But to the public, MacArthur was a hero, whereas Truman was a mere politician, and a deeply unpopular one at that. In the year after he fired the general, his approval ratings were the lowest ever recorded of any president then or since. He left office with no savings and no pension. In the years that followed, presidents were understandably leery of taking on popular generals.

Another popular general, Dwight Eisenhower, then won landslide victories over Adlai Stevenson in 1952 and 1956. But Eisenhower was unusual among military leaders in that he was deeply worried that the United States was becoming a garrison state. When he took office, defense accounted for nearly 60 percent of federal government spending. But, when confronting the two perennial controversies in civil-military relations, war powers and weapons procurement, even Ike opted not to fight a two-front war.

As we have seen, he threatened the use of nuclear weapons to end the Korean War, and would go on to give military commanders unprecedented powers to initiate a nuclear attack at their own discretion. But at the same time he expanded the nuclear arsenal—arguing that nukes offered more bang for the buck—Eisenhower tried to cut other kinds of weapons systems. The role of ground forces would mainly be to keep order in the continental U.S. after the Air Force had finished waging nuclear war. Army generals such as Matthew Ridgway, James Gavin, and Maxwell Taylor bitterly protested what they described as a dangerous overreliance on nuclear intimidation. What if the Soviets refused to be intimidated?

Eisenhower answered such objections by giving military

commanders independent authority to initiate nuclear war at the first sign of Soviet aggression—even if the Soviets attacked with conventional weapons. "What would happen, in effect, would be that General Gruenther would use atomic weapons in the event of sudden attack by the Soviets on NATO," Eisenhower explained to his National Security Council, naming his friend, the commander-in-chief of the U.S. European Command. "We would have to 'hang him' afterward if we didn't approve."

Eisenhower was probably trying to be humorous, but the fact that he was giving military commanders—not just in Europe, but around the world—the power to strike first with nuclear weapons could not have been more serious. No less important, this authority was a closely guarded secret, to the point where, when Kennedy succeeded Eisenhower, military commanders would swear that these orders did not exist. Even decades later, government censors redacted this section about Gruenther from the official record of Eisenhower's meeting.

No commander was more assertive in pushing for secret powers to plan and initiate nuclear war than the head of the Strategic Air Command, Curtis LeMay. Unlike the European Command, or Far East Command—where the different services were "unified" and the commander also had to take account of the interests of regional allies—SAC's purview was global in scope but only reflected the parochial view of the U.S. Air Force. Many in the air force continued to believe it would be better to initiate an attack on the USSR while the United States still had an overwhelming advantage. In the meantime, they provoked Moscow with overflights ostensibly meant to prevent any surprise attack—overflights that were secret even to senior civilian officials. LeMay told the B-47 aircrew that clashed with Soviet MiGs in 1954 that he would have awarded them Silver Stars for gallantry in action, but that would have required Washington's approval, and "I'd have to explain this mission to too damn many people who don't need to know."

At a SAC briefing that same year, other military commanders were told that "the exact manner in which the SAC will fight the war *is known only to General LeMay and that he will decide. . . .*" LeMay had shown the same kind of independent initiative when he firebombed Tokyo in 1945. Rather than inform civilian officials beforehand, he presented them with a fait accompli. LeMay did not stop firebombing Japanese cities until he ran out of napalm. Now he would not even share war plans with the other services. Amazingly, this meant that in a nuclear war the United States would have been conducting uncoordinated attacks on hundreds of targets in the USSR—air-force pilots and naval aviators would have been hitting the same targets (or hitting each other).

LeMay's arrogance about his secret plans for nuclear war was all the more infuriating to the other armed services because he was also outfighting them in the other major theater of civil-military strife: Pentagon appropriations. Eisenhower was still trying to rein in military spending, and at this point the air force was the big winner. Its share of the defense budget rose from roughly 30 percent in 1950 to more than 45 percent by 1955. To fight back, army generals used strategic leaks. Ridgway wrote one final attack on Eisenhower's "Massive Retaliation" strategy upon resigning as army chief of staff. But when he was told to classify it, the report instead ended up in *The New York Times.* His successor, Maxwell Taylor, similarly attempted to undermine Eisenhower's authority when he told reporters about a top-secret proposal for a three-billion-dollar army-run missile defense system, hoping the publicity would force Eisenhower to drop his opposition.

The air force was still not satisfied with the dramatic growth in weapons procurement. In an effort to drum up support for even more B-52's, classified intelligence was leaked that grossly overstated projections of Soviet bomber production, spreading fear about an impending "bomber gap." Eisenhower despaired when he thought about how he could stop the leaks. He had already personally warned everyone on his National Security Council that he would order the FBI to investigate whoever leaked information from their deliberations. When some members suggested the United States have its own Official Secrets Act, the president observed, "You could read all this classified data in the newspapers anyway." He and the NSC talked endlessly about how to restore control. "If he were the Secretary of Defense," Ike suggested, "he would 'cut some throats with a dull razor.'"

It proved impossible to restore discipline, because more and more officers were coming to realize that, if ever caught leaking secrets or otherwise defying their superiors, they could obtain better paying positions in the private sector. By the mid-1950s, it was estimated that more than two thousand of them each year opted for these golden parachutes. Unlike Truman, who made George Marshall secretary of defense, and Omar Bradley head of the Veterans Administration, Eisenhower took care to appoint civilians to the top positions in the Pentagon. But two of his appointees would be forced out of office over accusations that they had engaged in corruption with defense contractors. A lot of corruption was perfectly legal, such as when corporate boards—many with business before the Pentagon—hired recently retired generals and admirals, including Bedell Smith, William "Bull" Halsey, and Omar Bradley. When LeMay himself finally retired, he became an executive for a California defense contractor and bought a four-acre home in Bel Air fit for a movie star.

Eisenhower sought the help of private citizens—scientists, business leaders, and university administrators—to try to get balanced advice about the unending demands for more military spending. In 1957, when he was advised that the government should spend forty billion dollars on fallout shelters, he appointed a committee led by Rowan Gaither, the head of the Ford Foundation, to study civil defense. After Gaither had to step down for health reasons, two defense contractors on the committee took charge: Robert Sprague of Sprague Electronics, and William Foster of Olin Mathieson Chemical Corporation. They came back to Eisenhower with an even bigger bill: forty-four billion, or $383 billion in 2020 dollars. But instead of fallout shelters, their report pushed guided-missile batteries and ICBMs as a higher priority (Sprague Electronics would supply the missile guidance systems).

Nowhere in this report did the authors reveal the most startling fact discovered in the course of their study. It showed just how far the military had pushed forward on that second front: gaining independent authority to start a nuclear war. Dissatisfied with the anodyne, "chamber of commerce"–type briefings he was receiving from LeMay, Sprague insisted on visiting SAC headquarters in Omaha, Nebraska. When finally shown a map revealing both where bombers were based and how much time it would take for them to get airborne, he calculated that a surprise Soviet attack could destroy them all. LeMay then took Sprague to an even more secret room, where SAC received reports from reconnaissance planes overflying the USSR. If the Soviets were massing for an attack, LeMay vowed, "I'm going to knock the shit out of them before they get off the ground." Sprague questioned whether LeMay's plan went against national policy. "No it's not national policy," LeMay said. "But it's my policy."

If Sprague was untroubled by what LeMay told him, it may be because Sprague himself wanted to go even further. He recommended delivering an ultimatum to Moscow demanding it disarm or face attack. Eisenhower declined to take the advice, and refused to ramp up military spending. The president knew that the committee was overstating the danger. So Foster leaked their report. Eisenhower was furious to read the details of this top-secret report in *The Washington Post*. Administration critics in Congress used it to redouble efforts to increase Pentagon purchasing from military contractors. The president told John Foster Dulles, "This experience had proved," he thought definitively, "the unwisdom of calling in outside groups."

Unfortunately for Eisenhower, and the country, some of those on the inside were completely unhinged. Thomas Power, who personally led the attack on Tokyo and succeeded LeMay as commander of SAC in 1957, was even more aggressive in pressing for both more nuclear weapons and more authority to use them. Power insisted that even the generals under him should be able to order the use of nuclear weapons without prior approval from their superiors. When civilian strategists briefed him on the idea that the United States might consider sparing Soviet cities so as to reduce the risk of retaliation against American cities, Power erupted. "Look. At the end of the war, if there are two Americans and one Russian, we win!"

Even Power's subordinates, like General Horace Wade, had their doubts. "I used to worry that General Power was not stable," he told an interviewer some years later. "He had control of so many weapons and weapon systems and could, under certain conditions, launch the force. Back in the days before we had real positive control, SAC had the power to do a lot of things, and it was in his hands, and he knew it." Wade knew that these were the kinds of concerns that led McNamara and Kennedy to insist on electromechanical locks. They did so not just to prevent a foreign power from seizing American nukes, but also "to keep it out of an individual ['s hands] that might not be completely stable."

But commanders like LeMay and Power rose to the top because all agreed on the need to avoid a nuclear Pearl Harbor, to the point where generals constantly prepared to strike first. In a rare photo of the War Room from the time, the display board shows SAC bomber routes sweeping up and over the North Pole, and nuclear detonations across the USSR. Remarkably, no one has pulled the curtains closed to conceal the map. What is even more amazing is how it is titled: "TYPICAL *First Strike*." The ideas of LeMay and Power were just more extreme, more unstable, versions of Eisenhower's own.

In 1958, after hearing reports of increasing Soviet nuclear capabilities, Eisenhower reluctantly approved a plan to release 400-foot-high reconnaissance balloons from aircraft carriers in the Pacific, which would take photographs while overflying the USSR. A sticking point was the use of timers to initiate the balloons' descent, which Eisenhower rejected out of concern that they would not be reliable enough to ensure a safe recovery in Western Europe. Each balloon's payload weighed thousands of pounds, and hundreds of smaller balloons had already been lost in the USSR in an earlier program. But the air force countermanded Ike's orders, and one of the balloons came crashing down in Communist Poland. The air force tried to avoid informing the president. But Eisenhower did discover they had disobeyed direct orders, and insisted that all money budgeted for the program be impounded. He observed how there was "disturbing evidence of a deterioration in the processes of discipline and responsibility within the armed forces." In view of the "obvious" harm to national security, he wanted "action to be taken at once," starting with a formal investigation. When another balloon was recovered in the Soviet Union, Ike vowed that he "would take the man who ordered that and fire him. There will be a great thing before the Supreme Court but in the meantime the man will suffer."

Eisenhower faced a dilemma. Overflights helped to show that air-force leaks were exaggerating the Soviet threat. Proving that Moscow was not building nearly as many bombers or missiles as the air force claimed seemed like the best way to resist the pressure for spending still more money on weapons, or even initiating a "preventative" war. But Eisenhower understood that violating Soviet territory "carried the danger of starting a nuclear war by miscalculation." After all, from the Soviets' perspective, reconnaissance was indistinguishable from target acquisition, and target acquisition was exactly what the United States would do if it were actually preparing to attack. If the USSR attempted to do the same thing and overflew the United States, Eisenhower said he would declare war.

Luckily, the Soviets resisted these provocations, quite possibly because—as we have seen—they were able to intercept top-secret U.S. communications and count on timely warning of an actual attack.

But war by miscalculation was not the only danger created by a military that was pushing relentlessly for both more nuclear weapons and less civilian control over their use. Maximizing the American ability to detect and pre-empt a Soviet attack eventually led to multiple "fail-safe" warning systems, and a nuclear force that was primed like a "cocked weapon," as LeMay put it. Here again, secret procedures that were ostensibly meant to protect national security actually increased other risks—the risk of an accidental nuclear detonation.

In 1957, the USSR introduced its first ICBM, and Sprague and Foster warned Eisenhower that such weapons could soon destroy SAC's ability to retaliate. Eisenhower received this warning with stony-faced silence. But the next year, Power gained

To get bombers into the air as quickly as possible, SAC attached rockets to their fuselages and, for added thrust, injected water into the intakes of their jet engines.

the authority to launch armed and fueled B-52's kept ready for such a contingency—the alert bomber force—if he believed that a Soviet attack was imminent, arguing, as he and others had before, that time would be of the essence. In their need for speed, SAC pursued ever-more-extreme measures to get heavily armed and fully fueled bombers off the ground as quickly as possible. These modifications produced big billowing clouds of black smoke that followed the bombers as they roared down the runway. SAC also drilled crews to carry out "Minimum Interval Takeoffs," such that each succeeding bomber followed just fifteen seconds behind the last. Pilots had the terrifying experience of barreling down the runway with thermonuclear weapons and zero visibility, trying to maintain the precise intervals between the bombers, shaking and swaying through the preceding plane's wake turbulence.

Planes would crash and explode during these drills, and sometimes the bombs would burn, too. In some cases, the high explosives inside would detonate—without triggering a chain reaction, but with sufficient force to spew radiation over a large area. The crews that made it into the air had to fly for as long as twenty-four hours on airborne alert missions. In a B-47, with its cramped cockpit, this could be a grueling experience. The worst part was when the bombers linked up with an airborne tanker, and the pilot had to hold steady for as long as half an hour to keep the two planes connected without crashing into each other while highly flammable jet fuel flowed between them.

Hitting the runway with a nuclear weapon on board could also be dangerous. More than once, pilots jettisoned the payload rather than risk its explosion during a rough landing. Between 1956 and 1968, there were at least twenty-two accidents in which American airmen crashed while carrying nuclear weapons, crashed into a nuclear-weapon storage facility, jettisoned their weapons, or—in two cases—accidentally pulled the lever and dropped nuclear bombs.

Many of these incidents were kept secret at the time, and some still are, especially if they occurred in (or over) a foreign country. But secrecy was not an option when a bomb literally landed in someone's backyard, as happened to Walter Gregg in March 1958, wrecking his house and leaving a seventy-five-foot crater. The air force liked to insist that, even though it had dropped an atomic bomb on South Carolina, a nuclear detonation was impossible. It was true in this case, since the weapon and the nuclear "pit"—the fissile material itself—were kept separate.

But in other cases, like one at a SAC base in Morocco six weeks earlier, an actual detonation was narrowly averted. For the simple reason of wanting to add even more realism to a training exercise, the nuclear core had actually been inserted into the weapon. When the plane crashed, firefighters fought the flames for ten minutes before the base commander decided to evacuate all personnel and their families. The plane was carrying a ten-megaton weapon. In yet another accident, this one in 1961, the crew abandoned an out-of-control B-52 flying airborne alert near Goldsboro, North Carolina. Two multi-megaton bombs fell as the plane broke up, and only a single safety switch prevented a thermonuclear detonation. It could have clouded the air over several cities—including Washington—with lethal fallout.

The military's determination never to be caught by surprise thus created a whole series of surprises. And commanders' trying to keep them secret only compounded the danger. Risky policies and practices remained in place, like unexploded ordnance, long after LeMay and Power had left the scene. Airborne alert missions with fully armed nuclear bombers did not end until 1968, after yet another near miss. The true gravity of what transpired in this incident was not fully understood until many years later, when the Stanford political scientist Scott Sagan launched his own investigation, and discovered how close it had come to triggering a global thermonuclear war.

At the northernmost U.S. military installation in the world, in Thule, Greenland, 750 miles north of the Arctic Circle, the air force built a Ballistic Missile Early Warning System. The system was designed to detect any Soviet ICBM attack and relay the information back to North American Aerospace Defense Command (NORAD) headquarters in Colorado. A nuclear-bomb alarm was also installed, to deliver a warning if it detected a thermal flash, in the event that Thule itself was attacked. But fishing trawlers sometimes cut the underwater communications cable by accident, and Soviet trawlers could easily do it on purpose. SAC therefore assigned one B-52 from the airborne alert squadron to circle over the base. That way, there would always be an American plane in position to report any sneak attack directly to SAC headquarters, providing a final safeguard against loss of communications with both the base and the bomb-alarm system. The same plane would still be available for a nuclear-bombing run on the USSR. If it sounded the alarm, the SAC commander could then scramble all the bombers, release the B-52 and the rest of the alert force for their attack missions, and start launching ICBMs. This system was an attempt to account for all reasonable possibilities.

In January 1968, the pilot of the B-52 circling over Thule discovered that a fire had broken out in the aircraft's heating system. Thick black smoke wafted through the plane's cabin. Then, suddenly, the electric system failed. The crew bailed out, and watched as the unmanned—but fully loaded—bomber flew right over the base. It did a 180-degree turn, and started to come back around, still laden with four thermonuclear weapons. This all happened so fast that neither the crew nor the control tower relayed the news to NORAD headquarters in Colorado. The plane then crashed into sea ice just a few miles from Thule, and the munitions in all four of its bombs exploded.

If the plane had been carrying more primitive weapons, the impact alone might well have destroyed the base in a nuclear blast. But these bombs were designed to minimize the risks of going critical in an accidental detonation. In this system, two members of the crew would have had to turn electrical switches to arm the weapon.

But there were multiple ways in which the B-52 might have decimated the Thule early-warning system, set off the "fail-safe" bomb alarm, and in that way signaled what would have looked like a Soviet surprise attack. As the Yale political scientist Paul Bracken observed, the nuclear apparatus is an "enormously complex but stupid organism," which is "designed to kill even while being cut to pieces." In one possibility, the fire on the plane could have fused wires and closed circuits, arming the weapons. And if pre-armed bombs had dropped, they were designed to detonate. Furthermore, SAC had designed a "dead man switch," so that pre-armed bombs would *automatically* drop if the crew had bailed out. SAC did not want to waste even a single weapon if it could be made to explode anywhere on enemy territory. Here again, the system was vulnerable to short-circuiting, and precisely in those circumstances—a fire on board—when the crew might not be able to stop it.

It would even have been possible for a crew member to override deliberately what were supposed to be fail-safe systems. Such a thing happened in 1963, when a B-47 pilot reported what he said was sabotage to his superiors: someone had turned the two control switches that armed the bombs on board. It turns out the pilot himself was playing with the navigator's control switch and inadvertently turned it. Then he did something even stranger. He went to his own switch, broke the seal, removed the safety wire, and turned that one as well.

Why would a pilot play with a nuclear switch, and then turn a second switch, knowing it would arm a nuclear weapon? After the initial mistake, he would otherwise have had to fess up and file an official report. In a panic, he opted to make it look like actual sabotage. But the underlying reason for such behavior was the culture of the Strategic Air Command created by Curtis LeMay and Thomas Power. They subjected their men to countless hours of tedium combined with moments of terrifying stress, topping the system off with career-ending punishment for even minor infractions—in the case of Major Hering, even for questioning how they could be sure orders to start a nuclear war were legal.

Should we be surprised that some cracked under the strain? In a similar incident in 1962, a B-47 pilot pulled the wrong switch during a minimum-interval takeoff drill, disabling the water injection required to give the jet engines sufficient thrust. Rather than abort the takeoff, and admit he failed the exercise, the pilot decided to risk it. The plane lumbered down the runway and then crashed into a bridge abutment, killing all aboard.

More than anyone, it was General Power who created an atmosphere in which pilots were ready to risk death rather than receive demerits. He would publicly embarrass subordinates who did not measure up, and seemed to delight in destroying the careers of airmen guilty of any error. This is one reason why at least some of his subordinates worried that he was unfit to command. They knew that some of the most dangerous secrets were the ones subordinates concealed from their superiors.

How great was the danger that day in Greenland? SAC would have scrambled bombers at every base if it had lost communications with Thule, as Power had already done in a 1961 incident, when communications were down for just twelve minutes. It was only when he had definite confirmation of a false alarm from the backup B-52 flying over Thule that he canceled the alert. But if this backup—the very thing that was supposed to make the whole system fail-safe—had blown itself and everything else up in 1968, it would have looked from SAC headquarters as if the Soviets had started a surprise attack.

Of course, civilians in Washington might have overruled any immediate retaliatory strike, or at least tried to, especially if they were able to guess what had happened. But Sagan also found that, in fact, civilian officials might not have even known there was a B-52 with thermonuclear bombs flying over Thule: it was not on any of the maps that SAC had provided to them.

Thus, a secret plan, a secret mission, and secret screw-ups came perilously close to starting a global thermonuclear war, and this at a time in which—after years of relentless lobbying—the United States alone had procured some thirty thousand nuclear warheads. High readiness and zero tolerance for error had seemed essential to prevent a nuclear Pearl Harbor and maximize chances for victory. But in an atmosphere of top secrecy, this created unforeseen and unmanageable dangers.

The dirty little secret of civil-military relations did not just inflate Pentagon appropriations for world-ending weaponry by trillions of dollars, and increase the risk of nuclear war by miscalculation or accident. It also posed risks to the Constitution itself, and the bedrock principle that the military must answer to democratically elected representatives of the American people. As he neared the end of his presidency, Eisenhower realized that he was losing even the limited war he had undertaken to rein in defense spending. One crucial reason was that he could not effectively counter his adversaries' weaponization of secrecy and leaks to win political battles. While the president was sovereign over the security classification system, it was all too easy for senior officers who opposed his policies to use classified information to marshal support in Congress and manipulate public opinion. In his last battle, the air force and its allies in the defense industry leaked what was supposed to be classified intelligence, this time purporting to prove the Soviets were building far more missiles than the United States. And though the intelligence proved erroneous, the air force would actually promote the officers responsible for leaking it. Power even went public, claiming that Soviet missiles could cripple America's retaliatory force. He was doing an end run around the president for the specific purpose of framing the debate in the election of Eisenhower's successor.

Eisenhower had very publicly condemned the idea that generals could speak out in defiance of their commander-in-chief. Congress had already agreed to deny authorization for what Ike called "legalized insubordination." But in fact, once Power did it anyway, there was little the president could do to dispel the notion of a "missile gap," since he could not publicly acknowledge the secret overflights. And far from paying a personal price—recall how Eisenhower said he was inclined to cut throats with a dull razor—Power remained as SAC commander for four more years. When he retired, he, too, became a corporate board chairman—of Schick, Inc.

In his 1961 farewell address, Eisenhower warned about "the potential for the disastrous rise of misplaced power." "We must," he insisted, "guard against the acquisition of unwarranted influence, whether sought or unsought, by the military industrial complex." Even though the United States was nominally at peace after the Korean armistice agreement, the military still absorbed over 50 percent of the federal budget. The Pentagon's purchasing power amounted to nearly 9 percent of the nation's gross domestic product, which at the time was equivalent to the economic output of China, and three times more than the entire footprint of the federal government in 1914. Eisenhower thus ended his administration having ceded wide-ranging powers to the military to plan and even initiate nuclear war with little civilian oversight, while at the same time losing his long struggle to dismantle the massive peacetime military establishment.

With the incoming Kennedy administration, the opposite strategy was pursued. In fact, JFK rode to victory in the 1960 election by claiming that Eisenhower had let the Soviets take the lead in building nuclear missiles and supporting insurgencies all across the Third World. He sided with generals like Ridgway and Taylor, who insisted that the United States not only be invulnerable to a bolt from the blue, but also spend billions mobilizing conventional forces for every other contingency.

After his election, Kennedy brought Taylor back to the Pentagon as his chief adviser, and lavished money on the army so it could prepare for everything from counterinsurgency warfare in Southeast Asia to armored combat on the Rhine. The navy would get more supercarriers and ballistic-missile submarines. And Kennedy shoveled still more money to the air force for a thousand Minuteman ICBMs. He retained Power at SAC and elevated LeMay to become air-force chief of staff. If it actually came to nuclear combat with the USSR, these were the kind of battle-tested mass executioners he wanted at his side.

Kennedy and McNamara apparently thought that they, unlike Eisenhower, could keep LeMay and the other generals and admirals in line. "We thought we could reason with him," McNamara later explained. But early on, the administration began to realize that, in fact, there was a whole other side to civil-military relations, and Kennedy would have to fight to regain command and control of U.S. nuclear forces. He demanded answers to how he would exercise his authority as commander-in-chief, right down to who would answer the phone if he called the Joint War Room and ordered a nuclear attack on the USSR. Kennedy was appalled when he found out what would happen next. The military did not even want to explain their targeting plan, but it included not just destroying every city in the USSR, but those in Eastern Europe and China as well. "General," Kennedy asked the chairman of the Joint Chiefs, Lyman Lemnitzer, "why are we hitting all those targets in China?" Because, Lemnitzer answered, "they're in the *plan*, Mr. President."

Kennedy was amazed that the military had only one plan for nuclear war: to annihilate the entire communist world. The projections were shocking. The Pentagon estimated that, on top of half a billion fatalities in the USSR, China, and Eastern Europe, the fallout would kill another hundred million people in neighboring countries, most of them American allies. The strategists that McNamara brought into the Pentagon also discovered that there were many scenarios in which the military might attack without waiting for their superiors to give the orders. The civilians repeatedly insisted they receive copies of any standing orders that "pre-delegated" this kind of authority to initiate a nuclear strike. They were told that no such documents existed, because there was no such policy—until somehow, some time later, the documents surfaced. An air-force major based near the DMZ in Korea admitted that, even without any formal policy, a squadron commander who was already in the air would likely jump to the conclusion that they were under attack if there were a nuclear detonation at his base—even if it turned out to be an accidental detonation. He would immediately lead his group into Soviet and Chinese territory and start hitting them with nuclear weapons. In this way, if there were even one accidental nuclear detonation—among the many close calls during this period—it could have started general war between the superpowers.

The pre-delegation orders, like the complex "fail-safe" procedures to prevent a nuclear Pearl Harbor, thus lurked beneath the surface of civil-military relations in the 1960s, like more unexploded bombs. Realizing this, Kennedy tried to defuse the situation. He wanted to make sure that only he could issue an order to use nuclear weapons, and that if the moment came he would have options—like, for example, a plan that would specifically target Soviet nuclear forces. Unlike General Power, he was interested in the possibility of minimizing civilian casualties so as to stop an escalation that would lead to the destruction of America's own cities.

Civilian advisers were therefore sent out to SAC headquarters to gather information. "It was very unpleasant, very hostile," then Deputy National Security Adviser Carl Kaysen later recalled. " 'You bastards, it's none of your business' was just written all over all their faces." To the question of how military commanders might themselves order use of nuclear weapons without consulting their superiors, Power's deputy was nonplussed: "I can't imagine what you're talking about." During the two days they spent there, Kaysen began to wonder whether they would be "clapped in irons and never let out." Upon their return to

Washington, they warned McNamara: "It's worse than you think."

As the new and unseasoned president faced a series of international crises, his doubts about the competence, even basic rationality, of senior military leadership only increased. He felt he had to take responsibility when a U.S.-backed coup against Fidel Castro failed spectacularly at the Bay of Pigs. But in private he was angry that the generals did not push back against poor CIA planning. The military, for their part, considered Kennedy's decision to deny air support to be cowardly.

The Joint Chiefs came back with a plan for the U.S. military itself to invade Cuba. The chiefs—not the CIA—would develop a covert operation to provide a pretext for a full-scale invasion. The Pentagon proposed blowing up a U.S. ship in Guantanamo Bay, sinking a boatload of Cubans en route to Florida, or creating a bombing campaign in Miami or Washington they could blame on Cuba. America's top brass were actually proposing to drown refugees and bomb American cities.

After the discovery that the USSR had stationed nuclear missiles in Cuba in October 1962, Kennedy gathered his top advisers to discuss the U.S. response. Maxwell Taylor was allowed to participate, but not the Joint Chiefs of Staff. The president rejected their unanimous advice to carry out a surprise air strike and invasion. Instead, Kennedy was willing to make concessions to avoid war, even at the risk of appearing to abandon allies. In the meantime, he decided on a blockade in which navy warships would stop Soviet vessels on the high seas and inspect their cargo. After settling on this plan, he finally agreed to meet with his generals and admirals. The meeting did not go well. "This is almost as bad as the appeasement at Munich," LeMay fumed. "I just don't see any other solution except direct military intervention right now."

Kennedy did allow the chiefs to raise the readiness alert level of U.S. forces worldwide to DEFCON 3, two steps short of imminent war. He wanted to deter the Soviets from further escalation. But as the president readied himself to speak to the nation, LeMay wrote to Taylor recommending that SAC move to "maximum readiness posture," or DEFCON 2, the highest level short of actual war. Twenty-four hours after the alert, SAC would be ready to launch some twelve hundred bombers and 172 missiles, which together could deliver nearly three thousand nuclear weapons. Moreover, one eighth of the bombers would be kept in the air twenty-four hours a day. Raising SAC to DEFCON 2 meant that, if it came to war, these missiles and bombers were even more likely to land the first blows, and destroy both Soviet cities and Moscow's ability to retaliate. It would take time to achieve such readiness, but it would take even longer for the Soviets to realize what was happening—perhaps too long for them to do anything about it.

Taylor approved the plan, but without informing McNamara, National Security Adviser McGeorge Bundy, or the president himself that he was moving U.S. nuclear forces to DEFCON 2, the highest alert level in history. General Power broadcast this order to SAC bases all over the world without encrypting it. Power thus signaled to Moscow loud and clear that U.S. forces were getting ready to attack—if he was not actually trying to provoke the Soviets to do so first. The Soviets apparently put their own air-defense forces at a higher alert level, which went undetected. But, otherwise, Khrushchev did not respond in kind, perhaps reassured by what the KGB was able to pick up from its surveillance of the U.S. Embassy in Moscow. The Soviets did not call up the reserves, or disperse their own planes, or ready their own missiles. Like the Chinese during MacArthur's failed maneuver eleven years earlier, they refused to take the bait.

McNamara worried about what the military might do if he did not monitor its every move. He lived at his Pentagon office until the crisis was over, and insisted on being in the Flag Plot Room to supervise the quarantine personally. The chief of naval operations, Admiral George Anderson, bristled, and told McNamara that the U.S. Navy had been running blockades since the days of John Paul Jones. The secretary erupted, and ordered Anderson not to use force without express instructions.

Even with McNamara hovering over his admirals, U.S. naval forces engaged in a dangerous game of cat-and-mouse with a Soviet submarine squadron deployed to support the ships headed to Cuba. Anderson knew that, when batteries and oxygen ran low, each submarine would be forced to surface under the guns of U.S. warships—a humiliation for any captain. The Soviets were under strict orders to conceal their movements, maintain communications security, and only surface at night. Before the sub carrying the squadron commander submerged on the night of October 25, civilian radio broadcasts from the United States made its crew think war was imminent. U.S. warships began to circle the waters above them.

By the 27th, no fewer than five destroyers and an aircraft carrier were in pursuit of the commander's vessel, dropping grenades and "practice" depth charges. CO_2 levels on the sub reached dangerous levels, and temperatures topped 120 degrees Fahrenheit. Crewmen fainted from the heat. One of the officers recalled what happened next:

> We thought—that's it—the end. After this attack, the totally exhausted [Captain] Savitsky, who in addition to everything was not able to establish connection with the General Staff, got furious. He summoned the officer who was assigned to the nuclear torpedo, and ordered him to assemble it to battle readiness. "Maybe the war has already started up there, while we are doing somersaults here"— screamed agitated Valentin [Savitsky] Grigorievich, justifying his order. "We're gonna blast them now! We will die, but we will sink them all."

But the commander of the squadron, Vasily Arkhipov, talked the captain out of starting nuclear war. The sub surfaced with U.S. destroyers all around, and they flooded it with blinding light. When the Americans began to play big-band music, as if to celebrate, the Soviet sailors knew it was not the end of the world.

The next day, Khrushchev finally agreed to remove the missiles from Cuba. In his memoirs, the premier explained that he was afraid Kennedy might otherwise be overthrown in a military coup. He even quoted Robert F. Kennedy, who warned in a back-channel conversation with the Soviet ambassador that the U.S. military "could get out of control." "I don't know," RFK reportedly said, "how much longer we can hold out against our generals."

To be sure, this is Khrushchev's account, and even if the quote is accurate the implied threat could have been a Kennedy negotiating tactic. It also gave the Soviet premier a good excuse for backing down. But after the crisis, JFK himself heard direct evidence that at least some people in the Pentagon were out of control. According to McNamara, another admiral reported: "Anderson was absolutely insubordinate during the Cuban crisis. . . . He consciously acted contrary to the President's instructions." Kennedy could not believe it: "He wanted to sink a ship?" "He wanted to sink a ship," McNamara confirmed. Anderson held "that it was none of your business or my business to say whether he should or shouldn't."

The president came to believe the top brass were "mad." Even before the crisis over Cuba, he had already had to relieve Major General Edwin Walker of his duties commanding a U.S. Army division in Germany. Walker had reportedly been indoctrinating his men with propaganda from the John Birch Society—which claimed the fluoridation of water was a communist plot—and had publicly claimed that Harry Truman and Dean Acheson were "definitely pink." A congressional investigation revealed that Walker was not alone. Naval aviators, for instance, were being trained to "demand" that elected leaders "immediately establish a foreign policy based on Godly moral Principle." Rather than "coexistence with evil," they would "demand that our Nation take the offensive in the cold war with the objective of victory over communism."

Some senior officers not only directed subordinates to question civilian leadership and condemn the deterrence doctrine, they also joined with radical right leaders in attacking civil-rights organizations. Walker was offered a new assignment in Hawaii, but resigned his commission instead and returned to the United States. He personally led demonstrations against desegregation, including one in which armed protesters shot six federal marshals. The general was arrested for insurrection and seditious conspiracy. But, clearly, Walker was not the only military man with views that bordered on mutiny. Douglas MacArthur's chief aide, for instance, was a founding member of the Birch Society.

At least some of the top brass had a larger, even darker vision of the dangers facing American society, and insinuated the need for decisive action. Pentagon-run future-scenario exercises portrayed communism as a threat to white supremacy. Only a tiny percentage of these exercises have been made public, but we do have one from December 1962. Though it was organized two months after the Cuban Missile Crisis, it was set ten years in the future, in 1972. The scenario imagines a full-on "Red Dawn"–type communist invasion following a Soviet nuclear attack. The invaders install a Cuban–Black Power occupation government in the Southern states. This new government proceeds to carry out public lynchings of capitalists "in garish ceremonies in the Orange Bowl, before large crowds of drum-beating, chanting fanatics." In another scenario from the same exercise, "a gruesome cannibalistic orgy of Inter-tribal Mau Mau murder" eliminates all whites in Africa south of the Sahara. Chairman of the Joint Chiefs Maxwell Taylor welcomed a select group of influential civilians to participate in this exercise, including the *Twilight Zone* creator, Rod Serling. Shortly afterward, Serling would write the screenplay for *Seven Days in May*. The movie depicted how the Joint Chiefs of Staff would attempt to seize power to stop a president from negotiating nuclear disarmament. It was produced with the advice and encouragement of Kennedy himself.

Before he was assassinated, Kennedy said that his first advice to the next president would be to "watch the generals." Under Lyndon Johnson, McNamara and his team of civilian defense intellectuals continued attempting a "reconquest of the Pentagon," as Kennedy's court historian, Arthur Schlesinger, later described it. McNamara imposed hyperrational cost-benefit analyses on all manner of decisions, from weapons procurement to nuclear strategy. His "whiz kids" sometimes treated the generals with disdain, pitting them one against another and disregarding their views even when they were unanimous. The Cuban Missile Crisis also set the pattern for countless more military operations run out of the White House, most famously in Vietnam.

Mutual contempt between the White House and the Pentagon and their continuing struggle for control proved catastrophic when it came to advising the new president about whether and how the United States could ultimately prevail in Southeast Asia. Some of the chiefs were doubtful that they would win, but they did not want to cede influence, and they were reluctant to reveal their differences to civilian superiors. Their solution was to ask for more troops than they thought would be approved, thereby providing cover to pin any blame for a potential failure on the White House. Not realizing that even senior military leaders did not believe victory was possible, both LBJ and later Nixon accommodated these requests in order to avoid defeat, and promised further escalation if half measures failed.

Military power was thus employed in Vietnam in pursuit of an inherently contradictory set of bureaucratic and domestic political goals—goals that pitted senior military and political leaders against one another rather than against the ostensible enemy. The effect of this strategic incoherence was to maximize the ultimate cost of the conflict while minimizing any chance of actually prevailing. It culminated with Nixon and Kissinger using nuclear threats to cover the American retreat, what has been called the "madman theory" of nuclear brinkmanship: it is sometimes necessary, in order to de-escalate a crisis, to convince a foe that the ultimate decider might just be crazy enough to risk thermonuclear war. But, in fact, some military officials really did want to go all the way. In another Pentagon war-game scenario, a participant whose name was redacted from the record advised nuking North Vietnam.

In 1968, LeMay ran for the vice-presidency with the segregationist George Wallace. They campaigned on a law-and-order platform, and LeMay used his first public appearance in the campaign to advocate for the use of nuclear weapons if they proved necessary to defeat communism. They came relatively close to winning enough electoral votes to throw the election into the House of Representatives, where Wallace planned to use his kingmaker status to stop desegregation.

To this day, many still claim that the military could have won in Vietnam if only civilians had allowed them to fight unfettered—notwithstanding the fact that the United States dropped the explosive equivalent of five hundred Hiroshima-sized atomic bombs on Southeast Asia, and hundreds of thousands of Vietnamese, Cambodian, and Laotian men, women, and children perished during the two-decade-long struggle. But when one goes back and reviews the redacted parts of secret documents leading up to this debacle, it becomes clear that the Pentagon was planning to fight a whole host of wars in poor countries, producing contingency plans for counterinsurgency operations in Indonesia, Morocco, and Panama, and a first strike against China's nuclear facilities. If the United States had not experienced the wrenching trauma of Vietnam, the parts of the historical record that were previously redacted suggest that we would have experienced some other wrenching trauma, in some other part of the world.

In the aftermath of the Vietnam War, the United States adopted an all-volunteer military. Civilians with no experience of military service became increasingly deferential, and even reverential, toward those willing to serve. When polled, the percentage of Americans professing high confidence in the military rose steadily, and never dipped below 60 percent after 1989. Military leaders insisted there be "no more Vietnams"—future wars would have to be waged with overwhelming force and a clear commitment to total victory. And the different services closed ranks in the Pentagon, agreeing to work out their budgetary differences among themselves before presenting civilian superiors with a united front. Finally, they worked hard to develop friendly relations with sympathetic congressmen and senators, and mobilized their allies in Congress whenever they wanted to defy the White House.

At the same time, the Joint Chiefs resolved to destroy records of their internal deliberations, starting with the minutes of all their meetings going back to 1947. After 1978, they stopped keeping any notes of their meetings at all. It is as if America's most senior military leadership were running a numbers racket, committing nothing to paper. The few documents that happen to have survived—detailing covert violations of the territory of other countries, plans to stage attacks on the United States, and efforts to undermine civilian control of nuclear weapons—only suggest what else the Joint Chiefs might have hidden from us. The military appears to have calculated that the worst things we can imagine are not as bad as what they have actually covered up.

So when Americans are surveyed and asked which profession they trust the most, they might not realize just how much they are really trusting military officers when they put them at the top, outranking even doctors and teachers. Because the fact is, they have placed enormous faith in people who have been hostile to any outsiders seeking to exercise oversight. Would we be wrong to imagine the worst? The danger is not likely to be anything so dramatic as *Seven Days in May*. Nor is it reducible to the risk that military men will drag us into war, because the top brass pick and choose which wars they prefer to fight. When, as in the case of scenarios for saving the surrounded French garrison at Dien Bien Phu in 1954, they might welcome the risk of a larger conflict, generals claimed a single tactical nuclear weapon would be sufficient. But when instead an intervention does not fit their definition of the national interest, as in the case of stopping ethnic cleansing in Bosnia, generals claimed they needed 35,000 to 50,000 troops just to take the Sarajevo airport.

The danger is that, if the military is given too much deference, it is the generals and admirals—not elected leaders—who ultimately set national strategy. After all, why would the military seize power with all the attendant risk? Why not, instead, continue letting civilians take responsibility, but shape military options to limit presidential authority, use secrecy to cover up misdeeds and misappropriations from Congress and the media, and exercise a veto whenever a defense secretary threatens to disrupt their preferred way of doing business? The top brass still get to enjoy the esteem of a fawning public. They can retire after thirty years with 75 percent of their highest salary, plus whatever they can command in the private sector.

Colin Powell, for instance, bragged about how, as chairman of the Joint Chiefs, he orchestrated the conduct of the Gulf War, offering President George H. W. Bush only one option to end it. During the 1992 presidential campaign, Powell announced he would oppose any major military intervention in the conflict in Bosnia, as if that were his decision to make. He also implied that he would resign if Bill Clinton followed through on a campaign promise to allow gay people to serve in the military. In a White House meeting, Powell said he saw no parallel to the military's previous claims that Black people were not fit to serve in combat and would destroy unit cohesion. Marine Commandant General Carl Mundy insisted that for someone to identify themselves as gay was equivalent to saying "I'm KKK, Nazi, rapist." Clinton accepted as a compromise the "don't ask, don't tell" policy, and Mundy assured him that "we do not have witch hunts." Over the following sixteen years, some thirteen thousand gay, lesbian, and bisexual service members were investigated and thrown out of the military, losing their right to VA medical care and disability benefits. As for Powell, in just the first seven years of his retirement he amassed over twenty-eight million dollars from corporate boards, book deals, and speaking engagements. One reason his book deals were so lucrative was that Powell could disclose top secrets that lower-ranking former officials were legally prohibited from publishing.

Generals and admirals refuse to be accountable, even in the most literal sense: budgets and spending. Clinton's first secretary of defense, Les Aspin, insisted on the need for major cuts in spending to be based on a "bottom-up review" of the actual defense needs of the post–Cold War era. By the time the Pentagon was done with it, the review called for spending sufficient to fight not one but two wars simultaneously. Nevertheless, a steady stream of leaks undermined Aspin, and he was forced to resign after less than a year. The Defense Department has also, for decades, refused to comply with a legal requirement to report each year how it spends taxpayer dollars. Even Donald Rumsfeld—who blamed the erosion of confidence between military and civilian leaders on insufficient military spending—admitted that the generals and admirals could not account for millions of transactions amounting to trillions of dollars. Rumsfeld, like Aspin before him, tried to bring about a fundamental transformation in the Pentagon's missions, budgets, and contracting relationships with the private sector. He, too, was forced out, by a "revolt of the generals." In both cases, the media were led to believe it was because Aspin and Rumsfeld had risked the lives of servicemen by not committing adequate forces for overseas operations. But while both were flawed leaders who made themselves vulnerable, it was perhaps no less important that they were among the only secretaries of defense to attempt a frontal assault on Pentagon business practices.

In 2018, when the Pentagon finally submitted to an audit, the private accounting firm hired to do the job reported that there were so many errors and irregularities in the DOD's spending practices that an audit was impossible. An honest accounting would show that DOD reports to Congress are full of fabricated numbers, and the department routinely shifts appropriations around and holds funds in reserve when it can't spend the money fast enough. The deputy secretary of defense at the time—the Boeing executive Patrick Shanahan—was blasé: "We failed the audit, but we never expected to pass it."

The growing resistance to accountability is also true when it comes to the most solemn responsibility of all: planning for nuclear war. In 1960, SAC resisted allowing a civilian dispatched to their Omaha headquarters to review their plans for nuclear war. They finally yielded when they were told to accord their visitor with as much authority as the secretary of defense. But it had worsened decades later, when George H. W. Bush's national security adviser sent another civilian on a similar mission. He arrived with a signed document instructing SAC to give him the same level of access as would be given to the president himself. This time, SAC refused to let him see the plans. When asked what they would have done if the commander-in-chief personally insisted, they said they would have resisted the request as long as possible. If the president was adamant, they would let him see it, but change the plan the very next day. The deterioration in military discipline Eisenhower detected has thus continued, to the point where air-force generals feel they can defy the president himself.

Part of the problem is that many civilian officials have been unwilling or unable to assume *their own* responsibilities. For instance, President Bill Clinton managed to lose the "biscuit," the card containing the code to establish his credentials in the event of a national emergency. Apparently embarrassed, he pretended over months that he still had it in his possession. One can easily imagine what the people charged with the awesome responsibility of carrying out the president's orders concluded when they learned about his recklessness. What would have happened if there had been an actual emergency that required Clinton to take command? Such a scenario almost occurred in 1995, when the president's Russian counterpart, Boris Yeltsin, was presented with *his* nuclear briefcase because a Norwegian rocket was mistaken as the start of an American first strike.

But as much as people revere and trust the military, those officials can also be incompetent and accident-prone, and prefer to cover up real problems. Powell, for instance, helped whitewash the record of his own army division in Vietnam, denying a whistleblower's charges that it had massacred civilians without actually investigating these charges. When Seymour Hersh dug into it, he confirmed that Powell's division had actually killed more than a hundred innocents just at My Lai. We cannot know what else military officials have covered up if they destroy their own records. In his second memoir, *It Worked for Me*, Powell said he used a private e-mail address to communicate with his foreign counterparts and top advisers when he was secretary of state, but later claimed he did not save even one of these messages. (He apparently encouraged Hillary Clinton to do the same. It did *not* work for her.)

It is only when the military commits dramatic mishaps in full public view that the veil of secrecy falls away and we see something close to accountability, such as when naval vessels

THE MILITARY-INDUSTRIAL COMPLEX

repeatedly collided with slow-moving cargo ships in 2017. Less publicized problems at all three air-force bases operating Minuteman nuclear missiles are even more worrisome. In 2010, crews outside Cheyenne, Wyoming, lost control of a whole squadron of fifty missiles because of a computer malfunction. In the summer of 2013, the poorly trained security force at Montana's Malmstrom Air Force Base struggled to regain control of a missile silo after a simulated attack. The next year, nine senior officers—virtually the entire chain of command at Malmstrom—were fired when nearly half of their missile-launch crews were implicated in a cheating scandal on proficiency tests. Journalists found that the main problem was pressure to achieve a perfect score on the monthly tests, which was the only way officers could be promoted and escape this tedious and stressful work.

Others sought escape through drugs or alcohol. The next year, three more officers at Malmstrom were dismissed for using Ecstasy, cocaine, and amphetamines. Another captain, at Minot Air Force base in North Dakota, was sentenced in 2014 to twenty-five years in prison after being found guilty of leading a violent gang that drugged and raped women, including underage girls. The air force personnel security program had not even discovered his drug use and pattern of threatening behavior. Instead, he was exposed by a tip-off to local police from one of the women he had assaulted. In 2016, nineteen airmen came under investigation for drug use at the Wyoming base. Sixteen of them were part of the security force that was supposed to protect 150 nuclear missiles.

The rot in the missile force went all the way to the top. In 2013, the major general in charge of the entire Minuteman arsenal was relieved of duties after a drunken spree in Moscow. He drank heavily day and night during a three-day official visit and sought out "suspect" women, complaining "that his group had the worst morale and that the leadership wasn't supporting him."

When Pentagon secrets and self-serving leaks make it impossible to know whether these particular problems are just the ones we happen to know about, what does it really mean to "support our troops"? Preventing public scrutiny—even decades after the fact—is not just the policy of the Joint Chiefs. It pervades Pentagon culture. Even when presidential policy calls for the "automatic" declassification of twenty-five-year-old records, DOD officials find reasons to prevent the release of more than half of them.

At least part of the answer to what it truly means to support our troops in fulfilling their oath to uphold constitutional government is to make sure democratically elected civilians, both in the White House and in Congress, assume *their* constitutional responsibilities. The military would never have gained so much power if civilians had not let them have it. We need to "support our civilians," not because they can be trusted to be more sober or competent, but because—as the Founders understood—we cannot trust anyone with unaccountable power. As much as people admire the military, no one is perfect. Organizations that have impossible standards inevitably cover up their failings. Our system of checks and balances is meant to keep everyone honest and to expose such problems before they become a danger.

But there is a scenario still worse than an incompetent or intoxicated air force, one that outranks even the generals who command the Minutemen. Harold Hering, the major who was drummed out of the air force for asking questions about nuclear-launch orders, raised this issue all the way back in 1973: "How can I know that an order I receive to launch my missiles came from a sane president?"

Many Americans may be reassured by the fact that military officials—and former military officials—so often play key roles at the top of the national-security establishment. Generals and admirals are supposed to be "the grownups in the room" who will restrain an unruly president. In 2017, the commander of STRATCOM, the successor to SAC, even suggested that an order from the president to use nuclear weapons could be illegal if it did not follow procedures developed under the Obama administration, which require consultation with military advisers. Otherwise, General John Hyten implied, he would refuse to obey.

But, in fact, there are currently no legal checks or balances when it comes to the use—or abuse—of nuclear weapons. It is the president who makes and remakes policy. Even if a president decided to adhere to Obama's protocol, the advisers with whom he is meant to consult can be ignored or dismissed. Other than the laws of war—which both presidents and the Pentagon have ignored—there is no law prohibiting the commander-in-chief from launching nuclear weapons for any purpose whatsoever. Nor is there any law that would allow the military to refuse such orders. Hyten must know that, which makes it all the more significant that he would imply that it is actually generals like him who decide—not unlike MacArthur's argument that military leaders should ultimately answer only to their own conscience.

We may therefore be in a situation in which the refusal of military leaders to follow legal orders from a duly elected commander-in-chief may be the only guarantee against nuclear Armageddon—"may be" only because secrecy makes it impossible to know for sure. The circumstances in which the military might act in this way would be exceptional. But it is precisely in the most extreme situations that one learns where power ultimately lies. Unaccountable spending, secret military plans, collusion with private industry, and the refusal to keep a record of how all this gets decided at the highest levels are all manifestations of a slow and silent coup—not *Seven Days in May*, but almost eighty years of deterioration in military discipline. The dirty secret of civil-military relations—that our elected civilian leadership is not in fact in charge of the military—is becoming an open secret. The fact that we have come to accept it as the lesser danger is no less threatening to democratic accountability than is secrecy itself.

5

SURVEILLANCE

OTHER PEOPLE'S SECRETS

In 1991, a retired archivist named Daisy Suckley died in her family home in Rhinebeck, New York, just six months before her hundredth birthday. She had worked for many years at the FDR Presidential Library, mainly with photographs. Her family and the Roosevelts were distant relations, and she was able to identify people and events from the president's life better than any of the other archivists—whether photos of FDR treating European royalty to hot dogs in Hyde Park, cruising down the Hudson on the presidential yacht, or playing with children and his dog Fala. But she was always quiet and unassuming, and never boasted about having known the president.

When friends came to the old house and went through her things, they discovered a battered black suitcase under her bed. Upon opening it, they found it was filled with thousands of pages of letters, diary entries, and menus of meals she shared with FDR, from 1933 until the day he died. There were dozens of letters in his own hand, describing private moments they shared over the years. When scholars looked at the photographs anew, they began to notice someone who, until then, had always seemed to fade into the background at all the parties and receptions. But whether he was with Winston Churchill, or the Crown Princess of Norway, or King George II of Greece, or just playing with Fala, Daisy was close by the president's side. "It is certainly not in the simple & natural course of the life of a Suckley to be seeing, at first hand, the very core & hub of world history," she confided to her diary. "It is fantastic—But here I am!"

Roosevelt's friend kept his secrets all those years. They dispatched their letters through trusted go-betweens in specially marked envelopes. There is no evidence that anyone saw her diaries until after she had died. But once they were revealed, they showed that the president had confided in her some of the most important secrets of the war, from his clandestine meeting with Churchill off Newfoundland in 1941, to the timing of the D-Day landing. If Suckley had been a spy, or if someone had been spying on her relationship with the president, that hub of world history might have rotated in a different direction.

Spies have long pursued and exploited personal information and personal relationships to gather intelligence. For that very reason, governments normally screen people before entrusting them with top secrets. In this case, investigators might have worried about how, at the same time Suckley was becoming privy to highly sensitive information, her family was at risk of losing their home, and her relationship to the president made her vulnerable to blackmail. But background checks, by amassing this kind of personal information, can also create risks and opportunities for exploitation. What has changed since FDR's day is the scale and sophistication of both offensive and defensive forms of surveillance, and the sheer volume and variety of sensitive information that it generates. When China succeeded in hacking into U.S. Office of Personnel Management databases starting in 2013, it harvested information about the drinking, gambling, and drug-taking habits—indeed, anything uncovered in background checks—of millions of U.S. government employees and contractors. Former NSA Director Michael Hayden called the hack "honorable espionage work," and said he would have done the same thing. It is fair to assume that Hayden's NSA carried out comparable hacks of the personal information of people in other countries whenever it had the opportunity. As another former NSA director, Keith Alexander, explained, the government wants to be able to access all available information: "You need the haystack to find the needle."

Even when clandestine services are not seeking out personal information per se, but military and diplomatic intelligence, the NSA and its foreign counterparts often pursue such secrets by hacking into personal devices, or hacking into the companies that manage communications of every kind. They do the same for data gathered from space. When the National Reconnaissance Office vacuums up signals intelligence or imaging data, its sensors do not distinguish between government and private information. It is hard to imagine how someone in Suckley's position would be able to protect her secrets nowadays—not if she used a cell phone, and not when there are spy satellites orbiting overhead.

So, unless we keep all our private secrets hidden away, like that suitcase under Suckley's bed, they can become government secrets, both of our government and other governments, honorable or not. And, since the best intelligence has always been "all-source" intelligence, we need to be aware of all the opportunities governments have to collect our data. Whether it is from paid informants or multi-ton spy satellites or gargantuan antenna arrays, all of it becomes even more revealing when it is gathered together in a mosaic. We need to understand these things because, although learning state secrets through a personal relationship with the president is indeed "fantastic," the ability to protect our private thoughts and communications can be a very practical concern. In fact, it could be our last line of defense against the dark state. And when we see the full scope and power of state surveillance—and how it keeps adding up to even more than the sum of its parts—we can also see how that line keeps moving.

In this chapter, we will describe how the intelligence community has devised ever-more-ingenious ways to conduct surveillance, and artfully interprets and reinterprets legal restrictions to make this spying as secret and expansive as possible. Legal concerns go a long way to explain why officials treat their surveillance powers as special, even when compared with other top secrets. But they do not tell us why officials have gone to such lengths, to the point where they routinely operate outside the law. Though much of the scholarship on state surveillance has been produced by legal theorists, history demonstrates that it is the community culture—the beliefs and practices of secretive officials—that conditions behavior inside the dark state. And it is this history that is most helpful in determining how secure we should actually feel about depending on constitutional protections to stop "unreasonable searches and seizures."

In the concluding section we will turn the tables, and apply NSA data-mining techniques to the government's own internal communications. Since we cannot access the data it gathers about citizens through domestic surveillance, we will start by analyzing data about how it tracks internal resistance in an allied state, and demonstrate how one can mine the kind of metadata the NSA is permitted to gather from the communications of U.S. citizens. Then we will analyze a covert program to spy on people who aspired to come to the United States, which treated an entire ethnic community as potential subversives. In all these ways, we can start to see at least some of what lies on the other side of that last line of defense against the dark state.

In the hierarchy of top secrets, information about citizens derived from government surveillance has long had a special status. It could be considered the most secret of all the information the government gathers, in the sense that even the president— otherwise sovereign over all executive-branch secrets—cannot access it without appropriate legal authority. The names of citizens and permanent residents that show up in NSA surveillance are supposed to be "masked" before summarized reports are disseminated, even to the highest ranking officials. Only twenty people in the NSA have the authority to "unmask" them.

Officials with a clearance were themselves, until recently, generally not allowed to read an intercepted communication verbatim, even for foreign targets. When they are, they find its "raw" nature means the content can be even more "dramatic, entertaining, and juicy," as one State Department official put it. During the Cold War, for instance, the NSA learned about the health problems of Leonid Brezhnev, and the sex life of Nikolai Podgorny, his main rival, from intercepting their car-phone conversations.

The authority to intercept and listen to personal communications both at home and abroad derives from a legal framework that distinguishes between ordinary criminal activity and espionage or terrorism. Court orders might empower local law enforcement to surveil suspects of run-of-the-mill crime, but when national security is at stake, the extraordinary secret powers possessed by agencies like the NSA can be unleashed. And when the targets of surveillance are not U.S. citizens, those powers are even greater. But the lines are often blurred, as we shall see, and the surveillance powers of the dark state are sometimes turned on citizens, even when they are accused of ordinary crimes. U.S. courts long ago decided that foreigners have no rights whatsoever in protecting themselves against the NSA, but when even the private lives of citizens become the business of the government, then no one is safe, because only citizens can limit these powers and hold public officials accountable.

So, if the government routinely ignores its own rules about who can be surveilled and when, what actually makes information related to surveillance sacred in the hierarchy of top secrets? In practice, it is not so much personal information per se, no matter where it comes from. Officials have been remarkably careless in protecting private information that comes into their possession even when it concerns the people in the government's own personnel files, as shown by China's Office of Personnel Management hack. What is treated as special, above all, are the means the government employs to carry out surveillance. We have already seen how hacking and decryption methods have a privileged legal status, even more so than nuclear secrets. So, too, does the identity of undercover informants, the human side of surveillance. No matter how someone—anyone—comes to know the name of a covert operative or a confidential informant, it is a felony under the Intelligence Identities Protection Act for them to reveal it. Tapping phone lines, harvesting satellite imagery, and paying informants—of whom there are eighteen thousand just working for the Drug Enforcement Administration—all of these methods can form parts of a mosaic through which the dark state can see things that might otherwise be invisible.

But of all these surveillance methods, technical means to intercept and decrypt speech or text communications, or COMINT, have the greatest cachet. A 1952 National Security Council charter that applied to all foreign and domestic COMINT, from diplomatic cables to local phone calls, made clear that it was different: "The special nature of COMINT activities requires that they be treated in all respects as being outside the framework of other or general intelligence activities. Orders, directives, policies, or recommendations . . . shall not be applicable to COMINT activities, unless specifically so stated. . . ." Executive orders that required sharing intelligence and reviewing it for declassification therefore did not apply. Moreover, even this charter was classified top secret and withheld from the public for half a century.

Even more revealing of its special status is the fact that those who handle COMINT are members of an exclusive, even cultish group. Those who guard the secrets related to signals intelligence more generally—which also includes electronic intelligence, or ELINT—took steps to distinguish themselves clearly from those who could not access the different compartments from which they derive this intelligence. These compartments are designated with code words, so those with access are said to have "code word clearance" to see "code word material." The badges signifying this access have long been a status symbol. One particularly colorful example of the elusive naming system for this "sensitive compartmented information" is TALENT-KEYHOLE—the compartment containing photographic and communications intelligence from satellites. As a CIA study once put it, it "has the aura of a secret society. It has its initiation, its oaths, its esoteric phrases, its sequestered areas, and its secrets within secrets."

Similarly, within the NSA the process for giving someone access to its inner sanctum has been called "indoctrination." If the initiates pass muster, they too receive a special badge, without which they are barred from admission to NSA facilities unless under escort. During the Cold War, there were eighteen different gradations in color-coded badges conveying different levels of access, not unlike a Freemason's degree or a Scientologist's OT level. Any federal employee must take an oath to support and defend the constitution, but the oath administered to those who were given access to signals intelligence was far more severe and demanding. Inductees had to sign the oath, which included an acknowledgment that they had read and understood the drastic penalties for revealing code-word information. The oath not only committed them to conceal the mere fact that the NSA collected and analyzed signals intelligence, but also to turn in anyone who revealed such information. People may imagine that any government conspiracy must eventually be revealed through a deathbed confession, but officials who take the oath for code-word clearance vow to carry these secrets to their grave. As explained in a security manual on COMINT from 1952— the year the NSA was founded—the oath calls for "perpetual silence" because "it is of the utmost importance that complete and unconditional silence on all COMINT matters and activities be maintained for all time. . . ." After signing with name, rank, and serial number, the inductee raised his or her hand and solemnly swore once again, "so help me God."

That officials usually treat surveillance secrets more secretively—especially those related to "code word material" used for COMINT or ELINT—is also shown by the amount of time that passes before they leak. The entire government agency created to produce talent-keyhole material, the National Reconnaissance Office (NRO), was itself an official secret for more than thirty years. In 1961, Kennedy created it as a joint project between the air force and the CIA for the express purpose of both coordinating and concealing the development and operation of spy satellites. Not one publication even mentioned the NRO until 1971, even though it was regularly firing towering rockets into space. Two years later, it appeared in the *Congressional Record* in a list of other intelligence agencies, but this was inadvertent. Until then, a handful of the most senior committee chairmen had managed to conceal the very existence of this billion-dollar agency. The first time a president acknowledged— even indirectly—that something like the NRO existed, in 1976, he referred to it only as "special offices for the collection of specialized intelligence through reconnaissance programs."

It is likely that some surveillance programs have never been acknowledged, and might remain secret indefinitely. Digging deep in the archives, the historian might come across an intriguing lead, such as one that suggests that the secret power of surveillance trumped even the power of the military-industrial complex. It is a memo in the papers of Daniel Patrick Moynihan that references a highly classified study that analyzed all communications of field commanders up to and including Secretary of Defense McNamara, who was not told about the program. But both Moynihan and the source are dead, so for now this lead leads nowhere.

Until 1999, the most sensitive COMINT was automatically classified top secret. The "Top Secret" stamp and relevant code word had to appear on every page of every COMINT document. Since 1999, reports from the most secret surveillance programs have been designated "Exceptionally Controlled Information."

There are now thousands of these surveillance programs. Many are built around tools that have been developed to hack into IT systems and software and "exfiltrate" information. Some of the code words, like prism and stellarwind, became known— and notorious—after Edward Snowden revealed them in 2013. But the names of many more programs remain unknown to all but a select few. The cognoscenti just refer to them under the umbrella of "special intelligence."

But beyond the fact that it long went unacknowledged, has careful designations, and is restricted to certain officials according to careful rules, we know that "special intelligence" is special because of *unwritten* rules and unofficial processes that elevate it to an exceptional status. For instance, State Department officials know that including this kind of intelligence in a report guarantees it will be read. "The texts were placed between special covers, handled under lock and key, and hand delivered by special carriers," one State Department official recalled. Special intelligence "enjoyed almost immediate access to the highest levels of the government." A CIA study described how "few would have the temerity to take code-word material home, few even among those who take home other types of classified material."

Though the government only rarely pursues criminal charges when classified information is leaked, it makes an exception for this kind of information. It is impossible to know the exact number—indictments typically refer to "Sensitive Compartmented Information" without specifying the content of leaked documents—but a disproportionate number of prosecutions, dating back to Daniel Ellsberg and the Pentagon Papers, involved surveillance sources and methods. Time served in federal penitentiaries, then, is yet another measure of the special status of "special intelligence."

But what exactly did these officials leak that led to their prosecution? Crucially, they were not prosecuted because they improperly accessed and revealed information about private citizens, but because they revealed the *methods* used to conduct surveillance. In most of these cases, the accused divulged this information to raise awareness about real or potential government abuses. Conversely, even in the most obvious and egregious cases of abusing surveillance powers, such as when NSA officials spied on wives, girlfriends, and love interests for their own personal reasons, none were ever held criminally liable. At most, they risked losing their security clearances.

If there were any doubt remaining that denizens of the dark state protect at all costs surveillance methods over the private information of citizens, one need only consider the role of the NSA and other government agencies in creating a market that pays freelancers to produce tools that exploit software and hardware vulnerabilities. These tools might permit the buyer to watch people through their webcams, or listen to them through their cell phones, or hack computers even when the computers are disconnected from the Internet. Originally, the NSA purchased these tools for its own use. But by paying bounties it helped create a thriving market in which private corporations, police states, and criminal enterprises all participate. And rather than report all these vulnerabilities so vendors can "patch" them in a software update, the NSA picks the best of them to add to the Agency's own arsenal of cyberweapons. Even the best-informed analysts can only guesstimate what it now includes—the number and nature of these weapons is surrounded by the same degree of secrecy as once surrounded the nuclear arsenal.

So what explains this extraordinary secrecy? What has the government tried to hide from us, and how much of what's hidden is really *about* us—i.e., the surveillance of citizens? What are the costs and what are the benefits? And does this secrecy actually help keep us safe?

Intelligence from spy satellites, a simple bug, or an NSA "exploit" has unique qualities, since it can be available in near real-time, and can come unfiltered, unlike secondhand reports from more or less reliable informants. Moreover, American surveillance capabilities through technical means have long been second to none. It is understandable why intelligence agencies want to protect their best sources and methods when even the accidental disclosure of a code word can be costly. When *The New York Times* published a photograph in 1965 of the national security adviser reading a document with the code word "Top Secret Dinar" visible, for instance, the NSA had to switch to a new code word at a cost of over two million dollars. When it is not the code word, but the actual source or method that is revealed—such as listening in on Politburo car phones—that source or method becomes worthless. In the case of a covert operative or confidential informant, it could mean death.

When secrets about surveillance are no longer secret, deniability can still be useful—even when that deniability is implausible. By 1972, nearly twenty years before the agency would be officially acknowledged, NRO leadership already realized that total secrecy was becoming untenable. An article in *The Washington Post* had not only described its program, but revealed that it was plagued by cost overruns. But, at the insistence of CIA Director Richard Helms, the agency stayed undercover. Helms warned that any disclosure would lead to demands for further disclosures. Moreover, it was thought that official acknowledgment of the NRO's existence might lead some countries to try to challenge American satellite surveillance over their territory as a violation of international law. These satellites were not merely taking pictures from space—they were intercepting communications, a capability that could be thwarted by countermeasures if disclosed. The longer other countries were unaware of what U.S. satellites could do while orbiting overhead, the more the NRO could exploit their weaknesses. During internal discussions, agencies responsible for intercepting and deciphering signals intelligence had long emphasized the need to preserve other countries' "cryptographic naivete," which had been "so helpful to the U.S. COMINT effort." The same principle could apply to American citizens: as long as they were uninformed about the surveillance capabilities of their own government, the longer their government could exploit this naïveté. In the case of protesters in Detroit during the 1967 uprising, it probably did not occur to them that their own government would use a reconnaissance satellite to spy on them. This was just one of the examples provided by the National Photographic Interpretation Center when, in 1973, CIA Director James Schlesinger asked it to divulge "questionable" activity that violated the Agency's charter prohibiting domestic spying.

Secrecy and deniability also allow officials to escape even the conventional bureaucratic forms of accountability. Revealing the NRO's name and purpose, officials warned, "could lead to an effort to regularize the NRO in conformity with normal organizational structure and procedures of the DOD." The abnormally secret status of the NRO gave it abnormal freedom, such as in how it spent taxpayer money. The Pentagon concealed appropriations within its budget worth approximately six billion dollars today, with little or no external oversight, so that the NRO could roll over billions of dollars in excess funds to be spent on any purpose officials deemed appropriate. Accounting procedures were so weak and funding was so abundant that the NRO leadership itself had little sense of the Office's financial position. Consequently, Congress's constitutionally mandated power of the purse had no power over the NRO. When these dubious budgetary practices came to light after the end of the Cold War, both the director and the deputy director were removed from their posts. But until that point, the NRO had almost never received any public scrutiny. Even the Church

Committee, which exposed NSA and CIA malfeasance in 1975–76, had not looked into its activities. The NRO did not even have to answer Freedom of Information Act requests—there was simply nowhere to send them.

Back in 1955, Hubert Humphrey asked what price we pay for secrecy. We cannot know, even in the literal sense, what it costs to conduct secret government surveillance, since these costs are not revealed in public budget documents. Secrecy clearly has non-monetary costs as well, even in terms of the effectiveness of the agencies practicing it. The NRO leadership claimed that concealing their existence allowed them to be "efficient and streamlined." The selfsame secrecy makes it impossible to verify such claims. But a senior CIA official who spent many years working with the NRO came to the opposite conclusion: "The best engineering decisions are the ones debated in public," he observed. "The very worst are the ones hidden from scrutiny under the cloak of security." At the NSA, comparably secret and proudly independent, an internal study from the early 1990s also made the idea that secrecy created efficiency doubtful. The study found that it took ten days just to requisition paper clips, and employees had to wait four months for a new computer. When the NSA needed more paper clips—or anything else that required outside bids—it took an average of six months to issue a purchase order after all the bids were in. If anything, exemption from normal oversight and accountability made the NSA's bureaucracy even more sclerotic than that of the rest of the Pentagon.

Even setting aside the question of democratic accountability and organizational efficiency, strict compartmentalization of the code-word community created serious pathologies. As we have seen, the original sin of the dark state was failing to provide critical intelligence about intercepted Japanese communications to U.S. commanders at Pearl Harbor. In the decades that followed, officials were haunted by this failure and repeatedly referred to it in analyses of compartmentalization. Though aware of the many problems it created, they continued to keep knowledge about the means of surveillance in one compartment, analysis of the raw intelligence in a separate compartment, and policy making based on that analysis in yet another. But it was precisely when this information was most important that compartmentalization could be most disastrous.

As we saw in chapter 3, a U.S. Navy ship, the *Pueblo*, was carrying some of the NSA's most advanced encryption/decryption machines in 1968 when it set out on a secret mission to surveil North Korean military and naval forces. As one official pointed out afterward, "The intelligence analyst who did not know that the *Pueblo* was off North Korea prior to its seizure, and most did not, was not likely to have alerted his superior to some anomaly in North Korean naval activity." The captain of the *Pueblo* was aware that his vessel might be harassed even while it was in international waters, but, having received no specific warning, he was caught off guard when several PT boats and a sub chaser surrounded his ship. When he refused to heave to, the North Koreans started raking the deck with machine guns and naval artillery. Poorly trained technicians frantically set about hammering the cryptological equipment and burning the manuals while the captain played for time. He did not realize how much time it would take—the NSA equipment was literally in its own secret compartment. "I just had no idea of how damn much of this stuff there was on board," the captain later explained. The North Koreans captured all but a small percentage, including a working KL-7. They brutally interrogated the captured Americans about its operation and did not release them until almost a year later. This incident showed how compartmentalizing codeword intelligence could make it not only less useful, but more vulnerable. And what happened was hardly unique. "The list of such examples," a 1977 CIA study observed, "is endless."

Even in less dramatic, day-to-day business, compartmentalization has pernicious consequences. It makes it easier for the NSA to withhold intelligence it gathers from other agencies, if only to make sure it gets the credit. And since the NSA prefers having a direct line of communication with the president, its intelligence is more likely to be presented to the most senior policy makers without the context or analysis that would come from integrating it in all-source analyses. This is what happened in the months following 9/11, when Dick Cheney insisted that he and President Bush receive raw intelligence about terrorist plots. The daily report included dozens of different threats that had been extracted from billions of phone calls and electronic messages, satellite imagery, and human informants. "There was no filter," a senior NSC official recalled, and "most of it was garbage." But to those who did not know any better, it was terrifying, and disorienting. As another observed, the "sensory overload" day in and day out made senior officials "paranoid." Indeed, it pushed Cheney himself to go to the "dark side."

So, despite the cost, and the consequences, surveillance secrecy has long had a privileged status, and government officials have multiple reasons to keep it that way, some more legitimate than others. Technical means of surveillance can be uniquely effective in providing raw information in real time (or close to it), especially when the targets have no idea they are being surveilled. Treating these methods as special makes them exempt from normal accountability requirements. And it helps members of the secret code-word society maintain their cachet in a world in which millions of people have security clearances.

There is a yet more compelling reason to treat these surveillance secrets differently, which we can see most clearly when we probe the history of surveillance. The capabilities and accomplishments of government surveillance have long been top secret, because, in essence, when it comes to light, this surveillance may turn out to be illegal. For many years this was literally true, as we shall see: a bizarre interpretation of the law held that spying on citizens was allowable provided it was not disclosed in courts. Even now, the information it produces is supposed to be limited to counterintelligence, and not freely shared with law enforcement. In fact, much of what the NSA does depends on extremely fine legal distinctions that, in practice, it has proved either unwilling to honor or incapable of doing so. Surveillance has always been *borderline* illegal, even when it does not cross the line, both because intelligence agencies are continually pushing the limits of what's permissible, and because the public usually wants to outlaw these practices as soon as it learns what they are.

As we have seen, the very first efforts to conduct government surveillance in peacetime, after World War I, revealed that it could not be continued if it had to be publicly reported and justified. J. Edgar Hoover only kept his job at the Justice Department's Bureau of Investigation by lying to the Senate, denying his role in organizing mass roundups and deportations of alleged subversives. Hoover also had to promise to end political investigations as a condition for becoming director of the FBI, but he continued them in secret. His secret surveillance didn't stop there. In 1939, the Supreme Court ruled that the Communications Act of 1934 barred federal agents from intercepting communications, and precluded any prosecutorial use of the communication, or even use of evidence that resulted from the intercept—what Felix Frankfurter called "fruit of the poisonous tree." But Hoover decided the law actually allowed wiretapping, just as long as the FBI kept it secret. In fact, Hoover was suspected of surveilling the Supreme Court itself.

George Marshall also decided to ignore the law in building up the Signal Intelligence Service (SIS) when he was army chief of staff. "We knew it was illegal," one army cryptologist later recalled, "and therefore we better keep quiet about it." The FBI and the army worked hand in hand, with the FBI breaking into embassies in Washington—what were called "black bag jobs"—and handing the codebooks over to the SIS. Private companies like RCA and Westinghouse went along, and regularly provided the SIS with international cables. In 1938, when Hoover presented a plan to Roosevelt to vastly expand domestic surveillance, he advised it be done with "the utmost degree of secrecy" and without notifying Congress, precisely because Congress might otherwise shut it down. FDR approved the plan.

The president did not immediately give Hoover all the funds he needed, but he did back him up when Attorney General Robert Jackson tried to stop FBI wiretaps. By 1941, it was an open secret. Without quite admitting the practice, Roosevelt implied that it was limited to those "engaged in espionage or sabotage." In private, he wrote that the Supreme Court was right to prohibit wiretapping, since "it is almost bound to lead to abuse of civil rights." These were extraordinary times, which justified extraordinary measures. But with the president's order, Hoover now felt he had carte blanche to intercept communications of anyone he deemed subversive.

Illegal surveillance unleashed an infernal dynamic. The more the government ignored the law, and expanded the drag-net beyond spies and saboteurs, the greater the potential consequences of eventual exposure. This made secrecy ever more important. But the more secret these programs were, the more tempting it was for officials to continue expanding them. As Justice Louis Brandeis pointed out when considering state surveillance back in 1928: "Crime is contagious: If the government becomes a law-breaker, it breeds contempt for the law; it invites every man to become a law unto himself."

Thus, illegal surveillance ended up serving many self-interested and partisan agendas. After World War II, Hoover continued building up a massive system for conducting surveillance, and used it to curry favor with presidents, and conversely—as in the case of John F. Kennedy—blackmail them. Using what he learned, he attempted to manipulate American politics in line with his own goals. For instance, Hoover's FBI wanted to prevent the emergence of a Black "messiah." Worried about the support Martin Luther King, Jr., attracted, the director studied King's sex life and tried to break up his marriage, at the same time stoking rivalries with other leaders. In an anonymous letter—only recently unredacted—an FBI agent posing as another Black American suggested that King should commit suicide.

Hoover not only bugged King, he also kept files on the sexual transgressions of congressmen and senators, and happily shared them with President Lyndon Johnson. The president stayed up at night reading these files and loved gossiping about what he learned. Johnson also insisted that the NSA give him the raw transcripts of its best intercepts, and notify him immediately as soon as they were available.

Most of the officials receiving surveillance reports guarded them more closely. Robert F. Kennedy was embarrassed when LBJ revealed the contents of FBI tape recordings. As attorney general, Kennedy himself had ordered the FBI to conduct hundreds of wiretaps, including the surveillance of Martin Luther

KING,

In view of your low grade, abnormal personal behavoir I will not dignify your name with either a Mr. or a Reverend or a Dr. And, your last name calls to mind only the type of King such as King Henry the VIII and his countless acts of adultery and immoral conduct lower than that of a beast.

King, look into your heart. You know you are a complete fraud and a great liability to all of us Negroes. White people in this country have enough frauds of their own but I am sure they don't have one at this time that is any where near your equal. You are no clergyman and you know it. I repeat you are a colossal fraud and an evil, vicious one at that. You could not believe in God and act as you do. Clearly you don't believe in any personal moral principles.

King, like all frauds your end is approaching. You could have been our greatest leader. You, even at an early age have turned out to be not a leader but a dissolute, abnormal moral imbecile. We will now have to depend on our older leaders like Wilkins a man of character and thank God we have others like him. But you are done. Your "honorary" degrees, your Nobel Prize (what a grim farce) and other awards will not save you. King, I repeat you are done.

No person can overcome facts, not even a fraud like yourself. Lend your sexually psychotic ear to the enclosure. You will find yourself and in all your dirt, filth, evil and moronic talk exposed on the record for all time. I repeat - no person can argue successfully against facts. You are finished. You will find on the record for all time your filthy, dirty, evil companions, male and females giving expression with you to your hidious abnormalities. And some of them to pretend to be ministers of the Gospel. Satan could not do more. What incredible evilness. It is all there on the record, your sexual orgies. Listen to yourself you filthy, abnormal animal. You are on the record. You have been on the record - all your adulterous acts, your sexual orgies extending far into the past. This one is but a tiny sample. You will understand this. Yes, from your various evil playmates on the east coast to   and others on the west coast and outside the country you are on the record. King you are done.

The American public, the church organizations that have been helping - Protestant, Catholic and Jews will know you for what you are - an evil, abnormal beast. So will others who have backed you. You are done.

King, there is only one thing left for you to do. You know what it is. You have just 34 days in which to do (this exact number has been selected for a specific reason, it has definite practical signfficant. You are done. There is but one way out for you. You better take it before your filthy,abnormal fraudulent self is bared to the nation.

When the FBI released a letter that agents sent to Martin Luther King, Jr., with surveillance recordings, it "sanitized" the parts that, among other things, alleged they proved King was a "filthy, abnormal animal."

King, Jr., apparently because of King's close association with former communists. "Bobby Kennedy was the biggest tapper of all," Richard Nixon complained, when his own operation was later revealed. But, unlike LBJ, Kennedy had kept quiet about it, reflecting the typical attitude of the Washington establishment.

Outside the Beltway, most Americans continued to think of wiretapping as criminal or at least disreputable. As Brian Hochman has shown, it was most commonly associated with financial crimes and divorce cases. For decades, members of Congress friendly to law enforcement had tried to pass legislation to create a legal framework but failed every time. By the mid-'60s, growing concerns that the government might be surveilling citizens without legal sanction had created momentum to pass a law that would explicitly prohibit wiretapping, except in cases where there was a clear national security interest. At the same time, the Supreme Court ruled that government bugs and wiretaps were subject to the same restrictions that had long prohibited unreasonable searches and seizures, forcing the FBI to discontinue hundreds of active surveillance operations.

In 1968, the momentum shifted in the other direction. A backlash against Black civil rights protests gave law-and-order advocates the opportunity they needed. Their champion in the Senate, staunch segregationist John L. McClennan, urged giving authorities the power to stop Black protests before they started: "You could bug a room or a hall in which [Stokely] Carmichael was meeting, in which [H.] Rap Brown was meeting, where they were inciting to riot, telling people to get their guns, 'Go get whitey' . . ." Conservative jurists like chief justice William H. Duckworth of the Georgia Supreme Court insisted that "concerned and thinking people throughout America are alarmed when our highest court constantly throws roadblocks in the path of enforcing the law against criminals" (which, for Duckworth, included Black people who sat at whites-only lunch counters).

Of course, the FBI was already carrying out surveillance and sabotage against the civil rights movement. But anxiety that the government was not doing enough to crack down on Black activists was instrumental in McClennan's successful effort to include language authorizing wiretapping in the Omnibus

TELCON
The President/Mr. Kissinger
7:00 p.m., June 1, 1973

P: Hello.

K: Mr. President.

P: You had told me that McGeorge Bundy had the affrontry to tell you that
      Bobby Kennedy in that period didn't have any taps.

K: That's right, yeah.

P: Have you heard the figures?

K: Al mentioned them to me.

P: Let's get away from the bullshit. Bobby Kennedy was the greatest
      tapper. 300 in 1963 -- almost 300 --. 250 in the rest. And I'm
      getting the names and I'm going to publish the names next Thursday.

K: I think --

P: And let their assholes know that they're going to get this, Henry.

K: I think you should, absolutely.

P: Because they have done us in on this thing. Now the biggest tapper
      was Bobby Kennedy. Now Johnson doesn't appear to be so big but
      he had the Secret Service do it. And I've ordered Rowley to give me
      the names of the Secret Service taps and I'm going to put those on it
      too.

K: I think --

P: They started it. They want to have a gut fight; they're going to get
      one, Henry, you understand.

K: I think so.

P: They think they know how to fight but they've never fought anybody
      before. But, you see, Bobby Kennedy was the biggest tapper of all.
      Now I want you -- now this is not going to go out till Monday but leak
      it to somebody. Talk to one of your liberal friends and say we've
      got a blockbuster coming out. Now, will you do that?

K: Certainly I can.

Kissinger recorded Nixon, Nixon recorded Kissinger, but both
agreed Bobby Kennedy was the biggest tapper of all.

Crime Control and Safe Streets Act of 1968, and he also carved
out a controversial exception giving the president broad powers to use surveillance to thwart subversion or hostile acts of a
foreign power. The increasingly routine use of wiretaps, now
legitimated with a duly signed warrant, changed the way the
public thought about state surveillance more generally, such that
many came to accept the potential for abuse as the price to be
paid for public safety. Henceforth, outrage about government

surveillance would only erupt when it seemed to include what Duckworth had called "concerned and thinking people" and not when it targeted communities that had long been subject to over-policing.

Between 1965 and 1975, the FBI opened more than half a million files involving more than a million Americans. They at least had a mandate to investigate illegal activity, but other agencies, like Army Intelligence, did not. The cover provided by security classification made it possible for Army Intelligence to accumulate information about hundreds of thousands more people, notwithstanding a strict prohibition on domestic spying. The original justification was to support units deployed in response to civil disturbances. But Army Intelligence eventually assigned some fifteen hundred agents to work full-time against civil-rights groups and antiwar protesters. The best summary of the Pentagon's domestic surveillance program, and how egregious it was, is provided on the Pentagon's own Web site:

- Military counterintelligence special agents established, maintained, and disseminated files on civil rights activists and organizers. These were not legitimate DOD targets.
- Counterintelligence special agents penetrated organizations such as the "Resistors in the Army" and the "Friends of Resistors in the Army" and recruited members of these organizations as informers. These organizations posed no foreign threat.
- So called "dissidents," actually U.S. persons who were exercising their First Amendment rights, were placed under surveillance and their movements were observed and recorded. These U.S. persons were not legitimate DOD counterintelligence targets.
- Radio communications of civil rights and antiwar demonstrators were intercepted by military intelligence personnel. The interception of these communications was improper.
- Using media cover, military counterintelligence special agents infiltrated the 1968 Democratic National Convention in Chicago. There was no legitimate Defense investigative purpose for this action.

- Information collected by Defense elements was routinely transferred to civilian law enforcement authorities without evidence of criminal activity or relevance to the law enforcement missions of the receiving authorities. This activity was improper.

With the encouragement of Presidents Johnson and Nixon, the CIA organized its own domestic surveillance operation, "Operation CHAOS," even though the 1947 National Security Act prohibited the agency from exercising any "internal security functions." CIA personnel would later claim it was legitimate to investigate whether foreign powers were taking advantage of domestic discord to infiltrate and manipulate protest movements, and correctly point out that some protesters hoped to incite a violent revolution. But with approximately 160 "assets" working around the world over several years, the CIA found that, if anything, American dissidents were taking advantage of foreign governments by obtaining international conference invitations and free flights and hotel stays. The real damage to national security would be self-inflicted, as CIA Director Helms himself worried when he delivered a report on the surveillance of American students to Kissinger: "This is an area not within the charter of this agency," he wrote, "so I need not emphasize how extremely sensitive this makes the paper. Should anyone learn of its existence it would prove most embarrassing for all concerned."

Even after it was revealed that the CIA spied on citizens, the Agency covered up the fact that the targets included congressmen, redacting this part of a 1974 document when it was first declassified. The NSA, for its part, targeted U.S. senators in the late 1960s and early 1970s, along with journalists and antiwar activists. Even as late as 2008, the NSA did not want to reveal the names listed in an agency history. When the redaction was finally lifted, in 2013, it showed that they included the man who would become the first chairman of the Senate Intelligence Committee, Idaho Democrat Frank Church. A Bronze Star–winning army-intelligence officer in World War II, Church had become increasingly critical of official secrecy and Cold War national-security policy. The NSA also intercepted the communications of Howard Baker, a prowar Republican, who later became Ronald Reagan's chief of staff.

Without more information—which the NSA will not provide—one can only speculate as to the motivation. Was it merely to satisfy the curiosity of Presidents Johnson and Nixon about what both allies and adversaries were saying about them? Or were they conducting surveillance on senators to make sure they stayed reliable? One thing is clear: Congress could not exercise effective oversight of intelligence agencies if these same agencies were gathering information revealing the private lives of these same congressmen and senators.

The NSA took care to cover its tracks, disguising intelligence reports arising from domestic surveillance to make it seem that they came from covert agents, another example of how different modalities of surveillance worked together, in this case concealing illegality. The reports were printed on plain paper with no markings indicating their origin, and delivered directly to the White House. Even an NSA lawyer thought the program was "disreputable if not outright illegal." In fact, Justice Department investigators determined that both the NSA and the CIA had violated criminal statutes, and informed responsible officials of their Miranda rights. But the DOJ advised against prosecution, because the accused would claim they were only following orders, and "subpoena every tenuously-involved government official or former official." The "buck-passing" would not end until even the president was implicated. "While the high office of prospective defense witnesses should not enter into the prosecutive decision, the confusion, obfuscation and surprise testimony which might result cannot be ignored."

When NSA officials testified before the Church Committee, senators were amazed to hear them claim that they had not violated any law. The Watergate revelations made it even more obvious that the intelligence community was grossly abusing the national security exemption in the recently passed Omnibus crime bill. It also ignored the 1974 Privacy Act, which required that agencies give notice of what information they were collecting about citizens. Now Congress passed the Foreign

Intelligence Surveillance Act (FISA), which created the Foreign Intelligence Surveillance Court. Starting in 1979, lawyers for the FBI, the NSA, and other intelligence agencies had to go to this court to get warrants authorizing physical searches or surveillance in the U.S. FISA promised to subject surveillance programs to scrutiny as never before. But if there was any hope for true oversight, it was dashed in the first year of the Reagan administration.

In 1981, only two years after the FISA Court's implementation, the new president gave the intelligence community the authority to gather virtually any information it wanted from overseas. This included any data from and about U.S. citizens, as long as that data was gathered "incidentally." The full scope and implications of this executive order became apparent in a still-secret White House legal opinion written, appropriately enough, in 1984. It argued, "Once evidence is constitutionally seized, its dissemination or subsequent use raises no additional Fourth Amendment question." So, if the NSA "incidentally" collects personal information about a U.S. citizen from an overseas data center, which it is allowed to do under this executive order, and finds some pattern or anomaly in that data, it can hand the information over to the FBI. Ever since its inception, this interpretation has been used to authorize the bulk collection of communications according to rules developed by the executive branch with no input from the courts or Congress.

Meanwhile, for those surveillance programs that were supposedly subject to the FISA Court, the ultimate independence of the executive was also swiftly assured. Government lawyers make the case for domestic surveillance, and are expected to act in good faith, only seeking warrants as part of duly authorized investigations of foreign espionage or sabotage. But no one argues the other side. FISA proceedings have therefore been likened to a modern-day Star Chamber, seventeenth-century England's notoriously oppressive special court. The comparison, though, is not quite fair to the latter. Whereas the Star Chamber allowed members of the public to enter the court and witness the proceedings, the FISA Court meets in a locked, guarded, and windowless room designed to keep its deliberations completely invisible to any but the initiated. This is the place where the secrecy of the executive branch of government meets the secrecy of the judicial branch—and then overpowers it. From 1978 to 2000, a period in which the annual number of FISA applications quadrupled, and the government began to request e-mail intercepts, cell-phone tracking, and Web browsing histories, there was only a single instance—out of over thirteen thousand cases—in which government lawyers did not get what they wanted. In that one case, the court "modified an order *and authorized an activity for which court authority had not been requested.*" As the FISA judges observed:

> It is self evident that the technical and surreptitious means available for acquisition of information by electronic surveillances and physical searches, coupled with the scope and duration of such intrusions and other practices under the FISA, give the government a powerful engine for the collection of foreign intelligence information targeting U.S. persons.

How do we explain this unrivaled winning record for government lawyers arguing before the FISA Court, with 13,102 wins, no losses, and one instance in which the referees themselves kicked the ball into the net? Was surveillance a rare example of flawless performance by government bureaucrats working in secrecy, without a single instance of overreach or mismanagement? It would be amazing, considering all the abuses in the years leading up to the passage of FISA, and the fact that almost no one involved in all that illegality had suffered any serious consequences. It would be even more amazing considering that the intelligence agencies themselves regarded complying with FISA to be a complex challenge.

In fact, FBI headquarters in 2000 finally admitted to a large and rapidly growing number of "mistakes" by field agents, including unauthorized videotaping, experimenting with software that intercepted the wrong subjects' e-mail, and listening in on the wrong cell phone. Violations such as these were not just harmless mistakes, not when we recognize the crucial distinction between ordinary law enforcement and the extraordinary powers accorded agencies like the FBI and the NSA for purposes of counterintelligence. One of the main purposes for which Congress created a secret court that issued secret rulings was to allow the government to fight off foreign powers, but at the same time to prevent the government from turning this "powerful engine" against ordinary citizens to make criminal cases. Yet the FBI admitted in 2000 that there had been at least seventy-five cases in which agents crossed this line, whether by making "erroneous" assertions in the original application to the court, or by using surveillance for law enforcement.

Despite the obvious problems the government was having in conducting lawful surveillance even within the incredibly loose guidelines created by the Foreign Intelligence Surveillance Act, it would keep expanding the scale and scope of these operations. This is all the more striking when one considers that these years—just after the end of the Cold War—were a time in which the United States was unusually secure as the world's only superpower. But this was also a period in which personal computers and cell phones became ubiquitous, and the Internet created enormous new opportunities for data gathering. The infernal dynamic therefore led officials to keep seeking new surveillance powers: the risk of exposure—especially as the extent of surveillance kept growing—made secrecy ever more important. But the more secret these programs were, the more tempting it was to continue expanding them. The secrecy itself made the intelligence more valuable, since the targets were unsuspecting, and this in turn made induction into this secret society all the more desirable. Those admitted discovered a culture that tolerated illegality and spurned even the idea of being accountable to the public.

To take one example, in 1985, a group of journalists and scholars formed a nonprofit organization called the National Security Archive. They became increasingly effective in using FOIA requests to obtain records that revealed a range of illegal or dubious government activities. Archive lawyers, some former Justice Department attorneys, won a series of hard-fought cases, preventing the Reagan administration from destroying e-mail back-ups, and forcing the FBI to release documents showing how the Bureau told librarians to spy on borrowers. But most of its FOIAs were for decades-old historical documents, and at no point did anyone accuse the National Security Archive of anything worse than creating work for the officials who had to process their requests. The archive also helped organize scholarly conferences with former government officials, and became a trusted and moderate voice on the need to accelerate declassification.

The FBI responded by putting the National Security Archive under surveillance. The records documenting this are heavily redacted, so it is difficult to determine the extent of the effort. But it appears to have started in 1989, when FBI Director William Sessions sent a cable classified secret assigning this job to the Washington field office's intelligence division. The reason? He was concerned about how effectively these American citizens were using the Freedom of Information Act. FBI surveillance continued for at least fifteen years, and included both "mail covers" (authorizing the FBI to copy envelopes going to and from the archive) and "Positive Intelligence" from "an extremely sensitive and reliable source of continuing value." In FBI parlance, this almost certainly meant a wiretap; all the redactions make it impossible to know for sure. In 2005, when the National Security Archive submitted FOIAs to the FBI to see if it had any records on the organization, the FBI claimed it had no such records. This response was only legal if it was *still* investigating the group.

So efforts to push back against government surveillance, even the exposure of illegal surveillance, did nothing to deter or discourage the continued expansion of these programs. Instead, officials targeted the organizations that tried to hold them to account, and found new ways to exploit their quasi-legal powers to aggregate even more data. If anything, the fact that no one ever paid a price for crossing even clear red lines emboldened officials to push still further.

The FBI already had the authority to use "pen register" and "trap and trace" devices. In the case of the National Security Archive, these methods enabled it to log what numbers its staff dialed even without showing probable cause. But now, with a new program called "Carnivore," it sought to interpret existing statutes to cover Internet communications. This would have allowed the FBI to see all subscriber data of the archive's Internet service provider, even if the archive was not a court-designated target.

There was already a body of case law holding that citizens cannot expect the government to refrain from accessing information about their communications if that information has been entrusted to a third party, like the telephone company that places the calls. But when these cases were decided, practically every phone was a landline, and every call was a voice call. As communications technology changed and people began living every aspect of their lives online, government lawyers adamantly defended the same proposition: Americans had no reasonable expectation of privacy when the government was collecting information *about* their communications—i.e., metadata—rather than the content of their communications. When the existence of the Carnivore system was revealed in July 2000, members of Congress questioned its legitimacy and legal basis, and vowed to develop new legislation.

But, rather than induce caution, pushback from Congress only caused government officials to make greater demands. A Pentagon panel, the Defense Science Board, expressed interest, similar to that of the FBI, in aggregating the metadata of Internet communications, including the specific Web sites visited, and routing information that revealed the physical location of targets. But the NSA did not have the authority it wanted to collect large volumes of communications metadata—including the communications of citizens—from U.S. Internet service providers. In the Defense Science Board report, the authors anticipated that only a "sophisticated attack" on the United States would make it politically feasible to challenge Fourth Amendment protections. When such an attack happened, the authors predicted, "the legal regime needed to respond to the attack will likely be put in place quickly by politicians anxious to be seen as part of the solution."

It was only one year later that the 9/11 attack occurred. The Bush administration quickly presented Congress with draft legislation that granted sweeping new surveillance powers. Attorney General John Ashcroft warned that new terrorist attacks were imminent, and if Congress did not pass the proposed bill it would have to bear responsibility for them. Just as predicted, politicians anxious to be part of the solution quickly pushed through the USA PATRIOT Act with scant debate. It included a provision little noticed at the time, section 216, that changed what was permissible with pen-register and trap-and-trace devices to permit more programs like Carnivore, so the government could search through communications metadata from millions of citizens.

As the powers of surveillance programs grew, so, too, did the number of FISA warrants granted, more than doubling between 2000 and 2005. But this publicly reported data did not actually show the full scope of surveillance. In yet another example of legal sophistry, the Bush administration had decided that—because he was the commander-in-chief—the president could authorize the FBI and the NSA to spy on citizens *without* a warrant. Another little-noted provision of the PATRIOT Act made it easier to do this through the use of so-called National Security Letters (NSLs), which compel companies to give access to user data without any prior approval from the FISA Court. Whereas previously a senior Justice Department official had to certify that there was evidence to believe a target was an agent of a foreign power, now any FBI field office could issue an NSL merely because the desired information was deemed relevant to an investigation.

So, in the case of the National Security Archive, suppose the FBI Washington field office asked the FISA Court for a warrant, claiming that Cuba or Russia might exploit its conferences on the history of the 1962 Cuban Missile Crisis to gather intelligence. In such a scenario, the judges might decide that the facts were too thin, or that the surveillance might violate the staff's First Amendment rights. FBI agents could still order Verizon to turn over its data using an NSL. We don't know if this happened to the National Security Archive, but this is exactly what happened to others subject to FBI investigations during this period, when agents refused to take no for an answer. The data demanded through an NSL might include the phone numbers and e-mail addresses of anyone who connected with staff members, and the Web site addresses the staff visited when surfing the Internet—both at home and at the office. Not only would Verizon be compelled to comply, it would not be able to disclose that they were doing so to the archive or to anyone else.

In total, there were about eighty-five hundred NSLs in 2000. From 2003 through 2005, it averaged close to fifty thousand a year. In fact, a report from the inspector general found that it was impossible to determine the true number, "because an unknown amount of data relevant to the period covered by our review was lost from the OGC [Office of the General Counsel] database when it malfunctioned." The report showed the figures the FBI gave to Congress "significantly understated" the Bureau's use of NSLs during this time period. Not only that; audits of these requests showed that almost one in ten of NSLs issued by FBI field offices resulted in violations of the FBI's own rules, typically when agents did not report that the NSLs had yielded more data than was legally authorized. For FBI headquarters the violation rate was well over 50 percent, because in most cases the Bureau was unable even to establish whether the NSL resulted from an authorized investigation.

Once revealed, the practice of warrantless surveillance of the communications of thousands of citizens provoked an angry public reaction. This rancor focused on the NSA more than the FBI, since most people had assumed the NSA would not be so bold as to spy on Americans—not after the pushback in the 1970s, the last time such activity had been exposed. Some NSA officials told journalists that they had not participated because they feared criminal prosecution. Bush administration officials anticipated this reaction as well, having reportedly rejected the idea of obtaining legal sanction from Congress because they concluded that there would be too much opposition. Congress responded in 2005 by requiring reporting on the use of NSLs, including any legal violations, and in 2008, by amending FISA explicitly to require warrants for domestic surveillance. At the same time, it conveniently gave telecom companies *retroactive* immunity from lawsuits for cooperating with the government.

So had the NSA learned its lesson? And would the FBI now

U.S. Department of Justice

Federal Bureau of Investigation

In Reply, Please Refer to
File No.

2004

President

Dear ▮▮

   Under the authority of Executive Order 12333, dated
December 4, 1981, and pursuant to Title 18, United States Code
(U.S.C.), Section 2709 (as amended, October 26, 2001), you are
hereby directed to provide the Federal Bureau of Investigation
(FBI) the names, addresses, lengths of service and electronic
communication transactional records, to include existing
transaction/activity logs and all e-mail header information (not
to include message content and/or subject fields), for the below-
listed email address:

   ▮▮▮▮▮▮

   In accordance with Title 18, U.S.C., Section 2709(b), I
certify that the information sought is relevant to an authorized
investigation to protect against international terrorism or
clandestine intelligence activities, and that such an
investigation of a United States person is not conducted solely
on the basis of activities protected by the First Amendment to
the Constitution of the United States.

   You are further advised that Title 18, U.S.C., Section
2709(c), prohibits any officer, employee or agent of yours from
disclosing to any person that the FBI has sought or obtained
access to information or records under these provisions.

   You are requested to provide records responsive to this
request personally to a representative of the ▮▮▮▮▮▮
▮▮▮▮ of the FBI. Any questions you have regarding this request
should be directed only to the ▮▮▮▮▮▮ Due to
security considerations, you should neither send the records
through the mail nor disclose the substance of this request in
any telephone conversation.

In a National Security Letter, the Department of Justice demands the recipient turn over personal information about a surveillance target, with the assurance that it is not infringing on the target's First Amendment rights, but at the same time prohibits the recipient from exercising those same rights to reveal the existence of the letter.

be prohibited from spying on American citizens without a warrant just because they had filed Freedom of Information Act requests? In fact, the intelligence community was once again using a workaround. The NSA had obtained a FISA Court order that permitted it to harvest telephone metadata from millions upon millions of people—the numbers they called, when they called them, and from what locations. It was also collecting equivalent metadata from e-mail, including the IP addresses of the devices from which the e-mails were sent. The program did not have a catchy name, like "Carnivore," but it was yet another example of how, in fact, officials were *omnivores*—continually seeking out new sources of surveillance data both at home and abroad, from citizens and noncitizens alike.

The NSA obtained this new power by promising the court that personnel would be trained to follow rules to prevent fishing expeditions. Among them were requirements for "reasonable suspicion" that the data would reveal terrorist connections, as well as strict auditing controls to prevent broad dissemination. This would appear to protect an organization like the National Security Archive. But in 2009, the FISA judge Reggie B. Walton found that NSA officials had misrepresented how the system worked, allegedly because no one at the NSA really understood the overall system architecture, leading to "daily violations." The NSA promised to make changes, but after new violations Walton was "deeply troubled" at what he described as a pattern of "serious and widespread compliance problems."

Some judges had also begun to point out that, with the proliferation of connected devices and information-gathering apps, the quantity and quality of information the government was obtaining through metadata was completely unprecedented. The government's defense, that case law from the era of telephone switchboards ought to apply, came under new scrutiny. In 2012, the case *United States v. Jones* raised questions about the secrets that might be revealed just from tracking the movements of someone's car with a GPS device. Did Sunday drives end at a church or a strip club, what hour did the driver finally make it home, and what other addresses might they have stopped at along the way? As Supreme Court Justice Sonia Sotomayor pointed out, the URLs people visit while surfing the Internet are even more revealing. An individual observation might not be conclusive, such as someone googling information about safe and unsafe doses of medications. But when combined with another observation, such as when the same individual looks for directions to visit a hospice, it creates a composite picture. "The Government can store such records and efficiently mine them for information years into the future," Sotomayor pointed out, "to ascertain, more or less at will, their political and religious beliefs, sexual habits, and so on."

This is known as the mosaic theory—that, like little pieces of tile arranged to form a composite whole, otherwise innocuous observations made individually can generate insights about a subject when put together. But government lawyers will take a different stand on the mosaic theory depending on whose information it is being used to defend. When it pertains to an individual's right to protect their privacy, they have argued vigorously against it. But when it comes to protecting the government's own secrets, they have argued vigorously, and successfully, *in support of* a mosaic theory. Ironically, this is especially true in the case of protecting the secret powers it has to invade our privacy. All the way back in 1978, in the case of *Halkin v. Helms*, they persuaded judges that, "in this age of computer technology," it was too dangerous to disclose even the phone numbers the NSA and the CIA might be monitoring, since "seemingly innocuous information can be analyzed and fitted into place to reveal with startling clarity how the unseen whole must operate."

The plaintiff in this case, an antiwar activist named Adele Halkin, was not even allowed to know if she was under NSA surveillance. In her case—and hundreds of others that cited *Halkin v. Helms* as settled law—the idea that metadata might form a mosaic led judges to deny citizens information about government surveillance. So citizens cannot mount a constitutional challenge because they cannot prove they are under surveillance—even, remarkably, when they have proved that the people they were communicating with were under NSA surveillance.

In fact, the whole point of harvesting metadata is to put social networks under surveillance. As of 2021, more than two hundred and thirty thousand people have been formally targeted by the NSA. We do not know who these people are, and may never know. But, according to its own rules, the NSA could gather not just any phone number that one of these people contacted, but also any number with which they are connected by a third party—even a customer-service number used by millions of other people.

The idea that the mosaic theory is no less applicable to government surveillance of citizens as it is to citizens' efforts to monitor their government has been gaining traction in the courts. But rulings to rein in surveillance by law-enforcement authorities left the NSA's program largely untouched. One of the only changes Congress imposed in recent decades was to require the intelligence community to report the extent of their surveillance. These reports showed that, by almost every measure, the scope and intensity of government surveillance continued trending upward even after the Snowden revelations and the outrage that followed. The CIA could not even provide a good-faith estimate of how many times it accessed raw surveillance data on American citizens.

Other figures speak to the continued flourishing of surveillance activities in the post-Snowden era, such as the massive increase in the collection of what are known as call detail records, or CDRs. A record of the numbers and a stamp of the time when someone calls or texts together with routing information might seem relatively innocuous, but when fitted into place with many other CDRs and other kinds of surveillance data it can be quite revealing. And since the cellular antenna indicates the location of a call with increasing precision, it has proved all too easy to use this data to identify particular individuals. There are many, many ways a government could use such data, both legitimate and illegitimate. It could count people who might not otherwise show up in a census, but also identify those who failed to file a tax return. It could be used to model the spread of disease, or quarantine diseased individuals. The appeal of CDRs is apparent from the jump in their collection, which went, in the single year 2016–17, from 151 million to more than half a billion records.

Congress did allow provisions of the USA PATRIOT Act used to authorize bulk metadata collection to expire in 2020, including the CDR program. Subsequently, it was revealed that, despite costing one hundred million dollars, the information gathered had resulted in only one FBI investigation—with no information provided as to its nature or outcome. But the intelligence community retained an array of other tools, such as National Security Letters, FISA warrants, and pen registers, which are used to collect vast amounts of Internet metadata, such as URLs and e-mail headers. Perhaps most striking are the new kinds of surveillance hardware the dark state has also continued to develop, including drones equipped with two hundred cameras that can continually track multiple individuals across an entire city, giving the military the same capabilities imagined in Hollywood thrillers.

To be sure, for all these surveillance tools to outfit a truly Orwellian state, harvested data would have to be aggregated. But that is precisely what the intelligence community aims to achieve. The FBI maintains a "Data Integration and Visualization System" that draws from hundreds of different databases, and hundreds of millions of pages of records. When the FBI sought to exempt its "Data Warehouse" from the protections afforded by the 1974 Privacy Act, it had to give the following overview of the system's capabilities:

> Records may contain investigative and/or intelligence information that has been replicated and/or extracted from other FBI systems; obtained from open source or commercial databases; and lawfully collected by the FBI or other government agencies such as the Departments of Defense, Energy, Homeland Security, State, and Treasury. These records include, but are not limited to, biographical information (such as name, alias, race, sex, date of birth, place of birth, social security number, passport number, driver's license, or other unique identifier, addresses, telephone numbers, physical descriptions, and photographs); biometric information (such as fingerprints); financial information (such as bank account number); location; associates and affiliations; employment and business information; visa and immigration information; travel; and criminal and investigative history, and other data that may assist the FBI in fulfilling its national security and law enforcement responsibilities.

In introducing the system in 2011, the then director of the FBI, Robert S. Mueller III, reported that new capabilities might include "geospatial tools and cross-case correlation." It was subsequently discovered that FBI agents routinely use the system to search for metadata the NSA has collected, including what was "incidentally" collected about citizens, notwithstanding the basic principle that this kind of surveillance should only be employed against citizens when there is credible suspicion of espionage or terrorism. The NSA's own reporting has revealed that it has repeatedly violated citizens' privacy protections; it attributes this to "technical irregularities." So, here again, if the FBI had continued its investigation of the National Security Archive—it refuses to say one way or another—its agents could have accessed NSA data revealing staff communications with people abroad. They could have disclosed what they learned from the database with a whole host of other parties, including local law enforcement.

Over the last century, much about U.S. surveillance has changed. In Hoover's day, the FBI director had wide-ranging powers to conduct surveillance against citizens he suspected of being "un-American." Now there is a complex legal framework meant to create clear limits, both to prevent arbitrary abuse of power and to protect bedrock principles. But that framework has proved completely unworkable, at least for its ostensible purpose. If anything, it has worked both to legitimate and to conceal government surveillance powers—powers that are far more extensive, and interconnected, than ever before. And these powers can be, and have been, used against American citizens just for exercising their right to request information from their government.

A culture of secrecy and poor record-keeping has assured that much about America's vast surveillance programs will remain unknown. So how can we know what the government might be doing with all this data? For instance, should we believe the government lawyer who argues that giving up our metadata makes little difference to our personal privacy, or should we agree with the government lawyer who argues that giving up metadata can create a "mosaic" that might reveal many secrets?

We no longer need to speculate. Luckily, we can do our own research, but this time using *government* metadata. We don't have access to enough data to analyze what the intelligence community gathered to track the political activity of American citizens. The NSA has released relatively few documents, even from seventy years ago, and nothing that might reveal "sources and methods." And the FBI typically only releases individual surveillance files and not aggregate data that we can mine to reveal the larger whole. But we can analyze how U.S. Foreign Service officers abroad monitored political dissent in other countries, because, although the State Department does not release the content of still-classified cables, it does release all the metadata. We will use that to examine a particularly important case study, the Iranian Revolution, and then go on to demonstrate how this kind of metadata can be mined to identify other significant events. Finally, we will look at what kinds of metadata are most sensitive even now, and in that way find our way to a surveillance program that targeted those who have aspired to come to the United States, perhaps believing that it is a country that does not surveil its citizens.

In a series of experiments at History Lab, we started with just two kinds of metadata—the date and the subject—to see whether algorithms could automatically detect important events, much as agencies might try to do with citizens' personal metadata. The government has for years funded their own research in this area because of its many applications. For instance, intelligence analysts have long been interested in improving their ability to track political protests to predict when a surveilled community might revolt. The most famous example came in 1978–79, when Iranians rose up against the secret police and overthrew the Shah, America's longtime ally. Jimmy Carter, with egg on his face, claimed, "The rapid change of affairs in Iran has not been predicted by anyone as far as I know."

In fact, when we analyzed State Department cables and CIA reports from the period, they showed that U.S. diplomats in Iran had been closely tracking protests as they became more frequent and more violent. CIA analysts, on the other hand, were asleep at the switch. There was no increase in their reporting about Iran until the situation was out of control.

Tracking the direction and frequency of communications is a form of traffic analysis, which has long been a tool for signals intelligence. Even though we don't have access to the message text in the State Department cables that are still classified, traffic analysis can point the way to important insights. What could we learn if, like the NSA, we could mine a massive collection of metadata—i.e., *all* the State Department cables from the 1970s?

To that end, an MIT professor named Rahul Mazumder developed a statistical technique to identify sustained bursts of activity above the normal baseline, a technique first invented to identify events from e-mail metadata. Columbia's High Performance Computing Cluster computed the results, using some twenty-six hundred cores to process 1.7 million cables in less than an hour and rank-order almost five hundred "bursts" from 1973 to 1977. This analysis enabled us to analyze whether, as with the Iranian Revolution the CIA failed to predict, officials failed to see when important events were unfolding. Some, like the Fall of Saigon in 1975, produced a steady escalation in the frequency of communications related to Vietnam, a peak, and then a gradual decline. For others, such as a 1974 military coup and invasion of Cyprus, you can tell they occurred with little warning because of the spike in the number of cables.

This radically inductive method was uncannily effective in identifying historical events from the 1970s, matching a Berkeley historian expert in this period in a head-to-head competition. Could we also mine this metadata to find some of the top secrets from the same period—just as the government uses our communications metadata to reveal private information? In so doing, we also hoped to reveal what parts of the surveillance engine remain secret. To answer that question, we built a classifier, the same kind of tool we used to identify documents with radioactive content. Only we built this one to identify the words that would "predict" that cables would not be released at all, using just the metadata, without knowing what makes the content of these cables sensitive even now.

Among the top twenty words are "Asmara" and "Amberley." Examining the few cables containing these words that have been declassified, we now glimpse what had been deemed sensitive for all those years. It turns out that "Asmara" referred to an NSA facility in Ethiopia that intercepted satellite signals. The specific purpose of "Amberley," on the other hand, is less clear, though we do know that it was a U.S. base in Australia and was discussed in declassified cables in the same context as Pine Gap, a center for gathering surveillance data. The Australian prime minister would not discuss Amberley's activity at all—and even fifty years later, the government still does not want us to see what's in these cables.

Among the top five predictive words, one finds "Harvest," which refers to the code name "Olive Harvest." Cables with "Olive Harvest" in the subject line refer to aerial reconnaissance flights by U-2 spy planes along the Golan Heights. In 1974, Kissinger negotiated a deal to share this imaging data with Israel and Syria to reduce the risk for both sides of another surprise attack or an accidental war. The flights continued long after, and continue to be classified.

But of all the words, the most sensitive is "Boulder." If the subject line of a cable includes that word, it is 129 times more likely to remain classified than a cable without it. There are almost seven thousand of these still-secret Boulder cables. When we plotted the network connecting who sent and received these messages, the same way the FBI might try to distinguish a social network from a target's cell-phone metadata, it was clear that the very same agency, the FBI, was deeply involved, and their cables mainly concerned embassies in the Middle East like Amman and Cairo—right at the center of the spokes.

So what was "Boulder"? And why was it the most sensitive term in the entire lexicon of U.S. diplomacy? I've asked this question of audiences at several universities, including Harvard, Yale, Stanford, Cambridge, and the Sorbonne. Every time I've asked the assembled historians and political scientists if there was anyone who could explain it, I've met with puzzled expressions—no one could guess what "Boulder" meant.

In reading the relatively small number of cables that were released, almost all of them before 2002, one finds telltale clues: they consist largely of biometric data about visa applicants, like their hair and eye color, in order to check their names—presumably against a watch list. It turns out that "Boulder" was the name of another classified surveillance program. This one started after the 1972 Munich Olympics, when the Palestinian Black September group killed Israeli athletes. Thousands of people with Arabic-sounding last names who applied for American visas were investigated by the FBI as potential terrorists. The Bureau also investigated untold numbers of American citizens—according to one official, "any Arab or others of a suspicious nature"—including their political beliefs and what groups they belonged to. Contemporaries understood they were being targeted, but they could not get official confirmation, and never knew the full scope of the operation.

Most of the Boulder cables had not originally been classified. But six months after 9/11, while the Bush administration was dramatically expanding terrorist watch and no-fly lists, and the FBI was intensifying surveillance of Muslim communities, White House Chief of Staff Andrew Card ordered additional scrutiny for even unclassified material if public release risked endangering homeland security. After this order went out, very few Boulder cables became public.

In this way, the history of surveillance intended to thwart terrorism—particularly relevant after 9/11, and likely to produce useful lessons—was apparently deemed too sensitive to discuss. Still, officials were happy to unload a stack of hay that hid the few needles they left behind.

But mining the metadata can now give us a "meta" view not just on things the government did not want us to know from long ago, but also on things—such as surveillance programs—that it is still trying to keep secret right now. One striking fact is how often these programs have focused on marginalized communities—whether the Eastern European immigrants that Hoover helped round up during the Palmer Raids, the Black civil-rights activists he hounded during the 1950s and 1960s, the Arab Americans investigated as potential terrorists during the 1970s, or the Muslim communities who were targeted after 9/11. But the agencies mainly responsible for this surveillance, the FBI and the NSA, were (and are) among the least diverse in the entire federal government. As late as 1996, more than 87 percent of NSA employees were white. It was only then that its leadership began to recognize how homogenous organizations have a harder time understanding the rest of the world.

This chapter has focused on how these agencies have targeted citizens, since only U.S. citizens and their representatives in Congress and the courts can stop it. But that is obviously harder when the targeted communities are also ones that are denied the ability to exercise their civil rights, and when organizations are targeted for FBI surveillance merely because they asked the Bureau for information. We also need to realize that the NSA, FBI, and other agencies have the legal authority to discover everything about any "non-U.S. person," or, indeed, any citizen who might be connected to someone who has fallen under suspicion. The surveillance to which these persons are subjected could include not just the telephone numbers and e-mail addresses they contact, and when and where they are contacted, but also the *content* of *all* their communications: their Web browsing histories, their credit-card transactions, their medical and psychiatric records, and everything that might be pulled out the back door of their devices and operating systems, whether from Facebook, Instagram, or their phone's own cameras and sensors. The places from which these agencies can draw now include the massive data centers Google, Amazon, and Apple have built all over the world.

Much of the debate about government surveillance has been led by lawyers, and focuses on legal theories, as if a legal analysis can explain what officials actually do, notwithstanding the long history of their routinely violating the law with total impunity. The culture of secrecy—its rituals, its ethnography, its belief systems—offers a much deeper understanding of these programs, and how and why they have so consistently operated outside the law. It also helps explain why this surveillance regime has been so resilient and so resistant to reform. Exposure of abuses, and occasional counterattacks, have only made it stronger, and bolder. After all, responsible officials have largely escaped any meaningful discipline even when they targeted the very people who are supposed to exercise oversight over them, right down to the present day. In one particularly egregious instance from 2014, CIA officials hacked the Senate Intelligence

Committee staff's computers. They wanted to stop the senators and staffers from accessing a secret internal Agency review that confirmed that CIA torturers had lied about the effectiveness of waterboarding. The Agency's inspector general barked, but the caravan moved on. In 2019, another inspector general found that FBI officials had systematically misrepresented and omitted key facts in applying to the FISA Court to surveil a former Trump campaign adviser, Carter Page. Only one faced charges, for actually doctoring evidence in the FISA application, but he was sentenced only to probation. Under Trump, the Justice Department turned around and secretly obtained communications metadata from Apple in order to investigate the House Intelligence Committee chairman, Adam Schiff. In each case, one side or the other expressed outrage, but all of them were simply variations on a theme. If the CIA and the FBI surveil political opponents, when they must know their actions will garner special scrutiny, how do they behave toward people without political power in cases that are unlikely ever to be reviewed?

Long ago, Senator Frank Church became famous for helping uncover CIA assassination plots and other covert operations. But he said that what he discovered about state surveillance was more disturbing, and more dangerous:

> . . . that capability at any time could be turned around on the American people and no American would have any privacy left, such [is] the capability to monitor everything: telephone conversations, telegrams, it doesn't matter. There would be no place to hide. If this government ever became a tyranny, if a dictator ever took charge in this country, the technological capacity that the intelligence community has given the government could enable it to impose total tyranny, and there would be no way to fight back, because the most careful effort to combine together in resistance to the government, no matter how privately it was done, is within the reach of the government to know.

Church ended on a hopeful note: "I don't want to see this country ever go across the bridge." "That" he said, "is the abyss from which there is no return."

But when you consider how much surveillance we are not allowed to know about, authorized in secret courts that issue secret rulings, or by White House lawyers with no judicial or congressional oversight, how would we even know if we are already on the other side of that bridge, looking back?

6

WEIRD SCIENCE

SECRETS THAT ARE STRANGER THAN FICTION

In 1978, a CIA official came upon a set of documents dating from the First World War. They were much older than the CIA itself. They were due—past due—for "automatic" declassification. But after looking at them, this official decided that the documents were too dangerous to be released to the public: "continued protection is essential to the national security." So they were locked away again for another quarter of a century.

After the end of the Cold War, more people began to learn of the existence of these mysterious documents. Watchdog groups filed a lawsuit in federal court demanding to know what was in them. But government lawyers managed to fight them off, and the documents were kept under lock and key.

Finally, in 2011, the CIA director himself, Leon Panetta, released a carefully worded statement. He announced that new technology had finally made it possible for the Agency to reveal what had been hidden for nearly a century: "When historical information is no longer sensitive," he said, "we take seriously our responsibility to share it with the American people."

So what was the big reveal? Did the documents disclose the names of heretofore unsuspected spies operating at the highest levels? Did they uncover the existence of a decades-old deep-state conspiracy? No. The documents contained recipes for making invisible ink.

For Steven Aftergood of the Federation of American Scientists, Panetta's vague reference to new technology was a rationalization to reduce public embarrassment. By the 1970s, digital encryption had rendered invisible ink obsolete. The CIA had invoked national security and secret research to guard something that might, at best, have provided a temporary distraction at a child's birthday party.

Measuring the extreme age of certain secrets, like comparing the age of nuclear secrets and UFO secrets, can tell us things about what the government still does not want us to know. In some cases, especially with science and technology, the secrets can be surprising, even strange, as we saw with the counterintuitive design of the Hiroshima bomb. But whereas the atomic bomb is still dangerous, in many other cases uncovering secret research and technology only reveals the embarrassing weirdness of the dark state, even—especially—when it claims its methods are scientific.

Government scientists and engineers themselves do not always hide their magical thinking, instead choosing to associate their work with myth and legend. When, during the Cold War, a group of professors first came together to advise the Pentagon on emerging technology, they called themselves the Jasons, as if they were Argonauts. The cryptonym for breaking Japanese codes was "magic," reflecting a persistent tendency to associate cryptology with the occult. When consultants from the RAND Corporation devised what they considered a more scientific method for predicting future threats, they called it Delphi, suggesting they had become oracles. The most senior officials help cultivate these myths. "If ever legends and stories of American technological genius were deserved and not yet realized," former CIA Director Robert Gates has declared, "they would be about scientists and engineers—the wizards—of CIA. . . ."

Is it any wonder that it is so hard to get at the truth of secret science and technology, considering that the scientists themselves engage in mythmaking? The rest of us are discouraged from demanding to know what they do in our name, both because myths are more alluring than facts, and because the imagery implies that their work is inexplicable—at least to nonscientists. But it is important that we try. As we shall see, "the pursuit of the magic weapon" is "the distinguishing feature of modern American defense," as James Fallows once observed. When it can take almost a century for the public to see these secrets, and they turn out to be underwhelming, we have to confront the question: Did the resources invested in developing secret weapons and spy gear truly serve to protect national security? Or have government scientists spent this whole time chasing a chimera?

To be sure, some of the most important components of any modern arsenal did start out as secret feats of science and engineering, including radar, spy satellites, and stealth aircraft. As Arthur C. Clarke postulated in his famous third law, "Any sufficiently advanced technology is indistinguishable from magic." Fortunately, historians can usually tell the difference between science and fiction, because we have the great gift of hindsight. Even more important, we can see *why* government officials went to extremes in covering up the bizarre things they devised when they thought no one was looking. The usual explanation is that staying ahead of all possible enemies requires pursuing the most advanced technology. But that is not the whole story. As we shall see, pursuing secret weapons is both costly and risky, and can actually undermine national security. It continues because it is part of a larger strategy, one that is enormously lucrative for defense contractors, and one that also allows public officials to accrue unaccountable power. The secrecy also helps them to avoid embarrassment, and they have a lot more to be embarrassed about than just ninety-year-old invisible ink, including research that most people would consider dangerous or even grotesque.

This chapter will describe a lot of magical thinking, and many bizarre experiments, but research at the limits could be a very serious business, literally. Harnessing the profit motive to make secret weapons was one of the main drivers in the rise of the modern military-industrial complex. As far back as the nineteenth century, the Royal Navy—at the time the greatest in the world—had to partner with private companies to perfect the torpedo and other high-tech weapons of the day. Similarly, the U.S. Army hired major corporations like DuPont and Union Carbide to build and operate the massive plants required to produce the materials for the atomic bomb.

Scientists can be quite businesslike in combining risky and expensive research with the very material considerations that make this research possible, and potentially lucrative, especially if they can keep it secret. Professors often conceal data and experiments until their work can be patented or reviewed for publication (by peers who also prefer to remain anonymous). Leo Szilard, the Hungarian physicist who pushed FDR to start the Manhattan Project, even tried to patent the nuclear reactor and make it his personal intellectual property, if only to exert some control over its future development. We have seen how other scientists bristled at information controls of any kind, whether public or private. Such controls seemed to stifle the spirit of free inquiry upon which innovation depended—especially for free spirits like Richard Feynman and Niels Bohr. But others were more accepting. The committee that General Groves convened to create a policy on declassification was chaired by Oppenheimer and made up entirely of scientists. Its members realized that their research had many commercial applications. Private contractors like Dow Chemical and General Electric were also pressing to be released from wartime restrictions.

So secret science is very much a part of the history of state secrets in America—a very big part. It has been driven by competition between the great powers, in this case the fear that the Nazis would be the first to build an atomic bomb, but also the mixed motives of interested parties—not least the scientists themselves. After the Manhattan Project, thousands more of them would work with security clearances, undertaking classified projects on contract with the Department of Energy, the CIA's Directorate of Science and Technology, the Defense Advanced Research Projects Agency (DARPA), and IARPA, DARPA's equivalent in the intelligence community. Some were inspired by patriotism. Others believed that government backing would allow them to work on the very hardest problems with all the resources available to a superpower. Rather than countless stress-filled hours writing grant applications, one short meeting with the right officials could yield millions in research funding.

Covert work continues to be done in secret laboratories, reported in secret conferences, and published in secret journals. Sometimes, we see civilian spinoffs from military-funded research that benefit humankind, such as miniaturized transistors, global positioning systems, and the Internet, which started as ARPANET, so named for the defense agency in which it originated. The U.S. biowarfare program also helped in the development of vaccines, as long as they were demonstrably useful to "warfighters," such as those for anthrax and Ebola.

But even though the serious business of government-funded science and technology is an essential part of the history of state secrecy, we should not assume that secret government programs have been essential in creating successful technologies more generally. Nor should we underestimate the capacity of researchers to use government money to do things they would have done anyway. Perhaps the most important innovation of all, ARPANET, with its protocols for a decentralized communications network, was not secret research. Though ARPANET demonstrated for some of its early backers how communications could work after a nuclear war, data scientists were already highly motivated to develop some means to connect their computers quickly and reliably. The early Internet was built in a remarkably transparent fashion, creating a culture of openness that survives to this day.

Pentagon largesse doubtless played a significant role in the particular ways these technologies developed. The civilian spinoffs, in turn, have long been used to justify Pentagon appropriations. But many of these things—and perhaps many more—might have been invented anyway, and adopted faster, if they had been developed without all the strings attached to government secrecy. A lot of valuable taxpayer-funded research is still classified, or even forgotten, benefiting no one. One outside historian, when given a security clearance and commissioned to write a history of the research and development of military lasers, was astonished to find that the technical reports alone amounted to fifty cubic feet. But much of the information for his research was locked up in separate and incompatible information systems, unknown even to scientists and engineers working on related projects. The secrecy requirements were so severe that, in the event this historian was intercepted while transporting classified tapes of interviews with government scientists, he was prepared to eat the tapes rather than let them fall into the wrong hands. "Secrecy," he concluded, "clogs the arteries of our scientific and technical information systems."

Slowing the deployment of new technology can have enormous consequences. The physicist Leo Szilard estimated that compartmentalization within the Manhattan Project added eighteen months to the development of the atomic bomb. If the United States had not gone to such lengths to (unsuccessfully) conceal the atomic-bomb program, it might have had a nuclear option to defeat Nazi Germany months before the D-Day landings.

Sclerotic state science and technology is also incredibly costly. Altogether, the U.S. government devotes more than half of its R&D spending to the military, and has been doing so for more than forty years. This is proportionately more than three times more than any of its allies spend. Even accounting for the difference in the size of their economies, the American military R&D effort is three times greater relative to that of the U.K., five times greater than that of France, and twelve times greater than that of Japan. The United States accounts for a whopping 81 percent of military R&D among all the countries in the Organisation for Economic Co-operation and Development put together.

The opportunity costs are incalculable. As much as we may value the crumbs that fall off the Pentagon's banquet table of top-secret research, what might be achieved if more of this research were done out in the open, and actually devoted to benefiting humankind? Instead of prioritizing planetary threats like global warming and emerging viruses, government scientists have filed hundreds of patent applications for ever-more-advanced methods of mass killing. The Atomic Energy Commission (AEC) even patented ways to poison a city's water supplies more effectively, which the proud inventor called "an improvement in the art of toxic warfare . . . wherein bodies of water are the targets and wherein it is desired to effectively contaminate same." Some things may have been kept secret *because* they were so shameful, like a report to the president about a program to weaponize Q fever and other kinds of bacteria "capable of reducing enemy will to resist."

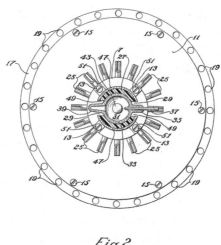

Fig. 2

WITNESSES.

Ralph Corbli Smith

Paul A. Glaister

INVENTOR.
DONALD F. HORNIG
BY

Robert R. Cavenee

Some secret military technology could be strangely beautiful, like this triggering device to detonate simultaneously the charges to initiate a nuclear reaction. The patent description only referenced its use in "certain types of ordnance." The inventor, Donald Hornig, personally armed the first atomic bomb.

Putting so much of America's scientific talent to work on secret weapons and spy gear does not necessarily serve national security even when U.S. forces deploy advanced technology against an unwitting enemy, and it actually works. We have seen, for instance, how the army radar that detected the Pearl Harbor attack made no difference because of inadequate training and interservice rivalries.

Our adversaries have demonstrated how rapidly deploying low-tech armaments can be highly effective, like arming insurgents with AK-47's, boarding planes with box cutters, and swarming social media with bile-spewing bots. Whereas the U.S. intelligence community gives top priority to billion-dollar "technical" assets, such as spy satellites and quantum computers, Russian spies seem to learn more by bribing "human assets" with cash payments, or paying programmers to hack our computers. Moscow reaped a remarkable return on these small investments. Tipped off by the CIA agent Aldrich Ames, for instance, the KGB "turned" American assets in the USSR and fed them false information. And what was the goal of this KGB disinformation campaign? To fool U.S. decision makers into believing that the Soviets were spending far more on military R&D than they really were. The CIA admitted that false reports of Soviet progress in developing new fighter aircraft and cruise missiles did "clear cut damage" to U.S. decision making on programs that cost billions of dollars. The man ultimately responsible had expensive taste—Ames took to wearing tailored suits and bought a new Jaguar. But buying spies bespoke suits is much cheaper than trying to build magic weapons.

Competition for money also fuels interservice and intelligence-community rivalries. For instance, in the 1950s, when the air force began to war-game future scenarios for nuclear conflict, and tried to show how aircraft carriers would be sitting ducks, the navy judged the games to be a "transparent campaign" to obtain more funding for more strategic bombers. The commander-in-chief of the Pacific Fleet was no less transparent about his own calculations: he wanted to show that carriers could play a role in a nuclear war, and not just in smaller conflicts. "The money contest is big league," he declared, and "We must stay in [the] majors."

But the serious business of building secret weapons ultimately depends on magical thinking, as the air force's own flagship program from the period amply demonstrated. Not satisfied with the B-52 Stratofortress, SAC wanted a supersonic bomber, the B-70 Valkyrie. A 1958 *Air Force Magazine* article explained that the name, from Norse mythology, evoked the "maidens of extreme beauty, who ranged the heavens on their steeds, choosing those who were to die in battle and bearing the fallen heroes back to Valhalla." It quoted an aeronautical scientist describing the research that made the Valkyrie possible as "strange and wonderful." It would be much more than a Mach 3 bomber, the author insisted.

The B-70 could be a:

- Supersonic transport.
- Money-saving recoverable booster for space projects.
- Space interceptor to query and investigate foreign satellites in orbit.
- Ballistic missile launcher.
- Supersonic nuclear-powered aircraft.

As if all that were not enough, the four-man crew and their ten-megaton hydrogen bomb would enjoy "living-room comfort" while cruising at some fifteen miles above the Earth at two thousand miles an hour, with optimum temperature and pressure and extra legroom.

> The B-70 would "encapsulate" the individual. In an emergency, the capsule would eject, its chute opening at a preset altitude. The capsule would be equipped with a boat for water landings, and clothing and food suitable for either arctic or desert survival.

But after almost ten years of R&D, the program produced a grand total of two planes. General Electric staged an aerial photo shoot with one of them, surrounded by several other warplanes with GE engines. The company wanted to show off how successful it had been selling its products to the Pentagon. But the B-70 collided with one of the other aircraft, a Lockheed F-104 Starfighter, sending both of the unfortunate pilots to Valhalla. The second Valkyrie was then towed down a highway to its final resting place, to be made into an exhibit at the National Museum of the U.S. Air Force. The program cost for that one museum piece was $1.5 billion, $13 billion in today's dollars, or roughly double the price of its weight in gold. (The "Dyna-Soar" it was supposed to boost into space proved to be priceless—the program cost billions but did not produce even one working prototype.)

The next air-force attempt at building a strategic bomber, the B-1, took some twenty years, eventually producing one hundred planes that were notorious for high maintenance costs and low reliability. By 2019, only six of the remaining sixty-two were considered mission-capable. They are permitted to fly a maximum of three hundred hours a year, but never at low altitudes. The B-2 stealth bomber also took decades to develop, and cost three times its weight in gold when twenty-one were finally deployed in the 1990s. The air force awarded the contract for a replacement bomber in 2016. Even sympathetic observers thought the official estimated price of the new bomber—half that of the B-2—was completely unrealistic. The actual price the air force agreed to pay Northrop-Grumman was classified. Spokesmen claimed that disclosing this secret would only benefit America's adversaries. A large-scale RAND study of dozens of weapons programs found that—on average—the Pentagon ended up paying 74 percent more for aircraft than it had originally budgeted.

The museum-bound B-70 Valkyrie: thirteen billion dollars' worth of roadkill

The lack of realism in initial cost estimates provided to Congress was the single largest reason.

Defenders insist that, even if the Pentagon cannot or will not tell us what these magic weapons cost, keeping a technological edge is essential for national security. That is why it has to keep pushing the envelope, whether testing titanium exoskeletons for foot soldiers, or robotic mules to carry all their high-tech gear. But true security requires a strategy that integrates the different means and ends essential to defend the country, and does not lose sight of the human beings who are on the front line (and the many other human beings who back them up). A titanium exoskeleton does little good for a soldier if he must live in vermin-and-mold-infested military housing that sickens him and his entire family. And a robotic mule won't get the soldier anywhere if, after all his training, he resigns when a medically discharged buddy commits suicide outside a VA hospital for lack of decent care. While the Pentagon is trying to build drones that can surveil entire cities—including American cities—it cannot even ensure that soldiers receive their paychecks because of archaic payroll systems. Chasing after a technological chimera thus diverts funds from adequate pay and training for troops, decent hospitals for their wounded comrades, and better schools for their children—and all children.

In all these ways, a strategy centered on developing secret weapons and spy gear—no matter how long it takes, and no matter how much they cost—can actually undermine national security. So why, after all this, is America's national-security strategy squarely based on magical thinking? If it's not invisible ink, then what is the real secret here?

It comes down to three things: money, power, and—not least—secrecy itself. Rather than a means to make America safe, each of these has become its own reward for the denizens of the dark state, and all are even more rewarding when they form an interlocking and impenetrable system.

More than any other factor, the pursuit of secret weapons and spy gear is what makes America's intelligence and defense establishments incredibly expensive. Out of total military spending, which includes personnel costs, operations and maintenance, etc., the United States spends 40 percent more than NATO guidelines on the equipment it purchases from defense contractors—i.e., missiles, vehicles, naval vessels, etc. And the cost of cloaking military research and development doubles the appropriations required to produce these weapons. The expenses include not just the direct cost of creating secure environments and communications systems, and background screening and training, which itself drains the talent pool. There's also the higher cost of noncompetitive contracts, and the clogged arteries that result from compartmentalized, noncirculating research.

For many of our leaders, the extreme cost of magic weapons is a feature, not a bug. In a world of no-bid contracts and "cost-plus" accounting, which guarantees profits for contractors, constantly upgrading the requirements of a new weapon or surveillance system ensures an ever-expanding revenue stream for the future paymasters of senior military leaders.

A strategy centered on secret science and engineering also gives power to technologists. Whether for good or ill, they have been the only ones able to seriously challenge military men in their own domain, because they can invoke an authority that trumps combat experience. In essence, if new high-tech weapons are assumed to revolutionize warfare, then hard-won experience in more conventional combat can be made to seem irrelevant. As one of Robert McNamara's "whiz kids" retorted when a general pointed out his lack of combat experience: "General, I have fought just as many nuclear wars as you have." Even in a blood-and-guts counterinsurgency conflict like Vietnam, Jason scientists could sway multibillion-dollar Pentagon decisions and actually dictate military operations, such as when they pushed a program to use a vast network of sensors to interdict communist supply lines.

Finally, the chimera strategy also puts a premium on secrecy. After all, once the secret is revealed, and the mythical beast is made real, it can be more cheaply imitated. Then these weapons—whether nuclear bombs or zero-day exploits—can be turned against the United States. But this secrecy, like money and power, has become an end in itself. Knowledge is power, and secret knowledge—especially the knowledge that comes from vast systems of surveillance—gives our leaders the power to remain unaccountable to anyone without a "need to know." We might have to wait ninety years before they let us read the invisible ink.

Keeping research on weapons and surveillance systems secret does sometimes contribute to American security. But so, too, can stopping further progress in military science. For instance, in one of the unredacted documents History Lab discovered, the physicist Isidor Rabi revealed to President Dwight Eisenhower in 1959 that the Soviets had not yet realized the need to shield their H-bombs, a vulnerability the United States might use in wartime to render 99 percent of them ineffective. To Rabi, this meant the United States should push for a moratorium on all further nuclear testing, notwithstanding the objections of the generals.

In some cases, misinformation can be more effective—and much cheaper—than actual military research. In the 1970s, a legendary Pentagon technologist named Andrew Marshall masterminded efforts to fool Soviet Intelligence as to the priorities and accomplishments of American military research. For instance, the United States engaged in a complex disinformation operation to give the impression that it was covertly developing biological weapons, which helped to provoke the Soviets to embark on a program that eventually employed some sixty thousand scientists and technicians to mass-produce anthrax and smallpox. The idea was not simply to "outspend" the USSR—a simplification that is sometimes used to credit Ronald Reagan with winning the Cold War. It was to induce the Soviets to spend on the wrong things.

But in trying to fool adversaries, we sometimes fool ourselves. When Reagan announced a plan to build a system to defend against nuclear-ballistic-missile strikes, critics derided the project as an expensive fantasy inspired by *Star Wars*. It depended on hundreds of missiles intercepting hundreds of other missiles—

the equivalent of spraying bullets to knock down other bullets, except that ICBMs travel ten times faster. The Pentagon planned to make this seem plausible by running a rigged experiment: it would deliberately blow up a test missile as the experimental heat-seeking interceptor came near. But the interceptor did not even come close to its target in the first three tests. The army finally decided to make the test missile an easier infrared target by first heating it before it left the launchpad, and then having it swing around mid-flight to present itself broadside to the interceptor's sensor. These measures doubled the size of the target.

In press conferences and congressional testimony, Pentagon spokespersons described the result as a big success for American technology, the first time a missile shot down another missile. They did not reveal to any member of Congress that, to make the project work in wartime, the Pentagon would first have to convince the Soviets to make their missiles easier to hit. It was from such results that the Pentagon was able to secure tens of billions more in research on anti-missile systems. Secrecy thus incapacitated Congress, giving the Pentagon the power to unlock appropriations. "You're always trying to practice deception," the secretary of defense who approved the program, Caspar Weinberger, later explained to a reporter: "You are obviously trying to mislead your opponents and to make sure that they don't know the actual facts."

But who are the "opponents" here, and who ultimately pays the price when such deceptions nullify constitutional checks and balances? Consider the landmark case of *United States v. Reynolds*. It started when, in 1948, a B-29 testing new electronic equipment caught fire. Some of the crew bailed out, but three Radio Corporation of America technicians on board died in the crash. Their widows, led by Patricia Reynolds, sued to find out what happened and get compensation to care for their now-fatherless children. But the secretary of the air force filed a sworn affidavit insisting that the mission was highly classified, and that even the accident report would, if revealed, endanger national security. The case went all the way to the Supreme Court. A majority of the justices sided with the government, explaining that "air power is one of the most potent weapons in our scheme of defense," and "newly developing electronic devices have greatly enhanced the effective use of air power." They also ruled that judges could not ask to review what the government is trying to protect, even in their own chambers. Military experiments "must be kept secret if their full military advantage is to be exploited in the national interests."

United States v. Reynolds has been cited in succeeding cases more than 840 times, typically to uphold the government's legal authority to conceal what it is doing without answering to anyone. But when the 1948 accident report was finally released, it revealed nothing about military research. It did reveal that the three RCA technicians had never been briefed on emergency procedures. What's more, the plane itself was unfit to fly, since a known defect that caused the fire had been left uncorrected. With no way of knowing these facts, the widows had been forced to settle their case, and even take less compensation than they were originally offered. So, having allowed these men to die through its own negligence, the air force cheated their widows and children, and perpetrated a fraud on the Supreme Court itself. In this way, the Pentagon used the hexing power of technology as a secret weapon to fight off judicial oversight.

Perhaps only a president has a fighting chance to make officials more accountable, but not if they, too, are fed disinformation. In the 1980s, for instance, the CIA gave the White House the inflated assessments of Soviet research and development. CIA officials knew that their sources were suspected double agents. But they did not want to divulge that fact, lest readers disbelieve what they said. Thus, when faced with facts that risked undermining the national-security rationale for an ever-expanding program of secret research, officials chose to risk misleading the president.

The power of secrecy to prevent accountability created a space for officials to engage not only in magical thinking, but in truly villainous behavior, starting with fooling sick people into becoming guinea pigs in government experiments. In 1945–47, Manhattan Project researchers injected eighteen people with plutonium. Supposedly, the subjects had terminal diagnoses, but it turned out that many of them were not terminally ill—at least not until they were given doses that, in some cases, were high enough to be carcinogenic. One of those injected was only five years old. Even in 1972, as part of a follow-up study, researchers were instructed to tell survivors that the original study had been an experimental treatment for their illnesses (which it was not) and to "*never* use the word *plutonium*." In another study, in 1946–47, a group of alcoholics and homeless people were injected with increasing doses of uranium, all to determine the dosage level that would injure their kidneys.

One could argue that government scientists had an urgent duty to better understand nuclear radiation in the first years of the atomic era, and it would be anachronistic to expect them to have obtained informed consent for all their studies. But in fact, as early as 1946, the trials of Nazi doctors like Josef Mengele had already made experimentation with nonconsenting subjects notorious. For the chief U.S. prosecutor at the Nuremberg war-crimes trials, Telford Taylor, it seemed obvious that only "sinister doctrines" could lead to "macabre science," concluding that "a nation which deliberately infects itself with poison will sicken and die." In April 1947, American doctors submitted recommendations to the U.S. Counsel for War Crimes in Nuremberg that would form the basis of the Nuremberg Code for ethical research. During these same years, army scientists who were researching biological weapons took care to obtain explicit consent from volunteer subjects and brief them about the potential dangers of the experiments.

Government scientists who instead poisoned unsuspecting children and homeless people understood that they might have to answer for their actions. On the very same day that the ethical research recommendations were submitted in Nuremberg, Oliver Haywood, an Army Corps of Engineers colonel advising the AEC, pointed out that acknowledging human experiments "might have adverse effect on public opinion or result in legal suits." Haywood therefore recommended that any documents related to the poisoning of unsuspecting human subjects be classified (or reclassified) as secret. But when defending policies on secrecy, Truman administration officials insisted that they did not classify information to shield officials from embarrassment, but only to uphold national security.

In 1950, a senior AEC scientist was explicitly warned that human radiation experiments had "a little of the Buchenwald touch." But this research not only continued, it greatly expanded in scope. After all, the public was unsuspecting, and secrecy shielded those responsible from having to answer for their actions. The AEC and the Pentagon actively suppressed public discussion of the dangers of radiation, and deliberately downplayed the effect of fallout following nuclear detonations. One reason is that detecting radiation in the atmosphere continued to be an important source of intelligence on Soviet nuclear testing. Officials also worried that greater understanding of the poisonous nature of radiation would make nuclear weapons seem like chemical and biological weapons—which were widely stigmatized in both civilian and military circles—making it harder to legitimize plans to use them in future conflicts.

But researchers took care to target people who were less able to resist these experiments, or to be believed if they publicly protested. In 1953–54, an AEC study injected radioactive iodine in seven newborn boys. Six of them were Black. The following decade, a Pentagon study at the University of Cincinnati subjected over one hundred cancer patients to whole-body radiation to determine how it would affect soldiers on the battlefield. Most were Black, and their average length of schooling was six years. They were not told that they risked severe nausea and disorientation, and several died. The AEC paid MIT researchers to feed radium and thorium to elderly people. The subjects thought they were signing up for research that would keep them healthy. Another AEC-funded study irradiated the testes of inmates at the Oregon State Penitentiary to determine the effect on testicular function. The inmates were required to have a vasectomy afterward "to avoid any possibility of contaminating the general population with irradiation-induced mutants." As a congressional committee later concluded, government scientists were using fellow citizens as "nuclear calibration devices."

Having first irradiated individuals, government researchers began to experiment on whole army units. This research included conducting war games around nuclear detonations to test both the levels of destruction and irradiation, and the physical and emotional impact on American soldiers who might have to fight on nuclear battlefields. With each exercise, the army pushed to move infantrymen ever closer toward ground zero. An hour after the blast, they would be ordered to march single-file to within five hundred yards of the crater, close enough to see dazed and scorched rabbits and lizards. The army petitioned to raise the permissible radiation exposures to more than double what the AEC allowed for its own workers. In 1956, the air force sent five B-57 crews right through irradiated clouds twenty-seven times in six different H-bomb tests in the Pacific. Some of these men received exposures three times greater than the annual maximum dose deemed safe for workers. One AEC health expert observed that the military acted as if levels of radiation that "might hurt other people" did not apply to air-force personnel.

An estimated two to three thousand of the servicemen involved in these nuclear experiments were studied more closely as research subjects. They included paratroopers subject to poly-graph tests before and after they were ordered to march into a nuclear-blast zone, before anyone had even checked the site's radiation levels. Only a little over a third of the paratroopers admitted that they had any concern about the situation, com-pared to 79 percent of those in a control group, who did not actually face the danger. The blood-pressure readings of the study subjects were significantly higher when they were asked about it. In one test, over a third of the subjects recorded heart rates of a hundred beats per minute or more.

And yet, even as their hearts were pounding, these paratroop-ers fell in line and followed orders, marching to ground zero. "Nothing to get panicky about," one observer said before a test, summing up the soldiers' attitude. "Nobody's lost any sleep over this at all." If the observers were accurately recording what the men said, it may not have just been a normal reluctance to dis-play fear in front of one's fellow soldiers. All of them had sat for several hours of "indoctrination lectures" intended to reassure them that the tests were safe. Afterward, the observers reported

Forward, march!

that the soldiers had a touching faith in government scientists. "We wouldn't have been afraid anyway," one observer related, "because we know the Army couldn't afford to take risks." "I don't think the government would risk the lives of the troops," another added. Decades later, it was deemed impossible to measure the effect of radiation exposure on these men's cancer rates, because government researchers had not even preserved the data. But it was clear that, taken as a whole, "atomic veterans" had elevated rates of thyroid cancer and leukemia.

Training often involves taking risks, and such risks must be set against the potentially greater risk of sending untrained troops into battle. But preparing soldiers for the rigors of battle is different from experiments with unknown hazards. Even the organizers—let alone the troops—did not know the level of risk in these experiments. It would take years for symptoms to start showing up. Moreover, secrecy made it impossible to have an informed discussion about what level of danger was acceptable, or to help veterans manage the risk through early screening, diagnosis, and treatment. Altogether, over two hundred thousand military personnel were exposed in these nuclear tests.

The AEC also started to treat whole communities of American citizens—men, women, and children—as test subjects, and kept that fact secret even when officials knew the experiments jeopardized the subjects' safety. In 1949, scientists deliberately released radioactive iodine into the air from the plutonium-reprocessing plant in Hanford, Washington. They wanted to test a theory about how they might observe the Soviet nuclear program. But because of faulty methods and unpredicted weather, the radiation plume extended hundreds of miles, from northeastern Washington to south-central Oregon. In nearby towns, radiation was measured on vegetation at levels hundreds of times higher than what was considered tolerable at the time. The level in Walla Walla, some fifty miles away, was as much as five times higher than what would now be considered too radioactive for milk or food consumption even during a nuclear emergency. And yet officials rejected suggestions that they should issue a health warning.

Even the 1949 incident accounted for only 2.3 percent of the total radiation released from the Hanford plant for the period of 1944–1951. But officials seemed more worried about public discussion of the hazard than about the hazard itself. As one physicist put it, "Not all the residents will be as relaxed as the one who was recently quoted." And what did this proud citizen say? "Living in Richland is ideal because we breathe only tested air."

Some government-funded military research now seems less sinister than strange. And, when we look back, certain of these

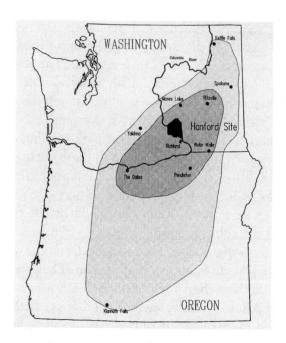

Oregon milk or Washington apples? Pick your poison!

experiments can even look silly. But the men responsible were deadly serious at the time, and there were commonalities uniting all these efforts—whether scientists aimed to control minds or control the weather, defoliate the Vietnamese countryside or irradiate the upper atmosphere. Government officials tried to make such research secret, even when it did not start out that way. This made it possible to experiment on unwitting subjects and evade external oversight. But it took men of extraordinary hubris and recklessness to exploit their freedom of action and seemingly infinite resources to the fullest. They expanded these programs—sometimes by orders of magnitude—without stopping to measure the harm or consider unforeseen consequences, and sometimes without even verifying whether their research was producing valid results.

For instance, scientists had long speculated about whether it might be possible to use airplanes to seed clouds in order to accelerate the formation of rain droplets, and experimented with dry ice and the chemical silver iodide. In 1946, Irving Langmuir believed he had achieved a breakthrough, and began to seek military funding. Generals and admirals—including Dwight Eisenhower himself—attended his cloud-seeding demonstrations. He excitedly pointed out that, in one day, even an average hurricane unleashed as much energy as four hundred twenty-megaton bombs. In 1947, Langmuir seeded clouds in the path of a hurricane that was heading out to the Atlantic, curious about whether he might be able to deflect its course. It doubled back and slammed into Savannah. The military eventually took over this research and classified it as top secret, and Langmuir directed hundreds of experiments across the United States and off its coastal waters—experiments that were poorly controlled, and never substantiated his sweeping claims.

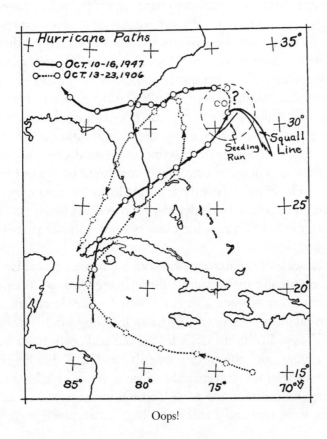

Oops!

During the Vietnam War, the Pentagon ran an enormous covert operation to seed clouds over the Ho Chi Minh Trail so as to bog down communist efforts to supply the Viet Cong. American planes made thousands of cloud-seeding sorties, but no verifiable data demonstrated any increase in rainfall. Subsequently, the U.S. government repeatedly denied or stonewalled when asked about the operation.

Unable to stop the insurgents and weapons streaming down from the North, the U.S. military sought to deny them cover so as to bomb and strafe them more easily from the air, spraying poisonous herbicides all across the Vietnamese and Laotian countryside. The consequences would be more dramatic than those induced by cloud seeding, and prove impossible to conceal. U.S. military planners initially intended the herbicide program to be covert and "experimental," but the South Vietnamese government instead decided to announce it publicly, again using the word "experiment." Robert McNamara advised President Kennedy to expand the program so it could "test all conditions."

These "experiments" and "tests" eventually dumped eleven million gallons of Agent Orange and other herbicides over some ninety-three hundred square miles, turning crops black and killing more than a third of Vietnam's mangrove trees. But for the five years of the operation, the U.S. military did not even evaluate how people were reacting to being dosed with dioxin, a highly toxic chemical compound contained in Agent Orange. They would go on to develop multiple forms of cancer, and their offspring had severe birth defects, such as spina bifida and anencephaly, a condition in which one is born without parts of the brain and skull.

The scale of the nuclear-weapons testing program also escalated, eventually involving all those living downwind of these detonations in Nevada and the South Pacific. It continued to be shrouded in secrecy, notwithstanding lingering uncertainty about the predictability and safety of radiation exposures outside testing areas, and the urging of AEC and U.S. Public Health Service experts for greater public disclosure. The effects of just one such experiment, the 1954 Castle Bravo test in the Marshall Islands, were two and a half times larger than planned, produc-

ing fallout over seven thousand square miles of ocean—far outside the exclusion zone. Hundreds of Pacific Islanders had to be
hastily evacuated. Officials still tried to keep the incident secret,
but that became impossible when a crew of Japanese fishermen
came ashore with severe radiation sickness. As for the islanders, they became subjects of a long-term study of the resulting
tumors and leukemia.

Despite this experience, Pentagon planners set their sights
ever higher. As we have seen, in the early Cold War period some
scientists hypothesized that a barrage of nuclear detonations in
the atmosphere could disable incoming warheads as they passed
through the resulting radiation belt. From August to September
1958, the government hastily organized a series of experiments
to test this concept, detonating 1.7-kiloton nuclear bombs at
increasing altitudes. Operation Argus, named after the all-seeing,
unsleeping Greek god with a hundred eyes, left a cloud of elec-
trons trapped in the Earth's magnetic field for weeks afterward.

The effect turned out to be too weak to stop incoming warheads, but would prove dangerous when, after a temporary suspension of nuclear tests, the Pentagon resumed this research on
a much larger scale—almost a thousand times larger. In 1962,
it launched a 1.4-megaton weapon 250 miles over the Pacific.
"Starfish Prime" produced a brilliant aurora, which could be
seen in New Zealand and Brazil. The explosion created an electromagnetic pulse that disrupted communications, set off burglar
alarms, and knocked out hundreds of streetlights in Honolulu,
some eight hundred miles away. The damage had only just
begun. One by one, orbiting satellites began to malfunction as
they passed through the newly formed radiation field. It fried
their electronic circuitry and damaged their solar arrays.

It still seems strange that scientists and engineers thought
it was a good idea to conduct experiments at such a large scale,
gather little or no data about the damage, and then escalate by
orders of magnitude. The first radiation testing involved eighteen people in 1945–47; it expanded to over two hundred thousand military personnel in the 1950s. Herbicide spraying covered
fifty-seven hundred acres in 1962, and 1.7 million acres in 1967,
the year the U.S. government first interviewed the subjects of

*"But how do you know destroying the inner
Van Allen belt will create havoc until you try it?"*

their experiment. In the case of the upper-atmosphere tests, the weapons used went from 1.7 kilotons to 1.4 megatons.

Did all of these "experiments" at least add to the sum total of human knowledge? Many of the radiation studies on human subjects produced no scientific papers, or even records of exposure that would have been required for follow-up research. The cloud-seeding work was not well controlled, and the government's own project officer judged the 1958 upper-atmosphere nuclear tests to have been "poorly-instrumented." In addition, the "meager data" gathered from them was kept classified for a quarter-century. As for Starfish Prime, many of the satellites it put out of commission were being used for scientific research. It crippled Ariel I, Britain's first satellite, and disabled Telstar, the famed communications satellite. In total, the experiment damaged or effectively destroyed fully a third of Earth's fleet of satellites, and the radiation belt it created lingered for years afterward.

Although proponents of secret science like to focus on examples in which it has benefited society, insiders from the very beginning of the Cold War worried that the best minds would not be drawn to work that they could not even talk about. Secrecy protected those involved from embarrassment or criminal prosecution, but it also made it much harder to vet experimental protocols, validate the results, or replicate them in follow-up research. One research manager at a Department of Energy weapons lab would later admit, "Far more progress is actually evidenced in the unclassified fields of research than the classified ones." The physicist Robert McCrory, whose own lab received millions in funding in partnership with Lawrence Livermore, Sandia, and Los Alamos National Laboratories, was even more blunt: "Some of the work is so poor that if it were declassified, it would be laughed off the face of the Earth."

We can only guess what, specifically, McCrory had in mind when he said this. There are all too many possibilities. Collectively, they lend credence to the oft-stated concern that secret programs became a refuge for second- and third-rate minds. The wizards of Langley, for instance, considered it a "remarkable scientific achievement" when they managed to prove that cats could be "trained to move short distances." According to a CIA veteran, Victor Marchetti, this achievement was part of a program to determine whether cats could be turned into surveillance devices:

> A lot of money was spent. They slit the cat open, put batteries in him, wired him up. The tail was used as an antenna. They made a monstrosity. They tested him and tested him. They found he would walk off the job when he got hungry, so they put another wire in to override

that. Finally they're ready. They took it out to a park and pointed it at a park bench and said, "Listen to those two guys. Don't listen to anything else—not the birds, no dog or cat—just those two guys!" They put him out of the van, and a taxi comes and runs him over. There they were, sitting in the van with all those dials, and the cat was dead!

The CIA nevertheless commended the "energy and imagination" of the team, and considered them potential "models for scientific pioneers."

It could be argued that a sprawling research program purposely designed to push the envelope will, over several decades, inevitably produce some strange and low-quality research. But in some cases it is possible to make a side-by-side comparison of U.S. government research with research commissioned by another country that had fewer resources but the same goal. For instance, during World War II, American and British forces both used dogs to detect mines. It was delicate, dangerous work, and the dogs sometimes proved unreliable. Both governments therefore mounted research projects in the early 1950s to evaluate and improve dogs' ability to locate mines.

The British just wanted "the facts" and sought out a "trained scientist." They selected Solly Zuckerman, an anatomist expert in animal behavior. He designed the experiment to eliminate the possibility that human handlers were unconsciously influencing the dogs' performance. This required systematically isolating the specific biochemical and physiological factors that might explain success or failure, since either could prove important when mines were odorless. Zuckerman had a strong personal motivation—he had seen the devastating impact of blast injuries when he conducted wartime physiological research with the survivors. His larger agenda was to develop more rigorous experimental methods in animal research. Zuckerman found no solid evidence that dogs could be relied on to detect buried mines.

The U.S. Army, on the other hand, hired a "parapsychologist" named J. B. Rhine. It is not clear why—all the army records were later destroyed. Though his training was in botany, Rhine had become famous for his experiments—never replicated—in extrasensory perception (ESP) and psychokinesis. For Rhine, the study was an opportunity to prove that ESP really existed; he had already gathered a collection of amazing stories of animal ESP. Rhine once again convinced himself that dogs possessed special powers. Army officials found in follow-up work that the results were random, and another study proved to be a complete failure, marked by a "rather conspicuous refusal of the dogs to alert." But Rhine used the army money to seed new research, and found new customers. The Office of Naval Research funded a decade of work on ESP in homing pigeons. In other studies, one of Rhine's colleagues tried to influence a cat telepathically to select one dish of food over another. But here, too, even Rhine admitted that the results were "not spectacular." Alas, the cats proved "elusive."

The U.S. government would spend several decades on the larger program of mind-control research. And Rhine was a paragon of scientific rigor compared with some of the other researchers on the government payroll, who espoused theories of extraterrestrial and ghostly visitations to explain ESP, and were hired by the U.S. Army to consult on psychedelic mushrooms. The CIA's Project MKUltra involved a whole series of experiments on unwitting subjects, using a range of different drugs in order to manipulate them into saying and doing things against their will. It was given carte blanche to operate without the normal Agency accounting controls or need for written contracts. Once again, researchers rapidly escalated their trials with little understanding of the effects. In the first round of an experiment conducted at the New York State Psychiatric Institute, one of the patients, Harold Blauer, was given 0.4 mg of methylenedioxyphenyl-isopropylamine, a drug similar to Ecstasy. The next dose was sixteen times stronger, and Blauer was dead in thirty minutes. When the family took legal action, government lawyers threatened witnesses with prosecution under the Espionage Act. Decades later, CIA Director Stansfield Turner admitted that "some unwitting testing took place," but testified to Congress that the subjects were "criminal sexual psychopaths confined at a State hospital." In fact, Blauer was a tennis pro who voluntarily sought treatment for depression after a divorce.

The CIA also experimented on its own personnel. In one case, the head of MKUltra, a chemist named Sidney Gottlieb, dosed the attendees of a joint Agency-army retreat with LSD. One of the unwitting subjects, an army biochemist named Frank Olson, was traumatized by the experience. Until then, Olson had been an outgoing and devoted family man. Afterward, he sank into depression, overcome with feelings of shame, and would not return home. He told his army supervisor that he wanted to quit or be fired.

Gottlieb was likely alarmed upon being warned about this situation. MKUltra had been approved by the CIA director himself, Allen Dulles, who called the program "ultra-sensitive." But Gottlieb reportedly had not obtained prior authorization before drugging Olson and the others. As an internal Agency report later noted, participants in this work well understood that their methods were "professionally unethical" and legally dubious, and would provoke "serious adverse reaction" from the public if ever revealed. Gottlieb therefore had a powerful motivation to make certain Olson told no one about what the CIA had done to him.

Gottlieb and his deputy decided to take Olson to see a New York doctor. The man had no psychiatric training but did have a top-secret CIA security clearance and experience with LSD. The doctor plied Olson with bourbon and sedatives, and took him to see a performance by a magician, whom Gottlieb was interested in hiring to help dose more unwitting targets. Olson's public behavior became increasingly erratic, and he said that the Agency was "out to get him." The doctor said he would take Olson to a sanitarium to be treated by CIA psychiatrists. But that night, Olson "fell" from the tenth floor of the Statler Hotel in Manhattan.

Gottlieb's deputy was sharing the room with him, and claimed to have been asleep when it happened. His story was that Olson had just crashed right through the window, without opening it first, or even raising the shade. We may never know what happened in that hotel room. But at the time, the CIA was training its assassins to first ply their victims with drugs or alcohol, and advised, "The most efficient accident, in simple assassination, is a fall of 75 feet or more onto a hard surface."

The CIA was clearly prepared to kill innocent American citizens. Six weeks after the Agency covered up what happened to Olson, a CIA mind-control team went on its first foreign assignment. The mission was to slip "artichoke"—likely LSD—into the drink of another unwitting subject and induce him to attempt an assassination of a prominent politician or American official. The artichoke team was primed for action, proudly noting that they "were ready when called upon for support, even though the operation did not materialize." Most of the MKUltra records were later destroyed, so we cannot know what other missions might have aimed to achieve. But CIA mind-control research went on for more than a decade, involved some eighty different institutions, and would eventually cost approximately ten million dollars—about a hundred million in today's dollars.

A whole new mind-control program started up in 1972, this time led by the Defense Intelligence Agency (DIA). The goal of this new program was "to determine whether anomalous mental phenomena (i.e. extrasensory perception and psychokinesis) existed and the degree to which such phenomena might be applicable to problems of national interest." Like MKUltra, it went on for many years, and cost many millions of dollars. How many exactly is still difficult to determine. But a single California contractor, SRI International, would eventually receive $11.3 million (or about $36 million in today's dollars).

Even escape artists and magicians saw that the government was being rooked, and patiently explained to officials how time-worn tools of their trade could easily trick someone into believing in ESP. So, too, did the scientists at DARPA, who concluded that the Israeli illusionist Uri Geller, the DIA's star pupil, was a "charlatan." They thought it was "ridiculous" that Geller had fooled the U.S. government into using taxpayer dollars to see whether he could bend spoons with his brain. They pointed to a host of problems with the ESP and psychokinesis experiments, above all the fact that the people paid to conduct them had a financial incentive to produce positive results.

In 1985, the army commissioned a blue-ribbon panel from the National Research Council to evaluate the program. The panel concluded there was "no scientific warrant for the existence of parapsychological phenomena" such as "remote-viewing"—

sensing the location or appearance of things through sheer mental effort—or psychokinesis. Nevertheless, over the following decade the army conducted between fifty and a hundred more such experiments. In 1995, another review of the remote-viewing program was commissioned, this time by the American Institutes for Research (AIR). Once again, the reviewers found that, because of flaws in the research designs, there was no clear evidence demonstrating the existence of the paranormal.

But the AIR report found something even more damning. After some twenty-five years of experiments, the reviewers concluded, "In no case had the information provided ever been used to guide intelligence operations." Even if some people really do have ESP that cannot be explained by science, the point of the program was not to use government resources to explore the Twilight Zone. It was to support actual missions that would safeguard national security. Yet, despite all the time and money spent—not to mention the human costs—the government's venture into the paranormal proved useless for any legitimate intelligence purposes.

Why, then, did the intelligence community and the Pentagon go to extremes in pursuing such embarrassing "research"? For the same reason why they felt they had license to control the weather and alter the upper atmosphere: because, under the cloak of secrecy, their hubris and magical thinking ran wild. Moreover, controlling people's minds was a prize that was just too tempting to resist. And although the government may have given up on telekinetic spoons, it did not give up on that larger goal. During the first decade of the "Global War on Terror," the CIA pursued mind control through more direct methods— i.e., "enhanced interrogation." The program employed psychological abuse, stress positions, and waterboarding not just to make people talk, but also to discover scientifically rigorous and reproducible methods for compelling subjects to submit to the will of interrogators and lose all sense of personal agency. Just like MKUltra, the enhanced-interrogation program was conducted as a series of "experiments." Here is how the CIA's Office of Medical Services, in a top-secret 2004 document, described the protocol for recording the application of "treatments" to "subjects":

In order to best inform future medical judgments and recommendations, it is important that every application of the waterboard be thoroughly documented: how long each application (and the entire procedure) lasted, how much water was used in the process (realizing that much splashes off), how exactly the water was applied, if a seal was achieved, if the naso- or oropharynx was filled, what sort of volume was expelled, how long was the break between applications, and how the subject looked between each treatment.

The CIA hired a retired air-force psychologist named James Mitchell to enact these methods. Mitchell, too, saw himself as a scientist. As an informed source recounted to the journalist Jane Mayer, after Mitchell took over a case, he told the FBI agents that an interrogation "was like an experiment, when you apply electric shocks to a caged dog, after a while, he's so diminished, he can't resist." When the agents argued that the subject of this experiment was a human being and not a dog, Mitchell retorted, "Science is science."

Waterboarding, "diapering," and stress positions ultimately proved no more effective than ESP or psychokinesis, as the CIA's own internal reviews concluded. Many of the victims had already provided valuable intelligence to their interrogators before they were tortured, and once the waterboarding began, many offered false information in order to make it stop. But the waterboarding did not stop until Mitchell's company was paid eighty-one million dollars.

Secrecy was at the core of all these research programs, starting with the goals they were intended to serve. Whether surveillance cats, magic mushrooms, psychics, or enhanced interrogation, many of the government's most bizarre experiments were intended to reveal secrets. Secrecy was also part of the protocol, because the experiments depended on deception. And it is hard to imagine that any of this research would have happened were it *not* secret. The Pentagon and the CIA have only declassified a small percentage of the original documentary record, and virtually nothing that might reveal "sources and methods." How much more may still be classified, or has been destroyed, as occurred with so many of the MKUltra and "enhanced interrogation" records?

We should be able to trust public officials to use science and secrecy to support a strategy that truly serves national security and upholds democratic values without treating human beings as lab rats or calibration instruments. But, as the Harvard historian of science Peter Galison points out, these two concepts are fundamentally opposed. Science aims to uncover and secure knowledge, whereas secrecy conceals knowledge and surrounds it with misinformation. A strategy that is based on science must therefore keep secrecy to the absolute minimum. Science, after all, is a team effort, wherein cumulative and sometimes rapid advances depend on the free flow of information.

This was already clear over fifty years ago, when the Pentagon's Defense Science Board convened a task force on secrecy. Even in research areas where the United States had a lead, and where the technology was vital to the national defense, the members agreed that sharing knowledge more freely would enhance security. This is what happened when the government lifted wartime restrictions on disseminating knowledge about microwave electronics and computers. The idea was to achieve "security by accomplishment"—i.e., prioritizing technological progress. If, instead, scientists continued to be censored to maintain "security by secrecy," it would be harder to recruit and motivate the best minds, learn from the achievements of others, and expose incompetents and charlatans through rigorous peer review. One member judged that, if the tendency to classify more and more research continued for another decade, "our national effort in weapons research will become little better than mediocre."

Five decades later, the metastasizing problems arising from government support for secret research in pursuit of magic weapons are impossible to conceal. A lack of accountability clearly led to long delays and extortionate costs. Under the cloak of secrecy, government researchers conducted grotesque or ridiculous experiments that harmed countless numbers of people. Perpetrators went unpunished, and victims were left with little recourse—in some cases, because research protocols made it impossible for them to know they had been victimized. And much of the research contributed little or nothing to scientific knowledge or national security.

All this would be just tragic if it were only history. But, alas, this history tarnished the reputation of science itself, creating dangers that we will be living with far into the future. Recall how, back in the 1950s, people had tremendous confidence in government research, like those paratroopers who marched toward the mushroom cloud, or the Washington State resident who felt relieved to live in a place where government scientists tested the air. That had started to change by the 1970s, when CIA mind-control research first came to light. But even in the 1980s, government officials were able to dissuade editors at national newspapers from investigating the radiation experiments, by both playing to their patriotism and pretending it was not worth their attention.

This did not change until Hazel O'Leary became secretary of energy in 1993. A daughter and granddaughter of doctors, O'Leary had grown up in segregated Virginia. She was the first woman and the first person of color to hold this high office. Unlike her predecessors, upon hearing of how her department had experimented on poor and sick people, she announced that she was starting an investigation, and declassified a vast trove of documents. This shocked Washington, but O'Leary thought it was the only way to restore trust in the government's ability to manage a host of technological challenges, like storing hazardous waste and dismantling nuclear weapons.

But the damage was already done. By this point, government scientists in biohazard suits had already become the favored bogeymen in countless Hollywood thrillers. Is it any wonder that, rather than believe officials who say their research serves the public interest, many people now struggle to distinguish science from fiction? Should we deride the suspicions they have about information provided by government spokesmen—whether about vaccines or global warming? By invoking the authority of science for the very worst human-rights abuses, and concealing the evidence or destroying it outright, government officials sowed doubts about everything scientists do. As these doubts have grown, all of humanity has become less secure.

The consequence of this secrecy is therefore not only what we are not allowed to know, or the fact that we don't even know what we don't know. Too many Americans now distrust science itself. So they know even less than they can, and should, just to ensure their own survival.

7

FOLLOWING THE MONEY

When you consider the costs and risks incurred in the name of "national security"—whether the subversion of democratic accountability, a whole series of undeclared wars, surveillance of private communications, experimentation on unwitting citizens, or an arsenal of weapons that can destroy the world—you have to ask yourself: *What is it all for?* Is there some bigger secret overshadowing all the rest, even bigger than the dark state itself, that could explain why—after all of this—the American people do not *feel* very secure?

One after another, every president since FDR has assured us that it's not just about national security, but the fate of freedom itself. America's mission is to defend democracy, and democracy has many enemies. Were it not for the huge, secretive apparatus of departments, agencies, and private contractors, the world would be even more dangerous than it is now, and democracy itself might not survive.

But before Roosevelt took office, before the CIA and the NSA even existed, another president offered a different take on America's mission: in 1925, Calvin Coolidge said, "The chief business of the American people is business." The idea has often been boiled down to an even pithier expression, "The business of America is business," a catchphrase as much for critics as for supporters. Coolidge's successors seldom spoke so plainly, but as they erected a vast national-security state, many critics came to believe that it was really designed to serve a hidden agenda: to protect and promote capitalism.

According to this way of thinking, the idea of defending democracy is just political cover for a constellation of private actors who use the dark state to defend plutocracy. America's "security" has become ever more costly because the Pentagon and the intelligence community subsidize their profit-seeking. The problem, in other words, is not that foreigners hate freedom, as is so often said when some Americans pay with their lives. Instead, most anyone would hate surrendering their economies to a global elite of financiers and industrialists, which seems to be the cost of doing business with the United States.

When you consider the kind of people who are typically put in charge of U.S. foreign policy, this position cannot be dismissed out of hand. It is no secret that the top ranks of the State Department and the Pentagon are filled with corporate lawyers, financiers, and CEOs—men like James Forrestal, Dean Acheson, John Foster Dulles, Robert McNamara, George Shultz, James Baker, Dick Cheney, and Donald Rumsfeld. Similarly, for decades now, presidents have chosen ambassadors for the most prestigious postings from among their wealthiest backers. The relationship is so clear and so consistent that researchers have been able to develop a price list for each ambassadorship, enumerating the contributions any would-be diplomat has to make to the president's campaign or party for a particular post. (For the Court of St. James, it ranges from $1.1 to $4.3 million.)

Why would we expect such people to stop defending (and advancing) corporate interests if that's how they gained power in the first place? Moreover, the aforementioned corporate elites are just the ones we already know about—the ones who exerted influence through public office. Critics would argue that there are other individuals—private individuals—who work behind the scenes advancing hidden agendas, and some of their most crooked deals might never come to light. We have seen how the military-industrial complex itself is a money-making operation— not least for former generals and admirals—especially when it pursues a strategy centered on the procurement of secret weapons. It does not help that so much of this history is hidden from the public decades after the fact. Long-simmering suspicion of secret machinations behind American foreign policy boils over whenever another overseas intervention is contemplated. Protesters spill into the streets, vowing there will be "no blood for oil." They point out that it's usually poor people who must kill or be killed when it's a "rich man's war." As the former CIA agent Philip Agee argued: "US national security, as preached by US leaders, is the security of the capitalist class in the US, not the security of the rest of the people—certainly not the security of the poor, except by way of reinforcing poverty."

In this chapter, we will test these arguments about the "business of America" by analyzing actual data: First, how big and how profitable is the business of building America's arsenal? Is it so remunerative that the military-industrial complex provides its own explanation for U.S. foreign policy? Conversely, if we investigate how foreign policy is made day to day, how much of it is really *about* business—not just the business end of all these expensive weapons, but efforts to promote cross-border trade, foreign investment, and international commerce of every kind? No less important, is this economic agenda hidden, as critics argue? Are the American people being misled as to who is really in charge?

By analyzing millions of government records, we can determine whether and how all this might change over time. We will expose what subjects were most secret in the declassified record of U.S. foreign relations in the 1950s and 1960s, when the military-industrial complex was at its biggest as a share of the country's peacetime GNP under both Republican and Democratic administrations. We will also examine another corpus—orders of magnitude larger—of records from the 1970s, when national policy seemed to whipsaw from the cynicism of the Nixon administration to the idealism of the Carter years. This will include hundreds of thousands of still-classified State Department records. We will combine these techniques to survey U.S. history as a whole with others that zero in on the most sensitive episodes and individuals who have been systematically erased from the official record. They provide a new perspective even for celebrated cases that have long been cited to prove that capitalism itself can be a covert operation: CIA efforts to overthrow democratically elected governments that tried to opt out of a U.S.-centered global economy by nationalizing foreign-owned assets. We will follow the money and combine forensic accounting with a close reading of redacted and unredacted documentary evidence to answer the classic question for solving crimes: who profited?

Taken as a whole, do covert operations represent a viable business model, enriching the people privy to classified information? To the extent that the business of America really is business, subsidized by the U.S. government, did the government actually help businesses succeed—i.e., by profiting the particular firms it promoted abroad—and was secrecy essential to their success? Once we have peeled back the layers of this larger problem, we can grapple with the core question: does all of this make most Americans better off? In a democracy, this question represents the ultimate bottom line.

Our first question is whether the business of preparing for and prosecuting wars itself explains a large part of U.S. foreign policy. Whoever is directly or indirectly employed by the military-industrial complex, or enriched by it, is clearly incentivized to support the current national-security strategy, and to continue concealing its inner workings. Weapons production is not an insignificant part of U.S. industry, accounting for about 10 percent of manufacturing output. Moreover, it is consistently profitable. During periods of growth, like 2001–7, defense hardware firms have outperformed the S&P 500.

But though defense procurement accounts for 10 percent of manufacturing, manufacturing itself only accounts for about 11 percent of the total U.S. economy. It is an even smaller percentage of the U.S. workforce, less than 10 percent, down from more than 30 percent in the 1950s. Further, the defense sector may be consistently profitable—in part because it has shed workers—

but its profits are not particularly impressive. A profit margin of 10 percent means a good year for firms like Lockheed Martin, General Dynamics, and Northrop Grumman. This makes them more like utility companies than the corporations capitalists look to as leaders, such as Apple, Amazon, and Alphabet.

Arms manufacturers have also shown little inclination to find new customers even when appropriations fall, such as at the end of the Cold War. They doubted their capacity to make as much money producing other kinds of goods. Instead, these periods saw consolidation, with larger firms swallowing smaller firms, such as in the 1990s, or diversifying beyond weapons manufacturing to provide government services, a growing trend over the last decade. Perhaps the poster child for this particular trend is the software startup Palantir, which found a valuable niche in promising to integrate siloed government information systems. But after a strong start, it has yet to take off. It has not cracked the top ten U.S. contractors in market capitalization, or the top hundred defense firms worldwide in revenue. And Palantir has yet to turn a profit.

One might have expected such a technology-intensive sector to be more lucrative, when you consider how military R&D can spin off civilian products. But, again like utility companies, defense contractors are highly regulated. The government often classifies even nonsensitive research, and imposes controls on the export of products with potential military and intelligence applications, hindering the rapid development and mass production of new technology. This was a continuing source of tension in the development of computers and networking. There are important exceptions, such as DARPA's funding for research on machine learning. And machine learning more generally is what helped firms like Amazon and Alphabet become so profitable. But they were able to commercialize this technology precisely because most of the research was never classified. Spending to improve the technology in warplanes and warships not only has few civilian applications but also imposes opportunity costs on the larger economy. This capital would likely have generated more innovation and more profits if it had been invested in directly productive sectors of the economy.

If the research-and-development work of government contractors is not especially lucrative for the companies themselves, does it at least help industry in general? Other countries use their intelligence capabilities to support the civilian economy directly, such as through industrial espionage and technology theft. But, although we will see later how U.S. intelligence agencies and private corporations sometimes collude in covert operations, the government does not typically share information with American companies to help them compete. In fact, the involvement of U.S. companies in supporting government surveillance has generally been *bad* for business. When the Snowden revelations came to light, the reputational damage to Silicon Valley was estimated to cost U.S. firms anywhere from $35 to $180 billion. The real figure is incalculable. And in none of Snowden's leaked documents was there any indication that anyone in the government considered the massive risk that the intelligence community's collection practices represented for the most dynamic part of the American economy. Did they really think it could be kept secret forever?

It is certainly hard to make a business case for America's many wars, notwithstanding bromides about the freedom of navigation or the rule of law. If anything, Vietnam, Iraq, and Afghanistan were costly distractions for international commerce, excepting, again, the companies that directly profited. For instance, in August 2021, the CEO of Fluor Corporation, David Edward Constable, told investors that the company had "successfully completed our assignment in Afghanistan"—an assignment that included $3.8 billion in contracts in the preceding six years. Kabul fell nine days later. Building an Afghan military around complex equipment that could only be maintained by foreign technicians was indeed a successful business strategy. But did the fourteen *trillion* dollars the Pentagon spent overall from 2001 to 2021—one-third to one-half of it for contractors—represent a profitable investment for the rest of the private sector?

Iraq, with all its oil riches, would be the most plausible case, but the facts of U.S. involvement there are particularly revealing. If the Bush administration's invasion and occupation had really been a war for oil, you would expect that American corporations would have won all the contracts to control Iraq's oil fields.

Instead, the biggest fields went to non-U.S. firms—in fact, many of the contracts went to firms based in China and Russia.

It is therefore implausible to think that capitalists have all been complicit in the secret machinations of the military-industrial complex. In fact, there has long been a business argument against government surveillance, excessive military spending, and open-ended overseas commitments, from "America First" opposition to FDR to the Koch brothers' libertarian critiques of the foreign-policy "Blob." The surveillance state and perpetual war might benefit some well-connected contractors, the argument goes, but when the government picks winners, we all lose. The Kochs spent large sums to advance these arguments, and so, too, have other capitalists with otherwise opposing politics, like George Soros. Moreover, far from buying and selling politicians, many wealthy people experience political contributions as a shakedown, and politicians are past masters at taking money from rich contributors without necessarily delivering the goods.

So the military-industrial complex cannot, by itself, explain national policy. This is especially true if one takes seriously the ideology that underlies this entire way of thinking, which is based on the assumption that political power is ultimately a function of economic power. The business of building weapons is just not big enough, and the U.S. economy is too diversified to support such a narrow agenda. Rather than looking at the defense sector as emblematic of capitalism writ large, it is better understood as a highly regulated industry with relatively low returns on investment. In fact, it may even be a money loser for the economy as a whole, considering the costs—including opportunity costs—of building secret weapons, fighting forever wars, conducting global surveillance, and controlling technology exports. The collateral damage all this inflicts on the "made in U.S.A." brand is beyond measure.

If the economics of the military-industrial complex don't explain foreign policy, then could it be the other way around? Could national-security policy—including the military-industrial complex itself, but also diplomacy, intelligence gathering, and foreign aid—be seen as secretly serving private economic interests more generally, above all by promoting international trade and investment? Though political crises and military operations attract all of the attention, could it be that much of the business of everyday foreign policy is actually *about* business?

There is no easy answer to this question. Most presidents do not describe the business of America as business, at least not in public. Many higher-up officials take a pay cut to work in Washington, and take umbrage at the suggestion that they are shills for corporate interests. Even cynical calculations to start or prolong wars can be made in service of idealistic goals, rather than just greed. Lyndon Johnson, for instance, refused to accept defeat in Vietnam because he thought that doing so would endanger his program to build a Great Society in America. Coolidge himself insisted, in that same 1925 speech, that, at their core, Americans are idealists, and value some things even more than wealth.

To get at the true motivations animating American foreign policy, historians typically discount what politicians say in public and read lots of once-secret documents. The most important are gathered together and published by the State Department in *The Foreign Relations of the United States* (*FRUS*). By law, State Department historians have access to every government archive, and must certify that *FRUS* constitutes a "thorough, accurate, and reliable" account of U.S. foreign policy. In order to ensure that the government is meeting its mandate, an outside committee of scholars with security clearances reviews what gets redacted and which documents get left out. It takes about thirty, forty, or even sixty years for cables, memos, and transcripts to appear in *FRUS* volumes, which is usually enough time to permit the release of even highly sensitive records.

But *FRUS* now totals more than three hundred thousand documents, and overall an estimated 1.4 *billion* pages of documents have been declassified since 1980. No one person could read even a fraction. Instead, historians have to read selectively, dipping into a few *FRUS* volumes, and then branching out to look in the archives. In evaluating their work, we are limited to what the researchers have chosen to tell us about what they found. We have no way of knowing what they might have missed, ignored, distorted, or—in some cases—made up.

There is a new and better methodology for getting some perspective on otherwise impossibly big questions like defining the "business of America." It is called "distant reading." Instead of scrutinizing particular files and selecting a few documents to represent the larger whole, it involves surveying entire collections with computers to inventory and analyze their contents. In recent years, the State Department has published all the *FRUS* volumes in digital form. That means we can now start looking at the complete official record of U.S. foreign relations. We have already seen how one distant-reading technique, topic modeling, can be used to calculate the "half-life" of state secrets, and to confirm that secrets about nuclear weapons are much more closely guarded than secrets concerning UFO sightings. In this case, we can use it to identify which topics are the most discussed and which are the least, and then calculate how much policy makers concerned themselves with international trade and investment.

We programmed an algorithm to divide this corpus of *FRUS* documents dating from 1932 to 1980 into distinguishable topics and then assigned each a name after reading the highest scoring documents for each one. They included everything from the Arab-Israeli conflict to the establishment of diplomatic relations with China. The largest topics account for ten thousand or more documents, and the smallest (like Portuguese decolonization and Norwegian security) account for fewer than two thousand documents each.

So which topics dominate *The Foreign Relations of the United States*? It turns out that the top three topics are all business: international financial diplomacy, the Export-Import Bank and foreign credit, and the balance of trade. So, too, are many of the other topics, each of which makes up a smaller but still-significant part of "the people's business." These include shipping, commodities trading and regulation, import and export controls, and foreign property, as well as distinct topics for several commodities, including disputes over oil, the steel trade with Europe, foodstuffs, and rubber production.

So the data supports the idea that, for half a century—years that witnessed World War II, the Korean and Vietnam Wars, superpower détente, and a renewed Cold War—U.S. policy makers actually focused on American trade and finance more than on any other set of issues.

But recall that, for critics, prioritizing trade and investment is wrong not just because they believe that other issues, like human rights and the environment, are more important but also because this business is conducted in secret, and on behalf of a relatively small elite. Topic modeling gives us different ways to determine whether that turns out to be true. For instance, by reading the documents most characteristic of a particular topic and then calculating how many of these documents are classified, we can get a sense of which topics were the most secret.

Topics by Number of Documents in
The Foreign Relations of The United States

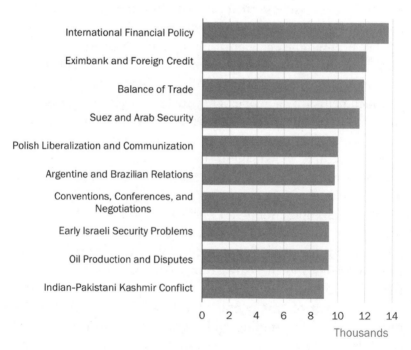

It is not *all* about the money, but economic-related topics are at the top of the agenda in the official record of U.S. foreign relations.

Some of these documents related to business were indeed secret, or even top secret. For instance, the top document for international financial policy was an "Eyes Only" 1947 cable that included highly sensitive information about Britain's precarious financial situation after World War II. "Please guard this information with extreme secrecy," the U.S. ambassador sending it wrote, "and take every possible precaution to insure against leaks." However, the two top documents regarding the Export-Import Bank and the balance of trade are not even classified. One concerns a loan by the bank to China for purchasing American cotton, and the other relates to a dispute over flax imports from the USSR. This is hardly the stuff of spy thrillers or conspiracy theories.

When we examine the proportion of documents for each topic that were classified, the picture seems even clearer. If you exclude unclassified communications—and ones whose clas-

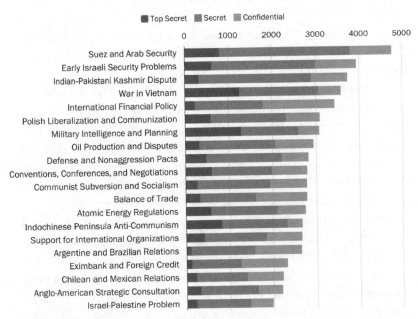

Topics by Number of Secret Documents in
The Foreign Relations of the United States

■ Top Secret ■ Secret ■ Confidential

0   1000   2000   3000   4000   5000

Suez and Arab Security
Early Israeli Security Problems
Indian-Pakistani Kashmir Dispute
War in Vietnam
International Financial Policy
Polish Liberalization and Communization
Military Intelligence and Planning
Oil Production and Disputes
Defense and Nonaggression Pacts
Conventions, Conferences, and Negotiations
Communist Subversion and Socialism
Balance of Trade
Atomic Energy Regulations
Indochinese Peninsula Anti-Communism
Support for International Organizations
Argentine and Brazilian Relations
Eximbank and Foreign Credit
Chilean and Mexican Relations
Anglo-American Strategic Consultation
Israel-Palestine Problem

Economic diplomacy falls down the rankings when you count secret documents: many others turn out to be more sensitive.

sification level is not clear—and just tally the number of top-secret, secret, or confidential communications, these finance and trade topics are no longer among the largest ones. The Suez Crisis, Israeli security, Indo-Pakistani border wars, and Vietnam all inspired more classified communications. Instead of being ranked one, two, and three, the top trade- and finance-related topics drop to rank five, twelve, and seventeen. Even among the classified records within finance and trade, relatively few were classified at the highest levels compared with other topics.

But distant reading, when applied to an entire corpus spanning several decades, misses what can only be discovered when we study the historical record more closely, such as the impact of different presidential policies, pivotal episodes, and particular individuals. Nefarious dealings, and the extremes to which the government might have gone to serve particular business interests, do not necessarily leave behind a big paper trail. Some documents released in *FRUS* are heavily redacted. There are whole volumes of other documents that have still not been published, usually because the State Department historians cannot get other agencies—typically, in the intelligence community and the Pentagon—to clear them. We don't know what lies beneath those redactions, or what is in those documents that have not been released, and may never be released.

In the past, this problem would have been the end of the inquiry, and the beginning of endless speculation about conspiracies and cover-ups. But here again, by combining big data and big computing, we can continue peeling back layers that conceal answers to the question of what might still be secret even now. We won't find all the answers, of course, but we can get measurably closer to the truth.

One way to find out what—or who—is still being concealed in the official record is to calculate the percentage of documents that have redacted text within each topic. The same technique can also show whether there's a difference between Democratic and Republican presidents. In this case, we looked at the Eisenhower years, 1953–60, and the Kennedy and Johnson administrations, 1961–68.

For the 1960s, the topics with the highest and lowest percentage of redactions clearly indicate their level of sensitivity for the Kennedy and Johnson administrations. The topic with the highest percentage is defined by the words "source," "arms," "area," "mission," "information," "officers," "base." (This time we did not assign the topics names, but let the topic models' top words speak for themselves.) When you look at the documents in this cluster, they concern matters like a covert bombing campaign in Laos, and U.S. and Soviet arms shipments to Africa. Material concerning military strategy and arms exports is obviously highly sensitive. The topic with the smallest percentage of redacted documents relates to "aid," "million," "assistance," "economic," "countries," "Japan," "foreign." Documents in this topic are thirteen times less likely to be redacted than the highest-percentage topic. We can also infer, by the sheer volume of policy memoranda, meeting minutes, and diplomatic cables, that, of the two, the "aid," "million," "assistance" topic took much more of the time and energy of U.S. government officials. It contains twenty-five times more documents than the one on covert operations and arms shipments. It is just not particularly sensitive to the U.S. government, which reviewed and released almost all these records in the 1990s, with very few redactions.

In the Eisenhower years, the topic with the smallest percentage of redactions again relates to foreign aid and trade. Its characteristic terms start with "foreign," "exchange," "bank," "department," "export," "market," "grant." Clearly, one of the least secret topics of the Eisenhower administration's foreign policy concerned international business. But the topic with the highest percentage of redactions is more complex, and highly intriguing. It is defined by the words "oil," "day," "man," "times," "companies," "arabia," "construction." Many of the documents most representative of this topic relate to covert operations. A large number also concern U.S. oil companies, including some that characterize their relationship to the CIA. When you read them, you realize why the algorithm clustered these documents together: they discuss things like how oil companies can help manipulate the number of barrels per day shipped to countries, such as Guatemala and Cuba, that had seized American-owned assets—countries that, crucially, were targeted for regime change. The algorithm has led us right to what could be critical evidence of the dark state colluding with corporate interests. Does it, finally, prove that U.S. foreign policy has been a foot soldier for global capitalism?

Even without this new evidence unearthed by data mining for redacted documents, the 1954 campaign to overthrow the government of Guatemala has long been a notorious example of how the hidden hand of bribery and extortion—not the "free market"—is what best explains the way the world works under U.S. hegemony. In studying this event, historians usually focus on the role of one American corporation, the United Fruit Company. It is understandable, considering that several members of the Eisenhower administration had connections to the company. In fact, people in Central America called it El Pulpo—"The Octopus" —because it seemed to have its tentacles in everything. UFCO owned 42 percent of Guatemala's land, and turned much of the country into a vast banana plantation. It had benefited from the support of Guatemala's longtime dictator, Jorge Ubico Castañeda, who helped UFCO drive competitors out of business. The company owned almost all of the railways and port facilities, and thus the only practical means of traveling between the Atlantic and Pacific coasts, or transporting goods to market. It also owned the telegraph and telephone systems. Even in Guatemala City, the capital, UFCO could control communications.

So there are good reasons to look more closely at UFCO and Guatemala to find out what happens when a revolutionary movement challenges U.S. corporate interests. But when the focus narrows in this way, UFCO can start to assume mythical proportions—in literature as much as history. In Gabriel García Márquez's 1967 masterpiece, *One Hundred Years of Solitude,* he recounted the true story of how striking banana farmers in Colombia were massacred by soldiers called in at UFCO's behest. The company's power seems insuperable, with their man in Colombia even controlling the weather, summoning a whirlwind in the novel's climax to blow the grieving town into oblivion. The Chilean poet Pablo Neruda, in his 1950 collection, *Canto General*, described UFCO's local confederates in places like Guatemala and Colombia as "bloodthirsty flies." The company itself is depicted as a force of nature, its ships laden "with the treasures from our sunken lands."

So not only has UFCO's role in the 1954 Guatemala coup long been notorious, the company has loomed large in how critics imagine the impact of capitalism in shaping North-South relations across the entire hemisphere. Historical research on the 1954 coup usually starts ten years earlier, with an uprising that overthrew the UFCO-supporting dictator Ubico—one of Neruda's "flies." The new government was democratically elected and progressive, and initiated a series of social reforms. Over the following years, it built schools, enforced labor regulations, and supported union organizers. In 1951, one of the leaders of the 1944 uprising, a brilliant Army colonel named Jacobo Árbenz Guzmán, was elected president in a landslide. With his people behind him, Árbenz started to challenge UFCO directly. He announced his intent to build a road from the Atlantic to the Pacific to break UFCO's railway monopoly. He passed an agrarian-reform law that expropriated nearly half of the company's land holdings, compensating them at the same low valuations UFCO had long used to underpay its taxes. Now, and for the first time, many Guatemalan farmers did not have to work on company plantations, but could instead till their own fields. UFCO executives reacted with growing fury. The value of their Guatemalan holdings was equivalent to 15 percent of the company's market capitalization. In response, they fed stories about communists in the Árbenz government to the media and the State Department, and UFCO demanded that Washington take action.

Though they are usually downplayed in this UFCO-centered account, which credits the company with the power to distort American perceptions and policy on Guatemala, some of these stories were actually true. Árbenz personally considered himself a communist, though he thought Guatemala wasn't yet ready for communism. So, too, did his top advisers. Some held influential positions in his administration, such as the heads of the National Agrarian Department, which was responsible for redistributing expropriated land, and the government information agency. They seemed to go out of their way to thumb their noses at Washington, praising the progress realized under communism in Eastern Europe, and mourning the death of Stalin.

So, in the summer of 1953, Eisenhower approved a plan to overthrow Árbenz's government. In Diego Rivera's "Glorious Victory," a mural depicting how this decade of democracy ended in a military dictatorship, UFCO is once again depicted as driving events. Secretary of State John Foster Dulles, his CIA director and brother, Allen, and Ambassador John Peurifoy dole out dollars to their chosen client, Colonel Castillo Armas, over the dead bodies of Guatemalan revolutionaries. Indigenous farm workers trundle bananas up the gangplank into a big white ship with an American flag emblazoned on the prow (and, more faintly, "UFCO"). It is as if the coup were a drug deal, only for tropical fruit instead of cocaine.

But was it really about the bananas? And does it make sense to attribute this kind of power to just one company, however well connected? Turning back to those heavily redacted "oil," "day," "man" documents, we find that many concern another coup—on the other side of the world—that has a surprising connection back to Guatemala. Less than a year earlier, Eisenhower ordered the CIA to help overthrow Iranian Prime Minister Mohammad Mosaddegh after he nationalized British oil holdings and attempted to reduce the country's dependence on global energy markets. Administration officials worried that his government would instead come to depend on communist support. Once Mosaddegh was removed, local communists were arrested, and the State Department brokered a deal in which American oil companies gained control of nearly half of a new consortium that had exclusive rights to develop and export Iranian oil.

So what happened in Guatemala was consistent with a broader policy to prevent communists aligned with Moscow from taking over countries that were politically and economically integrated with the West. But the two coups were not just variations on a theme. There were important causal connections, which we can see when we zero in on one of the top documents in that most heavily redacted topic. Far and away the largest number of redactions in that document covered up the name of the "man" in "oil," "day," "man." Examining it more closely reveals just what a conspiracy looks like when it finally comes to light but the government still does not want you to be able to identify the conspirators.

When the original volume of *The Foreign Relations of the United States* that pertained to Guatemala was released in 1984, there was not one document that even mentioned the CIA plot to overthrow its government—Operation PBSUCCESS—perhaps because the CIA was then plotting to overthrow the government of Nicaragua. This particular document was not released in a new volume until almost twenty years later, and has been overlooked by scholars until now. It shows how the CIA recruited executives from oil companies to help squeeze the Guatemalan government.

Like many other countries at the time, Guatemala was heavily dependent on U.S.-owned tankers and refineries to import oil and gas. The document describes a meeting in New York organized by the chief of the CIA's Western Hemisphere Division in the Directorate of Operations, J. C. King, and a mysterious, nameless "Mr. [*name not declassified*]." They met with the special assistant to the president of one of these oil companies (very likely Esso, now Exxon, or Texaco, both of which were headquartered in or near New York City). Apparently, they were meeting because the CIA's contact at the company could "no longer be relied on." Perhaps hoping to win their confidence, the oil man promised to disclose nothing to anyone except the company president, at which point the CIA man and his mysterious associate got to the heart of the matter: They wanted to know if it was possible to begin reducing Guatemala's supply of oil until it was depleted. They also wanted to find out who would need to know about it. The oil man immediately began to describe how this could be handled without raising suspicion, and kept to a small circle inside the company. Though much of the document is still redacted, the details reveal the atmosphere of bonhomie between men who share the same sense of what it means to be a "loyal American," building trust by comparing their military service and second homes.

More than that, the fact that the document remained classified for so long shows how careful the CIA was to closely guard information about the ways in which public officials conspired with private businessmen, and how the U.S. government still does not want to come clean. Decades later, the historian Piero Gleijeses interviewed one of the CIA planners, Richard Bissell, and showed him proof of a meeting between CIA Director Allen Dulles and representatives of one of Guatemala's oil suppliers. Bissell explicitly denied that they had even considered squeezing Guatemala's stockpile. In fact, when more documents were declassified, they showed how it was part of the plan all along: the CIA was calling in favors, pressing the beneficiaries of one coup to help with another.

The threat of being cut off from fuel supplies weighed heavily on Árbenz as renegade elements of the Guatemalan military, led by the U.S.-backed Colonel Castillo Armas, gathered across the border in Honduras. He had little doubt that his army could defeat them in battle, but he could not see any way of winning the endgame. The United States "could cut off our oil supplies," he told his top adviser. "The economy could not withstand it, nor would the army."

In June 1954, as the insurgents prepared to invade, Árbenz invited Esso's man in Guatemala, Roberto Saravia, to a meeting at the presidential palace. He wanted to know about how many days of fuel supplies were on hand, how fast they were being drawn down, and whether there were any new deliveries on the way. He also asked if Guatemala could purchase a million gallons of gasoline in barrels. Saravia told him it was impossible, and then went to the U.S. Embassy to report everything Árbenz had told him. A week later, Guatemala's foreign minister also asked to meet the Esso representative, and pressed him on what he knew about efforts to cut off fuel supplies. Saravia denied knowing about any such plans.

So the CIA worked hand in hand with oil companies to convince Árbenz that, at the same time Guatemala was about to be invaded, his fuel supplies were running out. What happened in 1954 therefore involved many players, and at this point it is far from clear that all this was orchestrated just for UFCO.

If we want to understand who—or what—was driving events we have to try to identify the man in "oil," "day," "man," Mr. [*name not declassified*]. This is the classic technique for resolving this kind of mystery, asking the question "*Cui bono?*" If we can identify that person, the one who ultimately benefited, he might be able to tell us why Árbenz was finally driven from power.

Narrowing down a list of suspects requires sifting through many thousands of secret documents. In that one heavily redacted document, there may be as many as seven names of CIA operatives or CIA assets. Alas, exposing even one of them may violate the Intelligence Identities Protection Act. But we have seen how algorithms can automatically match redacted and unredacted versions of documents. It is also possible for algorithms to automatically extract people's names from thousands of snippets of unredacted text using another distant reading technique, "Named Entity Recognition." When applied to all the documents researchers have managed to get declassified at presidential libraries since the 1970s, it allows us to reveal which names are *disproportionately likely* to be blacked out, and then rank them in a list of "America's Most Redacted" during the period when Eisenhower was president. It does not necessarily give us the identity of the specific person who helped orchestrate the Guatemalan oil embargo, but it reveals the *kind of* people who otherwise would remain "Mr. [*name not declassified*]." You can see the list in the figure on the following page.

We have already seen one of these names, that of the Iranian prime minister, whom the CIA helped overthrow after he nationalized foreign-owned oil assets. CIA Director Dulles was even more intent on taking down Patrice Lumumba, the charismatic elected leader of the Republic of the Congo, who aroused American anxieties as a potential leader of national-liberation movements across Africa. The head of MKUltra, Sidney Gottlieb, was sent to Katanga to poison him.

Others on the list who also died of unnatural causes, like

"America's most redacted" (from top, left to right): Charles Malik, Lebanese representative to the United Nations; Ismet Inonu, former President of Turkey; Faisal bin Abdulaziz Al Saud, Crown Prince of Saudi Arabia; Patrice Lumumba, first Prime Minister of the Republic of the Congo; Mohammad Mosaddegh, Prime Minister of Iran; William Pawley, businessman and former ambassador; Louis Joxe, secretary general of the French foreign ministry; Harmodio Arias Madrid, former President of Panama; Willy Brandt, mayor of West Berlin; Azzam Pasha, Secretary-General of the Arab League.

King Faisal of Saudi Arabia, were key allies of both the United States and American oil companies. The French diplomat Louis Joxe likely made the list because he was *too* friendly with Washington. In 1958, the Eisenhower administration secretly tried to use the International Monetary Fund and the Export-Import Bank to force France to withdraw from its colonies in North Africa. This was something that Joxe actually favored, but which many in Paris suspected was intended to give U.S. corporations control of Saharan oil fields. Joxe's name—which he shared with a son who became prominent in French politics—was redacted in documents that might have led his countrymen to suspect him of disloyalty.

So there are different reasons why the U.S. government would conceal someone's name when releasing decades-old documents, and not all of them involve multinational corporations or secret U.S. economic diplomacy. Even when they do, these episodes sometimes turn out to be complex. In the case of the Saharan oil fields, for instance, there is no evidence that U.S. companies were impelling the government to push France out of Algeria, but not because they weren't greedy. At the time, energy markets were glutted, so U.S. companies concealed the extent of reserves they already controlled across the border in Libya in order to avoid any pressure to invest in their development. Even Vice President Nixon considered it embarrassingly cynical. Much of Libya's population suffered from malnutrition at the time. After peanuts, their chief export was scrap metal they stripped from World War II–era armored vehicles.

Thus, just as the oil cartel kept secrets for the dark state, and used its monopoly power—far more powerful than bananas—to punish communists, the dark state sometimes kept secrets for big oil. And uncovering the underlying meaning of these redactions requires more than a superficial reading of economic history. In no case is this more true than that of the only American among "America's most redacted"—William Pawley.

When he finally died of a self-inflicted gunshot wound, the *Miami Herald* described Pawley as "a swashbuckler in a gray flannel suit." In public, he was a tremendously wealthy businessman who entertained presidents and movie stars at his various estates, whether poolside in his waterfront Miami Beach mansion, or in the boxwood gardens of an 860-acre northern-Virginia horse farm. But in secret, Pawley had a decades-long career organizing covert operations, from working with Franklin Roosevelt to maneuver the country into war with Japan through the back door, to advising Richard Nixon on how to punish countries that tried to expropriate U.S.-owned assets. One discovers upon looking at one of these unredacted documents that Eisenhower might have given Pawley overall responsibility for U.S. foreign policy in Latin America if he had not already been notorious by 1960 for being a "friend of dictators." So Pawley continued working behind the scenes, in secret. And the full scope of his work—including the crucial role he played in the Guatemalan coup, and again in Cuba—was not revealed until long after he died.

Pawley could be said to have been part of America's burgeoning military-industrial complex almost from birth—starting with his boyhood in Cuba, where he worked in his father's business, supplying the U.S. Navy base at Guantanamo, and continuing when he attended military school in South Carolina. As a Florida real-estate speculator, he gained and lost a fortune, then recouped it by selling airplanes for Curtiss-Wright. After becoming president of China's national airline, it was Pawley who convinced Roosevelt to organize the covert operation that supplied the nationalists under Chiang Kai-shek with American pilots and planes to attack the Japanese, the "Flying Tigers." Pawley himself was well compensated for sales commissions on all the aircraft Curtiss-Wright began shipping to China, skirting the Neutrality Act by treating it as a private venture. Thus, even before the CIA existed, before the government had an official classification system, Pawley was already running clandestine missions for the White House.

As far back as the 1930s, critics already saw characters like Pawley as exemplifying how—as the legendary marine general

Smedley Butler put it—"war is a racket," conducted for the benefit of wealthy insiders. Butler would have known about the business of America. He famously complained about how—in China, Mexico, Haiti, Cuba, Nicaragua, Honduras, and the Dominican Republic—he had been made to serve oil companies and UFCO as "a high class muscle man for Big Business, for Wall Street and the bankers." In fact, Butler warned that businessmen were prepared to turn the United States itself into a military dictatorship to protect their wealth and power.

But to Pawley, U.S. entrepreneurs represented America at its best, and when their overseas investments were endangered, this presaged danger for all Americans. He thought the U.S. government should therefore protect American businesses abroad, and the businessmen, in turn, should work in league with U.S. diplomats, soldiers, and spies. At a time when the United States had little or no intelligence network abroad, businessmen would thus serve as an early-warning system for foreign threats, and serve as assets for covert operations—especially when their own assets were at risk.

Truman decorated Pawley for his work in China. But after communists took over, and the new government in Beijing nationalized foreign-owned assets, Pawley grew increasingly disenchanted with Democrats. In 1952 and 1956, he raised millions of dollars to elect and then re-elect Eisenhower president. He became a regular visitor to the White House, and Eisenhower grew to love fishing for bass from a ten-acre man-made lake at Pawley's Virginia estate. By that point, Pawley controlled vast holdings across Central and South America, including bus companies in Miami and Havana, and oil and mining companies in the Dominican Republic.

So, when Eisenhower was uncertain about whether the CIA plan for Guatemala would work, he called Pawley at his Miami mansion and asked him to come to Washington. Pawley took an office at the State Department and, together with the U.S. Steel representative for Latin America, reviewed and approved the operation. It is not clear what part Pawley might have played in the effort to impose an oil embargo, though he did work with the navy to embargo arms shipments to Árbenz. He also assumed a decisive role when, two weeks after Guatemala's foreign minister pressed the Esso representative to resume fuel deliveries, it seemed like the CIA plan was unraveling.

Despite Pawley's angry protestations, CIA Director Dulles had only authorized the shipment of three fighter-bombers for the insurgents' air force, likely in fear that a full squadron of U.S.-supplied P-47 Thunderbolts would make the American role too obvious. But by June 22, five days after the rebel forces crossed into Guatemala, two had been lost in action, and the third had crash-landed in Mexico. One of their main targets had been Guatemala City's fuel depot. That morning, they had finally succeeded in taking out one of the gas tanks, shooting it full of holes and setting some sixty thousand gallons ablaze. A source told the CIA that attacking the other tanks would eliminate the government's gas supply. The CIA station chief in Guatemala City continually urged aerial attacks on the capital, insisting that his contacts in the army would not otherwise move against Árbenz: "Bomb repeat Bomb."

As the insurgents' invasion stalled, even CIA planners lost confidence. Dulles agreed that Colonel Castillo Armas was hardly capable of defeating the Guatemalan army unassisted. At Pawley's urging, the CIA director decided to double-down by dispatching three more fighter-bombers, and the two men went to the State Department seeking immediate approval.

In an unpublished memoir, Pawley recalled what happened next. Unfortunately for the CIA director, his brother, the secretary of state, was not in town. So they saw a new assistant secretary, an international lawyer named Henry Holland. He flat-out refused to allow the delivery of additional planes. He seemed pleased that the whole operation—which he considered dishonorable—was about to fall apart. To Dulles and Pawley, the need for action was urgent, but Holland responded in lawyerly fashion: "It's not quite that simple, old boy." He pointed out that, since there was a civil war in Guatemala, arming insurrectionists to attack a sovereign government was clearly illegal. "Dammit," Dulles exclaimed, "I can't work like this!"

So the three men went to see Holland's immediate superior, Undersecretary of State Bedell Smith. Holland carried three heavy law books into the meeting, but they made little impression on Smith. Recall that he, too, had overseen covert operations when he was CIA director. But, rather than allow himself to be overruled, Holland wanted the president to decide.

Holland, Dulles, and Pawley went to the White House, where they were ushered into the Oval Office, Holland still carrying his three law books with him. He started to explain the complexities, but Eisenhower interrupted him. "'Henry,' he said, 'put away the law books. Let's discuss this from a practical viewpoint.'"

Eisenhower then turned to Dulles, and asked what chance Castillo Armas had of prevailing without air support. As Pawley writes in his memoir,

> *"Nil," Dulles answered.*
> *"And if we supply them?"*
> *"Perhaps twenty percent."*
> *Ike turned to me.*
> *"Bill, go ahead and get the planes."*

Pawley told the Nicaraguan ambassador he needed to immediately approve the funds necessary to pay for three more fighter-bombers to be leased to the insurgents. The ambassador said this approval would take several days, whereupon Pawley went to his own bank and withdrew $150,000. Then he drove the ambassador to the Pentagon, the two walked inside, and Pawley opened up his briefcase to start handing over stacks of bills. One can only imagine how Pentagon officials reacted. But they proceeded to count the money, and the Nicaraguan ambassador went ahead and signed the contract. That same evening, the planes flew to Panama, and went into action the next day. Now the CIA gave the pilots new orders: whereas before they had only had permission to strafe the gas tanks, now they could blow them up.

In the end, they did not have to. Resuming bombing runs on the capital was enough to make senior Guatemalan army officers realize that the United States would not give up, and they began to defect. One of them, Carlos Enrique Díaz, a friend of Árbenz, convinced the president that by resigning he might still be able to save the revolution. But when Árbenz ceded his place to Díaz, the United States demanded the new president accept a cease-fire, declare martial law, and arrest the remaining leaders or face an "all out bombing attack." Díaz quickly gave way. Árbenz's supporters were subjected to humiliation and reprisals. Árbenz himself spent the rest of his life in exile, wondering if he could have done more.

As Diego Rivera intuited when he painted this "glorious victory," the centerpiece of the whole operation was the American threat of inflicting death, destruction, and inevitable defeat—which he represented with a carefully balanced, unexploded bomb with Ike's grinning visage. And the artist was not wrong in showing the CIA handing out bribes to seal the deal—some of these officers really were paid off to form a junta. But the mural is misleading in the way it balances all the violence depicted on the right side of that bomb with bundles of bananas being hauled off to the UFCO ship on the left, as if it were all about the bananas. U.S. officials colluded with several companies and corporate elites, not just UFCO. All of them preferred to act covertly and in concert, and none wanted to see any confiscation of foreign-owned assets succeed. But rather than acting to ensure America's banana supply, they worked at the behest of an administration that was determined to prevent communists from realigning any country with Moscow. Eisenhower was not doing their bidding, as would become even more clear in the aftermath of the coup, but he did protect their identities. In Pawley's case, his name was systematically scrubbed from the official record, to the extent that the president's appointment book was doctored to remove mentions of his visits to the White House. That is why his name is missing from almost every account of the Guatemalan coup—including Eisenhower's own.

The defeat of the Guatemalan Revolution, coming on the heels of the overthrow of Mosaddegh, only emboldened Pawley and his co-conspirators. Shortly afterward, the president asked him to serve on a panel to review CIA covert operations. All four members were from the corporate world, including a senior partner at Milbank, Tweed, and the founder of an accounting firm who also led several corporate boards. Even the panel chair, General James Doolittle—of the famed 1942 Doolittle Raid on

Tokyo—had long since left active duty and was then a vice president and a director at Shell Oil.

Like management consultants, the four businessmen praised CIA leadership but also advised that it cut costs by eliminating less productive employees. But most of all, they told Eisenhower that the CIA had to be more ruthless:

> There are no rules in such a game. Hitherto acceptable norms of human conduct do not apply. . . . We must develop effective espionage and counterespionage services and must learn to subvert, sabotage and destroy our enemies by more clever, more sophisticated, and more effective methods than those used against us. It may become necessary that the American people be made acquainted with, understand and support this fundamentally repugnant philosophy.

As we have seen, the CIA's Project MKUltra was already plotting assassinations. After the Guatemalan coup, and this endorsement, the Agency would go even further in targeting foreign leaders, as in the case of Lumumba. But Eisenhower did not ask the American people if they supported such a policy. After all, even the proponents told him it was repugnant. Instead, when a new revolutionary government, this time in Cuba, expropriated foreign-owned assets, including some of Pawley's own properties, Eisenhower once again tapped him to help organize a covert operation. Together with the CIA, Pawley developed much the same business strategy as the one used against Árbenz seven years earlier: working with other businessmen to sabotage the Cuban economy and help arm an insurgency. The CIA even set up their training camp in Guatemala. Eisenhower said he knew of "no better plan," and his only worry about it was that it would become publicly known. "Everyone," he told a group of the government's highest-ranking officials, "must be prepared to swear that he has not heard of it." Even thirty years later, the CIA did not want to reveal how "a group of New York businessmen" was "organized as cover for this activity," and redacted this part of the planning discussion.

When the plan finally came to fruition under Eisenhower's

successor, and it failed spectacularly at the Bay of Pigs, critics like Pawley were all too ready to blame Kennedy for underinvesting in air support. The CIA launched a new operation to assassinate Castro, Operation MONGOOSE, while Pawley backed his own band of saboteurs. They were among the first to warn that the Soviets were deploying nuclear missiles on the island. Even after the crisis was resolved and the missiles were removed, Pawley continued backing anti-Castro schemes, such as one effort to kidnap Soviet soldiers so they could testify that the communists were violating the agreement that ended the Missile Crisis. Pawley was not one to give up easily.

———————————

So there is ample evidence, across multiple cases, demonstrating both the deep involvement of private interests in illegal operations, and systematic efforts to cover up these efforts decades after the fact. There is also evidence to suggest that this was not just a matter of operational security. Did they cash in on this secret information? Those deemed to have a "need to know" the CIA's plans could benefit from trading on what they knew. Of course, it is hard to prove insider trading in such a cold case. But, recently, a team of economists studied fluctuations in stock prices for companies affected by these CIA operations. They analyzed the four aforementioned CIA coups (successful and unsuccessful) against governments that had expropriated the property of American or multinational companies—in Iran, Guatemala, Cuba, and Congo—plus Chile. In the last case, the International Telephone & Telegraph Corporation even offered to pay the CIA a million dollars (about $6.7 million in 2020 dollars) to overthrow Salvador Allende, the country's elected leader.

The team found that, in the case of Guatemala, United Fruit's stock rose in value right after the operation to overthrow Árbenz was approved. In one week, an inside trader would have realized a 3 percent return. Of course, United Fruit was just one of twenty companies with confiscated assets in the five countries included in the study. But the study also showed overall increased trading activity and abnormally high returns among these companies after these coups were authorized.

Should we be surprised? It's not for nothing that people called the CIA "the Company." Many of its first officials were recruited from Wall Street. Conversely, former CIA Director Bedell Smith went on to join the UFCO board of directors in 1955. So one can easily see how UFCO-connected officials or collaborators like Pawley might have cashed in on insider knowledge of these hostile takeovers.

For some, this might be enough to prove that the core, the rotten core, of the dark state was capitalism, QED. And if anything, Philip Agee was unfair when he dismissed the CIA as "nothing more than the secret police of American capitalism." Rather than rent-a-cops, "the Company" could be seen as a rather effective hedge fund, with a diversified portfolio—far more expansive than fruit—and a reasonable rate of return.

But there is one problem with this conclusion: none of the above facts prove that Washington was acting at the behest of American businesses, or that it actually helped them, even in a notorious and seemingly clear-cut case like Guatemala. As it turns out, in 1951, the Justice Department was planning to file an antitrust suit to force UFCO to divest itself of its utility-and-railway monopoly in Guatemala. Truman's National Security Council decided to delay the case, because the State Department worried it would have "serious foreign policy implications." But on the very day when the CIA-supported insurgency invaded, Secretary of State Dulles took up the question in an NSC meeting:

> On balance it might be positively advantageous to U.S. policy in Latin America if the suit were instituted. Many of the Central American countries were convinced that the sole objective of United States foreign policy was to protect the fruit company. It might be a good idea to go ahead and show them that this was not the case, by instituting the suit.

His brother, Allen, advised a one-month delay, "by which time the situation in Guatemala would have been clarified."

Sure enough, as soon as Árbenz was out, the Justice Department filed suit, beginning years-long litigation that ultimately forced UFCO to sell its Guatemalan holdings and end its efforts to maintain a monopoly. This was the beginning of a long decline in the company's fortunes.

We have seen how oil companies helped the CIA overthrow Árbenz, and it would seem like an obvious quid pro quo after the Agency helped these companies gain a foothold in Iran. But, in fact, they had been reluctant to make the risky Iranian investment, during a time when the market was already glutted, and insisted the Eisenhower administration formally request their involvement. They, too, were under threat of antitrust litigation, and proceeded only after the Justice Department provided assurances this expansion would not increase their legal exposure.

In other cases from the same period, the U.S. government did little to help companies recover expropriated property. In 1952, the Marxist leaders of Bolivia nationalized tin mines owned by multinational corporations, which until then had played a dominant role in the country's export economy. Corporate lobbyists in Washington railed against the government in La Paz and its plans to redistribute their property. Bolivia paid lip service to the principle of offering "prompt, adequate and effective compensation," but only because the Eisenhower administration insisted the country would not otherwise attract more foreign investment. It then became one of the world's biggest recipients of U.S. foreign aid per capita. Six years after the nationalization, the frustrated U.S. ambassador complained he had seen "nothing but words and no action" to compensate the mining companies. Eisenhower nevertheless stuck with the policy of supporting Bolivia, hoping to show that the United States would help different kinds of governments—even Marxist ones—as long as they did not signal allegiance to Moscow.

In the case of the Árbenz government, aligning with Moscow was the cardinal sin, not challenging UFCO. As Holland explained to the Bolivian ambassador, even if Guatemala had paid every dollar that the company claimed it was due, Eisenhower's policy "would not change one iota." Árbenz's top communist adviser did not disagree: "They would have overthrown us even if we had grown no bananas."

So, rather than the CIA's working as "high class muscle man for Big Business, for Wall Street and the bankers," even a Republican administration could use big business as long as these businessmen made themselves useful, and then throw them under the bus as soon as doing so served Ike's definition of the national interest.

Moreover, covert ops were not common enough, or successful enough, to constitute a viable business model, at least as far as one can determine from the information the CIA has released to the public. Fifty such operations have so far been acknowledged. A large number of them involved propaganda activities, such as subsidizing anticommunist cultural organizations, student groups, and media outlets like Radio Free Europe. It seems unlikely that capitalists got rich from the CIA funding of French literary magazines (and it is equally unclear whether such work was really essential in saving capitalism). In fact, one of the CIA's favorite partners was the AFL-CIO, which used CIA money to support anticommunist labor organizations and anticolonial trade unions.

The CIA's explicitly political interventions in other countries usually centered on funding pro-American candidates and political parties rather than training and arming insurgents. This includes the CIA's very first covert operation, an attempt to influence the 1948 elections in Italy. As for the more violent operations, the CIA has acknowledged authorizing paramilitary activities in twenty-one countries, including China, the USSR, Indonesia, Tibet, Bolivia, and Angola. Though we may hear a lot about the CIA's "successes," like Guatemala, Iran, and the Congo, more than 60 percent of their paramilitary operations failed to achieve their objectives, according to the Agency's own historian.

So while there is circumstantial evidence that some engaged in insider trading at the expense of those who lacked access to classified information, it would seem they would have been more likely to lose money than make money. The more violent operations were not usually successful. Even when they were, policy makers could sell out private-sector interests when it suited them.

This analysis is based on the operations that have been acknowledged. How can we know the number or nature of other operations that have not yet been revealed? The possibility of a gap in our knowledge should make us skeptical about the CIA historian David Robarge's claim that precisely 86 percent of CIA covert operations were intended to "promote or protect democracy or resist dictatorship or dictatorial forces." As for *The Foreign Relations of the United States*, the very fact that it is the *official* record of U.S. policy will make it untrustworthy to skeptics. Moreover, even though three hundred thousand documents is a lot of documents, that number is still only a tiny fraction of the original documentary record. Every single one of the documents in *FRUS* was hand-picked by a State Department historian, and as such still reflects what that historian thinks was important (or should have been important) in U.S. foreign policy.

Fortunately, for those still not convinced, there is one more body of evidence available for analysis, the biggest of all, and it is the same one that Chelsea Manning and Julian Assange drew from in what they called "Cablegate." We will examine their charges in chapter 9. But Manning's cables are less than 1 percent of the records in the State Department Central Foreign Policy Files (CFPF), and it is a quirky and nonrandom sample (very few cables involving Russia, for instance). If, instead, we examine the CFPF records that have been released from 1973 to 1979, when the State Department started using the same electronic records system, there are more than three million.

Crucially, this collection includes the metadata for hundreds of thousands of still-classified records from these same years. Though the full texts were withheld, because of either national security or personal privacy, this metadata includes the "from" and the "to," the date, subject, classification level, and TAGS. TAGS, or "Traffic Analysis by Geography and Subject," categorized each cable to help officials carry out research on the State Department's far-flung operations. TAGS includes everything from Internal Political Affairs (PINT) to VIP Travel Arrangements (OVIP) to Embassy Security (ASEC). Each cable was assigned one or more TAGS, so that each record could be sorted according to subject, country, or organization.

This National Archives collection so far encompasses just seven years of State Department diplomacy, but if you have to choose any seven consecutive years to represent the full range of U.S. foreign relations—from the most "realist" to the most idealist—the period 1973–79 really is ideal. It starts in the era of Nixon and Henry Kissinger, who were famous for détente with the USSR but infamous for their secrecy and cynicism. After the Ford interregnum, it continues into the presidency of Jimmy Carter, who initially championed transparency and human rights. It ends with the Iranian Revolution, a renewed Cold War, and a big new covert operation in Afghanistan, where the United States began to arm the mujahideen to fight the Soviets and defend Persian Gulf oil.

The 1970s therefore provide an extreme test of whether business interests are paramount regardless of who occupies the White House. And whereas until now we have been peeling the layers of the onion, from public statements to secret documents to (un)redacted text, analyzing the CFPF allows us to see the whole onion, all at once: what diplomats were doing day to day, hour by hour, country by country, on more than 140 different subjects.

It turns out that, by far, the biggest category of State Department communications, fully 37 percent, relates to business and economics, including military sales and assistance. By contrast, all communications related to politics and policy amount to just 21 percent. But business and economic communications are much less likely to be secret, whether at the time they were delivered or when they were reviewed for declassification decades later. Of the thousands of communications related to trade and investment, only about 2 percent were classified as secret or even confidential. Moreover, just 2.5 percent have been withheld, a third of the number withheld among the politics and policy messages.

To be sure, there was some variation over time. In 1977, Carter vowed to pursue "a foreign policy that is democratic, that is based on fundamental values, and that uses power and influence . . . for humane purposes." Sure enough, during his presidency the number of communications related to social issues like the environment and family planning doubled, from 5.7 percent in 1974 to 11.7 percent in 1979. Communications specifically related to human rights spiked particularly dramatically in 1977, almost tripling in number from 1976. The percentage of State Department communications related to economics and business declined, from 39.5 percent under Nixon and Ford to 34.7 percent under Carter.

One might imagine William Pawley turning over in his grave. In fact, in January 1977, two months after Carter's election victory, he killed himself after a long illness. Right up until the end, he railed against environmentalists and anyone who opposed the procurement of new weapons systems. But Pawley could rest easy. Under Carter, American diplomats still spent far more time on business and economic affairs than on things like human rights, a category that never even reached 2.5 percent of the total. Though Carter was a born-again Christian, he was also a businessman. He staffed the senior ranks of his administration with fellow members of David Rockefeller's Trilateral Commission, which was dedicated to deepening global economic integration. As we will see in the next chapter, the supposed idealism of the Carter administration was a political campaign strategy

The World According to the State Department

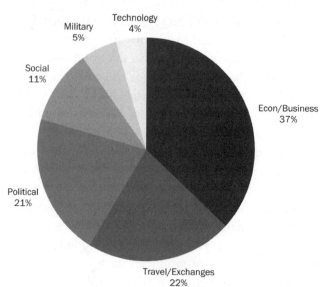

that had little effect in places that really mattered to American policy makers.

Nevertheless, exporters argued that Carter's State Department had the wrong priorities, and was not doing enough to help U.S. businesses. They wanted commercial attachés to be trained and rewarded for assisting American exporters, and not shifted from job to job and country to country like other Foreign Service officers. The Carter administration agreed, and almost seven hundred personnel were transferred from the State Department to the Commerce Department. During the Reagan years and right up to the present day, the U.S. Commercial Service has taken the leading role in championing U.S. business interests.

Thus, analyzing millions of diplomatic communications from the 1970s, including still-classified cables, confirms what we found studying the official record of U.S. foreign relations during the 1950s and '60s. Under both Democratic and Republican administrations, both those who prided themselves on their "Realpolitik" and those elected on a platform of idealism and transparency, business promotion and economic diplomacy have been at the top of the agenda. For the most part, that agenda is not hidden. And when it appears a president is giving insufficient attention to business affairs, corporate lobbyists will take action, reaching inside departments and agencies to assert their interests.

Long after Nixon, Ford, and Carter left office, presidents from both parties have continued to promote American businesses while claiming their foreign policy creates economic opportunities for all Americans. They have even tried to sell wars to the public as good for the economy, as when George H. W. Bush's secretary of state, James Baker, claimed the Gulf War was really about "jobs, jobs, jobs." But even after emerging victorious with few American casualties—and much of the cost of the war borne by Gulf states—Bush became vulnerable when the U.S. economy sank into another recession.

In 1992, another Southern Democrat defeated Bush's re-election bid in a campaign premised on the belief that "it's the economy, stupid." Upon taking office, Bill Clinton followed through on his promise to create a National Economic Council, signaling that his administration would not prioritize defense and foreign policy over economic policy. But, in fact, economic policy had been a priority all along, certainly when compared with things like human rights, for Democratic as much as Republican administrations. In the rare cases when this involved the use of covert operations, individual companies could be used as tools, but it was always part of a larger strategy to defend and advance capitalism.

All this gets us closer to a full accounting of the relationship between capitalism and U.S. national-security strategy, and closer to the bottom line: even if the priority given to American business is no secret, has it benefited most Americans, or only a select few? This is the hardest question of all, but we can tackle it in two parts.

First, we need to know whether business promotion actually benefits anyone. Hard-core capitalists might well ask whether the government would be more effective if it simply got out of the way. In fact, economists have been able to show that just establishing consulates or embassies is associated with a 6 to 10 percent increase in exports, and setting up an export-promotion agency in another country correlates with a 12 percent increase. If we directly measure the effort these consulates, embassies, and agencies are making over time, we can get an even more precise estimate of the difference it makes. Diplomats have been dismissed as "striped-pants cookie pushers." But when you read what they do from day to day, you find that they actually spend a lot of time pushing U.S. exports.

Of course, diplomatic work benefits some firms more than others. Small and medium-sized companies will likely need more government help than will big multinationals, and start-ups more than older firms with long-standing trade relationships. The government can provide otherwise expensive information about market conditions in foreign countries as a public good. It can also help settle disputes before they reach the stage of a formal complaint—something that could be particularly costly to a smaller company.

Overall, we found that each 10 percent increase in communications about trade promotion predicted a 3.56 percent increase in trade. So, if the United States had a thousand trade-promotion communications with a country over the course of a year, and exported ten billion dollars' worth of products—about as much as we export to Ireland and Peru—ten more communications would predict an increase in exports of $35.6 million.

To be sure, correlation is not causation (it is only correlated with causation!). But there are good reasons to believe that the work of diplomats to promote exports really does promote exports. The results hold up even when we exclude individual countries that might have had a disproportionate impact on the data. We also find that trade promotion in different countries correlates with export levels for all years when we examine them individually, so the effect is consistent over time.

Ultimately, someone has to pay for all the striped pants and cookie pushing. But the cost of embassies and diplomats is tiny compared with the value of international trade. The State Department budget in 1978 was about $1.4 billion. U.S. exports that year totaled about $136 billion. Our findings indicate that, if the State Department had increased trade promotion by about 4 percent, the resulting increase in exports would have generated overseas sales for U.S. businesses in excess of the entire departmental budget.

The relationship between trade and diplomacy—and the fact that both work better when they are transparent—should not be so surprising. It would not surprise the business leaders who have benefited from this long-standing and very public bipartisan policy, and who rallied to defend appropriations for trade promotion when they were under threat at the start of the Trump administration. On the other hand, surrounding international trade negotiations in secrecy can provoke a backlash. In the case of the Trans-Pacific Partnership—the terms of which Congress members were not even allowed to discuss, under threat of prosecution—secrecy led to repudiation by leaders of both parties.

But the fact that the government has been effective in promoting international trade seems to be a secret to many Americans. When they are surveyed, most seem to think that the State Department is in the business of giving away American money. In poll after poll, responders regularly estimate that a quarter of the federal budget goes to foreign aid. That would amount to about $1.11 trillion, or more than twenty times the current size of the State Department budget. In the federal budget, less than 1 percent, or $39.2 billion, actually goes to foreign aid, a tiny fraction of the amount Americans assume is allocated for that purpose. In fact, historically, most of it had to be spent purchasing goods and services from firms headquartered in the United States, another form of export promotion. This proportion has declined in recent years, in part because the "Buy American" requirement was a notoriously inefficient form of corporate welfare. But even though more of these funds are now being spent abroad, about two-thirds of American foreign aid still goes through U.S.-based organizations, whether contractors, NGOs, churches, or universities.

So there is compelling evidence that the business of America really is business. It can sometimes be a very shady business. But, compared with other aspects of American diplomacy, most of this business is out in the open. Most amazing of all, even if Americans don't know it, when it comes to promoting trade and investment, the government actually seems to know what it is doing.

But what, in the end, does that do for most Americans—say 99 percent of Americans? The second part of our bottom-line question is really much bigger than the first. Does promoting the "business of America"—and American businesses above all—convey benefits beyond the wealthy 1 percent? Measured per capita, Americans are much more prosperous than before the period of U.S. hegemony. But the very top income stratum has reaped most of these gains, and controls an increasing proportion of stock, real estate, and liquid capital. This is especially true during the last fifty years, a period that also saw a threefold increase in the relative importance of international trade in the U.S. economy. Americans may have seen gains in their standard of living, some of them hard to measure with economic statistics.

But opening up the U.S. economy has also made many feel more insecure, since more and more jobs can be outsourced, even the middle class are becoming poorer relative to their richest countrymen, and the policies that our leaders insist are necessary to defend the American way of life put us on a permanent war footing. All this may help explain why so many Americans think that the U.S. government gives their money away: they simply do not see how U.S. foreign policy benefits them personally, do not know critical information about that policy because it is kept from them decades after the fact, and do not feel they have much say in the matter.

The very wealthiest Americans, the William Pawleys of this world, have grossly disproportionate power to shape public policy through campaign contributions and political lobbying, and see tangible benefits from their participation in a global economy that runs under American hegemony. Even if most of the political class is not directly invested in the military-industrial complex, and even if some personally believe our current national-security strategy is too costly, it continues because they allow it to continue. And while it does, the dark state absorbs about half of all discretionary federal spending, squeezing out programs that would directly benefit poorer Americans, like improved childcare, education, and public health.

So this is why our question of who really benefits is not only hard to answer, it is impossible. Or, rather, it is impossible for any one person to answer in a book, no matter how much data they deploy. Whether the relatively small gains most Americans see from U.S. economic hegemony are worth all the costs and risks of maintaining this power over the rest of the planet can be answered only by hundreds of millions of people deciding for themselves, in democratic elections. But Americans do not have a real choice if they do not know what they are voting *for,* and what they could be voting *against.* That, in the end, is the core problem, but it actually starts at the top, with the president's sovereign power to decide what the people are allowed to know and when they are allowed to know it. Unpacking *that* problem can finally explain how this whole system of government secrecy has spun out of control.

8

SPIN

After the Japanese attack on Pearl Harbor, American forces continued to suffer a series of crushing defeats, culminating with
the surrender of the last U.S. forces in the Philippines. Officials
in Washington feuded over what to say about the fighting. In
June 1942, Roosevelt formed the Office of War Information to
coordinate and tighten control of what some critics were already
deriding as government censorship and propaganda. Three
months later, the OWI issued new rules to unify and rationalize
a government-wide system for identifying and protecting sensitive information. They expanded what could be legally protected
to anything related to the national defense but also prohibited
unnecessary classification and reserved the higher gradations of
secrecy for only those things that could cause serious harm if
revealed. The new regulations affirmed the "need to know" principle, and stipulated how secret information would be carefully
labeled and communicated to the minimum number of people.

That same month, FDR went on a two-week cross-country
tour, ostensibly to inspect how industries were mobilizing to
produce war materiel. The real reason Roosevelt was traveling
was to help Democratic candidates in the 1942 elections, since
Republicans were expected to make major gains in the House and
Senate. He wanted to control the press coverage, so he decided

to make up his own rules. He used an OWI ban on reporting troop movements to keep his own whereabouts secret. In this way, he limited the press pool to three wire-service reporters, and required that they keep silent until he returned to the White House. Even then, the reporters would have to submit their copy for approval. It was the first time in history that the media were prevented from reporting on an extended presidential tour, one that would take Roosevelt to twenty different cities.

"You know, I'm not supposed to be here today," Roosevelt told fourteen thousand cheering shipyard workers in Portland, who apparently had a need to know. "So you are possessors of a secret—a secret even the newspapers of the United States don't know. I hope you will keep it a secret. . . ." As the crowd laughed, the journalists fumed, but there was nothing any of them could do about it.

Whether he realized it or not, Roosevelt was setting an example of how to use this new system that was supposed to protect national security to advance his own partisan interest. After all, these were his rules, because the OWI was his office. But as

FDR's secret mission

his coast-to-coast tour amply demonstrated, the scope and variety of what could be classified—along with the number of people who might also manipulate official secrecy—were growing at a dizzying rate, as dozens of shipyards, plane factories, and military bases filled with war workers and service members. Though Roosevelt meant it as a joke, it was actually true: many thousands of people—more every day—were coming to know things the government was officially classifying as dangerous information that could aid the enemy. They were subject to disciplinary action, even prosecution, if they broke the rules. But as a practical matter, the president could not control what they would do with all these secrets. Moreover, any president who hoped to win voters' trust could not be seen to be hiding behind a system designed to deny them information.

In this chapter, we will see how every president since Roosevelt therefore tried to have it both ways: they use executive orders to control what the public is allowed to know about "national security," and the OWI rules served as the template. Every element—from standardizing gradations of secret information, to delimiting who would have access to those secrets, to mandating procedures for safe handling—has appeared in all subsequent orders on national-security information. But at the same time, presidents have kept presenting themselves as open and accessible, because appearing open is how they can appear honest, and thus worthy of the public trust. To manage the news, and make it work to their advantage, they disclose information—including classified information—to push their preferred issues, whether overtly, using the "bully pulpit," or covertly, through authorized leaks. On the other hand, politically appointed officials all across the executive branch continue to classify and thereby conceal not just dangerous information that could threaten national security, but many things they simply prefer that the public ignore, whether elite cynicism, illegal surveillance, managerial incompetence, or military insubordination.

But as that vast military-industrial complex continued to grow, after a brief pause following the atomic bombing of Japan, so, too, did the number of officials who could classify information and leak it for their own reasons. After conjuring the power of secrecy, and setting it loose, presidents found that it had a power all its own. Thousands more people, many career civil servants, began creating their own secrets, and jealously protecting them, making it harder to identify and protect what mattered to the president personally. At the same time, they could leak whatever they liked, undermining the president's ability to manage the news cycle. The Espionage Act seemed like a worthy scepter to enforce sovereign presidential power over secrecy. But the capaciousness of the law made it unwieldy. A law that could actually stop leaks by criminalizing a journalist's disclosure of classified information—a real official secrets act like the one in the United Kingdom—would make it much harder for presidents to have "plausible deniability" in planting information they want to reveal. It would also entail negotiating with Congress to define and delimit secrecy, and depend on courts to interpret and enforce its provisions.

So every president since FDR has continued trying, and failing, to control the dark state through executive fiat. In principle, their sovereign control over secrecy both enhances—and hides— executive power. But by trying to have it both ways, insisting the president has autonomous power over national-security information while pretending to be transparent, presidents have created the worst of both worlds: a system that denies us the information we need to hold public officials accountable, but does not actually protect information that really could endanger national security. Meanwhile, the denizens of the dark state can continue working in the shadows, learning more and more about *us*, while continuing to make certain we learn as little as possible about *it*.

Roosevelt was a master of public relations, but he was also a deep believer in secrecy, for legitimate purposes and otherwise. In some cases, he had good reason to worry that the media might endanger national security. When the *Chicago Tribune* reported that America's victory at the Battle of Midway resulted from advance knowledge of the Japanese plan, it was appropriate to launch a grand-jury investigation to determine whether and how the reporter had learned about U.S. code breaking. The *Tribune* claimed he had simply guessed at the right answer. In fact, a naval officer had shown him intercepted Japanese communications, and there was a strong case for convicting both of them under the Espionage Act. The navy decided that producing witnesses with direct knowledge of what happened was not worth the additional risk of alerting Japan about the breach. This was an early example of a recurring problem: prosecutors sometimes drop cases because the discovery process and a public trial will further expose sensitive information.

But Roosevelt also went after reporters just for writing stories that criticized his administration, and sometimes put journalists he did not like under surveillance. He ordered the Justice Department to do a content analysis of reports and editorials from the *Tribune* group and Hearst newspapers to determine if they were repeating what Roosevelt considered Axis propaganda, while the FBI investigated possible Nazi connections. But lengthy investigations found neither propaganda nor Nazi connections.

When Roosevelt's investigations did not pan out, he resorted to public shaming. After first ordering the FBI to investigate how the *New York Daily News* was able to reveal the extent of the Pearl Harbor losses, he finally used a press conference to punish the offending reporter. He took out a German Iron Cross and awarded it to him in recognition of his service to the enemy. In fact, the Japanese did not need to read the *Daily News* to know what they had done to the Pacific Fleet; FDR was trying to keep this information from the American people. Even Roosevelt's own officials thought he was going too far in trying to stifle dissent.

The exigencies of a world war provided compelling arguments for controlling what defense-related information became public. But after the United States emerged as a global hegemon, Truman and all his successors had a harder time overcoming political and legal challenges to a system that was so out of keeping with the national tradition. As we have seen, following World War I and the Red Scare, the courts and Congress pushed back against censorship and surveillance and cut intelligence spending. In 1945, it was assumed that formal press censorship would disappear once again as the U.S. military demobilized and the Office of Strategic Services was dismantled. This turned out to be true, with the exception of nuclear secrets, as defined by the 1946 Atomic Energy Act. Even this had required long and difficult negotiations with Congress, which limited the scope to very specific types of information that could be construed as posing a life-or-death threat to the nation.

In 1947, with press freedoms largely restored, Truman doubled-down on a very different strategy: "secrecy at the source." This would become the policy for every one of Truman's successors. Using the unilateral power of executive orders, the president would assert sovereign control over how officials classified information, and thereby stop that information from ever reaching reporters.

If we look back at Truman's decision, it might seem to be of a piece with other Cold War policies. But it came well before the U.S.-Soviet rivalry became militarized. In 1947, the Cold War—a term that only started to become common that year—was largely a war of words. How could Truman expect journalists to believe he was just trying to protect national security when the experience of the real war that had just ended showed how often so-called secrets could be either ridiculous or self-serving? For instance, it was not just FDR who used official secrecy to conceal his movements. Army officers classified their stateside visits during wartime in order to avoid the criticism of enlisted men who spent years overseas without ever seeing their families. In fact, the very first draft of Truman's executive order proposed that the category of "confidential" include not just national-security information, but documents that would cause "serious administrative embarrassment."

Sure enough, when the draft order leaked, it provoked ridicule. Truman claimed that it was something cooked up by "some assistant secretary to an assistant secretary." In fact, the White House had specifically ordered the State-War-Navy Coordinating Committee to draft these rules, and they had been circulated to forty-six different executive agencies. Truman only dropped the plan when the opposition became too strong. The president himself was embarrassed when he had to hand the annual White House Correspondents' Association award to the journalist who broke the story.

That might have put an end to the Truman administration's push to control national security information were it not for another surprise attack—the communist invasion of South Korea, which was followed by another rapid mobilization. Truman's claim that secrecy was only ever intended to safeguard the nation started to have greater purchase. Even civilian agencies would have to safely handle sensitive information, so there was good reason to develop specific criteria. But a new draft executive order presented to him in January 1951 once again defined both "secret" and "confidential" classifications as covering not just information pertaining to national security, an extremely broad concept, but also anything that might be prejudicial to "the prestige of the nation." In the end, Truman approved a modified version of the new order that dropped "prestige" as something to be protected—indeed, it scarcely attempted to define what kind of information fit into the different categories. But it kept strict requirements for the handling of even "restricted" documents— the lowest level of classification.

The release of the new order ignited an explosion. Editors' associations called it "a dangerous instrument of news suppression." They knew that the policy of stamping documents "secret" or "confidential" without a clear definition of what those classifications signified had already proved self-defeating. It was pointed out that, during World War II, such requirements led officials to classify even newspaper clippings as restricted. "Our zealousness tended to make us overclassify more and more," one former OSS official recalled in a newspaper column. "This, of course, reduced the relative value of the classifications." Truman's order would lead to "galloping inflation" of classified material.

Truman had been warned by aides that his order would be "ridiculed" and would seem "like sheer nonsense from the public relations point of view." So they offered an array of explanations and justifications for the measures. But their contradictory nature only provoked more criticism. They claimed, for instance, that

The buck stopped here: Truman had to award Nat Finney five hundred dollars after the *Minneapolis Tribune* reporter exposed his administration's evasions and denials in attempting to create a security classification system.

greater control over classification would ultimately result in the public's receiving more information rather than less. But Truman went on to tell skeptical reporters that too much sensitive information was already reaching the public. When they asked if they should withhold information even if it was released to them by government officials, Truman dug in still deeper. He insisted that patriotic journalists should self-censor if they cared about national security.

As the columnist James Reston pointed out in *The New York Times*, "The administration's approach to public information is very much like a press agent's approach, to turn the flow of information on or off in accordance with the tactic of the moment, flooding the wire with news when it wants to put something over, and closing down on information if disclosure might prove embarrassing."

Indeed, critics' fears were already materializing. Almost immediately after the order, a senior official in the Office of Price Stabilization was caught issuing a directive to hide any information that "might prove embarrassing." Truman revoked this particular directive. But he could not police every government body newly empowered to create secrets, from the Commission of Fine Arts to the Battle Monuments Commission. Shortly afterward, the White House received a perfect example of overclassification from the Federal Trade Commission—a report on the international petroleum cartel that was stamped secret not because it had dangerous national-security information but, rather, because members had not read it yet. Instead of policing this misuse of the classification system, the White House just ignored the report. Excessive secrecy was not only providing cover for mere embarrassment, it was already undermining the secrecy system itself.

The administration also claimed to be following the advice of professionals to create rules that would combat espionage as the Cold War escalated. In fact, the security professionals in the FBI favored Republican-sponsored measures that Truman opposed, like forcing communists to register with the government. In public, the president continued to emphasize that only real experts—those with knowledge of real secrets—should decide counterespionage policy, not congressmen. But this implicitly meant that such professionals might judge that, for their own secret reasons, national security outweighed civil liberties, and no one—not Americans' elected representatives, perhaps not even the president himself—would be able to say anything about it.

FBI agents already had broad powers in deciding who was a security risk. They denied thousands of people clearance to access classified information—a condition of employment for an increasing number of government jobs. In many cases, it was only because they were judged to be sexually "deviant." Allegedly, this made them vulnerable to blackmail, even though lengthy investigations did not uncover a single example of a gay citizen who revealed official secrets because of blackmail. For immigrants, just having a relative living abroad could be grounds for denial.

Whatever contradictory justifications were offered to the public, and whatever the costs to individuals who became victims of arbitrary and capricious security policies, the overriding priority of the Truman administration was to maintain the executive branch's unfettered control over both secret information and the selection of who would have access to that information. So, at the same time Truman approved the new executive order, he also ordered that no one denied a security clearance would have a right of appeal. Secretary of State Dean Acheson judged that the ability to appeal a career-ending determination was "important only from a public relations point of view."

All the Truman administration's controversies over censorship and secrecy created the ideal conditions for a new president, from the opposition party, to promise a new day of openness and transparency. In his very first State of the Union address, in 1953, Dwight Eisenhower condemned secret diplomacy. In a press conference later that year, he also released the draft of a new executive order that would greatly reduce the number of agencies able to classify national-security information. When Eisenhower's attorney general, Herbert Brownell, announced the new order at a gathering of journalists, he embraced their criticisms of Truman. It was a "dangerous policy" to allow officials to follow the practice of "dictator nations" by using "national security to justify throwing a veil of secrecy over normally public matters."

But in private, Brownell's boss told the Cabinet that "the proposed order is really a public relations matter and that the Administration will benefit greatly by putting it through." Like Truman, Eisenhower believed many publishers acted in bad faith and were not really concerned with informing the public. When told that the vast powers of prosecution under the Espionage Act and the Atomic Secrets Act made journalists afraid, he said he wanted it that way, and went on to push for expanded wiretapping. As for his own officials, Eisenhower warned in a closed-door meeting that the FBI would investigate any leaks.

Eisenhower did eliminate the "restricted" category, which Brownell told reporters would reduce officials' tendency to classify everything. The president said in private that he was sure Moscow was already fully informed of everything with a restricted classification. But after the order was signed, defense contractors reported that it led officials to classify information at a higher level, rather than allow that information to be unclassified. When archivists later reviewed restricted documents from the Truman era to decide what could be released, they decided to treat them all as confidential. Thus, the higher classification just absorbed the lower one, so Eisenhower's gesture toward transparency only made these documents even more secret and further delayed their eventual release.

As for reducing the number of people who could create secrets, almost every president following Eisenhower would try to do the same thing, and for the same reason: they preferred to limit the power of secrecy to the people whom they appointed and who served at their pleasure. However, even after the new order, unauthorized leaks were as frequent as ever. Eisenhower's defense secretary, Charles Wilson, convened a committee of generals to find out why. They determined that senior officials had developed a "casual attitude" toward classified information, and journalists felt toward it anything from indifference to "active contempt." The main drivers in leaking were interservice rivalries and overclassification, which had reached "serious proportions." Even the "Top Secret" stamp was being applied far more broadly than the president's order had intended. But how could it be otherwise, when officials might be severely criticized for authorizing sensitive information to be released, but not for withholding it? "The act of classification is simple and expeditious," the generals agreed, whereas "declassification is involved and tedious." Few records were marked for "automatic" declassification, and most of the government was adding to the declassification backlog rather than reducing it. In just ten years, 1947 to 1957, the government created some seven hundred million pages of classified material. If stacked up in archival boxes, this pile of secrets would have been sixty-six miles high, and reach into space.

But when a congressional committee had tried to exercise its constitutional oversight responsibility to explore the same issues, the Pentagon spun a completely different story. Rather than acknowledging the casual attitude of senior officials detailed by its own internal report, Defense Department spokesmen claimed they took multiple steps to avoid needlessly piling up secrets, including authoring detailed directives and regulations, training and indoctrination, and "continuous staff supervision . . . to assure actual performance is in line with the policies." When required, "Corrective action is taken promptly." Asked how often Pentagon officials reviewed classified information in order to release it to the public, the spokesmen claimed, "The review is continuous." Whenever possible, documents were marked for automatic declassification at a specified future date. The only thing believable in their responses was the piddling amount of money they admitted to budgeting for declassification. It was $159,010, or less than $1.6 million today. The Pentagon spent twenty times as much on public relations.

When you closely study Truman's and Eisenhower's respective executive orders—and every other Democratic and Republican order that followed—what is most striking is not how they differ, but how remarkably similar they are. Truman's 1951 order, which Brownell called "dangerous" and dictatorial, insisted, "Security information shall be assigned the lowest security classification consistent with its proper protection." Eisenhower's revision insisted, "Unnecessary classification and over-classification shall be scrupulously avoided." Truman instructed officials to specify, along with the classification level, the date when declassification would be "automatic." So did Eisenhower. In his own order, announced to much fanfare in 1961, John F. Kennedy highlighted this notion of automatic declassification, winning favorable headlines for relaxing controls on information. In reality, Kennedy left Eisenhower's order largely unchanged. In his first State of the Union address, Kennedy promised he would not withhold anything necessary to keep Congress and the people informed. But a year later, even his friend Senator Mike Mansfield told him that little if anything had changed.

This is not a story of the "deep state" thwarting a president's best-laid plans to be more transparent. Upon gaining executive power, presidents recognize the political capital they can gain from defining what is secret while maintaining the appearance of transparency. Lyndon Johnson, for instance, was the first senator to introduce legislation to rein in overclassification, and as president, on July 4, 1966, he signed the Freedom of Information Act into law. But he could hardly have done otherwise. His press secretary, Bill Moyers, called the bill "a time bomb," but even the Pentagon thought the president had to go along "because of the great sensitivity of the subject." Not to be outdone in making himself available to journalists demanding more transparency, LBJ famously lifted his shirt to show the scar across his belly from a gallbladder operation. But behind the scenes, he referred to FOIA as "the fucking thing," and quietly sabotaged it. Justice Department lawyers helped write the House committee report so it would be applied as narrowly as possible. Johnson insisted that the law would not limit his ability to keep information secret, and sought to maintain total control over what became public. As he told future Secretary of State Cyrus Vance: "We've got the best bunch of leakers you ever saw over here, and I've got them in surplus, and if I need anything leaked, I'll leak it. But I sure as hell don't want my Joint Chiefs leaking it or my Defense people leaking it."

But when Johnson said this, he was responding to yet another unauthorized leak. He knew full well that no president could actually control what officials would classify, and what would leak, just by issuing executive orders. A full quarter-century earlier, Truman had acknowledged as much just days after issuing his own executive order. The *New York Times* columnist Arthur Krock had speculated that the president might not have even realized that it was his own officials who had leaked the classified information he criticized journalists for publishing. Truman wrote that it was Krock who did not realize that a president could not stop leaks out of the Pentagon. "You see, the Generals and the Admirals and the career men in government look upon the occupant of the White House as only a temporary nuisance who soon will be succeeded by another temporary occupant who won't find out what it is all about for a long time, and then it will be too late to do anything about it." But Truman put this unsent letter away in his drawer. Having conjured the powers of secrecy, and set them loose, he did not want to admit that he could not bring them under control.

No one tried harder to control the power of secrecy than Richard Nixon, and it ultimately destroyed his presidency. He sought recommendations from a Justice Department working group under Assistant Attorney General William Rehnquist, whom Nixon would later appoint to the Supreme Court. Rehnquist favored an official secrets act, which would make it simple to prosecute journalists for publishing classified information. But the group ultimately recommended against this step, for reasons the Pentagon Papers case—then being decided in the Supreme Court—would only reinforce. The justices' refusal to prevent the publication of this top-secret report under the Espionage Act showed that the White House would need to ask Congress to write a better law, and would still depend on courts to interpret and enforce it. That would mean sharing the power to define what constitutes a state secret, something no president has been willing to do.

Instead, Nixon tried to devise solutions he could implement on his own authority, such as brainstorming a new classification scheme with his counsels John Ehrlichman and Bud Krogh.

PRESIDENT: And maybe another approach to it would be to set up and remember I already mentioned to set up a new classification.

EHRLICHMAN: Right.

PRESIDENT: Which we would call what? Let's just call it a new classifica—Don't use TOP SECRET for me ever again. I never want to see TOP SECRET in this God damn Office. I think we just solved—shall we call it—Uh, John, what would be a good name? "President's Secure—" Or, uh—"Eyes Only" is a silly thing too. It doesn't mean anything anymore. Uh—

KROGH: We used "Presidential Document" before with one of the counsel we were working with, but that didn't—There's some—

EHRLICHMAN: How about—Uh, uh looking forward to the court case, I wonder if we could get the words "National Security" in it.

PRESIDENT: Yeah.

EHRLICHMAN: So that "National," uh, just say "National Security Classified" or "National Security—

KROGH: [Unintelligible]

EHRLICHMAN: Secret" or uh—

PRESIDENT: Well, uh, not the word "Secret" should not be used.

EHRLICHMAN: All right, uh, uh—

PRESIDENT: Because you see "Secret" has been now compromised.

In public, even Nixon felt the need to spin a different story and pretend he could issue an executive order in which words like "secret" and "national security" represented objective reality. He announced that his order would "lift the veil of secrecy which now enshrouds altogether too many papers written by employees of the Federal establishment." The order reduced the number of agencies with authority to classify information as top secret, limited the number of people entrusted with these secret powers, and accelerated the review and release of previously classified information. This meant that even top-secret information that was ten years old—namely, documents on the Bay of Pigs invasion and the Cuban Missile Crisis—could be released to the public unless officials found that doing so would risk national security.

On its face, Nixon's order seemed like progress. But what were presented as great innovations largely represented identical policies, only with stronger-sounding words: Whereas Truman wrote that the top-secret classification "shall be held to the minimum necessary," Nixon proclaimed, "This classification shall be used with the utmost restraint." If these proclamations actually restrained officials from overclassification, the effect would have been to help preserve the secrecy of the smaller number of documents the president actually cared about.

This also explains why Nixon favored automatic declassification. Taking old secrets out of circulation was another way to fight the inflation in secrecy that debased its value to the president and his closest advisers. He insisted that, under his 1972 order, declassification really would be automatic: "We have reversed the burden of proof: For the first time, we are placing that burden—and even the threat of administrative sanction—upon those who wish to preserve the secrecy of documents rather than upon those who wish to declassify them after a reasonable time."

It seemed like sunlight. But revealing the secrets of former presidents served to diminish their prestige relative to the current occupant of the White House. A fuller accounting of the Bay of Pigs and the Cuban Missile Crisis, for instance, could tarnish the reputation of the Kennedys. Just to make certain, John Ehrlichman asked Bud Krogh and Dave Young—two of Nixon's "plumbers"—to reach out and see to it that someone from "the political side of the house" could be in charge of declassifying these Kennedy-era documents, to ensure that whatever was released served "the best interests of the President."

So, even when talking the talk of transparency, Nixon was actually "weaponizing" declassification. At the same time, he was happy to use the public's continuing esteem for JFK, especially his crisis-management skills, to justify his own administration's secrecy. When Nixon had to defend his secret invasion of Cambodia, he said that Kennedy had also withheld information during the Missile Crisis in the interest of national security and to protect American servicemen.

In private, Nixon was realistic about his ability to control how countless unnamed officials would apply the new executive order, and treated the whole thing like a public-relations exercise. He called the interagency group that created it a "group of clowns." Instead, he resorted to illegal operations to identify and punish leakers, culminating in "dirty tricks" that—when revealed—forced his resignation.

In the aftermath, Gerald Ford promised "openness and candor," and even invited reporters into the White House kitchen to see him toasting his own English muffins. As a congressman, he had supported FOIA and attacked presidential use of executive privilege, arguing that all too frequently it was used to "cover up dishonesty, stupidity, and failure of all kinds." The English muffins were still warm when Ford vetoed a law that aimed to strengthen FOIA.

If ever a president seemed capable of finally bringing transparency back to the White House, it was Jimmy Carter. He told *Meet the Press* in 1976 that, if he was elected, one of his first acts would be to issue an executive order to "open up as many of the deliberations of the Executive Branch of government as possible," and join Congress in passing comprehensive sunshine laws. These promises seemed believable coming from Carter, a Sunday-school teacher. The man was so open he felt the need to tell a *Playboy* interviewer that he felt guilty for having "lust" for women who were not his wife.

But, once again, things appeared different from the perspective of the Oval Office. "I was shocked when I took office," he told a State Department audience six weeks into his term, "to learn about the number of different people who have access to highly secret, sensitive information. . . ." Just one "compartment" meant to contain cryptological secrets included some two hundred thousand people. But compartmentalization still denied information to the people Carter appointed to head departments and agencies, because even the president's closest aides had no way of knowing what information was hidden and whom they needed to ask to find it.

So, when Carter finally did issue his executive order on classification and declassification, a year and a half into his administration—not his first, but his ninety-eighth executive order—it limited the power to compartmentalize to heads of agencies, and reduced the number of agencies and officials who could classify information. Like all his predecessors since Truman, Carter was trying to gain control of the dark state, and prevent Congress or the courts from doing it for him. Congress had already overridden Ford's veto of the strengthened FOIA law, and Senators Joe Biden and Edmund Muskie threatened to pursue legislation if Carter did not follow through. To those within the administration who favored more comprehensive reform, internal opposition only put the political calculus in starker relief: "Does [the] President wish to abandon 'openness' program to Congressional action?"

As a result, some promising new elements survived the "time-consuming" and "frustrating" process of negotiating the new order with the Pentagon, the intelligence agencies, the State Department, and others intent on defending their autonomous power to compartmentalize secrets. One such reform measure required that officials consider whether, on balance, any potential harm from declassification might be outweighed by the benefit of keeping the public informed. Carter's order was also supposed, finally, to make declassification "automatic" after a specified period, usually six years or less. Only an agency head or those with a top-secret clearance could make an exception, and this was only to be done "sparingly."

Carter insisted that his new order would increase openness by limiting what was classified in the first place. It was part of a broader agenda to make America's conduct in the world less cynical and more transparent. In one of his most famous speeches as president, Carter promised that his administration's foreign policy would be based on human rights, and would also be a policy that "the American people both support and, for a change, know about and understand"—a swipe at Kissingerian cynicism and secrecy. Officials were instructed to err on the side of transparency whenever in doubt, and Carter proposed to create a new office—the Information Security Oversight Office—to make sure they did.

So did the Carter administration really take a principled stand for human rights, including Americans' right to know how his administration managed the country's foreign policy, military posture, and intelligence gathering? Did officials classify less information, and did declassification actually become the default policy, to the point where it became automatic? Surely, this was the moment when the power of principle would finally have some impact in limiting the sway of the dark state.

We can now answer these questions with actual data from millions of State Department cables and other official documents from the 1970s, many of them still classified. We have seen in chapter 7 how Carter's State Department started *talking* about freedom and democracy far more than under his predecessors, with a significant jump in communications related to human rights. Critics argued that American diplomats were going around the world hectoring allied governments, cutting off U.S. arms shipments to those who failed to meet Carter's standards. The Georgetown University political scientist Jeane Kirkpatrick maintained that the administration's efforts to push democratization only undermined allies facing internal unrest, like Iran and Nicaragua, since this kind of browbeating meant nothing to communist dictatorships. Kirkpatrick's critique was so popular among Republicans that, when Reagan defeated Carter and became president, he made her the U.S. ambassador to the United Nations. Reagan claimed that his opponent had also failed to protect national-security information.

We would expect that, at the least, a relatively larger proportion of Carter-era diplomacy would be unclassified than that of the Nixon and Ford eras. In fact, there was no diminution in secrecy after Carter assumed office in 1977. If anything, the relative proportion of unclassified communications shrank. But what really stands out is how little change there is in classification practices over time.

What about the idea that Carter's foreign policy was based on human rights, even at the cost of risking relations with key allies? When we look at the data, we find that U.S. diplomats very frequently communicated about human-rights problems with regard to Latin American states like Chile and Argentina, accounting for fully one in ten cables concerning these countries. But some close Middle Eastern allies, like Jordan and Egypt, committed crimes against their own people that were just as bad or worse. Jordanians were tortured and imprisoned without trial, enduring months of solitary confinement in cells no bigger than

Proportion of Cables by Classification, 1974–1980

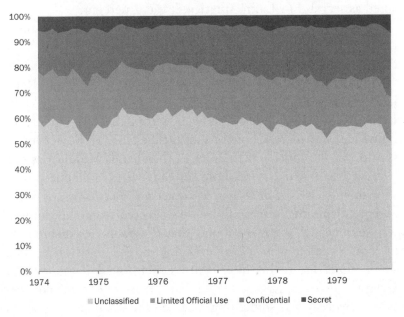

three feet by six feet. There were hundreds more political prisoners in Egypt. One university student held in a Cairo prison
was tortured with a stick inserted into his anus. Less was known
about Saudi Arabia, which exercised tight control over information. Nonetheless, accounts of abuse and executions reached
international reporters, including the public execution of a
Saudi princess and the beheading of her lover because of their
illicit affair. The flogging of two British contractors for brew-
ing beer, which was outlawed in Saudi Arabia, provoked outrage
among the British press and members of Parliament. But the
State Department showed little concern—less than 1 percent of
communications about these countries concerned human rights.

U.S. diplomats were also much more secretive when conducting business in the Middle East. An astonishing one in four
cables about Jordan were classified secret, which ostensibly
meant that—under Carter's policy—there was no doubt that, if
disclosed, any one of these communications would "cause serious damage to the national security." Almost 15 percent of all

cables about the United States' Middle Eastern allies were classified as secret. For Latin America, it was 2 percent.

Why so much less secrecy in U.S. diplomacy in Latin America during this period? Richard Nixon put it plainly in a 1971 conversation with his then Cabinet member Donald Rumsfeld: "People don't give one damn about Latin America now." Raising concerns about abuses with an ally was much less risky in Latin America because it was well within the U.S. sphere of influence, and there seemed to be little chance of Soviet intervention in the mid-1970s. On the other hand, Middle Eastern allies were involved in a whole series of wars and superpower showdowns. In the nearly five thousand transcripts of Kissinger's telephone conversations we collected from the time he was secretary of state, we found that the countries of Honduras and Ecuador were never even mentioned—not once. The single time one of his interlocutors mentioned Paraguay and Uruguay, in 1974, Kissinger found an excuse to end the conversation. Secrecy was something reserved for the issues and areas that actually mattered, such as war and peace in the Middle East, the secret bombing and invasion of Cambodia, back-channel negotiations that would lead to an opening to Communist China, and the many "dirty tricks" played on Nixon's domestic opponents.

All in all, Carter's order made little difference. On paper, it called for declassifying virtually all documents that were twenty years old or older—down from thirty years under the previous order. But departments and agencies were not given the resources to carry out this program. It peaked in 1980, when over ninety million pages were reviewed. Rather than automatically declassifying them, the reviewers kept 73 percent secret.

Another key element of Carter's plan, designating new documents for declassification on a specified date, had only been applied in one case out of ten. Rather than using their power to override the new directive "sparingly," officials had done so routinely. As for the idea that they would have to weigh the public interest in disclosure when deciding on declassification, even the Carter White House had called this part of the order, in internal deliberations, a symbolic step. Carter's national security advisor, Zbigniew Brzezinski, specified in writing that it would only apply in "rare" and "exceptional" cases. Government lawyers used Brzezinski's statement whenever their FOIA rejections were challenged in court. In not even one case did a judge require disclosure on the basis of this balancing test.

Carter did create the Information Security Oversight Office (ISOO), which was supposed to have the clout to police the classification practices of the entire federal government. The unanimous recommendation of the authors of Carter's new order had been to make it part of the office of the White House Counsel, Management and Budget, or the National Security Council. But no one wanted this impossible job. As a result, ISOO was tucked away in a corner of the General Services Administration, which was mainly concerned with things like building maintenance and purchase of supplies; there ISOO's staff of eleven would not get in the way.

Nevertheless, ISOO was able to gather data, which showed that officials classified information 50 percent more in five months in 1979 than in all of 1977. They blamed this puzzling response to Carter's order to err on the side of transparency on better reporting. But then the total increased again in 1980, when officials reported classifying information some sixteen million times.

By this point, Carter seems to have come completely around on the question of classification. His administration was ramping up military spending, and initiated an enormous new covert operation to support the mujahideen in Afghanistan. Casting about for some new way to categorize the most sensitive information—like Nixon before him—Carter and his administration tried an entirely new designation: "royal."

So even Jimmy Carter, the Sunday-school teacher, was ultimately unable to resist the temptation to exert sovereign control over state secrecy. As much as he championed human rights, he limited this crusade to the parts of the world that were least important to U.S. foreign policy, and was highly secretive in the areas, especially the Middle East, that mattered most. He did not back efforts to reduce overclassification and accelerate declassification with the requisite resources or White House supervision. If anything, by the end of his administration, the dark state was growing even bigger, and stronger.

As we have seen, Reagan campaigned against Carter for failing to safeguard national-security information, like sensitive new weapons technology. He called for amending the Freedom of Information Act "to reduce costly and capricious requests to the intelligence agencies" by running background checks on requestors. His party's platform also proposed criminal sanctions against anyone—not just government officials—who revealed U.S. intelligence sources and methods.

Yet, when Reagan took office, his staff did not pursue an American official secrets act. Their primary concern was to prevent any judicial oversight of what they wished to keep secret. So they crafted a draconian new executive order. It mandated disciplinary action for any official who did not protect classified information. Information would be classified even when officials could not identify any risk to national security, and they were explicitly told to err on the side of secrecy. The new order also removed any requirement to weigh these decisions against the benefit of keeping the public informed.

But Reagan knew that this was not a policy a president should be associated with personally. Even the authors of the new order did not try to defend it when invited to appear before Congress. Edwin Meese, counselor to the president, admitted in an unguarded moment, "There is way too much classification." As for Reagan himself, he deferred to Meese at a presidential luncheon when asked how the proposed order—along with another that expanded the CIA's domestic-surveillance authorization—squared with his promise to "get the government off the backs of the people." "I'm sorry," he said. "I'm eating."

Reagan normally relished Oval Office signing ceremonies, and made photo opportunities an art form. But his national security adviser, William Clark, advised handling the issuance of this order very differently when it was finally done: "To minimize criticism, I believe the President should issue the Order quickly, preferably this Friday when release would get caught up with the weekend news."

Even the limited extent to which Reagan, as a presidential candidate, insisted on the need to protect sensitive information was quite exceptional. Every other successful candidate has promised more transparency and accountability, only to abandon that promise upon becoming sovereign over state secrecy. The Clinton administration was initially supportive of Senator Daniel Patrick Moynihan's Commission on Protecting and Reducing Government Secrecy, and its recommendation that classification and declassification have a statutory basis, with real congressional oversight. But then a White House source told Moynihan that "the forces of bureaucracy were gathering" and he was being "slow rolled." In 2000, after five years of effort, all Moynihan got was a largely powerless "Public Interest Declassification Board," which presidents could safely ignore.

Still, when George W. Bush campaigned to succeed Clinton, he promised "a citizen-centered government, always listening and answering directly to the people." Using the Internet, everyone would be able to "drill through the federal bureaucracy to directly access information." Bush even promised to keep citizens informed proactively, such as by delivering push notifications with "the latest environmental regulations to an environmental activist"—subject, of course, to privacy protections. Instead, Bush gave several departments and agencies new powers to create secrets, reclassified and withdrew information that had previously been available on the Internet, and drilled through privacy protections with ever-more-intrusive forms of surveillance. The Bush administration cited 9/11 as the reason for its turn to secrecy. In fact, even before Al Qaeda carried out these attacks, the Justice Department was already preparing a new policy to eliminate the presumption of openness.

After campaigning against the excesses of the Bush-Cheney era, Barack Obama promised the most transparent administration in history. His personal media strategy was described as "full saturation," from direct messaging to supporters through social media to broadcast appearances on comedy shows. But his 2009 executive order on national-security information read like a greatest-hits list from previous orders: it reduced the number of people who could classify information, limited the amount of information classified at the highest levels, "automatically" declassified records from previous administrations, and ostensibly prohibited classification to "prevent embarrassment to a person, organization, or agency." Every single one of these measures had also appeared in Richard Nixon's 1972 order, and they still served the same underlying purpose: to shore up the president's own sovereign power over secrecy.

Another supposed reform was to instruct officials, "If there is significant doubt about the need to classify information, it shall not be classified." But the exact same language had appeared in Bill Clinton's 1995 order. The substance of it was much the same as what had appeared in Carter's. In all three cases, the number of times information was classified then *increased* the next year, and the year after that, and the year after that. . . . By the third year after Clinton's order, the number of times officials had decided to classify information had more than doubled, and then kept increasing. Three years after Obama's, it had grown by 74 percent. After so many decades of experience, how could a president who issues such an order have any doubt that officials would, in fact, err on the side of secrecy? Would it even be an error?

In fact, Obama really outdid his predecessors. In 2012, the number of new government secrets grew to over ninety-five million, an all-time high. At the same time, the Obama Justice Department prosecuted more people for unauthorized leaks than had all his predecessors put together. And by the end of his presidency, his media handlers had imposed draconian controls on reporters' ability to obtain unfiltered images and words out of the White House. Journalists reported getting hounded by administration officials for publishing unfavorable headlines, and noted that sources were terrified to talk about anything related to national security for fear of prosecution. When interviewed in 2013, thirty experienced Washington journalists said Obama went further to control information than any previous president.

When you get past the spin, you can see that both the promise of transparency and the betrayal of that promise increase executive power. There may be no better example than the most awesome power of all. In the past, presidents could only dispatch armed forces to kill someone when war had been declared and that person wore the uniform of the enemy. Even during the Cold War, it was exceedingly rare for presidents to order the assassination of particular individuals. But those were more innocent times, before many such killings could be carried out by remote control drones. In the present day, CIA armchair pilots compete with air-force armchair pilots to carry out hundreds of killings personally approved by the president. Year after year, the CIA under Obama would "neither confirm nor deny" that the president was killing people in this way. In court, the Agency quashed FOIA appeals by arguing that the very existence of the targeted killing program had never been acknowledged—it was a national-security secret and there was no "official information" about it in the public sphere.

But at the same time, anonymous officials used "pleaks"— leaks intended to plant favorable stories in the media—to spin their own version of the facts. They were quoted dozens and dozens of times touting the drone program to journalists, and assuring them that it had killed few civilians and many terrorists. Their position was that, as commander-in-chief, the president had the authority to kill anyone, anywhere in the world, in total secrecy—even if that person was an American citizen, and even if the attempt to kill the person killed others as well. Not only that, the public had no right to know the legal basis for these lethal powers—indeed, no right to know whether such a program even existed.

Obama finally acknowledged, toward the end of his presidency, that he had not paid sufficient attention to the dangers of this targeted killing program, at least early on. When the White House finally attempted to render an account, it guesstimated the number of civilian deaths from collateral damage as somewhere between 64 and 116, but offered no information about how it arrived at that range. Independent journalists detailed hundreds more: 474 in total. In a subsequent investigation of some thirteen hundred classified Pentagon reports, *New York Times* reporters found that the Pentagon only talked to witnesses two times, only once visited the site of a drone strike, and never found any wrongdoing. By talking to scores of survivors at nearly a hundred sites, the journalists found that the number of innocent men, women, and children killed in this secret program had been "drastically" underestimated.

So all the "pleaks" were completely misleading. And even after the drone program became public, and officials rendered an account, the organizing principle was still plausible deniability, the very opposite of democratic accountability. But now the goal was to plausibly deny the full extent of the government's deception, which was possible only because White House officials and their military and CIA advisers did not actually investigate how many innocents they were killing.

This Bush-Obama-era program was one of the first that Donald Trump fully embraced, and even expanded. He began his presidency attacking the "deep state" and portraying himself as a victim of FBI surveillance. He promised to release everything, from the last of the Kennedy assassination papers to the surveillance files of his own campaign. Unsurprisingly, he later found reasons not to. In fact, unique among post–World War II presidents, Trump did not change his predecessor's official policy on secrecy one iota. By declining to issue a single executive order on classification and declassification, he signaled that Obama's was entirely satisfactory.

In actual practice, he went even further than any president before him. He made it a habit to tear up official papers into tiny little pieces, and tweeted that every word he uttered to an adviser—every single one—was "highly classified." If Trump had followed through, this could have expanded the dark state to encompass every part of the executive branch. Everything that fell within the president's purview, everything he could touch—from the Agency for International Development to the Wilson Center for Scholars—would have been enveloped in the same cloak of secrecy.

Of course, this was the leakiest administration in history, and Trump was the leaker-in-chief. Other than continuing Obama's campaign against low-level unauthorized leakers, he did not try to obtain any legal solution to stop leaking generally, though his party controlled both houses of Congress. Even Ronald Reagan, the only president who promised more secrecy—and kept his promise—abandoned the one serious attempt to crack down on leaking. It would have involved requiring everyone, including

Cabinet secretaries, to document any meeting with journalists, and subject themselves to polygraph exams. It collapsed when Secretary of State George Schultz publicly rejected the plan.

Like nearly all his predecessors, Joe Biden promised "a recommitment to the highest standards of transparency." To take just one example of the urgent need for such a recommitment, over the previous eight years the backlog of FOIA requests had nearly doubled. But the Biden administration did not give policy making in this area any more priority than did the Trump administration. Advocacy groups found that no one in the White House was even working on the issue. A year into the Biden administration, his director of national intelligence, Avril Haines, acknowledged, "The volume of classified material produced continues to grow exponentially."

———————

As long as the dark state continues to surround itself with more and more secrecy, the White House cannot work *unless* it leaks, revealing secrets of the president's choosing to advance his agenda, while steering attention away from what's classified. Leaked information is the lubricant that allows it to spin. As the law professor (and former State Department official) David Pozen concluded, after years of research on leaking:

> The great secret about the U.S. government's notorious leakiness is that it is a highly adaptive mechanism of information control, which has been refined through a nuanced system of social norms. The great secret about the laws against leaking is that they have never been used in a manner designed to stop leaking—and that their implementation threatens not just gauzy democratic ideals but practical bureaucratic imperatives, not just individual whistleblowers but the institution of the presidency.

These secrets are great from a president's point of view, and terrible for everyone else. Leaks allow the chief executives and their most senior officials to have it both ways: They can maintain the useful fiction that all the information they have locked up is dangerous and will, if exposed to sunlight, explode (and possibly result in prosecution, *though only for more junior employees*). At the same time, they can make available only the information that puts themselves in the best possible light, without, in any legally binding way, acknowledging or expanding the public's right to know what the White House chooses to keep hidden.

The cost of this system includes not just the evasion of executive-branch accountability, both to the American people and to the other two branches of government. It also makes it almost impossible to identify and prosecute those who leak information that really can harm national security. Because reporters are quite secretive about their own sources, even at the risk of jail, there is usually no way to reveal who leaked information to them. Stopping leaks, therefore, would involve laws that punish the journalists who pass them on. But presidents have left the Espionage Act in place because it still serves to intimidate lower-level officials, setting an example through selective prosecution. Changing it, on the other hand, would open their powers of secrecy to the influence of Congress. Their overriding priority is to monopolize the control of secrecy, even more so than protecting the secrets themselves.

The modern presidency will not, therefore, reform itself, no matter what any candidate promises you. Every president has staked everything on a quest to achieve the capacity to change the world. Even the best of them believe they need more power to protect us and promote the general welfare. The worst of them fear that any weakness will leave them unable to protect themselves. But as long as the media remain free and independent, presidents have realized that they cannot hide something with nothing. So they promise to be transparent, only to spin tales that shroud the real story. When we unwind that thread, we find that it runs right through the history of the modern presidency, from Truman to Trump and beyond.

In the last century, the most important reversals in the expansion of the dark state only came about because the ostensibly coequal branches of government fought back. This history is much shorter, but it includes when Congress overrode Gerald Ford's veto of a stronger Freedom of Information Act, and the Church Committee exposed the intelligence community's misconduct. Other important victories came when court rulings prohibited prior restraint in the publication of the Pentagon Papers, and required the National Archives to save historic documents from destruction, as we shall see in chapter 10. But far more often, judges and elected representatives have abdicated their responsibility, because of either an overzealous faith in the cult of national security, or a lack of courage in meeting their constitutional responsibilities.

To be sure, the dark state would not have been so effectively defended—and expanded—if presidents had had to do it all by themselves. We have seen that many, many people working in government are deeply invested in preventing other people from knowing what they do. Some of the most notorious advocates of state secrecy only became that way when they, too, became invested in executive power. As a congressman in the 1960s, Donald Rumsfeld cosponsored the original FOIA legislation and railed against secrecy and spin. Similarly, when Dick Cheney went to Congress he argued that presidents—even Republican presidents—should not have an "excessive concern for secrecy." But even if Rumsfeld and Cheney had stayed true to their original convictions, any executive order must be interpreted and applied by many thousands of individuals who collectively make tens of millions of classification and declassification decisions every year. They go on protecting old secrets even when the temporary occupants of the White House would prefer that these be revealed.

But, ultimately, the chief executive has the most to gain from official secrecy, and the most to lose if he or she can no longer invoke national security to regulate the flow of information. Presidents therefore seek to maximize their authority over this unwieldy system. To the extent that executive orders promising reform are faithfully implemented, they would all increase the president's personal control. Presidents will typically want to preserve secret powers for the smallest possible number of people, ideally those they personally appoint and who serve at their pleasure. Any president will try to limit the information classified at the highest level, since too many bureaucrats creating too many top secrets debase the value of a president's own "royal" secrets. For the same reason, presidents will keep trying to take old secrets out of circulation, even—sometimes especially— when those old secrets prove embarrassing to a predecessor.

Every administration, including Reagan's, claims that it "recognizes that it is essential that the public be informed concerning the activities of its Government." It insists that its policies reflect an effort to "balance" the need for transparency with the need to protect national security. But it's all just spin—or, rather, it is about 90 to 95 percent spin, a reflection of how much of government spending on public information goes to public relations rather than declassification. In 1955—the same year the Pentagon spent $159,010 on declassification—it spent $2,987,412 on PR (about $29 million adjusted for inflation). By 1969, it was spending over $217 million in inflation-adjusted dollars for public relations. By 2016, it was $626 million, six times more than what *the entire federal government* spends on the systematic declassification program.

But Pentagon PR spending pales in comparison with what the government spends on protecting secrets. Back in 1955, the Defense Department claimed it would be impractical even to estimate the costs of all the "safes, locks, alarm and radio systems, guards, security investigations, the time expended by individual personnel." When Congress mandated the Information Security Oversight Office report in 1995 on the total cost of classification security, ISOO estimated it was $2.7 billion, more than 90 percent of it incurred by the Pentagon. In 2017—the last time ISOO even ventured to guesstimate secrecy spending—it was $18.39 billion. Comparing the sums expended between 1995 and 2017 suggests that the price of secrecy was increasing at four times the annual rate of inflation.

At the beginning of his presidency, Dwight Eisenhower famously bemoaned the waste represented by military spending:

> Every gun that is made, every warship launched, every
> rocket fired signifies, in the final sense, a theft from those
> who hunger and are not fed, those who are cold and are

not clothed. This world in arms is not spending money alone.

It is spending the sweat of its laborers, the genius of its scientists, the hopes of its children.

Eisenhower noted that just one bomber would pay to build a modern brick school in more than thirty cities. What can we say about spending $18.39 billion a year not for guns, not for butter, but just for secrets? That is enough money to build over a thousand new schools every year. Wouldn't improving education for millions of students make a greater contribution to national security, considering that these students will be our future diplomats, intelligence analysts, soldiers, scientists, and engineers?

The opportunity costs of the dark state are incalculable. But the direct cost of secrecy and spin may be even greater. Above all, it is the price we pay when we cannot know what our elected leaders are doing in our name. It is the bill that comes due when we have to learn history's lessons the hard way, over and over again, because even historians are not allowed to see secret documents from decades ago. Clearly, you cannot cover up something as big and ugly as unaccountable power with nothing, and that something—that secret, and that spin—gets bigger, and more expensive, every single year.

But what if most of what is concealed by the secrecy and the spinning is really just—nothing?

9

THERE IS NO THERE THERE

THE BEST-KEPT SECRET

Imagine you have been offered a government job, but you cannot start until you obtain a high-level security clearance. First, you have to fill out 124 pages of official forms and authorizations. You must describe in detail the dates and locations of all overseas travel over the last seven years. You also need to list every address where you resided for the last decade. And you are required to provide citizenship and employment information for all your family members and in-laws. Once you have completed this paperwork, investigators will run credit checks and contact your health-care providers.

Next, the interview. You are told, "It is imperative that the interview be conducted immediately after you are contacted." You will meet face-to-face, and may have to answer a lot of personal questions about everything from drinking and drugs to gambling, sexual preferences, and money problems. You might have to sign sworn statements, or even take a polygraph exam, knowing that examiners could grill you about your most painful experiences.

You will need to corroborate the information you provide, such as documenting every place you worked for more than sixty days. You will not only have to verify your degrees, diplomas, and citizenship, but also document the citizenship of family members, even if they are dead. Investigators will run checks on everyone you live with. Your former spouse, friends, neighbors, professors, and employers may also be pulled in, to be personally interviewed about potential character flaws. Depending on what they find, the investigation might be expanded to include your therapist or psychiatrist. They might also contact local law enforcement.

The process will take at least three months, and it might be more than a year before you will hear the final outcome. If you are found to have lied or withheld information, you are liable to a felony prosecution and five years' imprisonment. If, instead, you are simply denied your clearance, you may never find out why. The reviewers have broad discretion in determining who is trustworthy, and you have no legal recourse even if their questions and comments make it obvious that you have been the victim of prejudice. Even seemingly objective criteria for denial, like money problems or a record of being arrested—to say nothing of having relatives in other countries—results in some communities being underrepresented in jobs involving "national security." The government does not even collect data on the racial identity of applicants, making it hard to estimate the impact of these structural disparities.

But let us say you pass, having proved "unquestionable loyalty to the United States . . . strength of character, reliability, judgment, and trustworthiness." Now you have to be trained, or "indoctrinated," in how to handle different kinds of secret information. You must learn an alphabet soup of new acronyms, including everything from SAMI (Sources and Methods Information) to CNWDI (Critical Nuclear Weapon Design Information). After jumping through more hoops, you will be "read in" to classified programs, and go to work at a "SCIF," a Sensitive Compartmented Information Facility. Yours is steel-plated, wrapped in foil, insulated for sound, and shielded from electromagnetic radiation. Before you can enter the facility, you must put your cell phone in a locker, enter your PIN, expose an eyeball to the iris scanner, and then wait until the door slides open. If you accidentally set off the automated alarm systems, armed guards will respond in five minutes or less.

After you find your desk and settle in, a courier in military uniform arrives. He unlocks a briefcase and presents you with an opaque, sealed envelope. It has addresses on it but no names. Upon opening it, you find another envelope with a receipt attached. After you sign your name, the courier puts the receipt back in the briefcase, locks it again, and makes his exit.

You begin to examine that sealed inner envelope. This one has your name on it, and the name of the person and the agency that sent it to you. It is stamped top secret. When you open that envelope, you find a transmittal letter. This is also marked top secret, and includes formal notification that the attachment is highly classified. Even the different paragraphs of the transmittal letter start with the initials "TS," "S," and "C," since each paragraph is individually classified, or "portion marked." At the bottom you find instructions written for the person who, decades in the future, will decide if and when any of it can be declassified. It is marked OADR—"Originating Agency's Determination Required." The sender made sure there would be no automatic declassification.

Now they have your full attention. With anticipation, you eagerly flip over the letter and start rifling through the pages of the attachment. Every one of them is marked top secret, with the name of different "Sensitive Compartmentalized Information" control systems, code words for various "Special Access Programs," more qualifiers like "Very Restricted Knowledge" and "Risk Sensitive," and a range of "Special Dissemination Control" markings like "Restricted Data" and "No Forn" (no foreigners are allowed to know what you now know).

Finally, you realize what all the fuss is about. It's a three-day-old newspaper. And the instructions for declassification, when you might one day be able to tell someone what you have seen today without risking a felony conviction and ten years in prison? The date specified is twenty years into the future.

———————

Is it a joke? No. It may be the best-kept secret of all. Sovereignty is the core, the spinning core, of the dark state. It explains both the power of secrecy and the secrecy of power. But that core is encircled by a void. Once inside the silos and compartments, defended with intricate systems and armies of apparatchiks costing billions of dollars, you typically find that there is *no there there*. Most "secret intelligence" is not very secret, and much of what remains secret is not very intelligent. Otherwise intelligent government officials themselves may not know the difference, because the system itself—and the culture it breeds—conceals these critical distinctions.

In this chapter, we will survey this vast, vacuous expanse. Then we will use data to calculate the costs and risks of officials' continuing inability or unwillingness to identify more clearly the information that really does require safekeeping. This ranges from scandals like the Hillary Clinton e-mail affair to the continuing concealment—or loss—of huge numbers of records that should have been released to the public long ago. Finally, we will attempt to estimate the extent to which government officials might actually agree on what can and should be secret.

To take on the first dimension of this dark void, we will need artificial intelligence to estimate with any precision the amount of classified information that is not really secret, and how exactly that affects our ability to identify secrets that really do require safekeeping. But there is plenty of evidence of the enormity of this problem hiding in plain sight. When you start to look for it, you can see it everywhere. And the disappointment and bafflement you feel is how many, many people feel when they first see classified, secret information and ask themselves, "Really? Is that all there is?"

George W. Bush, for instance, started receiving briefings from the CIA at his Texas ranch while the outcome of the 2000 election was still in doubt. The "President's Daily Brief" represents the most important and urgent intelligence gathered day and night from all eighteen of America's spy agencies, which spend over fifty billion dollars every year. The PDB is handled with extreme care, and the distribution is limited to only a small number of the most senior officials. As the former briefer David Priess put it, it is the "most tightly guarded daily publication on the face of the earth." But after receiving the briefings for almost a month, Bush was puzzled. He suspected the CIA was holding out on him. "I'm sure that when I become president, you'll start giving me the good stuff," he said. But the briefer knew the president-elect would be disappointed. *"Oh shit,"* he thought, *"we've already been giving him the good stuff!"*

To be sure, some secrets really are important, surprising, or even strange. But those who are really in the know, know that many secrets are old news—literally. They include the newspaper reports that will be classified if they are passed around among officials. When intelligence-community reviewers went through Hillary Clinton's e-mail, for instance, they classified some communications as secret even when they concerned what was being reported in the press. There are sometimes good reasons for doing so. For instance, it is one thing for the United States to be flying lethal drones over another country in what is ostensibly, and officially, a covert operation. It is quite another thing for the government to acknowledge through the release of public records that it is killing citizens of that country—even if that acknowledgment is implicit from the media stories senior officials share among themselves.

But a lot of classified information really is "old news," and not just because it can't be publicly acknowledged. In 1971, Nixon complained, "The CIA tells me nothing I don't read three days earlier in *The New York Times.*" The president of the United States was comparing the President's Daily Brief with material most people would only find useful to housebreak a puppy. But it would be forty-five years before those 1971 briefings were declassified, and many are still heavily redacted.

President Truman made the same observation twenty years before Nixon. He said that 95 percent of American secrets were revealed in newspapers and "slick magazines." Truman did not pull this figure out of a hat: it was only a slight exaggeration of a highly classified CIA study. The study deserves close scrutiny, because it is still a sterling example of how many "top secrets" are not really secret, not when you know how to look for them.

The first director of the Agency's Office of Estimates, William Langer, came up with the idea. His office was responsible for producing the CIA's most important intelligence assessments for policy makers. Langer wanted to find out what his Soviet counterparts could learn about the United States just by exploiting public information. His designated target was America's order of battle, or the forces that could fight in the event of war. This included the strength and location of all ground forces, the position and performance characteristics of major combat vessels, and the readiness, range, payload, armaments, and airspeed of all military aircraft. This information would greatly benefit any enemy of the United States in planning an attack.

So who was chosen to uncover America's order of battle—something that had always been one of the most important secrets of all? Seventeen professors from Yale. The largest contingent were historians, like Langer himself, and the rest were from the classics, English, physics, biology, chemistry, and mathematics departments. Two had been junior naval-intelligence officers during the war, but none were real experts. They were best known for work on subjects like "Lord Hastings' Indentured Retainers 1461–1483," and "The Shrewsbury Drapers and the Welsh Wool Trade in the XVI and XVII Centuries." But the obscurity of their interests—their medievalism and early modernism—meant that they really knew how to use a large research library.

Ten weeks later, the Yale professors delivered six hundred pages of typescript and a thirty-page summary of their findings. To the amazement of Langer's deputy, Sherman Kent, the report included everything from the tactical organization of regimental combat teams to the physical addresses of 251 different army units. There were production schedules of new aircraft, as well as the deployment locations of nine classes of naval aviation—including the first Heavy Attack Wing capable of delivering nuclear weapons. U.S. capabilities in chemical, biological, and nuclear weapons each had their own chapter, including what specific agents American scientists were weaponizing, and where these weapons were being produced.

Kent judged the report to be 90 percent accurate. For instance, the authors overstated the size of the U.S. nuclear arsenal, guessing six hundred to twenty-four hundred weapons, with fifteen hundred judged the most likely number. In fact, in 1951 the United States had only 438 weapons. But, with more time, and a better-qualified physicist, Kent realized the team might have discovered this fact as well. It was supposed to be closely guarded, but information already existed in the public domain that would have made it clear.

A Sovietologist dressed up the report to read like a KGB intelligence product. It came as a total shock to Bedell Smith, the CIA director, and then to Truman himself. If this is what history professors could do over their summer break, what might the KGB and GRU accomplish, with all their wiles and ruthlessness, and with Lavrentiy Beria and Joseph Stalin cracking the whip? When asked by reporters what impact the study had, Truman said that this was what had prompted him to sign the executive order that created a vastly expanded peacetime secrecy system.

The president was wrong to think the professors' analysis was mainly based on leaks to slick magazines. It is true that press reporting was a useful source of national-security information. The Soviets themselves did not just wait until their issue of *Aviation Week* arrived at the embassy in Washington. They did their own reporting, on other reporters, such as by cultivating the personal secretary of Walter Lippman—the most influential newspaper columnist in the country. She regularly passed along her boss's best tips to the KGB. The Soviet's own news agency, TASS, served as a satellite listening post in the National Press Building.

But, according to Kent, the ultimate sources for most of the Yale report were the army, navy, and air-force public-relations departments. When he wrote about his experience with the Yale study more than two decades later, the departments still did not want Kent to disclose this embarrassing fact, even in a CIA report that he classified as secret. Apparently, the fact that Pentagon PR—not unpatriotic reporters—was the main source for useful military intelligence about the United States was too sensitive even to commit to paper.

All copies of the Yale report were locked up as soon as CIA Director Smith heard about it. The next day, a CIA official showed up in New Haven—in a car with medical license plates—and demanded to have all of the materials they had used. The medievalist replied that it would mean carting away Sterling Memorial Library.

An intelligence agency is actually not so different from a research library, albeit one with a very generous acquisitions budget and an unusually well-guarded rare-books-and-manuscripts department. America's oldest intelligence agency, the Office of Naval Intelligence, started as a library, and J. Edgar Hoover trained at the Library of Congress. When the CIA created a Board of Estimates to review and approve intelligence analyses before they were given to policy makers, five of the original eight members, including Kent himself, had doctorates in history.

The CIA continues to employ some very good scholars and librarians. But any researcher would struggle when asked to produce valid and useful information about a closed society. When analysts tried to do to Russia what Kent's scholars did to the United States, it was not so easy, and was even harder when analysts were not of the same caliber as the Yale historians. This brings us to the other dimension of the void encircling and obscuring the core of the dark state: alas, a lot of "secret intelligence" is not very intelligent. After 1945, there was tremendous pressure to determine the most important element in the USSR's order of battle for future conflict: how long it would take the Soviets to be able to deploy their first atomic bomb. The intelligence community's prediction each year was surprisingly consistent: it would take the Soviets five more years. The nuclear physicist Isidor Rabi charitably called it "a peculiar kind of psychology" when he recalled this period. "If you had asked anybody in 1944 or 1945 when would the Russians have it, it would have been 5 years. But every year that went by you kept on saying 5 years."

This kind of psychology is not so peculiar when you consider the analyst's predicament. In this situation, predicting that something will happen later rather than sooner is a safer bet. A false warning of a near-term development could be quickly debunked; if it happened repeatedly, it would quickly diminish an analyst's credibility. Overestimating the time expected, on the other hand, means an analyst might definitively be proved wrong only once. There is also safety in numbers, since individual analysts are less likely to be blamed for the mistake if they join a consensus estimate.

But, however understandable this might be in retrospect, the chair of the Atomic Energy Commission at the time, David Lilienthal, was still taken aback after reviewing secret intelligence on the Soviet program in 1948:

> The thing that rather chills one's blood is to observe what is nothing less than lack of integrity in the way the intelligence agencies deal with the meager stuff they have. It is chiefly a matter of reasoning from our own American experience, guessing from that how much longer it will take Russia using our methods and based upon our own problems of achieving weapons. But when this is put into a report, the reader, e.g., Congressional committee, is given the impression, and deliberately, that behind the estimates lies specific knowledge, knowledge so important and delicate that its nature and sources cannot be disclosed or hinted at.

We are still not allowed to see these "sources" and "methods," the "meager stuff" the analysts used to make up their spurious predictions. Is it because disclosing what the CIA actually knew, and did not know, would pose a "grave danger" to America's national security even three-quarters of a century later? Sir Humphrey Appleby, the mandarin of the classic BBC program *Yes Minister*, knew the answer: "The Official Secrets Act is not to protect secrets," he patiently explained, "it is to protect officials." Or, as the sociologist Max Weber observed more than a century ago, nothing is so "fanatically defended" as the official secret, since it keeps legislators "poorly informed," and hence powerless. It follows that the most fanatically defended official secret is the one that reveals that officials themselves are poorly informed, and pretending to a superiority they do not actually possess.

Thirty years after the Yale study, another professor was brought in by the CIA to consult on how the Agency was analyzing Soviet intentions, a brilliant political scientist named Robert Jervis. Unlike the Yale historians, Jervis obtained a security clearance. "With great excitement, I started reading the finished intelligence on the Soviet Union," he later recalled. "But soon was disappointed. I had expected both better raw information and better analysis. . . . With a few exceptions, the arguments and even evidence being mustered were quite similar to those available outside the government (in part because much secret evidence is soon made public)."

Another time, after reading intelligence on the USSR, Jervis learned about a startling development observed from Soviet missile tests. This information was guarded in the CIA's most protected vault, and Jervis made a mental note to avoid ever inadvertently revealing what he had learned. "I did not have to worry," he recalled. It "appeared in the next morning's newspapers."

Jervis also found that the CIA seemed completely uninterested in the possibility that at least some of what they learned about the USSR represented deliberate Soviet disinformation. It was well known that deception had long been a favored Kremlin tactic. The real question was what the Soviets wanted the Americans to believe, and why they wanted them to believe it. This in itself could be quite revealing. But Jervis found that almost no one wanted to investigate that possibility. He concluded that the cause of the CIA's lack of interest was probably that intelligence gathering was already so difficult that no one wanted to introduce another layer of complexity. It is also possible that some in the CIA had reason not to question what turned out to be Soviet disinformation, such as what spies compromised by Aldrich Ames would later spoon-feed their CIA handlers, which helped justify spending still more on Pentagon R&D.

Jervis made even more surprising and disturbing discoveries about the quality and secrecy of closely guarded CIA information when he started a new project: analyzing the CIA's failure in 1979 to notice that the Shah of Iran was about to be overthrown in a violent revolution. After almost a year of bloody demonstrations, CIA analysts were still claiming, "Iran is not in a revolutionary or even a prerevolutionary situation." It was not their failure alone. Even after the Shah declared martial law, the

Defense Intelligence Agency concluded that he "is expected to remain actively in power over the next ten years." There were some obvious reasons for their mistake. For one, few in the CIA responsible for understanding Iran spoke Farsi. The analysts also did not apply basic social-science methods in their work, such as hypothesis testing. Instead, they worked like journalists, relating to readers what their sources told them.

Perhaps it was no surprise, then, that hardly anyone at the CIA even read the classified political reporting on Iran in the run-up to the Revolution. A lot of top-secret information is simply ignored, because those with a need to know apparently don't really need it, know it's actually not valuable, or are too overwhelmed with other "top-secret" information competing for their attention.

Even after the hostage crisis, when this former ally became a bitter opponent of the United States, the agents the CIA assigned to cover Iran and its Islamic Revolution often turned out to be careerists and incompetents. One case officer, Reuel Marc Gerecht, who worked for the Agency from 1985 to 1993, described how his colleagues played a numbers game in pretending to recruit high-level assets. The CIA's performance-evaluation system rewarded those willing to pass off what they read in newspapers or plagiarized from State Department reporting as secret intelligence obtained from foreign agents. Lacking access to these clandestine intelligence reports, the diplomats typically did not even know they were being ripped off, and their reporting was credited to someone else. Unfortunately for them, "Diplomatic telegrams do not benefit from the boldly printed, highly classified code words that adorn Agency products." But there appears to have been some progress at the CIA after the Shah's overthrow. These CIA agents now made sure their work was "appetizingly packaged in bite-size morsels," making it easier for busy policy makers to digest than more in-depth State Department reporting.

The mere act of classifying information makes it seem more valuable. Psychologists have confirmed this in controlled experiments. In one study, when participants were told that foreign-policy information was secret, they were more likely to believe it to be of better quality and to give it more weight. The researchers also found that the participants judged other people's decisions more highly when told the decisions were based on secret information. One might suppose that government officials would be less credulous, since they see "secret" labels every day. But in a follow-up study by a different research team, this time with actual intelligence professionals as test subjects, participants in the experiment rated an intelligence estimate as more credible if it seemed to be classified. Here again, the only thing secret about it was the labeling.

So is it any wonder that officials will stamp something "Secret" or "Top Secret," even—or especially—when it is meager, old news, disinformation, or plagiarized? The intelligence community ends up fooling itself, because many with high-level security clearances tend to only pay attention to classified, compartmentalized information, and are unaware of how much of that information is actually public knowledge. Even if they suspect as much, it is more prudent for them to go on treating the information as secret so as to avoid any accidental disclosure. Sherman Kent, the CIA's top intelligence analyst, called such people "innocents," and said there are "a lot of them in the intelligence community."

But Kent was being charitable. David Lilienthal's blood-chilling conclusion about the lack of integrity, or even competence, in shoddy analyses rubber-stamped as secret has been substantiated time and again. In 1960, after five years of investigation, a congressional committee concluded that classification was not something that responsible officials used when there was no other way to guard information essential to national security. Instead, they found that secrecy was "the first refuge of incompetents." Five years later, a sociologist doing classified research for an army think tank found that any of his colleagues, no matter how junior, could manipulate the classification system for their own self-serving purposes, whether to hoard valuable intelligence, or to hide their own ignorance. "In such a context it is no longer possible to separate facts from lies, truth from fiction, research from gossip, or useful information from useless trivia."

In 1971, another disenchanted researcher at a Pentagon-funded think tank, Daniel Ellsberg, decided to expose the cost of government lies and secrecy by leaking an internal history of the Vietnam War, what came to be known as the Pentagon Papers. The Nixon administration took *The New York Times* to court to stop publication. In an affidavit submitted to the court, the *Times* journalist Max Frankel derided the mystique the public attached to state secrets as "antiquated, quaint and romantic." After years of trading secrets with presidents and senior officials, he concluded that Cold War spy scares had given the American public entirely the wrong impression:

> ... the Government and its officials regularly and routinely misuse and abuse the "classification" of information, either by imposing secrecy where none is justified or by retaining it long after the justification has become invalid, for simple reasons of political or bureaucratic convenience. To hide mistakes of judgment, to protect reputations of individuals, to cover up the loss and waste of funds, almost everything in government is kept secret for a time and, in the foreign policy field, classified as "secret" and "sensitive" beyond any rule of law or reason. Every minor official can testify to this fact.

Frankel was no radical muckraker. His one-time colleague Seymour Hersh considered him entirely too cozy with top policy-makers and too deferential to their claims to be protecting national security. But Frankel's high-level access is precisely why he was able to persuade the judges that it would be wrong to prevent the press from publishing the Pentagon Papers. His affidavit is still the single most authoritative account of how official secrecy actually works (and how it does *not* work).

Frankel had to put the normally unwritten rules of official secrecy in writing because the Pentagon Papers case was so exceptional. By laboriously Xeroxing thousands of pages of material, Daniel Ellsberg had carried out the first "bulk" leak of classified information, as Chelsea Manning and Edward Snowden would do again at even greater scales decades later. In each case, the purpose of the leak was to discredit the dark state itself. This violated the way things are supposed to work in Washington. As we have seen, leakers are usually high-level officials who trade only a limited amount of information to get a specific story told that advances their particular agenda or organizational interest. These officials have to persuade a journalist that their story is newsworthy, and make it appear somewhere it will be noticed, which has traditionally been a limited number of prestigious media outlets. But most classified information is too arcane, technical, or simply boring to appear in *The New York Times*, or even *Aviation Week*.

The same was not true of the Pentagon Papers. This high-level study was personally commissioned by the secretary of defense, and the subset of documents that were published were chosen because of their newsworthiness. Though they revealed much about the gross misuse of secrecy, they were hardly indicative of what most classified information actually consists of. On the other hand, the publication of 250,000 records from the State Department Central Foreign Policy Files on WikiLeaks, orders of magnitude more records than the Pentagon Papers, is another matter. Julian Assange called this data dump "Cablegate," and insisted that the "sensational" and "incredible stories" detailed therein would reveal "secret operations, deep-seated prejudices, national embarrassments."

Ironically, the State Department adopted this system that amassed millions of electronic records in place of paper files in response to the Pentagon Papers leak. After rejecting the idea of an American official-secrets act, the Rehnquist working group recommended systems with data indices that could unmask leakers by systematically tracking who had access to specific electronic records. Also ironically, as this database grew to become truly massive—containing twenty-six million records by 2006—it became feasible to leak far more records than was previously possible.

There certainly were some sensitive State Department cables that Assange himself apparently meant to protect, but failed to because of poor operational security. The leak revealed the identities of dozens of people who thought they could speak in confidence to American diplomats, such as human-rights activists and dissident intellectuals in China. Suddenly, they found themselves outed. But most of those quoted in the leaked cables had actually said many of the same things in open media. The secret was not what they said, it was that they said it to a U.S. diplomat in a private conversation. Consequently, the leak set off online manhunts and death threats directed at Tibetan and Uighur activists.

Assange claimed that exposing the high crimes of the U.S. government was worth the cost. But what crimes did WikiLeaks actually uncover in this trove of cables? Journalists made some headlines picking through them, but they were mainly about the plots and crimes of others, whether the Gulf states urging an American attack on Iran, the narcotics trafficking of senior Afghan leadership, or China's efforts to hack Google.

To be sure, it was embarrassing for Washington to have frank conversations exposed to public scrutiny, but was "Cablegate" really comparable to Watergate? Typically, the information in the WikiLeaks cables added some color to stories that were already well known to anyone who wanted to know, such as how the Yemeni government helped conceal U.S. missile strikes against the local Al Qaeda branch. "We'll continue saying the bombs are ours, not yours," Yemeni President Ali Abdullah Saleh said in one such cable, which *The New York Times* described as "breathtaking." It led a deputy prime minister to "joke that he had just 'lied' by telling Parliament" that Yemen had carried out the strikes. But all anyone had to do to uncover this secret was to read old newspapers—it had already been reported a year earlier in the very same newspaper. Soon, journalists stopped holding their breath and lost interest in reading the WikiLeaks cables. Only a tiny fraction of the cables ever seemed "secret" or interesting enough to merit a story in the media. That fraction is another measure of how little information that is classified secret is actually secret, or even news. The most important revelation from "Cablegate" was simply to confirm the banality of secrecy.

Opponents of government secrecy have a long history of contributing to the public's misconception about what secrecy typically consists of. Since the passage of the Privacy Act of 1974, subjects of FBI surveillance have managed to get many files released, and FOIA requests have secured the release of others. For a time, journalists eagerly reported the names of celebrities who were the subject of the Bureau's notice, from Marilyn Monroe to John Lennon. One compilation of FBI documents on writers was subtitled *Exposing The Secret War Against America's Greatest Authors.* But, as Daniel Patrick Moynihan later observed, the contents of the files were usually banal or silly, and the vast majority of the targets were not great authors, much less celebrities. So even the journalists stopped caring. There are important exceptions, such as COINTELPRO, when the Bureau infiltrated and disrupted both Black-nationalist and white-supremacist organizations. But the vast majority of informant reports and newspaper clippings were classified, then filed and forgotten. "Some war," Moynihan concluded. "Some secrets." He marveled at how, instead of revealing a series of new outrages, "The FBI's FOIA office was transformed into a genealogy service for the old Left"—a genealogy service with three hundred full-time employees.

To be sure, it is government obstruction, dissembling, and outright dishonesty that—more than any other factor—has engendered suspicion and encouraged conspiracy theorizing. The Kennedy assassination provides the ultimate example of how the tendency to conceal incompetence led the public to suspect that classified files are chock-full of criminal activity. One thing that is certain about the affair is that top officials resolved almost immediately to convince the public that there was no conspiracy. On the very day Oswald himself was killed, J. Edgar Hoover dictated a memo about how to "convince the public that Oswald is the real assassin." The next day, Deputy Attorney General Nicholas Katzenbach agreed that officials had to do everything possible to squelch suspicions: "The public must be satisfied that Oswald was the assassin; [and] that he did not have confederates who are still at large. . . ."

Did Katzenbach and Hoover seek to suppress speculation about the president's death because the Justice Department itself was implicated in it? Well, yes, in the sense that failing to keep tabs on Oswald was a colossal embarrassment for all concerned, and especially for the FBI. After all, while agents were closely observing Marilyn Monroe, they ignored a former marine who had lived in Moscow, came home with a Russian wife, and openly threatened FBI agents. Oswald even went so far as to leave a threatening note at the Dallas FBI office just weeks before the assassination (a note that FBI agents destroyed hours after Oswald was killed).

The CIA has been another suspect for theorists, who imagine the Agency must have engineered the assassination. But could the gang who couldn't kill Castro, or keep the plots to do so secret, kill the president of the United States and successfully cover it up for sixty years? Covering up their incompetence in failing to track Oswald was more than enough motive for the FBI and the CIA, as it had been on countless other occasions, on matters both great and (usually) small. But in this case, because of the insatiable public interest, layers upon layers of secrecy only created ever-deeper suspicion, even while it preserved the cachet of America's G-men and spooks.

None of this is to deny that government surveillance and some secret activities can be—and have been—outrageous and even dangerous. But the great majority of the 1.3 million government employees and contractors with top-secret security clearances are law-abiding bureaucrats. Even intelligence agencies attract their share of people who stay at their posts mainly because of the steady pay and benefits, while enjoying the vicarious glamour created by a relatively small number of real "shadow warriors." U.S. special forces, such as the SEALs, Delta, and the Green Berets, clearly need and deserve secrecy, even if it obscures their work and sacrifices. Though less than 1 percent of the active-duty military, they have accounted for more than half of all combat fatalities since 2015.

Contrast this record with much larger organizations, like the CIA, which demand and expect the same blanket protections for everything they do. True, they, too, have real secrets, and some of these secrets are really dangerous. The CIA's Memorial Wall has 137 stars carved into Alabama marble for all the employees who have died in the line of duty since the Agency was founded in 1947. Many of the stars have no name listed in the "Book of Honor," since they "must remain secret, even in death." The CIA director regularly appears before the Wall while giving speeches. "We in intelligence are not called upon to serve in safe havens," William Webster intoned in one such address in 1988. "Instead, we are asked to collect intelligence in areas that are distant and hostile, often at considerable risk to ourselves and our families." The head of the CIA's clandestine branch, Richard Stolz, joined Webster in emphasizing how secrecy made it important to see that these sacrifices were better known.

> Those of us here today know that [name redacted] and other foreign colleagues died in the service of their country and the CIA. Because we cannot speak of the work we do—just as [name redacted] could not speak openly of the work he undertook [words redacted] years ago—it is all the more important that sacrifices such as [redacted] are known to the men and women who serve this agency.

In this way, senior CIA leaders equate secrecy with honor, and all the CIA officials who ever refused to confirm or deny information that some other officials have leaked can associate themselves with the same secret-warrior status as [name redacted]. In fact, the book with the names of the dead was originally called "The Book of Honor and Secrecy." By 2016, CIA Director John Brennan declared that the Memorial Wall represented "the essence of the CIA."

But somehow the Memorial Wall was not deemed essential during the CIA's first twenty-five years. The decision to build it was only made in 1973, a year when no CIA officer died in the line of duty. Why only then? That was the year when Director James Schlesinger—angered to learn how Agency staff had been accessories to the illegal activities of Nixon's "plumbers"—directed every employee to report any activities that violated the CIA's legal charter. The resulting dossier, dubbed the "family jewels," was almost seven hundred pages long, and much of it is still redacted. It described domestic surveillance, break-ins, and assassination plots, and created unprecedented turmoil and recrimination. The higher-ups hoped the Memorial Wall would be good for morale. It was put in a place where every visitor would see it upon first arriving at CIA headquarters.

In fact, this Wall has always given a misleading impression. Working at the CIA is actually an extremely safe career choice. To put it in perspective, the CIA employs an estimated twenty-two thousand people, and it has lost on average fewer than two people a year. This includes some who died in vehicle collisions or commercial-airliner accidents while overseas, and others who died during a gallbladder operation or other medical complications. It is far more dangerous—twenty times more dangerous—to drive a cab than it is to work for the CIA. It is forty times more dangerous to haul garbage as a sanitation worker. And it is 140 times more dangerous to work on a commercial fishing vessel.

Thus, official secrecy can act like a big, warm blanket, covering up and giving comfort to people who might otherwise be exposed as doing rather mundane work, more or less well, more or less legally. How else to explain the way many intelligence officials react when someone tries to take their secrecy away?

The very idea "gives us psychological problems," as one Agency veteran, Gail Donnalley, confessed in 1974, the year the Memorial Wall was installed in Langley's lobby. "The ideal situation would be this," he said, "a complete and final removal of intelligence-related matters in terms of informants, agents, and employees from any aspect of public knowledge." The Wall would therefore serve to cover up everything that happened inside the Agency—indeed, make the Agency itself invisible. Instead, Donnalley reported, Nixon's issuing his executive order requiring that the CIA review records for declassification had a "traumatic effect" on rank-and-file intelligence officers.

Donnalley did not say what form this trauma took. But the psychological impact is easier to understand when you consider the central role secrecy plays in creating a sense of identity and solidarity, not just among those in the intelligence community, but among all those charged with defending national security. Though committing oneself to the defense of the nation is a worthy ideal, the actual work, as we have seen, is often mundane and disillusioning. The elaborate process of proving one's worthiness by divulging private information, the "indoctrination" and training that follows, the shared rituals and jargon, the isolation from other communities and sources of authority—these are all time-honored methods for creating esprit de corps. That they are oriented around protecting government information is what makes secrecy—far more than the ill-defined and oft-debated ideal of national security—the actual foundation of the dark state.

Rank-and-file denizens of the dark state find declassification "traumatic," but the most senior officials—political appointees or experts with careers outside government—know that decades-old records contain few if any important secrets. We have seen how, in 1970, the Pentagon's Defense Science Board's task force on secrecy warned that overclassification stifled innovation and protected incompetence. They judged that even closely guarded secrets only stayed secret for an average of five years, and the government could not count on keeping truly vital information from adversaries for more than one year. Over the longer run, classification was only effective in reducing the amount of information available to friends. They recommended reducing the amount of secrecy in military R&D by as much as 90 percent. Some members even argued, "we would have more to gain in the long run by pursuing a policy of complete openness in all matters." The members of this task force were not starry-eyed idealists. The leader, the physicist Frederick Seitz, was an ardent Vietnam War hawk, and one member, Edward Teller, was the proud father of the hydrogen bomb.

The most senior policy makers have repeatedly attested to the same reality: the information produced through secret sources and methods is not usually secret, and information that is actually secret does not stay secret for long. George Kennan judged that at least 95 percent of what the government needed to know was available from open sources. Howard Baker, the long-serving senator who became Reagan's chief of staff, said that, during his entire career, he had only learned one secret that remained a secret. Reagan's secretary of state, George Shultz, later recalled that he had already known the classified content of his CIA briefings from reading *The New York Times*, and over the following decade found that the Internet was making any desired information even more readily available. Former CIA Director Michael Hayden recently confirmed that only a "very narrow number of specific operational acts" actually stay secret for any significant length of time. When he was secretary of defense, Donald Rumsfeld went even further, concluding, "The United States Government is incapable of keeping a secret."

And yet, even after twenty-five years, when career CIA officials finally review records for "automatic" declassification to make available to the public what our adversaries learned long ago, they withhold close to 100 percent of anything involving "sources and methods" except when specifically directed to disclose them by the president or by an act of Congress. Even for its more anodyne research-and-analysis work, the CIA withholds 82 percent of these decades-old records. The Pentagon is little better, withholding 76 percent. The Department of Justice keeps more than 90 percent locked up. As a result, the mass of classified information keeps growing.

The government does manage to keep some secrets. Some of them are quite important, such as the identities of confidential informants who have not yet had their covers blown. Jervis relates that, after he was "read in" to certain programs, he was impressed with the information provided by particular spies and signals-intelligence exploits. Some of what Hayden called "specific operational acts" can yield enormous amounts of data, much of it quite personal. According to an NSA internal study, George W. Bush was impressed when his transition team began to hear their briefings, calling this material "great stuff!" The President's Daily Briefs were revised accordingly.

But the massive amounts of information harvested by the NSA and the other seventeen intelligence agencies through means that are more or less secret—less secret after the Snowden revelations—present the opposite problem for those who are trying to identify and protect the truly "top secrets": there is so much, it can be hard to identify anything that is actually useful.

Nowadays, the NSA is drowning in data. We have seen how, as of 2013, it was spending almost fifty million dollars just for basic research on "information overload." Just one information-technology company like Microsoft or Facebook can hold vast amounts of incredibly rich data. But that data is not typically organized to support even internal research—as insiders know all too well—much less aggregation and analysis by a government agency. This is a long-standing problem. As one CIA study concluded in 1977: "Conspiring against the integration of information in the Agency is not merely the codeword compartment but also the information explosion itself. . . ."

When it comes to signals intelligence, it is not that there is no there there. We know it is special. But there is so much, it is hard—even for the NSA—to know what might actually prove useful in all the petabytes of data it hoards and hides. It is even harder for officials to know what *other* agencies have, from other sources, and what they might have already given away. A 2008 interagency report for the Office of the Director of National Intelligence (ODNI) found that there was "uneven guidance, misunderstanding, and a lack of trust between Intelligence Community agencies and mission partners concerning the proper handling and protection of information."

Different officials will classify the same document differently, and make different redactions. The inconsistencies can make the whole classification process seem arbitrary or even irrational. But they can also be seen as reflecting the "bounded rationality" of different officials working in different parts of the government. What is top secret to a CIA agent, such as information obtained from a confidential informant, might not be for a State Department diplomat, who had the language skills to read the same information in a foreign newspaper.

In 1996, the Moynihan Commission on Protecting and Reducing Government Secrecy developed a proposal for a database of declassified documents, which would allow officials to know what had already been released. More than a quarter-century later, there is still no such system. As a result, officials within the same government department sometimes classify and declassify the same information differently. There are even cases in which the same official redacts the same record differently just a few weeks later, or the same document—already released in full—is redacted three different ways by three different officials. To err is human, and officials tend to err on the side of secrecy. The sheer volume of classified information means classification errors are inevitable, and at scale, these errors mean that the secrecy blanket actually has a lot of holes.

What is inexcusable is that, in all these years, the government has never conducted any rigorous study of the problem. It would be simple to start measuring reliability, and even identify the sources of error: Different officials could be asked to review the same information, and then one could measure to what extent they agree or disagree about what would cause "grave damage to the national security," and what they feel duty-bound to disclose to the public. If there is no effort to determine the degree to which officials can actually agree on what to classify or declassify, and no effort to identify clear errors, any executive order instructing them to err on the side of either secrecy or transparency is meaningless.

Academics have run studies on "inter-coder reliability" thousands of times on matters much less important. Whether they are analyzing Israeli attitudes toward the Iranian football team, or techniques for promoting preventive dentistry in Appalachia, self-respecting researchers know that they have to determine whether different people can generally agree on how to classify their data before anyone will trust conclusions based on that data. At a conference marking the fiftieth anniversary of the Freedom of Information Act, I asked a panel of government officials in charge of FOIA review if they had ever done such a study, to see whether their staff were consistent in what information they withheld or released. It took them a while even to understand the question I was asking. When the moderator explained it to them, one asserted that they already have too much work to do anything of the sort.

If officials cannot agree on what is secret, the dark state loses its reason for being. That would not be the end of it, of course, since, for many, secrecy has become an end in itself. But it would be impossible to cut it down to size, because there would be no way—even with artificial intelligence and supercomputers—to systematically identify the information that really does require safeguarding.

But in 2015, the government finally did run an inter-coder reliability study—quite by accident, and under duress. It started when the journalist Jason Leopold filed a FOIA request for Hillary Clinton's e-mails as secretary of state. Clinton and her aides had kept tens of thousands of e-mails on her private server. She insisted that none of them merited classification, which would have required safeguarding on a more secure system. But when Leopold appealed the FOIA denial, a federal judge ordered that the government had to release all of them unless the information was covered under one of FOIA's exemptions. Reviewers then had to go through each one to make their own assessment as to whether the e-mails needed to be classified.

As top State Department officials, Clinton and her aides were no less qualified to identify sensitive information than the people who were conducting this post-hoc review. The review therefore constituted a natural experiment, which would measure inter-coder reliability in classification. In the end, the reviewers decided that, of the 30,490 e-mail chains, 2,115 should have been classified. That amounts to 6.9 percent, or one or two e-mails out of the thirty-seven Clinton and her team averaged each day. Even if we accepted that all these e-mails should have been classified, is correctly identifying the other 93.1 percent as not meriting classification a failing grade? Recall how, in 2008, the very year that Clinton was picked to become secretary of state, the ODNI found government officials had conflicting information and inadequate communication on what information needed to be protected.

Moreover, Clinton and her team were also generating an untold number of communications using secure systems, including cables, secure telephone calls, and secure fax messages. Ordinary office workers average 121 communications a day. If the secretary of state averaged this many communications daily, the

6.9 percent error rate would drop to less than 2 percent. She probably had a lot more, which would make the relative proportion of underclassified cables even smaller. Of course, Clinton may have made many more errors in *over*classifying communications—i.e., keeping nonsensitive communications on secure systems, where no one will see them for decades to come. That would have been far more typical for a government official. But no one ever gets investigated for *that*.

The most important finding from this natural experiment—and the most devastating in terms of history, and the future of historical research—was how long it took to complete. As months went by, the *Times* ran stories puzzling over "why the State Department has struggled with the classification issues and document production." In fact, with a federal judge and Clinton herself urging a rapid review, the government had given it top priority. Some fifty officials drawn from all the departments and agencies with "equities" in Clinton's e-mails focused on this one task. Journalists just did not understand how page-by-page declassification worked, and how badly it worked. With no tools or technology to assist them, government officials had to treat each e-mail—even ones where Clinton had simply written "print this"—as if it might blow up the world.

In the end, it took almost a year to manually review and redact the fifty-four thousand individual e-mail messages. It took even longer for then FBI Director James Comey to decide that Clinton had been "extremely careless." If Comey had determined that it was "gross negligence," she could have been indicted. All this dragged on during the Democratic primaries, and the conventions, and continued into the last weeks of the 2016 campaign—when Comey reopened the investigation because he thought he might have missed some underclassified e-mails. For all the obsessive coverage by the media, no one ever stopped to ask an obvious question—by what standard was Clinton's behavior "extremely careless"? Did the average State Department official—did Comey himself—protect sensitive records on secure systems 100 percent of the time? When he was later found to have lied about using private e-mails for internal FBI communications—e-mails that were later withheld in full or heavily redacted—this only confirmed for Clinton's defenders that the whole affair was ridiculous. But is it really true, as some claimed, that secrecy is "random"? When Donald Trump was president, his opponents seemed quite certain that he was recklessly disclosing national-security information.

So how do we know what is normal, what is careless, and what is negligent when we have never established an official standard for correctly identifying national-security information? Is so much information classified that classification has effectively lost any meaning, encompassing "practically everything that our Government does, plans, thinks, hears and contemplates in the realms of foreign policy," as Max Frankel argued in his Pentagon Papers affidavit? Or can officials actually discriminate between sensitive and nonsensitive information, and are they "careless"—or criminally negligent—when they fail to do so?

This book has argued that, although there is indeed massive overclassification in our government, secrecy is not completely random or inexplicable. There are patterns in the way officials identify certain kinds of information as particularly sensitive. And if it is possible to identify the things that officials agree require protection, they could focus on protecting that information, and release everything else. It might even be possible to develop tools that could automatically rank records according to their sensitivity. But how can we prove it?

We devised our own experiment to determine whether there is a "there there"—that is, whether, as much as officials might sometimes disagree, there are patterns that make secrecy predictable. We would use artificial intelligence to model classified intelligence, training an algorithm with the collective wisdom of thousands of diplomats. We first gathered about a million State Department cables from the 1970s that were originally marked as secret, confidential, limited official use, or unclassified. With high-performance computers, we developed machine-learning algorithms to measure and compare the differences between communications in the classification categories. The algorithms are designed to detect patterns, such as who sent or received the message, and the words in the message itself. After "training" the algorithms with one part of the data, we tested them on the rest, then repeated the training and testing with different subsets of the data to measure and optimize performance. If there is something special about the most secret information, the algorithm should be able to rank automatically the ones that are most likely to be classified as secret.

The first thing we discovered, even before we started analyzing the data, was a lot of human error, starting with almost 120,000 cables that contain nothing but an error message explaining that the text of the original communication has been lost. There is *literally* no there there. The National Archives FAQ page describes these losses as resulting from technical problems. If that is true, and this first generation of electronic records is a harbinger, then the story related at the outset of this chapter would not culminate with the opening of a three-day-old newspaper, but of hundreds of blank pages—blank except for the scary classification markings. We will explore this further when we turn to archival destruction, the ultimate secret.

In our experiment, we were left with over nine hundred thousand diplomatic cables from 1973 to 1978 that still included the full text and many different kinds of metadata, including subject lines, keywords, and who sent or received them. We then started training a whole "ensemble" of state-of-the-art classification algorithms. The algorithms relentlessly and tirelessly tried out different combinations to produce the best possible performance, picking up on patterns that might be invisible to the human eye—like how a particular State Department office will classify messages with certain words, in messages about certain subjects, addressed to certain embassies.

We found that classification, though not always consistent, was hardly random. By calculating the relative frequency of different words in the message text and in the metadata, the algorithm could correctly sort 90 percent of the cables as classified (secret, confidential, or limited official use) versus those that were unclassified.

When you dig into the data, you can see the patterns that make classification largely predictable. With nothing more than the keywords—or "concepts"—officials assigned to each cable, it is possible to identify 84 percent of the classified communications. This is how they indicated which cables were meant for the highest-level officials, 87 percent of which were secret, and which ones were about sensitive topics, like arms-control negotiations. If these keywords indicated lower-level communications about subjects like civil aviation, scientific meetings, or, in one peculiar case, "meats," it was generally safe to predict that those communications would not be secret. (Though not always—the export of meat was "a subject which is extremely sensitive in Australia," as the American ambassador there warned in a secret, "Exclusive Distribution" cable.)

The machine is not always right. If we were able to access *all* the diplomatic cables from the period, including both those that were lost and those that are still classified, we would likely achieve higher accuracy. But even so, the results cannot be more accurate than the intrinsic consistency of the data allows. To the extent that humans misclassify their communications—or simply disagree about how they should be classified—so, too, will algorithms.

In our experiment, fewer than 11 percent of the cables that our algorithm identified as likely to be classified had *not* been marked as classified. But it turns out that a lot of these false positives resulted from human error rather than the limitations of the algorithm. This included cables that were originally secret when received at the State Department but that were re-sent to another post as unclassified, such as what Lebanese Christian leaders said about cease-fire negotiations with the PLO.

Meanwhile, a little over 16 percent of the cables the algorithm identified as unclassified were actually marked as secret, confidential, or limited official use. But, here again, inspecting these false negatives revealed a lot of human error, such as inconsistencies in the metadata we got from the State Department database and the actual markings that appear on the cables themselves. Hundreds of cables were mislabeled as unclassified, such as a report on the Japanese government's sensitivity about

U.S. inspection of its nuclear facilities. The message's text clearly showed it was meant to be confidential, and the algorithm was actually correct.

So it was not just Secretary Clinton who kept what should have been classified communications on nonsecure systems. It was also the officials responsible for protecting these sensitive State Department cables. Were these officials "extremely careless," or even criminally negligent? Obviously, the statute of limitations has run out. But after all these years, we should be wise enough to realize that expecting officials to recognize and protect sensitive information 100 percent of the time is a dangerous illusion, no matter how many billions of dollars you throw at the problem.

The more fundamental question is not where and how classified information is stored, but whether officials agree on what should be classified in the first place. When we looked at cables that were not simply mislabeled, and incorrectly counted as errors for the algorithm, we found many unclassified cables that seemed likely to have been highly sensitive at the time. This included, for instance, what a confidential informant told U.S. diplomats about the 1977 kidnapping of the son of the president of Cyprus. Other cables that were both labeled and marked as "secret" were almost certainly overclassified, such as miscellaneous travel reservations.

So we asked two experts with security clearances to give us their opinion. One was a historian named Richard Immerman, who for a time served in the Office of the Director of National Intelligence, and for several years chaired the State Department's Historical Advisory Committee. By an act of Congress, this committee has the responsibility to compare what the State Department declassifies with what it still keeps secret to verify that the published record of *The Foreign Relations of the United States* is an accurate and reliable record. The other was the political scientist Bob Jervis, the same one who authored the CIA's Iran study. At the time, he was the chair of the CIA's Historical Review Panel.

We gave these two experts the cables that the algorithm ranked as the most likely and the least likely to be secret, but that were *not* classified as the algorithm predicted. Without knowing the original classification—we redacted it from the copies we handed them—and without drawing on any of their classified knowledge, they were asked to sort the cables into two categories: those they thought should have been classified, and those they thought should not have been classified.

It turns out that, in most cases, they agreed with the algorithm, and disagreed with the original classification markings. Even after many years of experience dealing with classified information, they were amazed at how spectacularly wrong the original classifications were.

But the biggest problem of all, both for our algorithm and for democratic accountability, is how officials classify an enormous amount of harmless information. Note that our experiment included "Limited Official Use" records, 280,000 of them. In other parts of the government, this category has different names—more than a hundred different names, like "Controlled Unclassified Information," "Sensitive but Unclassified Information," etc. Unlike "top secret," "secret," and "confidential," it has no formal definition. When the George W. Bush administration attempted such a definition, the government's leading FOIA expert admitted it was "so broad that it is almost harder to think of information that does not fall within its scope than information that does."

If we leave these cables entirely out of the equation, it cuts the percentage of cables the algorithm misclassifies almost in half. Instead of 87 percent accuracy overall—taking into account false positives as well as false negatives—we get 93 percent. So officials' tendency to withhold information when they cannot offer any clear reason for doing so has a big, and now measurable, impact on our ability to distinguish sensitive from nonsensitive information.

This kind of technology could help. It should be feasible to develop a system that would capture and analyze classified and unclassified communication streams on the fly, much as spam filters do for e-mail systems. Like a spam filter, such a system would automatically label communications that are unworthy of classification (think "Meats"). Conversely, it would flag communications that are likely sensitive (think "Meats" + Australia + sent by ambassador). With enough data, it could automatically default to the predicted classification, requiring manual override if the sender wished to classify at a higher or lower level.

The same type of system could be used for accelerating the release of electronic records, harnessing data from previous declassification decisions to prioritize for close scrutiny records that are most likely to have sensitive national security or personal information. These systems could therefore "nudge" officials to classify or declassify communications appropriately. They would also reveal which officials tend to overclassify, making "top-secret" records that other officials leave unclassified even when they concern the same subject and have similar language. Classification and declassification systems could therefore be self-correcting, and become increasingly accurate as sources of error are continually identified and corrected for.

If the government began adopting machine-learning technology to assist officials in a more rational, risk-management approach to national-security information, the public might finally learn the best-kept secret of the dark state. People might be amazed at the vast quantity and low quality of most classified information—including *the most* classified information. But what remained would be more secure, both more secret and more intelligent. And we could finally focus on the core problem: how to keep our officials accountable when they claim sovereign power over what we, the people, are allowed to know about what they do.

The only problem is that this assumes that, after all these years, there is still something there.

10

DELETING THE ARCHIVE

THE ULTIMATE SECRET

If you ever go to the National Archives on the Mall in Washington, D.C., you can find the most important documents in American history: the Declaration of Independence, the Constitution, and the Bill of Rights. To approach the formal entrance, you must first climb thirty-nine steps up from Constitution Avenue. At the top, there are two massive bronze doors, each one nearly a foot thick, almost forty feet high, and weighing six and a half tons.

The documents are displayed inside a rotunda, more than seven stories tall, in a row of dimly lit cases. After lining up to look more closely, under the watchful eyes of armed guards, you will find that some are so faded they're scarcely readable. Long ago, before the Declaration of Independence was preserved in this way, sheets of damp paper were pressed against the parchment to create copies from the original ink. It also suffered from direct sunlight, and botched repairs with glue and Scotch tape. Now the physical security may seem even more impressive than the documents themselves. Each of them is suspended in an argon-filled titanium encasement, and at the first hint of danger, a mechanism will lower them down into a vault designed to withstand the blast of a nuclear bomb.

These are the most sacred relics of the American republic,

some of the first things we would want to save in the event of a national calamity. They are also our most public documents, on display for all to see and reproduced countless times. But they are surrounded by secrecy. Inside the National Archives—not just the building in Washington but also dozens of federal records centers and presidential libraries—there are millions upon millions of other records that are unlikely to be seen by anyone outside the government ever again.

True, government archives are in part places for citizens to

Don't get any ideas.

A scale model of the original, fifty-five-ton steel vault custom-built to protect the "Charters of Freedom." It was replaced in 2003 by a more secure Diebold system, but there is no public information about its design or construction.

explore the past. They afford a partial view into the government's inner workings, empowering scholars "to penetrate the mysteries of State," as the historian Lord Acton observed. But that access can be withdrawn, documents can disappear, and far more might be hidden than will ever be revealed. The first purpose of archives, after all, is to provide a place where powerful people can preserve their secrets. And, as Acton more famously observed, "Power tends to corrupt, and absolute power corrupts absolutely."

Now that more and more government records are electronic records—which number in the billions—no one may ever know all that lurks inside, and what might already be lost forever. But when we consider that presidents have been able to exercise nearly absolute power over what the public is allowed to know, it is already clear that the display cases in the rotunda are just a row of small windows into a very large vault. And if you could see all the way inside, you would realize that nothing, not even the Constitution itself, is truly secure.

To see fully how secrecy works, and how it has stopped working, we need to recognize that archives have always been at the core of the dark state, no less than cryptology, intelligence agencies, and surveillance systems. And that story is even older than America— thousands of years older. The most ancient archives, whether in China, Mesopotamia, Egypt, or pre-Columbian America, were the property of sovereign potentates. They existed for the purpose of amassing knowledge—and sometimes destroying it, when that knowledge proved dangerous.

When power shifts, archives are among the first things invading armies seek to control. Those who dream of ruling the world try to unite all of this secret knowledge. Napoleon treated archives of other European powers as trophies and hoarded them in Paris. Hitler followed suit, hauling French files measuring seven kilometers from end to end back to Berlin. After the Red Army crushed the *Wehrmacht*, commissars filled thirty freight cars with plundered archives and sent them on to Stalin.

In normal times, countries that have laws and institutions to safeguard the national patrimony task archivists with preserving the historical record. Their professional ethos is inspiring. As one of the most famous, Sir Hilary Jenkinson, attested in 1922:

> The Archivist's career is one of service. He exists in order to make other people's work possible. . . . His Creed, the Sanctity of Evidence; his Task, the Conservation of every scrap of Evidence attaching to the Documents committed to his charge; his aim to provide, without prejudice or afterthought, for all who wish to know the Means of

Knowledge . . . The good Archivist is perhaps the most selfless devotee of Truth the modern world produces.

But, however selfless, every government archivist has an internal conflict. Archivists are not only custodians of knowledge that they hold in trust for all who seek knowledge. They are also guardians of state secrets. Jenkinson imagined the archivist as being entrusted with materials selected by others—after all, he mainly worked with centuries-old manuscripts. State officials would decide what ought to be preserved. What "truth," what "evidence" they might have lost, destroyed, or decided to keep secret was not under Jenkinson's purview.

When the U.S. government began to accumulate an overwhelming mass of new records during World War II, every two years producing more records than in all of American history until 1934, archivists worked closely with other officials to destroy what they considered useless paper and make room for what really mattered. They, too, took possession of plundered archives, including lab notes and data from Japanese medical experiments on Allied prisoners of war. They were taken away from war-crimes prosecutors and classified top secret by Army Intelligence, who wanted to use this research in support of America's own biological-warfare program. But, ultimately, they were shipped back to Japan. U.S. Army archivists made no copies whatsoever.

The archivists' creed can therefore conceal darker arts. When all is said and done, government archivists are functionaries of the state. Their superiors can deploy whole armies and intelligence agencies to confiscate and control the historical record before any archivist even arrives on the scene. As the Czech novelist Milan Kundera once wrote, "The struggle of man against power is the struggle of memory against forgetting," and this struggle is a very unequal one. It can be so unequal, in fact, that those who have struggled to hold powerful people accountable would sometimes rather forget. For example, in 1890, abolitionists who led the new Brazilian republic ordered that all documents related to slavery be burned. The press cheered the decision, because former slaveholders would have no way to claim indemnification. Conversely, archives can be used like an arsenal against political opposition, which is why Napoleon, Hitler, and Stalin were so eager to seize control of them. In Eastern Europe, politicians regularly cite communist-era archives to smear or blackmail opponents they allege to have been police informants. In India, Hindu nationalists have mobilized mobs to attack mosques by claiming that they are righting historical wrongs committed centuries earlier.

In such cases, might all of us not be better off forgetting? The historian's creed stubbornly refuses this concession. First of all, who would get to decide what we are supposed to start forgetting, and where would that forgetting end? Furthermore, if there is no historical record, there is not even a chance for redemption—no chance for us to gain knowledge, or to find wisdom. If archives are not preserved, it is not just history that can disappear, but perhaps the very possibility of finding our way to a better future.

To return to Brazil, the National Museum, for instance, used to hold relics from communities of indigenous people that had otherwise vanished. It also contained recordings of languages that have since become extinct, and unique maps showing where these people once lived. But because of decades of neglect and a failure to invest even in a sprinkler system, all of that was lost without a trace in a 2018 fire. "That place was like a memory, a computer hard drive, that at any moment, any ethnic group, from any people, could access to get information, to know where they were, to not feel lost," one of the leaders of the Tupinambá people said in the aftermath. "What was there won't ever come back, no one can replace it." It was, as another put it, "like a new genocide."

Destroying historical records creates the ultimate secret, because effacing the last traces of the past makes that information secret beyond recovery—rendering it unknown and unknowable by any living being. In this chapter, we will see how this can happen not just through malfeasance, and deliberate vandalism, but also through neglect and indifference. Historically, forgetting the value of archives has been the greatest danger of all to the record of the past. And that neglect has been a function not of poverty but of poor leadership, not least in the United States.

One humid night in St. Louis, in July 1973, a motorist was passing a federal records center—the country's largest—and noticed a fire on the top floor. The building had no smoke alarms, no fire walls, and no sprinkler system. Instead, there were just row after row of file cabinets stuffed with millions of military records, lining corridors that were almost eight hundred feet long, stretching from one end of the building to the other.

Firefighters arrived quickly, but were driven back by the intense heat. As the flames raced down the corridors, metal file cabinets began to buckle and melt. When papers spilled out, they provided more fuel for the fire, which rose higher and higher, until the roof collapsed. The inferno blazed out of control for twenty-two hours, and did not end for four and a half days. Firefighters poured in so much water that a fire engine broke down. The top floor, which measured more than five acres—bigger than the flight deck of a Nimitz-class aircraft carrier—was completely destroyed, and with it approximately sixteen to eighteen million military personnel files.

In fact, we will never know the full scale of the catastrophe, because the government did not even keep an off-site index of the records stored there. As a result of this negligence, it is difficult to document the military service of millions of Americans—Americans who may be eligible for benefits, who may need to defend themselves against charges of "stolen valor," or who may simply want to find their final resting place in Arlington National Cemetery.

Though little noted at the time, an even bigger disaster was just beginning to unfold that same summer at the State Department in Washington. The government's first "Automated Data System" to store textual records became operational. It was the beginning of an era that some now call "the digital dark age."

The State Department had already conducted experiments with electronic records systems, to find out how they might be used to extract and store metadata automatically from the Central Foreign Policy Files. Electronic systems promised to improve managerial efficiency. Whereas previously orga-

Dustbin of history: the aftermath of the 1973 St. Louis records-center fire

nizations employed large numbers of secretaries and clerks to organize and access file systems, now they could maintain data indices to retrieve information with a few keystrokes—not unlike the "Memex" that Vannevar Bush imagined almost thirty years earlier. As we have seen, for the Nixon administration the main selling point was that these systems could more rapidly identify leakers. But they could also make workers redundant and save shelf space. It seemed possible to preserve on paper only those records with some ceremonial value, like treaties with original seals and signatures. Everything else could be stored on magnetic tapes.

But in the first years of the new system, large numbers of diplomatic cables started to go missing, for reasons the State Department has never been able to explain. Most of the missing cables do not date to when the State Department first set up the system, when one might expect officials would have been troubleshooting ways to transfer data reliably between different hardware and software platforms. Instead, they date to 1975–76, when then Secretary of State Henry Kissinger was coming under increasing criticism for amoral conduct. Intriguingly, the cables missing from the database tend to be more highly classified, and often involve Kissinger and his most senior staff. Electronic messages classified as "Secret" were more than three times more likely to go missing than "Unclassified" and "Limited Official Use" messages (22 percent versus 6.5 percent). Of the cables marked "CAT-C," intended for high-level attention, 62 percent are missing the actual words of the communication. Only an error message remains, e.g.:

> MRN: 1975JAKART014946 SEGMENT NUMBER: 000001 EXPAND ERROR ENCOUNTERED; TELE-GRAM TEXT FOR THIS SEGMENT IS UNAVAIL-ABLE

This particular record, an account of a meeting in Indonesia between Gerald Ford, Henry Kissinger, and President Suharto, survived because someone printed it out in hard copy, placed it in the correct file, and it was preserved for the archives. But there are almost no State Department cables in the database from the same period of December 1–15, 1975, the first of several conspicuous gaps. When the cable was finally declassified in full in 2001, it showed that Ford had given the green light to Suharto's plan to take "drastic action" against the people of East Timor, who sought independence after Portugal ended its colonial occupation. Kissinger advised Suharto to call his invasion self-defense, but delay it until Ford had returned to Washington.

Kissinger was incensed when, later that month, a U.S. Foreign Service officer sent a cable apparently confirming that Suharto's forces were using U.S.-supplied weapons to kill his political opponents, which was a violation of U.S. law. Kissinger worried about how many people had already seen the cable. "That will leak in three months and it will come out that Kissinger overruled his pristine bureaucrats and violated the law," he complained to his aides. "Everything on paper will be used against me." This second cable is one of the 119 sent from Jakarta that same month that are now missing from the State Department database.

Other notable gaps in the Central Foreign Policy Files

include March 18–31, 1976, when Kissinger supported the military coup in Argentina; May 25–31, 1976, when he favored the Syrian invasion of Lebanon; and June 1976, when he met with the prime minister of South Africa in the midst of the Soweto Uprising against Apartheid. Toward the end of Kissinger's term as secretary of state, he got a State Department lawyer to designate transcripts of his telephone conversations as "personal" records. Then he shipped them off to a vault at the Rockefeller estate in New York, where they could be protected by his wealthy patrons.

Kissinger knew all too well what might happen if he allowed all of these records to be turned over to the National Archives, as was required by law. In 1974, Congress forced Nixon out of office after discovering tape recordings of his secret dealings. That same year, it greatly strengthened the Freedom of Information Act, and after years of litigation the Supreme Court ruled that the Kissinger telephone transcripts were not his to remove, reaffirming the authority of the National Archives to recover them. But it was already too late for countless other records.

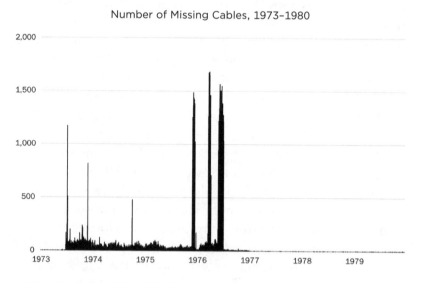

Nixon's secretary, Rose Mary Woods, became infamous for the 18.5 minutes of missing audio in the White House tapes. But that was all from one day in 1972. The gaps in the record of Kissinger's State Department span many weeks.

As we have seen, the Joint Chiefs of Staff decided to destroy all minutes of their meetings going back to their founding. The CIA destroyed records from multiple covert operations, including the coups that overthrew governments in Iran and Guyana. A former CIA historian described a "culture of destruction," where records of covert operations were routinely destroyed. As CIA Director Richard Helms was about to step down in 1973, he personally decided that all the files of Agency mind-control experiments should be destroyed: "Since the program was over and finished and done with we thought we would just get rid of the files as well," he explained, "so that anybody who has assisted us in the past would not be subject to follow up, or questions, embarrassment, if you will." Some of those who "assisted" were hardly capable of being embarrassed. Recall how Frank Olson, unwittingly subject to a CIA mind-control experiment, had "fallen" from the tenth floor of a Manhattan hotel.

All this archival destruction may have been an overabundance of caution. Ever since the 1953 *United States v. Reynolds* ruling, when the air force defrauded widows by claiming that an accident report proving its negligence could not be disclosed, federal judges have routinely denied FOIA requests for documents from the State Department, the Pentagon, and the CIA without even looking at them, all on grounds of national security. Recall that, in 1978, government lawyers even managed to convince judges to keep "innocuous information" classified because of how it might be pieced together into a mosaic.

But if documents are destroyed, even the slim possibility that they might eventually be revealed is eliminated. That is why, in 1986, a National Security Council official named Oliver North began deleting e-mails from his White House computer. He knew that the e-mails would show how he had been providing weapons and secret intelligence to Iran as ransom payments for hostages, then diverting the cash proceeds to arm the Contras in Nicaragua. The national-security adviser, John Poindexter, joined in the effort, and eventually the two of them deleted almost six thousand messages, and shredded many thousands of pages of documentation. Though Poindexter, who had received a Ph.D. from Caltech, knew his e-mails were being backed up on magnetic tapes, he also knew that the tapes were regularly recy-cled and were scheduled to be overwritten. But professional staff at the NSC, realizing the tapes contained e-mails of great and enduring importance, decided to put them aside so the records could be preserved. The recovered e-mails proved vital in con-victing North and Poindexter.

Nevertheless, on the last day of the Reagan administra-tion, officials on his National Security Council again sought to destroy their e-mails. When challenged, government law-yers claimed that whatever records were worth preserving had already been printed out. After years of litigation, a federal judge stopped them. He sided with the National Security Archive—the same organization of journalists and historians that would be put under FBI surveillance shortly afterward. They argued that electronic records are public records. Metadata also merits historical preservation, the judge agreed, because it would show which e-mails were actually read—revealing "who knew what information and when they knew it."

Fortunately, this case was decided during a brief period when, after America's historic triumph over communism, there was a bipartisan consensus in support of both modernizing archives and accelerating the release of Cold War–era records. It would show what could be achieved with just one favorable court rul-ing, and a modest investment by Congress in providing appro-priations to preserve historical records and release them to the public.

Dedicated National Archives staff set to work recovering the NSC e-mails and their metadata from over a hundred different hard drives. Torn tapes had to be spliced, creases ironed out, and moisture baked off in ovens. They succeeded in the end, and it set a precedent, showing that, with adequate resources, it was entirely possible to preserve important records, including elec-tronic records. Documenting the last years of the Cold War, and what kind of agreements were made at the time on the future of former Soviet states like Ukraine, would prove to be vital in years to come.

By the year 2000, the federal government was spending an estimated $231 million on reviewing and releasing classified

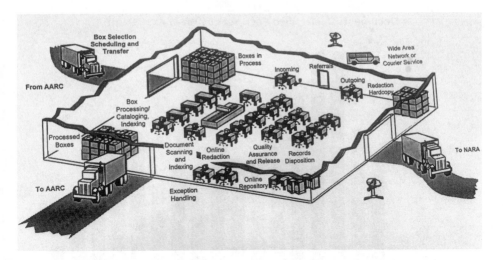

A CIA depiction of its "Declassification Factory," showing how records arrived from the Agency Archive and Records Center (AARC) and—after systematic processing—were shipped out to the National Archives and Records Administration (NARA).

records. Adjusted for inflation, that was equivalent to $349 million in 2020 dollars, and it did not include the (still-secret) figure for declassification by the CIA. But the post–Cold War push to release decades-old CIA documents was also impressive. The Agency established a "factory" where fifty-five experienced CIA officers systematically reviewed and redacted millions of pages of documents.

But in the years that followed, appropriations for declassification all but collapsed, shrinking to forty-nine million dollars in 2012. The CIA factory shut down, and the number of pages it released each year dropped off to almost nothing. The overall budget for the National Archives seemed to fare better, and even rose relative to inflation between 2000 and 2012, from $263 million to an all-time high of $423 million (both totals adjusted for inflation to 2020 dollars). But after 2005, a larger and larger proportion of this budget—fully 18 percent in 2012— was absorbed by Lockheed Martin in a botched effort to build a new Electronic Records Archive. It turned into an expensive fiasco, with an estimated cost in excess of $380 million, at least

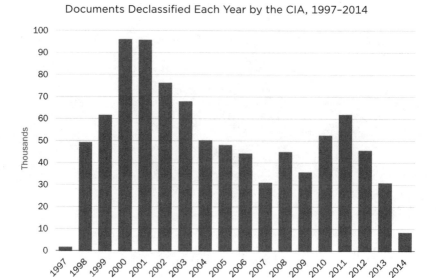

Documents Declassified Each Year by the CIA, 1997–2014

three times higher than estimated, for much less than was originally promised. After all the effort made to recover the e-mail
from Reagan's National Security Council, the National Archives
now cannot even review the e-mail from the George H. W. Bush
administration for declassification. It simply does not have anyone on staff who can reconstruct the data. Neglect, underfunding, and mismanagement have now done the work of intentional
destruction.

———————

Year after year, the National Archives budget has been shrinking,
to just $359 million in 2020. Fewer people currently work at the
National Archives than during the Reagan administration. And
yet their workload is far bigger: twenty-seven million cubic feet
of federal records awaiting review and processing, almost twice
as many as in 1985, and more than three times more cubic feet
of archival holdings. That load includes records from eight new
presidential libraries. And whereas there were thirteen million

electronic records in 1991, now there are 21.5 *billion*, with two billion more every year.

Even if their budget stops shrinking, archivists must cope with larger and larger data dumps from the entire federal government. In 2013, the Archives' inspector general found that—after the hundreds of millions handed over to Lockheed Martin—archivists could not assure the long-term preservation even of the electronic records it already had. Another inspector-general report found that management continues to use legacy systems for declassification and redaction that were due for replacement more than five years earlier. Archive staff could not even determine the age of these systems. Nevertheless, all federal departments and agencies are now prohibited from transferring paper records to the Archives. All records must be digitized if they are not already electronic records.

Recall how electronic records systems were supposed to be more efficient, part of a larger transformation that would eventually include networked terminals, and then personal computers. The cost savings came from not having to employ large numbers of secretaries and filing clerks, and reflected how this kind of work—mainly performed by women—had long been undervalued. But the true costs of eliminating these positions, and losing the institutional knowledge of the people who performed this labor, are tremendous, especially over the longer run. Electronic records systems permit particular kinds of queries to support certain functions deemed most important by managers, like internal audits. But the records themselves are no longer arranged in any humanly recognizable order, rendering traditional forms of archival appraisal—and historical research—obsolete.

What happens when archives are understaffed and underfunded, lack functional technology, and then face an avalanche of electronic records? We can already see the results by examining what happened to America's Central Foreign Policy Files—or what remained of them—after the State Department transferred them to the custody of the National Archives. In 2007, archivists decided there were still far too many of these electronic records—some twenty-six million—to review one by one in order to sort the wheat from the chaff. They began to experiment with sampling, looking at every "nth" cable to make generalizations about the historical significance of groups of documents. Alas, this method does not actually capture a representative sample, since the content and frequency of diplomatic cable traffic was hardly uniform. Undersampling weekends and holidays—when communications were normally less common but more likely to be important—could skew what was already a tiny selection. In the case of records related to passports, visas, and citizenship, for instance, they looked at just two hundred documents out of almost six million, a sample representing 0.003 percent, and then decided to delete all of them. In most cases, the archivists did not even read the full sample before deciding that a whole class of records should be permanently deleted. This included all the diplomatic cables on cultural diplomacy, educational exchanges, international sport, and scientific cooperation.

As Solon Buck, the second archivist of the United States, understood, records managers and archivists have always had to "weed" routine and duplicate documents to make room for the preservation of important papers. But these State Department records were small text files, millions of which could easily fit on a single thumb drive, rather than in an aircraft-carrier-sized warehouse in St. Louis. Moreover, a large and relatively complete set of seemingly routine records can present remarkable opportunities for research using distant-reading methods. With millions of cables on passports and visas, for instance, researchers might have been able to develop a vastly more sophisticated understanding of global migration. This opportunity is now lost forever.

Deleting immigration records also means deleting the stories just one such record might tell about a whole family's history. For instance, we still have some of the private letters of one of the greatest historians of the twentieth century, Marc Bloch. That is how we know that, in December 1940, he was offered an American visa that might have allowed him to escape occupied France, and the Holocaust. But he turned it down because he could not get visas for his mother and two grown children. He therefore decided to stay, and joined the Resistance. He was finally captured and executed in 1944, just before he could com-

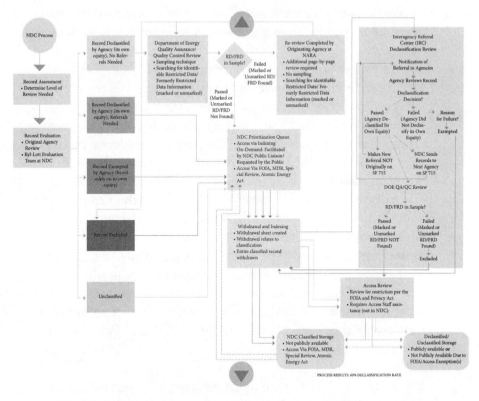

When the National Archives established a National Declassification Center, it was intended to streamline and accelerate the review and release of Cold War–era documents. But the process is still a Rube Goldberg machine.

plete a remarkable masterpiece, *The Historian's Craft*, which was to include a chapter on the history of the future. How many stories, how much future history, might be lost and impossible to recover because the National Archives are not preserving the records?

Even after culling millions of historical records without so much as looking at 99.997 percent of them, archivists still have millions upon millions of other diplomatic cables they have to review, page by page. Just checking for the presence of "restricted data" (nuclear information) is a multi-step, interagency ordeal. When you study the flow chart for this process, you wonder how anything ever gets released. If a record fails to pass at any point in a sixteen-step process, it goes back to the accumulating pile of government secrets, all of them stored in increasingly outdated systems.

The proportion of State Department cables that are being "withdrawn" rather than released has been rising. Whereas fewer than 15 percent of secret cables from 1973 were kept secret, in the most recent batch that underwent declassification review that rate has more than doubled. Many more withdrawn records were not classified when they were written. They might not even have been reviewed, because they were suspected of containing personally identifiable information (PII). Under the Privacy Act, the government must protect this information, and underfunded and overworked archivists have apparently been forced to use crude commercial software. It might flag records just because they have a nine-digit number, which may or may not be someone's Social Security Number, but not the eight-digit unlock code for launching ICBMs. Even so, there are many examples of government records available online that contain very private information, such as State Department communications about messy divorces and destitute Americans overseas.

It is unclear whether archivists have actually begun a systematic review of the top-secret cables, but for a different reason. Despite all the hundreds of millions the National Archives spent on an Electronic Records Archive, and the eighteen *billion* dollars the government spends on information security, there was no money for archivists who needed just one computer that was sufficiently secure to review all the most sensitive cables.

The few top-secret cables from the 1970s that have come out through individual FOIA requests already indicate why we need to see all of them. One from 1975 recently revealed the full magnitude of a diplomatic crisis with the Netherlands caused by Lockheed—the same company that failed to build a system to archive such records. The company paid the Queen's husband a million-dollar bribe to secure a contract to sell the Royal Netherlands Air Force a notoriously unreliable airplane, the F-104 Starfighter, which came to be known as "the Widowmaker." This was the same aircraft that had brought down one of only two copies of the B-70 Valkyrie in a midair collision. The cable shows that the blowback from the scandal risked the country's withdrawal from NATO.

Can we be sure the rest of these top-secret cables are secure? If they are, many would eventually be reviewed and released in the same document collection that Abraham Lincoln started in 1861, *The Foreign Relations of the United States (FRUS)*. As we have seen, State Department historians are required to compile the most historic documents, certify that these *FRUS* volumes constitute a "thorough, accurate, and reliable" account of U.S. foreign policy, and release them in a timely fashion.

But much has changed since Lincoln's time, when Americans could see what their diplomats were doing a year or less after negotiations were completed. Starting around World War I, the State Department imposed ever-lengthening delays on the release of diplomatic documents. With the Cold War, the delays became even longer, averaging twenty or thirty years. Now we are waiting as long as fifty years to see formerly secret cables, memos, and telephone transcripts. But at least in principle, all the most vital records are supposed to be included in these volumes, even if some are completely redacted.

Delays in Publishing the Official Record of *The Foreign Relations of the United States*

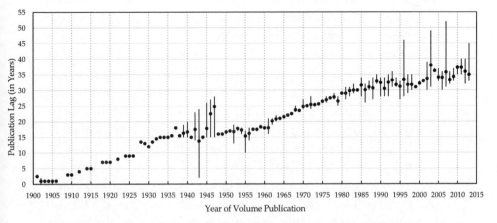

The circle for each year shows the average length of time before the State Department released documents recording U.S. foreign policy, starting with one to two years in the early twentieth century. The bars above and below show the range, which now may be as long as forty to fifty years.

The Decline in the Documentary Record

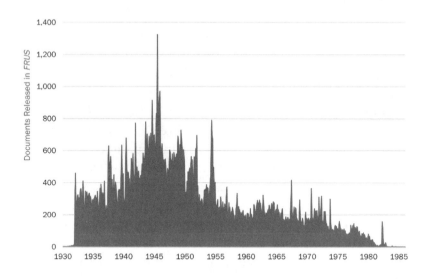

Other statistics are equally concerning. For example, we might have expected the official record of American foreign relations to have grown over the years. After all, the United States has established relations with 150 new countries since 1950, and engages in a vastly expanded range of international activities, from environmental regulations to cybersecurity. But the government is not only taking longer and longer to let us know what they are doing, they are also releasing less and less of that record every year. If scholars want to write about the 1970s, when climate change and international terrorism first appeared on the foreign-policy agenda, they find there are barely a quarter as many declassified documents about these topics as there are documents from the 1940s, on subjects like the Berlin crisis and the closing of the Iron Curtain. And in 2019–20, publication of new volumes almost ground to a halt, reportedly because the Pentagon was refusing to approve the release of Defense Department records. For instance, a collection of documents on basic national-security policy in the late 1970s was "under declassification review" for more than five years.

This is how the government treats what everyone agrees are the core collections recording our national and global history, collections that are stewarded by the State Department's Office of the Historian, with robust oversight by a congressionally mandated external committee. We can only imagine what will happen to the billions of e-mails and other records produced by every other government department and agency.

Some number of these records will never be reviewed or released, because they have been inadvertently lost or intentionally deleted. In 2021, the National Archives opened forty-five new cases involving unauthorized loss or destruction of federal records, up from twenty-eight in 2020. Many of these cases involve government officials' use of private e-mail or encryption services. But the practice has been going on for years, as Hillary Clinton and her defenders pointed out when she was found to have deleted tens of thousands of e-mails she deemed personal. Colin Powell, for instance, did not save any of his e-mails when he was secretary of state. Other Bush-administration officials used Republican National Committee accounts to avoid creating official records. Some twenty-two million e-mails were eventually recovered, but it may be impossible to determine how many more have been lost or deleted.

Clinton still insists, in her case, that the whole affair was just a big distraction from "the real issues." But how do we know what is real and what is false if government officials do not even keep records? And why is that not an issue for the Justice Department? According to the FBI inspector general, the reason Clinton was not prosecuted for the concealment, removal, or destruction of records was that the relevant law has "never been used to prosecute individuals for attempting to avoid Federal Records Act requirements." As of this writing, Trump is being investigated only for the improper handling of classified materials, not for tearing up presidential papers.

This is the real scandal, the "real issue" revealed by the Clinton e-mail affair and Trump's torn-up papers: the Department of Justice has for years refused to faithfully execute laws requiring that *all* government officials keep a record of what they do in our name. The more examples we find proving that both

Democratic and Republican politicians hide or destroy public records, the more obvious it should be that no issue could be more real, or more important. After all, the lack of trust in our government—well founded, in this respect—affects our ability to act collectively on any and all issues, no matter how urgent.

Some might suppose that everything, including messages our leaders try to conceal or delete, must be backed up somewhere—maybe even at the NSA. But during a 2013 visit, when I asked if NSA officials considered archiving data that might otherwise be lost to history for the sake of preservation, they reacted with surprise. It seems they never considered the idea. As for having the private sector take on that responsibility, companies like Google have no interest in archiving information if they can't make a buck from it. In fact, quite the opposite is true. Holding on to customer data is a legal liability.

Even when officials preserve their own information, archivists and historians find that the information may be unreadable if it was created with defunct software. If you doubt that we are living in what future historians might call a digital dark age, just try to open your oldest e-mail, or recover WordPerfect documents from a floppy disk.

By law, government departments and agencies must make public their own plans to preserve records, or designate them as "temporary," to be deleted after five or ten years. The most recent of such plans, proposed during the Trump administration but still pending approval, prompted one senior archivist to warn that "the situation is dire." To take just one example from the State Department, it proposed in 2018 that virtually all the papers of the undersecretary of state for economic affairs be designated as "temporary." That means the department was asking to delete rather than archive all meeting notes related to the enforcement of economic sanctions, all memos on congressional relations, such as the department views of proposed legislation, "involvement on major decisions regarding foreign aid to developing countries," relations with the International Monetary Fund and the World Bank, domestic and international banking and monetary policies, debt rescheduling, foreign-exchange markets and restrictions, and capital-market restrictions. If granted approval, department officials would get rid of "records reflecting company investments, legislation, voluntary notices of acquisition and other correspondence relating to mergers, acquisitions and takeovers by or with foreign persons." They also designated for deletion all records related to international aviation security and violations of FAA regulations.

Politicians like to claim that, someday, the "court of history" will redeem them. If the Trump administration really took pride in its efforts to rewrite trade agreements, it is hard to explain why his State Department proposed to destroy records related to anti-dumping efforts and the protection of intellectual property. It is perhaps easier to understand why Trump appointees at the Department of the Interior wanted to delete records about the enforcement of "health, safety and environmental laws and regulations." But all this is good news for anyone interested in evading economic sanctions, buying American strategic assets, selling us shoddy goods, stealing American intellectual property, or violating FAA safety regulations. Now even the court of history could be closed.

But any administration, no matter how responsible it is in designating important records for permanent preservation, cannot actually make that happen without adequately funding the National Archives. The last inspector-general report revealed that at the presidential libraries, the crown jewels of the National Archives system, archivists have not processed the majority of the paper records they have received, and estimate it would take decades to reduce the backlog. The backlog of electronic records is even more appalling. As of 2012, the presidential libraries held over three hundred million electronic records, over 95 percent of which were unprocessed. After Obama left office, the volume of unprocessed records became even more unmanageable. His administration's e-mails alone totaled another three hundred million records, which must be reviewed before they can be released. All the while, citizens keep filing FOIA requests, and keep waiting for responses. Even beyond the backlog of records that need processing, it will take almost 250 years at the government's current pace to process the FOIA requests for materials held at the George W. Bush Library alone.

The National Archives has all but given up. It quietly let it be known that the George W. Bush Presidential Library would be the last of its kind. Barack Obama will be the first president since Herbert Hoover not to have his own presidential library, but only a "center." The only historical records held there will be the ones on temporary loan and displayed in the center's museum. The plan now is for archivists to load up all the still-classified records from every presidential library onto trucks. They will drive them back to Washington, like an army in retreat, to make their last stand at the National Declassification Center.

Considering that the National Archives will no longer even accept paper records, what is to become of the vast trove of secret documents still held by the Pentagon, the CIA, the NSA, and every other part of the dark state? No one knows. In theory, government-history lovers might somehow find the money to carry out a vast archive-digitization project. What seems far more likely is that the National Archives' new policy will provide the justification to destroy irreplaceable records.

Years ago, much of the archive of the Drug Enforcement Administration was apparently lost—and perhaps destroyed—when the DEA moved to a new headquarters. The IRS cannot find two-year-old e-mails even under congressional subpoena, and after an investigation that required 160,000 hours of staff time and twenty million dollars. In some cases of archival destruction, it seems clear that officials have tried to cover up wrongdoing. How else to explain why Immigration and Customs Enforcement (ICE) wants to destroy records detailing the sexual abuse and death of undocumented immigrants? When the plan was first revealed in 2017, and the public was allowed to comment, tens of thousands of people posted critical comments, and dozens of congressmen and senators objected. The National Archives told ICE to temporarily delay the destruction of records of sexual assault and abuse, but allowed it to go ahead and start destroying records of detainees' complaints about civil-rights violations and shoddy medical care. The American Historical Association and the Committee for Responsibility and Ethics in Washington filed suit, and a federal judge agreed that the Archives had ignored the public and violated its own policies. But even after the practice was declared illegal, ICE officials accelerated the destruction of reports documenting how it had left detainees deemed to be suicidal or mentally ill in solitary confinement for months on end. Perhaps not coincidentally, they did it in November 2020, when Trump lost the election and a new administration was preparing to take over.

CIA director Gina Haspel was directly implicated in waterboarding detainees during the "Global War on Terror." She simply ignored legal requirements and clear instructions when she went ahead and destroyed the tape recordings of the torture sessions. During her confirmation hearings in 2018, Haspel dodged the question of whether torture worked, claiming, "I don't think it's knowable." Thanks to Haspel's decision to destroy federal records, there's a lot we will never know about what actually happened, and what we might have learned from it.

Some officials want to destroy history; others just don't seem to care. Perhaps the best example of this is what happened during the 2003 invasion of Iraq. As we have seen, conquering armies normally make it a priority to secure enemy archives. Such was the case not just for Napoleon, Hitler, and Stalin, but for American invasions as well. In World War II, Franklin Roosevelt deployed specially trained teams to protect historical manuscripts and other cultural treasures. In his message to the troops preparing to liberate Normandy, Dwight Eisenhower reminded them that they would be fighting around "historical monuments and cultural centers that symbolize to the world all that we are fighting to preserve."

But when American forces stormed into Baghdad on April 9, 2003, troops were deployed to guard just two government buildings: the Oil Ministry and the Ministry of the Interior. Iraq's National Library, which included the National Archives on the second floor, was left completely undefended. Baath Party loyalists quickly set the building ablaze. The library's director implored nearby U.S. troops to come protect the building, but they refused. When Donald Rumsfeld was asked about it, he offered no excuse or explanation, simply observing, "Stuff happens."

Back at the National Archives building in Washington, D.C., the symbols of open and accountable government—the Declaration of Independence, the Constitution, and the Bill of Rights—are still carefully protected behind those massive bronze doors. But behind the scenes, more and more of the substance—the record of what the government actually does in the name of the people—is being destroyed, deleted, or simply lost. The head of research at the National Archives admitted that the situation they face "boggles the mind," recalling the last scene from *Raiders of the Lost Ark*. "Spielberg got it right!" he said, when the film showed how a crate stamped "Top Secret" would simply be lost among thousands of other crates. But whereas that misplaced crate could be found again, much of what is now being lost is lost forever.

Other departments and agencies are starting to take matters into their own hands. The State Department, for instance, has reportedly begun experimenting with artificial intelligence, so algorithms can automatically identify which records to destroy. There can be no doubt that department officials face an immense challenge, not after their experience with the Clinton e-mail scandal. During her tenure, the department was already producing an estimated two billion e-mails a year. Information technology created this challenge, and information technology has to be part of any solution.

But rather than working with the National Archives, and teaming up with archivists and historians to develop and test new technology, the plan was reportedly to make currently serving officials read a random selection of contemporary records. This data would then be used to train algorithms to identify the records worth preserving automatically, and accelerate the destruction of everything else. Even those records the algorithm designates for preservation will not be turned over to the National Archives. The State Department will keep them in its own custody, and the National Archives will only have a "monitoring role." When I asked the spokesperson for the National Archives whether they had agreed to this plan, she said they had not even heard about it.

It is not clear what research the government is doing to test the idea of automated archival appraisal, and automated records deletion. Such a process is unprecedented in the annals of archiving. It is in conflict with the plain meaning of the Federal Records Act. It also goes against everything we know about history, at least since the time of Hegel. The whole point of allowing time to pass before rendering judgment is that it gives us some perspective, so we can look back at the past and see it more clearly. As Hegel put it, "The owl of Minerva spreads its wings only with the falling of the dusk." In other words, true understanding of a historical epoch is possible only as it is ending. Can State Department employees train algorithms to predict what future historians will want to know while that history is still unfolding?

To really know, you would need to run another experiment, and it would need to run for a few decades. You would have to keep a record of everything that happened in that time span and rate each record according to whether contemporaries agreed it would prove historic, banal, or something in between. You would then need to convene a group of historians to re-evaluate this record, many years later, and determine the accuracy of the initial predictions. Needless to say, the government is showing no interest in conducting such research.

So, in 2018, I joined with colleagues at Microsoft Research to run a simulation. We took advantage of the fact that State Department historians choose a tiny fraction of diplomatic cables—.09 percent—to include in *The Foreign Relations of the United States*. We used that collection to approximate the judgment of history—at least official history—as to what communications were truly historic. Were those documents the same as the ones contemporaries identified as important? To estimate that judgment of contemporary importance, we created an index that included how each cable was classified, whether it came with special handling instructions, the urgency with which it was dispatched, and who ultimately read and acted upon it—especially if it rose to the attention of the most senior officials.

In our experiment, we created a model using this index and tested it on the hundreds of thousands of cables in the full database to achieve the best possible performance in identifying which cables will become part of the historical record. For every cable the model correctly identified, there were almost ten that it missed (false negatives) and forty-four that turned out to be much less important than they had seemed at the time (false positives). Even when we used the most powerful computers available at Microsoft Research to train algorithms with the documents later picked by State Department historians—so they could "learn" what made communications historic—these algorithms missed more than four out of five.

So, unless the State Department has better data-scientists, we can already see what is likely to happen if government-engineered algorithms are turned loose on the documentary record: the great majority of important historical records will be destroyed, automatically, and much of what's left will be dreck. It is, in a very literal sense, the end of history as we know it.

Of course, and as we have seen, archives have always been at the core of the dark state, concealing what powerful people know and, no less important, concealing their ignorance. Intentionally destroying records of the past—whether selectively, or automatically—is the ultimate form of secrecy, since it makes this power over knowledge absolute, beyond even the court of history. But in a well-functioning democracy, archives are also supposed to provide a window into the government's inner workings, even if that view is—by its very nature—limited to the past. Keeping that portal open requires never-ending struggle, including pitched battles in courts and the public arena, but also a continuing investment in the people and the technology that keep archives "future-proof." Alas, we are losing this struggle, and we will never know all that we have lost, especially after it is gone.

Recently, a group of scholars gathered to consider the state of historical knowledge about the most futuristic part of our collective past, the space program. Inspiring stories like the one brought to life in the 2016 film *Hidden Figures* have shown that, decades later, we still have much to learn. Sending men into orbit and on to the moon was long celebrated as one of the greatest achievements in the history of life on Earth. But until that film—and the book it was based on—few Americans were even aware of the contributions made by Black women.

Alas, NASA seems to have little interest in documenting its own history. The assembled historians and archivists reported that, when the space program first began, NASA officials seemed not to care whether they preserved a historical record. So great are the gaps, it is not clear whether any archivist was around when the program first reached into space, and probed the universe beyond. Now NASA archivists must "constantly" justify the need for their work to agency leaders, and find themselves more and more overwhelmed by the challenge of saving digital records.

Is this how America's story ends? Will we travel to the stars, but not even know how we got there?

CONCLUSION

THE END OF HISTORY AS WE KNOW IT

This book began with a realization that it might be difficult, and perhaps impossible, to carry out serious research on official secrecy. But without at least making the attempt, we cannot begin to know what we do not know. And that unknowability is already a great and growing threat to our capacity to hold our government accountable and ensure that it can keep us safe. However, when I teamed up with data scientists and started to do the research, analyzing millions of electronic records and discovering how many more are missing, I realized that something even more elemental is at stake: The rise and fall of the dark state is just a preview of trends that will eventually touch us all. The exponential growth of information, much of it secret, all of it perishable, threatens history itself.

When I walked away from that foundation grant, I did not know how I would grapple with any of these challenges—and not just because of the scary warnings from the federal prosecutors. If the MacArthur Foundation had not stepped in, and gutsy data scientists had not stuck with me, the project would have been over before it had even begun. Even after getting that two-year grant, I worried we would run out of time and money before we could demonstrate the potential for taking a more rational, risk-management approach to state secrecy.

The biggest worry of all was that we might find that—as some critics have claimed—the processes by which officials select and preserve secrets is random and unpredictable. But, in fact, we were able to discover recurrent patterns, and also detect anomalies. Those patterns allowed us to build a whole set of tools that could be used to protect truly sensitive information while accelerating the release of everything else. And the anomalies, like human errors in both classification and declassification, showed that the current system serves neither national security nor democratic accountability. Along the way, we had also shown how making the documentary record more accessible to computational analysis could lead to new breakthroughs in exploring our country's history, and future. We had done all this using declassified documents and private funding. A government R&D program could create even more powerful algorithms by training and testing them with classified data.

In 2015, as we neared the end of the MacArthur grant, my colleagues and I boarded a train to Washington, D.C., so we could present our findings. I tried, and failed, to get them all to wear jackets and ties. They pointed out that conforming to everyone's stereotype of what mathematicians look like would only lend us more credibility.

When we got to Washington, no one raised any questions about whether we could be prosecuted for espionage. Instead, it seemed as if everyone—the State Department, the National Declassification Center, the CIA, the Public Interest Declassification Board, and the Office of the Director of National Intelligence (ODNI)—wanted to hear what we had been able to achieve. After all, the White House had specifically instructed the Defense Department and the ODNI to develop new technology for declassification. For my part, I needed to know whether the U.S. government was indeed going to join this effort. But after a whole series of meetings with officials intimately familiar with these problems, I discovered that their enthusiasm was always followed by a caveat of one kind or another. Until, finally, I realized the larger truth that underlay everything they were telling us.

We first went to Foggy Bottom, where we met the head

of the State Department's automatic declassification program. We presented our research on automatically detecting records with restricted data, which could relieve his staff of having to read every random document page by page in search of weapons schematics. He agreed that the need for this kind of technology was "frighteningly clear," and wanted to partner with us. But the State Department had no funds to pay for it. He gamely suggested we enlist students who could carry out this work for course credit. I was struck by the notion that declassification could be treated as a kind of school project, as if we could solve the problem with student-run hackathons.

At the biggest National Archives facility, in College Park, Maryland, we demonstrated how new software could automatically sort documents so reviewers could prioritize the ones most likely to merit their attention, and avoid the pitfalls of haphazard sampling. The director of the National Declassification Center stood up and said, in front of a big audience, that she would buy this technology "immediately." We explained that we wanted to make the tool open-access so anyone could use it for free and help us to improve it, but she said it had to be licensed to one of the National Archives' approved vendors—the same vendors who have been selling them dysfunctional electronic-records management systems.

Later, we went to the original, historic home of the National Archives on the Mall for a meeting with the director of Information Management Services at the CIA, along with officials from the Office of the Director of National Intelligence. They were not quite ready to invite us inside the CIA headquarters at Langley. Still, they were genuinely interested in our work and asked smart questions. The CIA official had already told me that he would rather use algorithms that make errors than continue relying solely on human reviewers, because at least the error rate would be measurable. But, although these officials told us how we could set up our tools so the CIA could actually use them— essentially, by letting Amazon host them in the cloud—there was no suggestion that the CIA would pay for their development.

Down the hall, in a high-ceilinged conference room, we appeared before the Public Interest Declassification Board.

This is the board Moynihan managed to create in 2000 after his long struggle to effect more fundamental reform. With members jointly appointed by the White House and the leaders of the Senate and House of Representatives, the board advises the entire government on how it should handle sensitive information and meet legal mandates to maximize transparency. Members have included federal judges, flag officers, and former members of Congress—all of whom have been given top-secret security clearances. The board was already on record insisting, "The government must study and pilot risk management principles" with "formalized, statistically-based processes." So we knew they would be interested. And they were genuinely excited by the results we were getting; the chair told me they wanted to have a follow-up meeting. Unfortunately, the board has almost no budget of its own, and no expertise in data science. Instead, they told us that the logical place for this kind of project was an agency known as the Intelligence Advanced Research Projects Activity (IARPA), which had been tasked to work with the National Archives to develop new technology to deal with the declassification problem.

This was not the first time we had heard about IARPA. Ever since we started our work, we had been hearing about this mysterious agency. It is modeled after the Defense Advanced Research Projects Agency (DARPA), which spends three billion dollars a year developing cutting-edge military technologies. IARPA performs much the same mission for the CIA, the NSA, and the rest of the intelligence community, and it is even more secretive. But it is known to fund dozens of research programs in areas like facial recognition and video surveillance tracking. Every one of its programs has a budget that is at least an order of magnitude bigger than that of our project. Given its expertise in high-performance computing and machine learning, it would make sense for IARPA to take the lead in organizing a program to apply data science to declassification.

With this in mind, I had set up our final meeting, with IARPA's deputy director for research, Catherine Cotell. As we said goodbye to the good people on the Public Interest Declassification Board, and walked past the massive bronze doors to hail

a cab on Constitution Avenue, we decided to take a few photos, and savored the moment. With its columned portico and imposing neoclassical statues, the U.S. National Archives is the most ornate building in all of Washington, and the ornamentation seemed to speak directly to our mission that day. On the western side, a sculpted figure representing *Heritage* holds an urn with the ashes of past generations in one hand, and with the other holds a baby representing the future. Beneath, chiseled words declare, "The heritage of the past is the seed that brings forth the harvest of the future."

We started to walk to the eastern side, in the direction of the White House, and stopped one last time to take a photo in front of a muscular, sixty-five-ton figure called *Guardianship*. It warns, "Eternal vigilance is the price of liberty." The youngest member of the team struck a vigilant pose, squinting in the bright sunshine. We laughed at how, in our own small way, we were also trying to be guardians—not just of secrets that really do require safekeeping, but of the historical record itself, and all it represents: the foundation of democratic accountability, the bedrock of all our liberties.

We were inspired to be there, the home of the Constitution itself, and were still basking in all the encouragement we had received for our own effort to ensure that future generations could learn from the past. It started to feel like all our work, all our meetings, had been leading up to this moment.

But now, headed back out to Maryland in the middle of rush-hour traffic, we really had to hurry, and discovered we could not even find on the map the particular building where we were supposed to present our work to IARPA. The address in Google Maps pointed to an unnamed structure right next to the "Applied Research Laboratory for Intelligence and Security." When our cab finally pulled up outside, we found a bunch of nondescript buildings in what looked like an office park. We correctly guessed that ours was the one surrounded by a steel paling with warning signs posted on both sides of the gate and guardhouse.

The cab driver did not want to get any closer, so we walked to the checkpoint and presented our credentials. Once inside, we were given a red "visitor escort badge." We were told to deposit all our devices in lockers, and to enter our Social Security Numbers into an electronic keypad. How did they even know our Social Security Numbers? I wondered, while the grim-looking sentries studied our expressions. Other than these guards, it seemed the building was practically uninhabited, and eerily quiet.

There was a lot of paperwork just to get one laptop past security, including a pledge not to attempt to connect to any network. I had sent our slide deck to Cotell earlier in the day, just in case. When she came out to greet us—emerging from a maze of empty cubicles—I knew we were headed into a tough meeting. "Did you send the right briefing?" she asked. "This does not look anything like the topic you described in our communication about setting up this meeting."

Cotell is a no-nonsense, MIT-trained materials scientist who specializes in lasers. She spent most of her career in the private sector, first with Bell Labs, and later with In-Q-Tel, a kind of venture-capital firm that uses CIA money to invest in technology start-ups. I knew she was not going to be a pushover. But her vexed reaction to the slide deck was mystifying. In putting it together, I had gotten advice from a computer-scientist colleague who had received DARPA contracts. We had presented much the same deck to the CIA and ODNI officials. Cotell herself had written that she had long been interested in ways to identify sensitive information automatically. I could not understand why she seemed so irked, and I struggled to read her expression as I began presenting our work.

It turns out that Cotell had spent years trying, and failing, to build her own system. But her system was built to *classify* information automatically, not declassify it. She told us that she had found that there were too many reasons why information might be classified, and it might be classified in dozens of different ways, depending on which "compartment" or "special-access program" it originated in. She wanted to see all we had, but was deeply skeptical that we could do any better than she had done.

Conceptually, building a classification engine presents the same challenges as a declassification engine. But I pointed out that more and more records are being withheld that were not classified to begin with. They might never even be reviewed, because crude software cannot accurately detect personally identifiable information (PII). Developing a more advanced, machine-learning-based solution to this one problem would remove one of the biggest obstacles to making more information available to the public, and at the same time more accurately identify and protect records that would violate citizens' privacy if released.

But now Cotell had the opposite objection. Detecting PII was a "trivial" problem, too easy for IARPA to bother with. It was focused on things like machine translation, or automatically rendering recorded communications in dozens of foreign languages into English. That work is indeed important: part of the NSA's "information overload" problem is that a lot of this information is in Arabic or Chinese. But wasn't it also important that the government be able to communicate with the public in plain English about previously classified programs? After all, taxpayers were the ones funding all of IARPA's research. Didn't people have a right to know what it had been doing with its black budgets? Cotell just stared at me blankly.

We soldiered on. Even if IARPA was only concerned with protecting national-security information, our research indicated that there was a lot of human error in both classification and declassification. Just to evaluate whether machines could help reduce the error rate, we first had to determine the frequency with which humans made such mistakes. Doing so only required a straightforward study, in which different officials would independently evaluate the same classified information. Such an experiment would establish what secrets officials within and across departments agreed required protection, what could immediately be released, and what fell into a gray area, requiring closer scrutiny.

Cotell laughed. She said she was sure that such a study would reveal that the level of inter-coder reliability in identifying state secrets was "terrible." We had finally found something we could agree on. To me the implication seemed obvious: we needed to run that study, and start helping all the people who face the immense challenge and responsibility of dealing with this mess—the people told to "automatically" review millions of secret records for public release, page by page, but with no consistent standard for what should have been classified in the first place. All of the people we met that day were looking for help, but had no way to help themselves. I wanted to help them. I thought I might have persuaded Cotell that she should, too.

Then Cotell just said it: she told me IARPA had no interest in developing technology to assist in the review and release of classified information. So it was not that it was too hard. It was not that it was too easy. She just did not care. "Why not?" I asked. Because, she said, it would bring an "insufficient return on investment."

At first, I did not understand what she meant. I was still thinking about those words carved into the National Archives building: "The heritage of the past is the seed that brings forth the harvest of the future." The IARPA building in which we were meeting was barely finished. Loose wires were still hanging out of the electrical outlets. IARPA was not even ten years old at the time. It had almost no history of its own. There was so much Cotell and her colleagues could gain from rigorous historical study of more than seventy years of U.S. government research and development—some of it brilliant, but too much of it weird and wasteful. How could she show no interest in learning the lessons from the past?

And what about the price of liberty? I had just come from meeting the people appointed by our elected leaders to guard American democracy against the threats that government secrecy poses: to our privacy and protection from state surveillance, to the principle of civilian control of military forces, and to our ability to prevent even presidents from exercising unaccountable power. I was still thinking, like them, that the intelligence community would feel some sense of collective responsibility, and could use a small part of its immense resources to help. Obama had specifically instructed the director of national intelligence—Cotell's bosses' boss—to build technology for declassification. How could Cotell just say she wasn't interested? Wasn't technology designed to maintain democratic accountability worth something, anything? To me, it seemed priceless.

But then it dawned on me. The fact that we cannot assign a dollar value to democratic accountability was precisely the problem. Cotell is one of a new breed of bureaucrats, the kind who want to think of themselves as venture capitalists, maximizing efficiency. But since there is no way for public officials to arbitrage concepts like democracy and security into profit and loss, she focused on cutting costs. Alas, the government spends so little on declassification—just a little over a hundred million dollars annually—someone like Cotell can't be bothered to deal with it. Even a perfect declassification engine that ran itself and cost nothing would only ever save a hundred million. The Pentagon spends four times that just on military bands. IARPA and In-Q-Tel would invest in building a *classification* engine because the government spends almost two hundred times as much on secrecy as on declassification, and could produce even more secrets if it found a way to make them automatically. Secrecy is what the government truly values, so that's where Cotell thought there might be a real "return on investment."

Cotell showed us to the door, and out to the parking lot. The sun had set, and it was dark outside. I looked around at the classified government-funded labs, and realized that the public might never know what they were doing in secret, or why they were doing it. After all, Cotell wasn't just speaking for IARPA. For several years now, the CIA has funded research at the University of Texas to explore the use of machine learning for declassification, but one of these researchers told me they operate on a shoestring, and none of their results have ever been published. Even worse, instead of focusing on declassification, they have started to work on "redaction integrity," developing countermeasures to prevent "malicious actors" from trying to uncover redacted text.

So what could we do? If the government would not do this work, and we could not work with classified data, then we could not definitively prove that a declassification engine could help, or even measure the full dimensions of the problem. Not long after the meetings in Washington, the White House Office of Science and Technology Policy invited me to write a report about what was technologically possible. But they wanted the report for their transition files, to give to the *next* administration—which turned out to be the Trump administration.

My meeting with the Public Interest Declassification Board was one of the last the board held before going into hibernation. It barely met over the following three years, perhaps because President Trump could not be bothered to appoint any new members when the old ones were term-limited out. The board's staff, the Information Security Oversight Office (ISOO), still came into work, but the ISOO director, Mark Bradley, stopped trying to come up with new ways to convey the same urgent message. His report for 2017 was fifty-eight pages long and full of useful data, as were all the annual reports dating back nearly forty years since ISOO was founded to serve as a watchdog and clearinghouse for information on official secrecy. But his 2018 report to the president was only four pages long, and Bradley said it would just repeat "many of the same points" as the preceding report: "I emphasized that users of this system inside and outside the Government rightly observe that its current framework is unsustainable, and desperately requires modernization.

The investment, adoption, and use of advanced technologies lie at the core of this transformation. . . ."

But none of these things are happening. And, for the first time in ISOO's history, the 2018 report was devoid of any actual data. After looking at the statistics that departments and agencies submitted that year, Bradley concluded that the figures failed to "reflect how agencies are actually operating in the digital environment." They were not even worth compiling. So, for the last three years, the public has had no information about the number of times officials classified information, no data on the number of pages declassified, and no clue how much the government has been spending on secrecy. Bradley is looking for ways to find out, but is hamstrung by cuts to his own budget. When asked what he could do about it, he said, "We're ringing the alarm bells as loud as we can." But those working at the Information Security Oversight Office now present little information, have no job security, and can't exercise oversight. Cotell, on the other hand, got a promotion to become acting director of IARPA, an agency with an annual black budget of hundreds of millions of dollars (the actual figure is classified).

If knowledge about the past depends on institutions' preserving the historical record and opening it to scholarly study, this truly is the end of history. As much as we might fear the dark state—with good reason—what may be even more disturbing is to recognize how its many pathologies resemble nothing so much as senile psychosis. For all the information it mindlessly hoards and hides, there have been too many instances in which the "official mind" has proved incapable of using what intelligence it has. Beyond the difficulty in recalling recently acquired information, officialdom is now losing even its long-term memory. Indeed, it is losing self-control—as revealed by the embarrassingly massive leaks of Manning and Snowden.

The conclusion is inescapable. The dark state can no more tell its own story than a man with dementia can write his own memoir. But that story must not be forgotten. As we have seen, for most of its existence, our government was extraordinarily transparent, unusually committed to preserving historical records, and dedicated to ensuring that voters were better informed than the subjects of other states. It was only during actual declared wars—dangerous confrontations like the independence struggles of the early republic, the Civil War, and World War I—that the federal government took on some of the features of the dark state. But once the danger had passed, Americans discarded the arms and armor, and renewed the pursuit of open and accountable government. That our political system has the proven capability to open, and close, and open once again—each time with a renewed commitment to expanding the rights of citizens—demonstrates that there's nothing inevitable or inescapable about excessive secrecy, illegal surveillance, or a massive military-industrial complex.

Moreover, we can now use data science to recover some of the memories of the dark state that might otherwise be lost forever. When we examine the surviving records with all available tools and technology, from old-school archival research to the latest machine-learning algorithms, we can also make out the broad patterns of official secrecy, starting with when the dark state was first conceived and born. It turns out that, from the very beginning, what's secret has been whatever serves the interests of the president and all those around him who are invested in executive power. Presidential candidates feel they need to promise maximum accountability. But as soon as they have gained office, they claim they will strike a balance between transparency and security. Then the full weight of the White House—and all the money and power of the dark state—shifts to the side of secrecy. The temptation has proven too alluring: ever since Pearl Harbor, policy and precedent have allowed presidents to conceal how ruthless and cynical they can be in dealings with other nations, develop unrivaled surveillance systems, and assemble an arsenal of secret weapons. But under the cloak of secrecy, the military can run amok and endanger us all, not least because generals and admirals use secrecy and leaks to advance their own agendas. And the code makers and code breakers have kept secrets even from the president, and routinely show contempt for Congress and the courts.

This history is therefore not reducible to a conspiracy theory. Presidents are clearly responsible for making policy on secrecy, and that policy is a matter of public record. No less important, it is no secret why the actual practices surrounding classification, concealment, and leaking have proved impossible to control. It is because presidents have refused to share responsibility for protecting truly sensitive information. Although presidents and their advisers sometimes engage in shady business, such as colluding with businessmen to overthrow other governments, they have generally not hidden the economic aspects of their agendas. For the most part, their promotion of capitalism has been out in the open, and—for that very reason—highly effective. Whereas money and power have become their own rewards for many of the president's minions, and secrecy has provided cover for astonishing hubris and horrific "research," the ideal that inspires most denizens of the dark state has been to let the rest of us sleep at night. Alas, the secrets they shared—the background checks and initiation rites, the cryptonyms and color-coded badges, the elaborate hierarchies ascending to ever-more-restricted knowledge—created an inward-looking culture that gradually became a cult.

It would be impossible to explain how all this happened without acknowledging something that is the opposite of secret, something so obvious that it too often goes without saying: white men designed the dark state and ruled over it long after other bastions of privilege had fallen. It could not have risen so quickly, or proven so resilient, if it did not draw strength from other, uglier elements of American history no less significant than our traditions of transparency and democratic accountability.

This book has celebrated how America avoided the trappings of coercive state power during the first 150 years of its existence. But that was before the majority of Americans were finally able to participate fully in national life. Aside from the brief Reconstruction period preceding the withdrawal of federal troops from the conquered Confederacy, white men had little fear that they would remain in control absent any serious foreign threat. But the searing experience of the Second World War—above all, the way it began with a resounding defeat at the hands of an enemy judged to be racially inferior—seemed to require an entirely new approach. After 1945, when antiracist and anticolonial movements began to advance around the world, including in the United States, insecure men walled themselves off from the rest of society and sought to avoid normal forms of democratic accountability, all in the name of national security.

The true nature of the dark state is perhaps best seen in government plans for nuclear war, which in Pentagon scenarios ended with Black Power governments massacring White people across Africa and the American South. The government constructed enormous underground complexes where thousands of senior officials would take shelter. They included a large facility for members of Congress, a five hours' drive from Washington. But elaborate continuity-of-government plans from the 1980s and '90s focused on protecting a commander-in-chief and teams of current and former officials. There was no plan for reconstituting Congress, in part to prevent any rival claim from the Speaker of the House, who was constitutionally next in line after the vice president. Long before, large-scale shelters in urban areas were deemed impractical, in part because of White concerns about sheltering with Black people if there was a breakdown in law and order. Instead, the government advised homeowners to build their own backyard shelters and expected urban dwellers to drive their personal automobiles away from cities in a time of crisis. Others would have to flee on foot (or, in one 1956 civil defense plan for Savannah, wait for segregated trains).

In more normal times, only those with a "need to know" would know about such plans. The FBI, which played the role of gatekeeper in determining who would be accorded a security clearance for some of the most important secrets, did not have any Black agents until the 1960s, other than those who served as Hoover's personal servants. Hoover would not allow even one woman agent as long as he lived. At the CIA, not one woman was allowed to enter the ranks of senior management until nearly four decades after the Agency was founded.

We have seen how a true outsider like Hazel O'Leary, when

finally given the opportunity to effect real change at the Department of Energy, was able to carry out iconoclastic reforms. But as late as the 1990s, other women and minorities who managed to get security clearances found the "cultural imperative" at places like the CIA was "Try not to 'stand out.'" It could not have been easy. When the CIA finally conducted this survey in 1991, nearly half of the women at the Agency said they had endured deliberate, unwelcome, and repeated verbal or physical sexual harassment, and well over half of Black employees said they had experienced pervasive racist behavior. Still, the number who filed even an informal complaint was "remarkably small." Despite their efforts to "fit in," Black employees tended to be hired at a lower level than whites with the same background, and women tended to be promoted more slowly. All in all, white men occupied fully 90 percent of the top four management ranks. When the 1991 study's authors asked the eleven most powerful CIA officials about the Agency's lack of diversity, they explained that women and minorities were "reluctant to take the risks necessary to advance."

In fact, these were precisely the people who took the biggest risks and made the greatest sacrifices out of sheer determination to serve their country despite this wall of suspicion and hostility. By this point, even the most pernicious forms of prejudice that excluded more than half the nation from fully participating in its defense had proved to be completely unfounded. For instance, a 1991 Pentagon study could not uncover a single instance in which a queer person betrayed secrets because of sexual blackmail. But even at this late date, as the Cold War was finally winding down, the military would ignore its own research and continue forcing openly gay service members to accept less than honorable discharges, while those who remained in uniform suffered extraordinarily high rates of harassment and sexual assault. And the CIA prevented its own report on the lack of diversity in its ranks from becoming public for fifteen years.

When new leaders began to acknowledge how this cultural insularity and homogeneity was self-defeating, and took steps to address it, it still proved remarkably resilient. In 2014, whites accounted for 89 percent of senior CIA managers, even though a survey showed that Black, Hispanic, and Asian men and women at the Agency were actually more highly motivated to be promoted. Decades after the "Lavender Scare," LGBT employees were still almost twice as likely to say that they had to hide aspects of their identity in order to be successful at the CIA. Altogether, only 27 percent of respondents said that work experience gained prior to joining the CIA was valued there.

One finds the same troubling legacy even in relatively new additions to the dark state, like the National Geospatial-Intelligence Agency. In 2018, the most prestigious assignments—like giving briefings in Ops Intel—were still disproportionately likely to go to whites, even though white people are already disproportionately represented in the management ranks. Similarly, white CIA professionals were disproportionately more likely than Black professionals to become heads of station or get other assignments that led to senior management. And at the NGA as well, Black employees were more likely to nominate themselves for promotion—and not be promoted.

This is not a culture that can readily recruit the best talent, or tolerate divergent viewpoints, or value information that comes from anything but its own secret sources and methods. Is it any wonder that, as we have seen, a lot of secret intelligence is not actually secret, and what is secret is often not intelligent? One reason for the pervasiveness and persistence of these problems—which senior leadership now fully acknowledges handicaps the effectiveness of the American military as much as the intelligence community—is the power of white male mentoring networks. Though other parts of American society are struggling to recognize and begin correcting for structural biases, the culture of secrecy—with its subjective security-review process, its focus on loyalty, its suspicion of outsiders—makes that even more difficult.

Historians are still surveying the full impact all this has had on American national-security policy, and the American people. We have seen how Black leaders were targets of the most persistent and malevolent forms of surveillance and disinformation campaigns. Marginalized communities were also more likely to be subjects of harmful and nonconsensual research. Even well-studied topics, like the Vietnam War, can appear in a new light when we notice how the obsessions of top policy makers with proving their own masculinity encouraged escalation, and see the impact of racial stereotypes in saving certain kinds of men for managerial roles while others were sacrificed in combat. More generally, there is substantial evidence to suggest that presidents viewed threats to national security not merely in terms of communist ideology and Soviet military power, but also in connection with the prospect of a global race war. At the same time that antiracism was winning victories in America and around the world, and growing numbers of women were choosing professional employment instead of motherhood, these men were increasingly anxious about the future of the white race.

Such fears, which were usually only expressed privately, were not all of a piece. They could lead to policies that seemed objectively progressive. FDR, for instance, wanted to accelerate decolonization because the "brown people in the East" resented white rule, and "1,100,000,000 potential enemies are dangerous." Truman and Eisenhower became co-chairs of the Planned Parenthood Federation of America. But this was to support its efforts to promote population control in poor countries. Eisenhower tended to group together what he called "the one and a half billion hungry people in the world." The "menace" they posed, he told his National Security Council, was "a constant worry to him and from time to time reduced him to despair." Whereas Eisenhower also concluded that the United States could no longer support colonial control, sharing Roosevelt's worry, his vice president, Richard Nixon, cautioned in another top-secret record that it would be naïve to hope for anything but an alliance with "strong men" in Africa, since "some of the peoples of Africa have been out of the trees for only about fifty years." For John F. Kennedy, the biggest threat was China: "The Chinese would be perfectly prepared, because of the lower value they attach to human life, to sacrifice hundreds of millions of their own lives. . . ." As for Lyndon Johnson, he felt even more menaced when he addressed American troops in Korea in 1966: "There are 3 billion people in the world and we have only 200 million of them," he warned. "We are outnumbered 15 to 1. If might did make right they would sweep over the United States and take what we have."

It would be too simple to draw a straight line from the kind of reasoning one finds in closed-door meetings to the places where the United States dispatched troops and weapons, and the millions who died in the wars that followed—overwhelmingly Asian, African, and Latin American men, women, and children. But the least one can say is that the secrecy of these deliberations did nothing to improve the quality of U.S. decision making. If anything, by reinforcing the homogeneous and insular nature of America's foreign-policy elite, secrecy gave free rein to their insecurity, ignorance, and prejudice.

Revealing the history of state secrecy can therefore open up new perspectives on the nature and purpose of high-level policy making. But to fully reconstruct what really explains American wars, diplomacy, and espionage, we need government officials to reveal the rest of their secrets. Even if it takes thirty, forty, or fifty years, this is the only way we can learn how we got where we are today. It also conveys a critical message: no one, whether well-meaning or ill-intentioned, politically prominent or operating undercover, can forever escape a historical reckoning. The wish to escape such a reckoning helps explain why, over and over again, the most senior officials have tried to destroy incriminating records and publish their own exculpatory accounts. By selectively disclosing self-serving secrets—a practice long abetted by the Pentagon and intelligence community's prepublication review process—they can monetize their privileged access to national security information for personal and political advantage. Scholars, for their part, have never stopped pushing for the timely release of state secrets, seizing on newly declassified documents to reveal what officials did not want us to know.

But as the government takes longer and longer to release fewer and fewer secrets, it has taken a staggering toll on historians' ability to study more recent events. Anyone doing archival research in the 1970s, 1980s, and 1990s had access to a far more complete documentary record, relatively speaking, for World War II and then the early Cold War than do scholars today for the late Cold War and post–Cold War era. You can see the difference this made by analyzing all the research articles published during these years in the field's top academic journal, *Diplomatic History*. It used to be that most scholars tended to discuss and debate the same historical period: the period for which previously secret information had just been released. In the 1970s, they studied the 1940s. In the 1980s, it was the 1950s. It was still recent enough that many of these scholars could personally recall the key events in reconstructing their history. Over time, there was also forward momentum: when documents about a later period of history were declassified, scholars turned to that period and provided fresh perspectives, uncovering parallels and connections so their contemporaries could have what historians call a usable past. So, as time moved forward, so, too, did historians.

But with the collapse of the declassification program over the last twenty years, these connections between the present and the past are increasingly distant and tenuous. Whereas, once, the release of large numbers of secret documents was so massive and revelatory that it drove new discoveries, now the declassification process is so halting and incomplete that it scarcely generates much interest among academics. Historians today are no more likely to study the 1970s than the 1950s or 1960s. The 1980s and 1990s, for that matter, are—with few exceptions—an undiscovered country. Of course, work on earlier eras might be as good as or better than more contemporary history. But there can be little doubt that even the 1970s—a period of nascent globalization, inflationary shocks, and perceived American decline—is far more relevant to our current predicament than the Eisenhower and Kennedy years. And might not serious study of the end of the Cold War help us avoid a new Cold War—or worse—with Russia or China?

Alas, along with a loss of focus, and the insights that focus might generate for the present, there is no longer much forward momentum. In the late 1970s, about half the published research in *Diplomatic History* referenced events that had taken place after 1941. Compare that with research in the last four years. It's forty years later, but that median year has only moved two decades. If this trend continues, in 2060 historians will have just begun to have access to the full historical record of the immediate post–Cold War era, and most of us will be dead and buried before documents like the Mueller Report and transcripts of Trump-Putin telephone calls are fully declassified.

Clearly, historians need new methods to recover the memories of the dark state and find out what is missing. The end of history as we know it can—indeed, must—lead to a new kind of history. That does not have to be a bad thing. Scholars should not, after all, keep waiting around for government handouts, especially considering how declassification itself can be a political instrument that presidents wield to advance their agendas. Even the man generally considered to be the first true historian, Thucydides, knew he could not simply parrot the self-serving accounts of generals and admirals. He is considered the father of our profession because he sought out original sources, weighed the evidence, and then "proceeded upon the clearest data." No claim, he wrote, would be included in his account of the Peloponnesian War unless it was "tried by the most severe and detailed tests possible."

Alas, standards have slipped. In recent years—the same years that have witnessed the decline in declassification—there has been a profound change in the way most historians work. You would never realize this from looking at their published scholarship. Their books and journal articles are still filled with footnotes that cite paper documents and the pages of print editions, giving the impression that they only ever work in archives and libraries, carefully reading one page at a time. The work seems to come out of a world in which information is classified and catalogued to reflect the accumulation of authoritative knowledge.

Would that that were the case. As the historian Lara Putnam has shown, scholars are actually becoming more and more dependent on online databases and search algorithms, just like everyone else, whether for historical newspapers or archival documents or research articles. When a search query yields some snippet or datum that serves the searcher's argument, they might never read beyond it to understand the broader context. And as Tim Hitchcock points out, historians typically have little knowledge of how the algorithms actually work, and why they often do *not* work, in ways that might be invisible to the unwary user.

Too many scholars are not, therefore, proceeding "upon the clearest data." Keyword searching for a supportive quote or anecdote is not a "severe" test. Alas, we have the worst of all worlds: Less and less of the historical record is arranged in files and described in archival finding aids, which would allow us to assess the context and significance of any particular piece of evidence. Instead, too many historians are exploring databases of digital documents with crude, off-the-shelf tools, then hiding their keyword searching behind the façade of deceptively authoritative notes and bibliographies. The result is increasingly superficial research, and this before the vast majority of scholars have even begun to face the challenge of analyzing social media and the World Wide Web as archives of global history. History as we knew it, in the sense of classical scholarship, is already ending. Most people just don't know it yet.

If Thucydides were alive today, this is not how he would work. The clearest data about American wars, diplomacy, and covert operations is the data that the researcher aggregates with well-documented methods based on principles of archival integrity, and then shares with the world. The most severe and detailed tests are the ones that we undertake in controlled experiments and then publish after peer review, inviting other researchers to refute or replicate our findings. If, as a society, we are prepared to make the requisite investment in this kind of research, the archiving, aggregating, and interlinking of historical data may bring the most revolutionary advance in our ability to explore the past since Leopold von Ranke first invented the graduate seminar and countries created public archives. Ranke taught his students to go from archive to archive and track down every available source. It was an impossible dream, but it inspired a lot of amazing scholarship. And that dream is now starting to become a reality—a *virtual* reality, made more real every time another document, film, or photograph is collected in archives accessible through the World Wide Web. We can begin to see that seamless web of history, of which secrecy forms a part, and we can start analyzing all of it—the visible and the invisible—simultaneously.

The realization of Ranke's dream, to see the whole web of history, depends on amassing data and analyzing it with artificial intelligence. Experiments with big (historical) data have the advantage of being transparent and replicable. The goal is twofold: to measure performance and to validate the results. Can the algorithm automatically identify what the government did not want us to know, and in doing so help reveal why the government did not want us to know it? How accurately can it identify which official authored this or that anonymous war plan? And what factors were predictive of a historical event? It is both possible and expected for researchers to share their data and their code so that other teams can rerun the experiment and improve on the results.

Since the data is never complete, and historians are hard to convince, history as a data science has to prove itself in the most rigorous way possible: by making predictions about what newly available sources will reveal. The less we are surprised by the new documents we find, and the artifacts we uncover, the more confident we can be that we are getting closer to the truth and can pose even more probing questions. Only now we can be precise in both specifying what we expect and measuring our confidence in making these predictions. To be sure, future historians will also be able to judge how, specifically, we were wrong. More important, they will be able to develop models that produce more accurate predictions. The kind of results described in this book represent the foundation, not the ceiling. Some of the techniques we used did not even exist twenty years ago.

This is how my colleagues and I were ultimately able to save our lab. We decided to call it History Lab, and give it a bigger mission. Instead of just building a declassification engine, our goal now is to preserve irreplaceable records, invent new tools to analyze them, and in that way build a new future for historical research. More and more organizations, like the Arcadia Fund, the American Council of Learned Societies, the Mellon Foundation, and even the government's own National Science Foundation and National Endowment for the Humanities, have come to agree on the urgency of this mission. With their support, History Lab has created a "data refuge" for millions of declassified documents and given it a permanent home at Columbia Library—a library that has survived longer than America itself. We call it the Freedom of Information Archive.

Data-driven history will go wherever the data leads us. But it already seems likely that it will pose a profound challenge to official secrecy. What future is there for official secrets when we can create a virtual archive of millions of formerly secret documents and start mining it for information—information the government itself cannot reliably access? With more and more data, there are no limits to what we might discover.

And that potential is precisely the problem. This book has been careful in showing what data science cannot do, at least not yet, which is often overlooked in the hype over "big data." But the main challenges to data-driven historical excavations of official secrecy are not technical in nature. They are political and even legal, and turn on a whole series of other questions that historians have never before had to consider. The most tantalizing hypothetical about history is now this: what if historians and data scientists joined forces to develop techniques that are so powerful and accurate that we can predict what would be revealed if a redaction were removed? In the worst-case scenario, this would present a tempting target for prosecutors. Alternatively, respected national-security experts worry that such techniques might provoke the government to withhold even more information from the public.

What is certain is that the government itself desperately needs to automate and accelerate archiving and declassification, which will otherwise collapse because of the exponential growth of classified data. Moreover, the technology that can "predict" what secrets are being withheld is precisely the technology that can tell government officials what documents they need to scrutinize more closely. We may therefore be witnessing the first stages in what could develop into an arms race, with algorithms that automatically withhold, redact, or delete documents pitted against algorithms that identify and reconstruct gaps in the official record. If these are the first stages in that arms race, you have just read the first pages of its history.

Remaking history is ultimately bigger and more important than government secrecy. If history reinvents itself as a data science, teams of researchers can start to probe the origins of urgent, world-spanning problems like nuclear proliferation, pandemic disease, climate change, and religious violence—

historical subjects far too big and complex for any one scholar to master alone. Connections across time and space—which might have taken a long time to come to light—can be made instantaneously. Rather than wait years before publishing them in scholarly journals and monographs, we can verify surprising findings and share them immediately.

In 1951, the science-fiction writer Isaac Asimov imagined a time when history and mathematics would become one and researchers would join together in a Foundation that could both predict and shape the future. Clearly, we are not predicting the future, as such, in the way Asimov imagined. We are only trying to find out if the past might be made more predictable. But if anything like a Foundation to discover laws of history ever comes to pass, this is how it will begin.

Acknowledgments

It seems like too little to merely acknowledge the many people who made this book possible. I might have listed them all as co-authors, like one of those physics papers with five thousand contributors, but I really do have to make clear that the errors and inaccuracies are my own. Anyone who reads beyond the first pages will see that the most original research was all done with collaborators who had skills and expertise that I lack. Some of the secrets we discovered are "royal," but in this book there is no "royal we." My colleagues answered my innumerable questions, patiently explained complex methods, and helped me combine energy and insights from three distinct realms of knowledge production, all of them quite new to me when I set out.

As my first guide to the world of data science, I am particularly indebted to David Madigan, a truly delightful and brilliant human being, who was both courageous and funny at times when the future seemed very dark. Long after the last grant is gone, he will still be my co-PI. Eric Gade started out as my student, then became an inspiration to me—determined, idealistic, and altogether decent even under difficult circumstances. I am also lucky to have had Ray Hicks by my side, with his unquestioned integrity and insistence on academic rigor. A number of distinguished data scientists were also unfailing in their support and encouragement, including Dave Blei, Julia Hirschberg, Katherine McKeown, and Duncan Watts. All were founding members of History Lab's steering committee, and they steered us through some strange and treacherous waters. In the years that followed, I was also fortunate to collaborate with some excellent mathematicians, engineers, computational social scientists, and digital humanists. Many were also willing to do the unglamorous and typically unrewarding work of applying for government and foundation grants. I'm thinking particularly of Ye Seul Byeon, Flavio Codeço Coelho, Daniel Krasner, Ben Lis, Rahul Mazumder, Thomas Nyberg, Owen Rambow, Rohan Shah, Renato Rocha Souza, and Arthur Spirling. Without them, the lights in History Lab would have gone out long ago.

While these days "big data" and artificial intelligence get all the buzz—and almost all the money—this book is also based squarely on less sexy but even more foundational forms of knowledge production: libraries and archives. From basic principles of provenance and original order, to the ethical complexities of appraisal, privacy, and access, to the daunting challenges of "future-proofing" ephemeral data, I was fortunate to have true masters teaching me, at each step learning how much more I did not know. In this book I have frequently described libraries as our most effective intelligence agencies—which they are. But they are intelligence agencies that also operate time machines, also known as archives. Without the people who command these vessels, we historians could never connect past, present, and future. Now that I have safely touched down once again, I wish to applaud these noble men and women, particularly the irrepressible Barbara Rockenbach, the inscrutable Rob Cartolano, the irascible David Langbart, the indomitable Ann Thornton, and the irreplaceable Michael Moss.

Finally, the most obscure and underappreciated kind of knowledge production concerns secrecy itself. Unlike data science and library science, there is not yet an organized field of information science dedicated to discovering how private, privileged, and national security information is produced, organized, and protected. So, when I set out to explore the history and future of official secrecy, I only gradually came to realize that I was following in the footsteps of formidable analysts and scholars. I'm thinking particularly of Steven Aftergood, Peter Galison, Margaret Kwoka, David Pozen, David Vincent, and Alex Wellerstein. They have all done highly original and painstaking work reconstructing the policies and actual practices of classifying, declassifying, and releasing information, without which I would not have known how to say anything that was either new or true. Richard Immerman and the late, great Bob Jervis, formidable scholars in their own right, played a different role, really a dual role, as both government advisers and academic watchdogs. They were able to teach me how and why this whole system is breaking down, and what might be done to fix it. Less high-minded people would have received me as an arriviste, and questioned whether my unconventional methods could really shed new light in this shadowy and byzantine realm. But every one of the aforementioned experts was genuinely curious and intellectually generous, and the excellence of their work continually challenged me to create something worthy of their respect.

I also have very specific and significant debts, for key passages and concepts that constitute essential pieces in the larger mosaic this book is meant to reconstruct. David Allen did much of the archival spadework that helped me to expose the unbroken chain of executive orders—and assertions of executive power—that helps explain much of this history. The historian Marc Trachtenberg had the original insight that redaction analysis could and should help scholars correct the intrinsic bias in the public record, and also had the well-earned confidence to reconsider the conventional wisdom about Pearl Harbor. At the risk of losing the nonacademic reader, I have also called out the names of other scholars wherever my debt was particularly large: e.g., Wellerstein on nuclear secrets, Galison on science, Pozen on leaks, Jervis on intelligence failures, and Scott Sagan on inevitable accidents. Scott and his Stanford colleagues also gave me a crucial boost of confidence at a critical stage, hosting me for multiple visits and affording me the opportunity to test my ideas in a series of talks with extremely smart interlocutors. I'm only sorry I can never repay my debt to them.

The attentive reader will note (in the notes) that some

of the most recent history about what is happening—or not happening—in declassification policy and archival preservation I learned from conversations and personal communications. This is because I was fortunate enough to have represented other members of the Society for Historians of American Foreign Relations (SHAFR) and the American Historical Association (AHA) in councils and committees where my colleagues and I tried to grapple with these problems. This includes the SHAFR Council, its Task Force on Advocacy, and the AHA NARA Review Committee. I was also privileged to serve—albeit briefly—on the Executive Committee of the National Coalition for History. However frustrating this work can be, I learned a great deal about why these problems are so challenging. I am grateful to my colleagues in SHAFR for entrusting me with these responsibilities and for their unwavering support, especially Kristin Hoganson, Julia Irwin, Barbara Keys, and Andrew Preston.

In trying to make a book about bureaucracy and data science more readable and relatable, I was lucky to be a member of a star-studded and extremely fun writing group, along with James Goodman, Nicole Hemmer, Jim Ledbetter, Dahlia Lithwick, Michael Massing, Natalia Petrzela, Claire Potter, Clay Risen, and James Traub. It was first organized and is still led by David Greenberg, who also shared his expertise on presidential spin. They gave me encouragement and enthusiasm when I needed it most, and the confidence to think I, too, could aspire to have a readership beyond the ivory tower.

But I would never have come even this far without my agent, Michael Carlisle, the best coach I have ever had. More than anything, I am grateful to him for helping me find a gifted and insightful editor, Edward Kastenmeier. At a time when many authors have all but given up on actually being *edited*, Edward took great care with every word and phrase but could also see the larger arc—at times, better than I could see it myself.

My biggest debt, in the very literal sense, is to those who accepted my grant applications, and agreed to fund the work of History Lab. They include Peter Baldwin, Michael Doyle, Mark Hansen, Ross Mounce, Chris Prom, and—not least— Eric Sears, as well as the many anonymous reviewers who either rated the applications highly or helped my collaborators and me make them better. I give you all an E (Excellent!). I was also fortunate to have the capable help of The Institute for Social and Economic Research and Policy, the home of History Lab. Thanks above all to my co-director, Tom DiPrete; our director of administration, Jo-Ann Rivera; and the wonderful staff, who managed hiring, lab meetings, workshops, and all too many last-minute grant applications. Sadly, I cannot thank any government declassifiers. David Allen and I filed Mandatory Declassification Review requests at the very beginning of this project, nine years ago, at several presidential libraries. I have not received any documents from any of them.

Alas, I have had all too many students over the years to thank them individually for their excellent questions and insights about "Secrecy, Privacy, and Surveillance"—a seminar I taught both at Columbia and the London School of Economics. Thanks to Arne Westad and his colleagues at the LSE, I was also privileged to deliver the Philippe Roman lectures in 2014–15, which is where I first worked out the ideas described in the introduction. And I have been lucky to have dozens more students join the team at History Lab since 2013. Just in the last four years, sixteen students contributed code to fifteen different projects. My own coding challenges, and the good-natured help I received from more advanced but much younger colleagues, like Nick Levine, left me deeply appreciative of the need and opportunity to rethink historical research. Several of these students have been my co-authors on papers and published articles, and the most distinguished alumni—and LinkedIn profiles—are listed at History-lab.org (do look them up if you are hiring!).

No one could have asked for better research assistants in writing a book. They were really much more than RAs. When I first had the idea of hacking the NSA, Martin Deeb signed on as my private investigator, and his gumshoe detective work still astonishes me. And when I thought I was nearly done drafting that and every other chapter, Michael Flynn got me thinking harder about American history, until I arrived at a very different, and better, point of view.

Thanks also to my friends (some of them in-laws) for listening to me when I insisted on revealing my secrets, especially Anna, Arvind, Chris, Darrin, Pete, Seth, and Tony, and to my own very extended family: sisters, Maura, Annamarie, Jeanellen; and brothers, Peter, Thomas, and Patrick; "out-laws" Tim, Joe-B, Mary, John, and Daniela. My father, Thomas J. Connelly, is no longer with us. But when I was barely old enough to operate the Xerox machine in his law office—already overflowing with papers—he was the one who first showed me a Freedom of Information Act request, and explained how he and other trial lawyers were using them to fight for civil rights. In the years since he first fell ill, my mother has become an ever more amazing model of sheer determination, making whatever obstacles I face seem small by comparison. Through it all, she has preserved my childhood home and everything in it until it's become its own sort of archive, filled with history, and love.

This is the legacy I hope to pass on to my unstoppable daughter, Lily Kovner, and it fills me with great pride to see how she is already just as strong-willed as her Irish forebears—another model for me to emulate. But for the same reason I could not be more grateful to Sarah. There is so much more that could be said but can't, which is why this book of secrets is dedicated to her.

Notes

Many of the cited sources are available on the internet, but URL addresses and website content are notoriously transient. For direct access to declassified documents referenced in these notes, more detailed explanations of the experiments, and links to online sources please visit history-lab.org/declassificationengine.

AEC	Atomic Energy Commission
AWF	Ann Whitman File
CFPF	State Department Central Foreign Policy Files
CIA	Central Intelligence Agency
CRS	Congressional Research Service, Library of Congress
DDEL	Dwight D. Eisenhower Presidential Library, Abilene, KS
DNSA	Digital National Security Archive, ProQuest
DOD	Department of Defense
DOE	Department of Energy
DOS	Department of State
FAS	Federation of American Scientists
FBI	Federal Bureau of Investigation
FISA	Foreign Intelligence Surveillance Act
FISC	U.S. Foreign Intelligence Surveillance Court
FOIArchive	Freedom of Information Archive, history-lab.org
FRUS	*The Foreign Relations of the United States* (Washington, D.C.: GPO)
GAO	U.S. Government Accountability Office
GPO	U.S. Government Publishing Office
HSTL	Harry S. Truman Presidential Library, Independence, MO
ISOO	Information Security Oversight Office, National Archives and Records Administration
JCPL	Jimmy Carter Presidential Library, Atlanta, GA

JCS   Joint Chiefs of Staff
JFKL   John F. Kennedy Presidential Library, Boston, MA
LBJL   Lyndon B. Johnson Presidential Library, Austin, TX
LOC   Library of Congress, Washington, DC
NARA   National Archives and Records Administration
NSA   National Security Agency
NSC   National Security Council
NRO   National Reconnaissance Office, Department of Defense
OSTI   U.S. Department of Energy Office of Scientific and
           Technical Information
PIDB   Public Interest Declassified Board
PQHV   ProQuest History Vault
RRPL   Ronald Reagan Presidential Library, Simi Valley, CA
USAF   U.S. Air Force
USN   U.S. Navy
USNA   U.S. National Archives
U.S. DDO   Declassified Documents Online

PREFACE: SHOULD THIS BOOK BE LEGAL?

ix Earlier that year: ISOO, *2012 Report to the President* (Washington, D.C., 2013), p. 7.

xiii Even in terms: Matthew M. Aid, ed., "Declassification in Reverse: The U.S. Intelligence Community's Secret Historical Document Reclassification Program," National Security Archive, Feb. 26, 2006.

xiv "Scholarship cannot": *Sweezy v. New Hampshire*, 354 U.S. 234, 250 (June 17, 1957).

THE RADICAL TRANSPARENCY OF THE AMERICAN REPUBLIC: A REINTRODUCTION

3 "growing mountain of research": Vannevar Bush, "As We May Think," *Atlantic*, July 1945; G. Pascal Zachary, *Endless Frontier: Vannevar Bush, Engineer of the American Century* (Boston: MIT Press, 1999), pp. 261–64.

3 "Memex": Bush, "As We May Think."

4 "A broad dissemination": Vannevar Bush, *Science, the Endless Frontier: A Report to the President on a Program for Postwar Scientific Research* (Washington, D.C.: GPO, 1945), pp. 29, 143–57.

5 Price worried: Byron Price to Harry S. Truman, Aug. 24, 1945, White House Central Files, Official File, box 1507, HSTL.

5   His own work: Zachary, *Endless Frontier*, pp. 269–71.

5   "put into a potential . . . freedom not to publish": "Remarks of Vannevar Bush," April 16, 1948, in *Availability of Information from Federal Departments and Agencies: Hearings Before a Subcommittee of the Committee on Government Operations*, 84th Cong., 1st Sess. (1956), p. 2159.

6   The eighty-one billion dollars: This is from 2017, and includes twenty-six billion for Pentagon "Operational Systems Development" (CRS, *Government Expenditures on Defense Research and Development by the United States and Other OECD Countries: Fact Sheet*, R45441 [2020], pp. 1, 4).

6   Some 1.3 million: National Counterintelligence and Security Center, *Fiscal Year 2019 Annual Report on Security Clearance Determinations*, April 2020, FAS.

6   But rather than making: The WikiLeaks and Snowden leaks have been the largest, when measured by volume of classified content, but leaks have also become more frequent (Senate Committee on Homeland Security and Governmental Affairs, *State Secrets: How an Avalanche of Media Leaks Is Harming National Security*, Senate Report no. 115, 1st Sess. [2017]).

7   Donald Trump railed: Annie Karni, "Meet the Guys Who Tape Trump's Papers Back Together," *Politico*, June 10, 2018.

8   In their official histories: For example, see Jennifer Wilcox, *Revolutionary Secrets: Cryptology in the American Revolution* (Fort Meade, Md.: NSA, 2012); "A Look Back . . . George Washington: America's First Military Intelligence Director," CIA, June 20, 2008.

8   "secrecy and despatch": Alexander Hamilton and John Jay, *Federalist Papers*, nos. 64 and 70. See also Daniel Hoffman, *Governmental Secrecy and the Founding Fathers: A Study in Constitutional Controls* (Westport, Conn.: Praeger, 1981), pp. 20–21, and Christopher Andrew, *The Secret World: A History of Intelligence* (New Haven: Yale University Press, 2018), pp. 295–96, 303.

9   "an example to the world": Hoffman, *Governmental Secrecy*, pp. 14, 24.

9   "friends of science" . . . "advances from persecution": Clarence E. Carter, "The United States and Documentary Historical Publication," *Mississippi Valley Historical Review*, vol. 25, no. 1 (1938): pp. 3–4.

9   In 1791, during Washington's: William B. McAllister et al., *Toward "Thorough, Accurate, and Reliable": A History of the Foreign Relations of the United States Series* (Washington D.C.: Department of State

Office of the Historian, 2015), pp. 35–37; Alexander Hamilton, *The Papers of Alexander Hamilton*, vol. 11, *February 1792–June 1792*, ed. Harold C. Syrett (New York: Columbia University Press, 1966), pp. 211–12.

9 "intelligence becomes interesting": George Washington, *The Writings of George Washington from the Original Manuscript Sources, 1745–1799*, ed. John C. Fitzpatrick (Washington, D.C.: GPO, 1938), p. 98. See also Andrew, *Secret World*, p. 309.

9 They developed a policy: McAllister et al., *Toward "Thorough, Accurate, and Reliable,"* pp. 11–12.

10 They did not change: Ralph E. Weber, *Masked Dispatches: Cryptograms and Cryptology in American History, 1775–1900* (Fort Meade, Md.: NSA, 2002), pp. 68–69.

10 In his spare time: David Kahn, *The Code-Breakers: The Story of Secret Writing* (New York: Macmillan, 1967), pp. 114–16.

11 an order of magnitude smaller: Paul Kennedy, *The Rise and Fall of the Great Powers: Economic Change and Military Conflict from 1500 to 2000* (New York: Random House, 1987), p. 154.

11 But even in the American West: Robert Wooster, *The American Military Frontiers: The United States Army in the West, 1783–1900* (Albuquerque: University of New Mexico Press, 2009), p. xiii.

11 "A popular Government": James Madison to W. T. Barry, Aug. 4, 1822, LOC. Though Madison's words are often cited to explain the freedom of information, he knew that information was not free. This quotation was just the beginning of a long letter arguing that universities must be supported, whatever the cost, since citizens needed "a knowledge of the Globe & its various inhabitants." Education might also create a healthy appetite for learning history, "an inexhaustible fund" for useful instruction.

11 The public demand: When Jefferson proposed a public-school system for Virginia, he explained, "Those entrusted with power have, in time, and by slow operations, perverted it into tyranny; and it is believed that the most effectual means of preventing this would be, to illuminate, as far as practicable, the minds of the people at large" ("79. A Bill for the More General Diffusion of Knowledge, 18 June 1779," Founders Online; original source, Thomas Jefferson, *The Papers of Thomas Jefferson*, vol. 2, *1777–18 June 1779*, ed. Julian P. Boyd [Princeton: Princeton University Press, 1950], pp. 526–35). See also Kenneth A. Lockridge, *Literacy in Colonial New England: An Enquiry into the Social Context of Literacy in the Early Modern West* (New York: Norton, 1974), pp. 68–69; F. W. Grubb, "Growth

of Literacy in Colonial America: Longitudinal Patterns, Economic Models, and the Direction of Future Research," *Social Science History*, vol. 1 (Winter 1990): pp. 456–57.

11 "Where the press is free": Richard R. John, *Spreading the News: The American Postal System from Franklin to Morse* (Cambridge, Mass.: Harvard University Press, 1998), pp. 154–55. Thomas Jefferson famously wrote, "The basis of our governments being the opinion of the people, the very first object should be to keep that right; and were it left to me to decide whether we should have a government without newspapers or newspapers without a government, I should not hesitate a moment to prefer the latter" (Thomas Jefferson to Edward Carrington, Jan. 16, 1787, in *The Works of Thomas Jefferson*, vol. 5: *Correspondence 1786–1789*, ed. Paul Leicester Ford [New York: Putnam, 1904], pp. 252–53).

12 "By travelling": Granger to James Jackson, March 23, 1802, in Walter Lowrie and Walter S. Franklin, eds., *American State Papers*, *vol. VII, Post Office Department (March 4, 1789, to March 2, 1833)* (Washington, D.C.: Gales and Seaton, 1834), p. 27. See also United States Postal Service Office of the Historian, "African American Postal Workers in the 19th Century." On barring Black people from carrying the mail, see John C. Calhoun, *The Works of John C. Calhoun*, vol. 2 (New York: Appleton and Co., 1853–54), p. 110; Brian Balogh, *A Government Out of Sight: The Mystery of National Authority in Nineteenth-Century America* (Cambridge, U.K.: Cambridge University Press, 2009), p. 223.

12 Jefferson therefore signed: John, *Spreading the News*, pp. 162–65; Jack Lynch, "Every Man Able to Read: Literacy in Early America," *Colonial Williamsburg Journal*, Winter 2011.

12 But in the nineteenth century: John, *Spreading the News*, pp. 257–71.

12 Henry "Box" Brown: Winifred Gallagher, *How the Post Office Created America* (New York: Penguin, 2016), pp. 141–42.

12 "arm themselves with": For a discussion of literacy, see Heather Andrea Williams, *Self-Taught: African American Education in Slavery and Freedom* (Chapel Hill: University of North Carolina Press, 2005), pp. 7–19.

12 When American ideals: John, *Spreading the News*, pp. 167–68, 278–79.

13 Federalists saw: Balogh, *Government Out of Sight*, p. 223; Jeremy Bentham, chapter 2 of his "Essay on Political Tactics," in *The Works of Jeremy Bentham*, vol. 2 (Edinburgh: William Tait, 1843).

13 When Andrew Jackson: Claudio Saunt, *Unworthy Republic: The Dispossession of Native Americans and the Road to Indian Territory* (New York: Norton, 2020), pp. 124–25.

13 The Choctaws well understood: Ibid., pp. 125–26.

13 "Our cause is your own": Walter H. Conser, "John Ross and the Cherokee Resistance Campaign, 1833–1838," *Journal of Southern History*, vol. 44, no. 2 (1978): p. 200. On Samuel Worcester, see Angela Pulley, "Cherokee Phoenix," *New Georgia Encyclopedia*, July 17, 2020.

14 But Jackson just ignored: Tiya Miles, "'Circular Reasoning': Recentering Cherokee Women in the Antiremoval Campaigns," *American Quarterly*, vol. 61, no. 2 (2009): p. 222.

14 Archived records have been: Steve Inskeep, *Jacksonland: President Andrew Jackson, Cherokee Chief John Ross, and a Great American Land Grab* (New York: Penguin, 2015), pp. 100–101. On property interests and the early-American political order more generally, the classic work is Charles A. Beard, *An Economic Interpretation of the Constitution of the United States* (New York: Macmillan, 1913), which gave rise to decades of heated debate. More recently, historians of economics have found support for his main argument—i.e., that votes on the Constitution aligned with the pecuniary interests of delegates. (Robert A. McGuire, *To Form a More Perfect Union: A New Economic Interpretation of the United States Constitution* [New York: Oxford University Press, 2003].) On presidential withholding of information, see Abraham D. Sofaer, "Executive Power and the Control of Information: Practice Under the Framers," *Duke Law Journal*, vol. 1977, no. 1 (1977): pp. 8–45.

14 "secrets of a very mischievous": Thomas Jefferson, "Memoranda of Consultations with the President," March 11–April 9, 1792, Founders Online.

14 "They are welcome": James Parton, *Life of Andrew Jackson*, vol. 3 (New York: Mason Brothers, 1860): pp. 606–7.

15 Cities like New York: Saunt, *Unworthy Republic*, pp. 187–96.

15 "opening to them": On Polk and his predecessor's defense of secrecy while seizing land from Native Americans and Mexicans, see Mark J. Rozell, *Executive Privilege: Presidential Power, Secrecy, and Accountability* (Lawrence: University Press of Kansas, 2010), pp. 34–37; James Knox Polk, "Inaugural Address," Washington, D.C., March 4, 1845, Avalon Project.

15 "monuments of the past": McAllister et al., *Toward "Thorough, Accurate, and Reliable,"* p. 14.

15   By 1850: Carrol Davidson Wright, U.S. Bureau of Labor, *History and Growth of the United States Census* (Washington, D.C.: GPO, 1900), pp. 39–50, 312.

15   The importance of public: James Gregory Bradsher, "An Administrative History of the Disposal of Federal Records, 1789–1949," *Provenance: Journal of the Society of Georgia Archivists*, vol. 3, no. 2 (1985): 1.

16   "develop the talents": Frances Smith Foster, "A Narrative of the Interesting Origins and (Somewhat) Surprising Developments of African-American Print Culture," *American Literary History*, vol. 17 (Winter 2005): p. 730.

16   "however unimportant": Frank Wells, Garrard Winston, and Henry Beers, "Historical Development of the Records Disposal Policy of the Federal Government Prior to 1934," *American Archivist*, vol. 7, no. 3 (July 1, 1944): p. 183.

16   In 1882, a young scholar: Michael G. Kammen, *A Machine That Would Go of Itself: The Constitution in American Culture* (New York: Knopf, 1986; 2017 ed.), p. 127.

16   Instead of a powerful: Alfred D. Chandler, Jr., *Scale and Scope: The Dynamics of Industrial Capitalism* (Cambridge, Mass.: Harvard University Press, 1990), pp. 53–54.

17   The passage: Andrew Delbanco, *The War Before the War: Fugitive Slaves and the Struggle for America's Soul from the Revolution to the Civil War* (New York: Penguin, 2019), pp. 8–9.

17   When the minister: McAllister et al., *Toward "Thorough, Accurate, and Reliable,"* pp. 17–19.

17   But Congress directed: Fred G. Ainsworth and Joseph W. Kirkley, *The War of the Rebellion: A Compilation of the Official Records of the Union and Confederate Armies*, vol. 135, *General Index and Additions and Corrections*, ed. John S. Moodey (Washington, D.C.: GPO, 1901), pp. v–vi. The page estimate includes the navy records, which were published separately. Lincoln's own papers, eventually deposited in the Library of Congress, are also voluminous, including some twenty thousand documents.

17   Moreover, the Union's: Eric Foner, *Reconstruction: America's Unfinished Revolution, 1863–1877* (New York: Harper, 1988), pp. 148–49, 154.

18   Other governments: Data from "The Correlates of War Project," Correlates of War, https://correlatesofwar.org.

18   Several European states: Richard Bach Jensen, *The Battle Against Anarchist Terrorism: An International History, 1878–1934* (New

York: Cambridge University Press, 2014); Faith Hillis, *Utopia's Discontents: Russian Émigrés and the Quest for Freedom, 1830s–1930s* (New York: Oxford University Press, 2021).

18 In 1873: Nicola Kay Beisel, *Imperiled Innocents: Anthony Comstock and Family Reproduction in Victorian America* (Princeton: Princeton University Press, 1997), p. 100.

18 All the while: Andrea Tone, *Devices and Desires: A History of Contraceptives in America* (New York: Hill and Wang, 2002), p. 39.

18 Absent any anxiety: Michael E. Bigelow, "A Short History of Army Intelligence," Army Intelligence Resources, 2012, p. 10, FAS.

19 As for diplomacy: Thomas G. Otte, *The Foreign Office Mind: The Making of British Foreign Policy, 1865–1914* (Cambridge, U.K.: Cambridge University Press, 2011), pp. 7–12; Robert Beisner, *From the Old Diplomacy to the New* (Arlington Heights, Ill.: Harlan Davidson, 1975, 1986), pp. 28–30. No matter how well qualified, Black diplomats were only ever appointed to a handful of consular posts, such as Liberia and Haiti (Allison Blakely, "Blacks in the Diplomatic and Consular Services," in *African Americans in U.S. Foreign Policy: From the Era of Frederick Douglass to the Age of Obama*, ed. Linda Heywood et al. [Chicago: University of Illinois Press, 2015], pp. 14–15).

19 One frustrated office-seeker: Candice Millard, *Destiny of the Republic: A Tale of Madness, Medicine and the Murder of a President* (New York: Doubleday, 2011), pp. 231–32.

19 With the advent: Desmond King, *Separate and Unequal: Black Americans and the US Federal Government* (New York: Oxford University Press, 1995), pp. 45–49.

19 Women filled: Cindy Sondik Aron, *Ladies and Gentlemen of the Civil Service: Middle-Class Workers in Victorian America* (New York: Oxford University Press, 1987), p. 5.

19 Relative to the size: International Monetary Fund, "Public Finances in Modern History," based on Paolo Mauro et al., "A Modern History of Fiscal Prudence and Profligacy," 2013, IMF Working Paper no. 12.

20 The exception: *An Act to Provide for Taking the Tenth and Subsequent Censuses*, S195, 45th Cong., 3rd Sess. (March 3, 1879); Margo J. Anderson, *The American Census: A Social History* (New Haven: Yale University Press, 1988), pp. 121–23.

20 "There ought to be": David Greenberg, *Republic of Spin: An Inside History of the American Presidency* (New York: Norton, 2016), p. 80.

20 But in 1916: Paul L. Murphy, *World War I and the Origin of Civil Liberties in the United States* (New York: Norton, 1979), pp. 81, 92–96; Anderson, *American Census*, p. 129.

20 "open covenants of peace": President Wilson's Message to Congress, Jan. 8, 1918, RG 46, Records of the United States Senate, USNA.

20 He failed to follow through: Sadao Asada, "Between the Old Diplomacy and the New, 1918–1922: The Washington System and the Origins of Japanese-American Rapprochement," *Diplomatic History*, vol. 30, no. 2 (2006): 223–24.

21 "has upset many": *Abrams v. United States*, 250 U.S. 616 (Nov. 10, 1919).

21 Arrested for speaking out: Edmund A. Kersten, *A. Philip Randolph: A Life in the Vanguard* (Lanham, Md.: Rowman & Littlefield, 2007), pp. 19–20. See also Beth Tompkins Bates, *Pullman Porters and the Rise of Protest Politics in Black America, 1925–1945* (Chapel Hill: University of North Carolina Press, 2003).

21 One exception: Tim Weiner, *Enemies: A History of the FBI* (New York: Random House, 2012), pp. 60–62.

21 He managed to: FBI, "*SIS. History*," pt. 1 (2004), pp. 5–6; James Kirchick, *Secret City: The Hidden History of Gay Washington* (New York: Henry Holt and Company, 2022), p. 69. It was not until the 1990s that the Bureau finally began to overcome its crippling lack of diversity (Rhodri Jeffreys-Jones, *The FBI: A History* [New Haven: Yale University Press, 2007], pp. 213–17).

21 "Gentlemen do not": David Kahn, *The Reader of Gentlemen's Mail: Herbert O. Yardley and the Birth of American Codebreaking* (New Haven: Yale University Press, 2004), pp. ix, 101, and see also Herbert O. Yardley, *The American Black Chamber* (Annapolis: Naval Institute Press, 1931), pp. 369–70.

21 Under the Communications: Bigelow, *Short History*, p. 10; Jeffreys-Jones, *FBI: A History*, p. 87.

22 At this point: Robert D. W. Connor, "The National Archives: Objectives and Practices," *Bulletin of the American Library Association*, vol. 30 (1936): p. 592; Jessie Kratz, "Survey of Federal Archives," *Pieces of History*, Oct. 6, 2014; "Transfer of War Department Records to the National Archives, 1937–39," R. D. W. Connor Papers, Louis Round Wilson Special Collections Library, University of North Carolina at Chapel Hill (hereafter Connor Papers), folder 866.

22 The United States still lacked: Rodney A. Ross, "The National

Archives: The Formative Years, 1934–1949," *Prologue*, vol. 16, no. 2 (1984): p. 38.

23 A new era: "Transfer of War Department Records."

23 "We have a right": Leech to Cass Canfield, Nov. 16, 1938, reproduced in "Transfer of War Department Records."

23 Connor won: "Lunch with the President, 1935," Connor Papers, folder 862.

24 "When my term": "Conference with the President, 1940," Connor Papers, folder 897.

24 "They care nothing": W. Fitzhugh Brundage, *The Southern Past: A Clash of Race and Memory* (Cambridge, Mass.: Harvard University Press, 2005), pp. 128–34.

24 "fleeing from": R. D. W. Connor, "The Rehabilitation of a Rural Commonwealth," *American Historical Review*, vol. 36, no. 1 (1930): p. 54.

24 Of the eighty-nine: Ross, "National Archives," pp. 35–37.

24 While Connor was in charge: Ibid., p. 37.

24 "The chief reason": Bradsher, "Administrative History," p. 13.

24 Roosevelt's own papers: FDR was worried about Republican investigations of his presidency. Connor was happy to support his plan, since it gave him face time with the president: "The words 'Franklin D. Roosevelt Library' were an Open Sesame to his office whenever I wanted to see him" ("Dedication of the Franklin D. Roosevelt Library, 1941," Connor Papers, folder 908).

25 "silences, erasures": Bergis Jules, "Confronting Our Failure of Care Around the Legacies of Marginalized People in the Archives," *Medium*, Nov. 11, 2016.

25 "Guardians of the Secrets": *Annual Report of the Archivist of the United States* (Washington, D.C.: GPO, 1934), p. 7.

25 Roosevelt could see: "Statutes at Large: 75th Congress Session 3, Chapter 2: An Act to Prohibit the Making of Photographs, Sketches, or Maps of Vital Military and Naval Defensive Installations and Equipment, and for Other Purposes," LOC; Weiner, *Enemies*, pp. 80–82.

25 In 1940: Exec. Order 8381, "Defining Certain Vital Military and Naval Installations and Equipment," March 22, 1940, FAS; Ernst Posner, "The Role of Records in German Administration," in *Archives and the Public Interest: Selected Essays by Ernst Posner*, ed. Ken Munden (Washington, D.C.: Public Affairs Press, 1967), p. 87; Rodney Ross, "Ernst Posner: The Bridge Between the Old World and the New," *American Archivist*, vol. 44 (Fall 1981): pp. 306–7.

25 When America entered: James Worsham, "Our Story: How the National Archives Evolved over 75 Years of Change and Challenges," *Prologue*, vol. 41, no. 2 (Summer 2009).

25 State Department historians: Peter Novick, *That Noble Dream: The "Objectivity Question" and the American Historical Profession* (New York: Cambridge University Press, 1988), pp. 301–4.

25 And the War and Navy: Milton Gustafson, "Travels of the Charters of Freedom," *Prologue*, vol. 34, no. 4 (Winter 2002).

26 "weeding out": Bradsher, "Administrative History," p. 13.

27 He expected that: Ibid., p. 9.

27 "in the capacity": "Remarks at the Dedication of the Franklin D. Roosevelt Library at Hyde Park, New York," June 30, 1941, American Presidency Project.

27 Those who could be depended on: Novick, *That Noble Dream*, pp. 305–9, quoting William Langer and S. Everett Gleason, and see also John F. Doherty to Kenneth P. O'Donnell, July 5, 1963, White House Central Subject Files, box 632, JFKL; Arthur Schlesinger to Boyd Shafer, Dec. 23, 1961, Papers of Arthur Schlesinger, Jr., White House Files, box WH 12, JFKL.

27 On the other hand: Alex Poole, "The Strange Career of Jim Crow Archives: Race, Space, and History in the Mid-Twentieth-Century American South," *American Archivist*, vol. 77, no. 1 (2014): p. 45. Whereas well-connected professors tapped friends to become OSS analysts and cultural attachés, John Hope Franklin was turned away when he volunteered to become a clerk in the U.S. Navy, notwithstanding his Harvard Ph.D. (John Hope Franklin, *Mirror to America: The Autobiography of John Hope Franklin* [New York: Farrar, Straus and Giroux, 2007], p. 105.)

27 That is how the War Department: Alan M. Kraut and Richard Breitman, *American Refugee Policy and European Jewry, 1933–1945* (Bloomington: Indiana University Press, 1987), pp. 126–45.

27 When surveyed: Steven White, *World War II and American Racial Politics: Public Opinion, the Presidency, and Civil Rights Advocacy* (Cambridge: Cambridge University Press, 2019), pp. 42–44; Survey 32: Attitudes of and Toward Negroes, March 1943, The American Soldier in World War 2, https://americansoldierww2.org.

27 Black servicemen: Thomas A. Guglielmo, *Divisions: A New History of Racism and Resistance in America's World War II Military* (New York: Oxford University Press, 2021), p. 246.

28 "because of race": Cornelius L. Bynum, *A. Philip Randolph and the Struggle for Civil Rights* (Urbana: University of Illinois Press, 2010), pp. 171–74.

28 "If you put all": Guglielmo, *Divisions*, p. 251.

28 But Truman only took: Bates, *Pullman Porters*, pp. 147–48; Kersten, *A. Philip Randolph*, pp. 79–83; "The Transformation of the Racial Views of Harry Truman," *The Journal of Blacks in Higher Education*, vol. 26 (Winter 1999–2000): p. 30.

29 What turned out: Daniel Patrick Moynihan, *Secrecy: The American Experience* (New Haven: Yale University Press, 1998), p. 73.

29 Within this dark state: The security-clearance process has evolved over the years, and in some cases administrative appeals are possible. But courts have provided little or no recourse. See David C. Mayer, "Reviewing National Security Clearance Decisions: The Clash Between Title VII and Bivens Claims," *Cornell Law Review*, vol. 85, no. 3 (2000): pp. 786–821; Louis Fisher, "Judicial Interpretations of Egan," Law Library of Congress, Nov. 13, 2009, FAS.

29 Even some kinds: On the large number of lesbian and gay people who worked in Washington before 1945, but were subsequently denied security clearances, see David K. Johnson, *The Lavender Scare: The Cold War Persecution of Gays and Lesbians in the Federal Government* (Chicago: University of Chicago Press, 2004), pp. 43–46, and Kirchick, *Secret City*, chaps. four and five.

29 In the years: An arrest record—even without conviction—can lead to such a denial, which has a disproportionate impact on overpoliced communities. See Paul R. Wassenaar, "Title VII—Racial Discrimination in Employment—Employers Use of Record of Arrests Not Leading to Conviction," *Wayne Law Review*, vol. 17, no. 1 (1971): p. 233. The government does not track security-clearance denials by race, but for a revealing study showing a clear correlation, see GAO, *Managing DOE: Further Review Needed of Suspensions of Security Clearances for Minority Employees*, GAO/RCED-95-15 (1994). The perception that Black people could not obtain security clearances gave senior officials an excuse not even to try appointing them. See, for instance, Michael Krenn, *Black Diplomacy: African Americans and the State Department, 1945–69* (London: Routledge, 1999), pp. 97–100.

29 "Every bureaucracy": Max Weber, *From Max Weber: Essays in Sociology*, trans. H. H. Gerth and C. Wright Mills (London: Routledge, 1948), p. 233.

29 In fact, many: "Even as the transparency laws of the 1960s and 1970s placed increasingly onerous demands on the domestic policy process," David Pozen writes, "they grew increasingly detached from the state's most violent and least visible components. While

the National Labor Relations Board continually runs into the strictures of FOIA [the Federal Advisory Committee Act, the Government in the Sunshine Act, and the Administrative Procedure Act], the National Security Agency runs riot." (David E. Pozen, "Transparency's Ideological Drift," *Yale Law Journal*, vol. 128 [2018]: pp. 100–65.) One reason is that this blanket of secrecy has also served to protect the interests of a host of corporate contractors, think tanks, and management consulting firms.

30 "Our present security": Commission on Protecting and Reducing Government Secrecy, *Secrecy: Report of the Commission on Protecting and Reducing Government Secrecy*, by Daniel Patrick Moynihan and Larry Combest, Senate doc. no. 105–2 (Washington, D.C.: GPO, 1997), pp. A48–A49.

30 "overclassification has": Committee on Classified Information, *Report to the Secretary of Defense by the Committee on Classified Information* (Washington, D.C., 1956), p. 7.

30 By 1961: Arthur M. Schlesinger, memorandum for McGeorge Bundy, March 20, 1961, Papers of Arthur M. Schlesinger, Jr., White House Files, box WH-12, JFKL.

30 a series of high-level reviews: Commission on Protecting and Reducing Government Secrecy, *Secrecy: Report of the Commission*, p. 2.

30 What we do know: PIDB, *Transforming the Security Classification System* (Washington, D.C., 2012), p. 17.

31 Altogether, the United States spent: ISOO, *2012 Report to the President* (Washington, D.C., 2013); ISOO, *2017 Report to the President* (Washington, D.C., 2018), FAS.

31 "coping with information overload": Barton Gellman and Greg Miller, "'Black Budget' Summary Details U.S. Spy Network's Successes, Failures and Objectives," *Washington Post*, Aug. 29, 2013.

32 The government estimates: PIDB, *Transforming the Security*, p. 17.

32 But at the largest: NARA, Office of the Inspector General, *Audit of Processing of Textual Records*, OIG Audit Report No. 13–14, 2013, p. 13. The most recent audit, from 2018, does not specify either the volume of backlogged records or the number of archivists who must process them, but notes that, "with staffing increases unlikely," they may need to work more than seven times faster to reduce the backlog (NARA, Office of the Inspector General, *Audit of Research Services' Analog Processing*, 18-AUD-11 [2018], p. 9).

32 Notwithstanding the exponential growth: Compare the data in ISOO, *Report to the President*, of 1997 with that of 2016: $150 mil-

lion in 1997 ($229 million adjusted for inflation), $107 million in 2016, and 204 million pages declassified in 1997 versus forty-four million in 2016.

32 The State Department is experimenting: Joseph Risi et al., "Predicting History," *Nature Human Behaviour*, vol. 3, no. 9 (June 3, 2019): p. 906.

34 Conversely, there are: Marc Ambinder and D. B. Grady, *Deep State: Inside the Government Secrecy Industry* (Hoboken: Wiley, 2013), pp. 190–92.

1 PEARL HARBOR: THE ORIGINAL SECRET

36 "surprise offensive" . . . "make it very certain": Franklin D. Roosevelt, "Address to Congress Requesting a Declaration of War," Dec. 8, 1941.

37 Altogether, "national security": Winslow Wheeler, "America's $1 Trillion National Security Budget," Project on Government Oversight, March 13, 2014.

38 Until then: Adam J. Berinsky, *In Time of War: Understanding American Public Opinion from World War II to Iraq* (Chicago: University of Chicago Press, 2009), p. 46.

38 Best-selling books: James Ledbetter, *Unwarranted Influence: Dwight D. Eisenhower and the Military-Industrial Complex* (New Haven: Yale University Press, 2011), pp. 21–25.

38 "full record": Franklin D. Roosevelt, "Fireside Chat," address, Dec. 9, 1941, American Presidency Project.

38 "ruse and cunning": Feis, *The Road to Pearl Harbor: The Coming of the War Between the United States and Japan* (Princeton: Princeton University Press, 1950), p. 5.

38 "final judgment": Gleason and Langer, *The Undeclared War, 1940–1941* (New York: Council on Foreign Relations, 1953), p. xvi. See also Peter Novick, *That Noble Dream: The "Objectivity Question" and the American Historical Profession* (New York: Cambridge University Press, 1988), p. 305.

39 The experiment involved: This is U.S. DDO, of which the publisher, Gale, gave permission for us to analyze as part of this project.

40 we came across this account: Henry Cabot Lodge, Jr., Memorandum of Conversation, June 26, 1954, U.S. DDO, unredacted version, doc. no. CK2349066468.

40 "Get me the president": This account is from ibid., and also from

John Martin, *Downing Street: The War Years* (London: Trafalgar Square Publishing, 1992), pp. 66–67.

41 Because the army chief of staff: Lori S. Tagg, "Intelligence, Japanese Attack on Pearl Harbor," U.S. Army, Jan. 4, 2017; *Pearl Harbor Attack: Hearings Before the Joint Committee on the Investigation of the Pearl Harbor Attack*, pt. 39, 79th Cong., 1st Sess. (1946), pp. 139, 228–29 (hereafter *Pearl Harbor Attack* with part and page number).

41 The State Department maintained: Memorandum of Conversation, June 26, 1954, U.S. DDO, redacted version, doc. no. CK2349309531.

42 "which reasonably could be expected": Exec. Order 12356, 47 Fed. Reg. 14874, April 6, 1982.

42 "old and tired": Lovett to Eisenhower, Jan. 24, 1952, U.S. DDO, unredacted version, doc. no. CK2349082002; John Charmley, *Churchill, the End of Glory: A Political Biography* (San Diego: Harcourt, 1993), p. 578.

42 "paper cities of Japan": Michael S. Sherry, *The Rise of American Air Power: The Creation of Armageddon* (New Haven: Yale University Press, 1987), p. 109.

43 "had long burned": David Reynolds, *In Command of History: Churchill Fighting and Writing the Second World War* (London: Penguin, 2004), p. 623. But, contrary to Reynolds's account, Churchill did leave in that, for the Americans, the Japanese attack represented "a vast simplification of their problems and their duty" (Winston Churchill, *The Second World War*, vol. 3, *The Grand Alliance* [Boston: Houghton Mifflin, 1950], p. 602).

43 It was only: *Pearl Harbor Attack*, pt. 39, pp. 226–29.

43 At a time: Reynolds, *In Command of History*, pp. 264–67.

44 Just ten days earlier: Peter Hennessy, *The Secret State* (London: Penguin, 2004), pp. 56–57.

44 forward deployment also brought: Fred Kaplan, *The Wizards of Armageddon* (Stanford: Stanford University Press, 1991), pp. 98–106.

45 "avoid any action": Hennessy, *The Secret State*, pp. 54–55.

45 "cause widespread": Memorandum of Restricted Meeting of Chiefs of Staff, Dec. 7, 1953, U.S. DDO, unredacted version, doc. no. CK2349558075; redacted version, doc. no. CK2349230668.

46 After the State Department lost: Henry C. Clausen and Bruce Lee, *Pearl Harbor: Final Judgment* (New York: Crown, 1992), pp. 45–46; David Kahn, *The Code-Breakers: The Story of Secret Writing* (New York: Macmillan, 1967), p. 29.

46 "back door" theory: Charles Callan Tansill's *Back Door to War: The Roosevelt Foreign Policy, 1933–1941* (Chicago: Regnery, 1952) is the best-known version of this argument, but the great Charles A. Beard's account is the most scholarly: *President Roosevelt and the Coming of the War, 1941: A Study in Appearances and Realities* (New Haven: Yale University Press, 1948). This line of argument was almost single-handedly revived by the historian Marc Trachtenberg in *The Craft of International History: A Guide to Method* (Princeton: Princeton University Press, 2006), chap. four.

46 "said that he would": Marc Trachtenberg, "Roundtable 5-4 on 'Democracy, Deception, and Entry into War,'" ISFF Roundtable 5, no. 4 (May 17, 2013).

46 U.S. forces escorting: Robert Dallek, *Franklin D. Roosevelt and American Foreign Policy, 1932–1945* (New York: Oxford University Press, 1979), pp. 285–92.

47 In April 1941: Daniel Ford, *Flying Tigers: Claire Chennault and His American Volunteers, 1941–1942* (Durham, N.H.: Warbird Books, 2016), pp. 35–38, 42–50.

47 Without U.S. oil: Edwin T. Layton with Roger Pineau and John Costello, *"And I Was There": Pearl Harbor and Midway—Breaking the Secrets* (New York: Morrow, 1985), p. 130.

47 "There will never": Sidney L. Pash, *The Currents of War: A New History of American-Japanese Relations, 1899–1941* (Lexington: University Press of Kentucky, 2014), p. 174.

47 But Ickes does not: Trachtenberg, "Dan Reiter and America's Road to War in 1941," in "Roundtable 5-4 on 'Democracy, Deception, and Entry into War,'" which also links to the original documents.

47 So Roosevelt's options: This is Trachtenberg's argument in *Craft of International History*, pp. 92–96.

48 Instead of intervening: Grew, *Turbulent Era: A Diplomatic Record of Forty Years, 1904–1945* (Boston: Houghton Mifflin, 1952), vol. 2, p. 1347.

48 "would simply drive": Patrick J. Hearden, *Roosevelt Confronts Hitler: America's Entry into World War II* (Dekalb: Northern Illinois University Press, 1987), p. 211. See also John M. Blum, *From the Morgenthau Diaries: Years of Urgency 1938–1941* (Boston: Houghton Mifflin, 1965), p. 377.

48 The announcement: Eri Hotta, *Japan 1941: Countdown to Infamy* (New York: Vintage, 2013), pp. 143–44.

48 Their policy up to this point: David J. Lu, *Agony of Choice, Matsuoka Yosuke and the Rise and Fall of the Japanese Empire* (Lanham, Md.: Lexington Books, 2002), pp. 12–13.

48 The agreement was supposed to deter: Jeremy A. Yellen, *The Greater East Asia Co-Prosperity Sphere: When Total Empire Met Total War* (Ithaca, N.Y.: Cornell University Press, 2019), pp. 28–45.

48 "at once": Trachtenberg, *Craft of International History*, p. 125.

49 "hat-in-hand": Grew, *Turbulent Era*, vol. 2, pp. 1302–4.

49 "has long been committed": "Memorandum by the Secretary of State," September 3, 1941, in "Japan 1931–1941," *FRUS*, vol. 2 (1943) pp. 588–92.

49 "conclusively and wholeheartedly": Grew Memorandum, September 6, 1941, in "Japan 1931–1941," *FRUS*, vol. 2 (1943), pp. 604, 608.

49 "accept the American terms": Grew, *Turbulent Era*, vol. 2, pp. 1321–33, 1359, and see also Trachtenberg, *Craft of International History*, pp. 104–5.

49 "no matter what": Feis, *The Road to Pearl Harbor*, pp. 252–53. See also pp. 259–60, where Feis answers the question of whether there was "some hidden wish to punish Japan" with another question: "Who is to know?" Gleason and Langer, for their part, quote the German ambassador as the authoritative source on Konoe's actual intent—even though Konoe refused throughout this episode to keep Berlin informed. They also refer to "Japanese records which became available after the war" without actually citing any such records, *Undeclared War*, 707.

50 "surrendering to the United States": Hotta, *Japan 1941*, pp. 170–71, 188–89.

50 Konoe kept trying: Hotta, *Japan 1941*, p. 179.

50 Interestingly, the Americans: Paul W. Schroader, *The Axis Alliance and Japanese-American Relations* (Ithaca: Cornell University Press, 1958), pp. 62–68.

50 "unbearable": Hotta, *Japan 1941*, pp. 201–2.

50 Tōjō therefore pushed: Dallek, *Franklin D. Roosevelt*, pp. 306–7.

51 "comprehensive Pacific settlement": "Memorandum of Conversation" and "Outline of Proposed Basis for Agreement," November 26, 1941, in "Japan 1931–1941," *FRUS*, vol. 2 (1943), pp. 764–70.

51 "maximum demands": Langer and Gleason, *Undeclared War*, p. 898.

51 "The question was": Langer and Gleason admit the wording was "infelicitous," but describe it as expressing Stimson's concern that the political situation did not permit the administration to parry the blow even though they saw it coming (*Undeclared War*, pp. 886, 898).

51 The words "without": That's why FDR and his closest advisers were "not too tense" upon receiving the reports from Pearl Harbor. Hitler was the main enemy, the United States would inevitably have to join the war, and "Japan had given us an opportunity," as one of the president's advisers recalled (Trachtenberg, *Craft of International History*, p. 129). As Roosevelt himself later said, "If the Japanese had not attacked the United States, he doubted very much if it would have been possible to send any American forces to Europe" (Roosevelt-Stalin Meeting, Nov. 29, 1943, in *FRUS, 1943*, vol. 3, doc. no. 365).

52 Roosevelt's most influential critics: Larry J. Frank, "The United States Navy v. the *Chicago Tribune*," *Historian*, vol. 42, no. 2 (1980): pp. 291–92.

52 "I am now painfully": Yellen, *The Greater East Asia*, p. 45.

52 The keynote: Even four years after Pearl Harbor, and after Hiroshima and Nagasaki had been destroyed, a poll showed that 23 percent of Americans wanted to keep on dropping atomic bombs on Japan before Tokyo had a chance to surrender (John W. Dower, *War Without Mercy: Race and Power in the Pacific War* [New York: Pantheon, 1993], pp. 36–37, 54–55, 98–110).

53 For that very reason: Both Marshall and the chief of naval operations, Admiral Harold Stark, urged Roosevelt to avoid war, advising, "The most essential thing now is to gain time," both for America to rearm and to give them the ability to focus on the main threat: Nazi Germany (Stark to Roosevelt, Nov. 5, 1941, *Pearl Harbor Attack*, pt. 16, pp. 2222–23).

53 "is not true": Thomas Schelling, foreword to Roberta Wohlstetter, *Pearl Harbor: Warning and Decision* (Stanford: Stanford University Press, 1962), p. vii.

54 These communications would have shown: Layton, *"And I Was There,"* pp. 115–17, 138–45.

54 "hostile action": *Pearl Harbor Attack*, pt. 39, p. 79.

54 It was locked: Ibid., pp. 228–29.

54 When the *Chicago Tribune*: David Kahn, *The Codebreakers: The Comprehensive History of Secret Communication from Ancient Times to the Internet* (New York: Scribner, 1996), pp. 604–5.

54 The army operated: *Pearl Harbor Attack*, pt. 39, p. 65.

55 Even after Japanese: The commander at Clark wanted to raid Formosa, but MacArthur only communicated with him through an intermediary for several hours after word came about Pearl Harbor, slowing the response (Arthur Herman, *Douglas MacArthur:*

American Warrior [New York: Random House, 2016], pp. 495–506).

55 as in August 2001: "Bin Ladin Determined to Strike in US," excerpt from the President's Daily Brief, Dec. 4, 1998, FAS.

55 In response to the Pearl: Brian Hochman, *The Listeners: A History of Wiretapping in the United States* (Cambridge, Mass.: Harvard University Press, 2022), pp. 85–86.

56 Thus, the same month: Melvyn P. Leffler, *A Preponderance of Power: National Security, the Truman Administration, and the Cold War* (Stanford: Stanford University Press, 1992), pp. 41–42; James F. Schnabel, *History of the Joint Chiefs of Staff*, vol. 1, *The Joint Chiefs of Staff and National Policy, 1945–1947* (Washington, D.C.: Office of the Chairman of the JCS, 1996), pp. 66–67.

57 Thomas A. Bailey: Novick, *That Noble Dream*, pp. 290–92, 305–9. As Novick points out, Bailey later qualified this claim. He did not mean that "people ought in all cases or even most cases to be deceived," only confirming his contention that presidents should deceive the public at least some of the time (*The American Pageant Revisited: Recollections of a Stanford Historian* [Stanford: Hoover Institution Press, 1982], p. 167).

58 "without provocation": George Bush, "In Defense of Saudi Arabia," speech, Aug. 8, 1990, in *The Gulf War Reader: History, Documents, Opinions*, eds. Micah L. Sifry and Christopher Cerf (New York: Times Books, 1991), p. 197.

58 "no opinion": "The Glaspie Transcript: Saddam Meets the U.S. Ambassador (July 25, 1990)," in *Gulf War Reader*, p. 130. See also Elaine Sciolino, "Envoy's Testimony on Iraq Is Assailed," *New York Times*, July 13, 1991. On green light, see Roger Simon, "Was the U.S. Signal Red or Green on Kuwait?," *Los Angeles Times*, Nov. 22, 1992. Ross Perot said that the Bush administration was guarding records of its instructions to Glaspie "like the secrets of the atomic bomb" (Jeffrey Smith, "State Department Cable Traffic on Iraq-Kuwait Tensions, July 1990," *Washington Post*, Oct. 21, 1992). As John M. Schuessler argues, Pearl Harbor was an illustrative example of how presidents have used false pretenses to start or expand wars the American people would not otherwise support (John M. Schuessler, "The Deception Dividend: FDR's Undeclared War," *International Security*, vol. 34, no. 4 [Spring 2010]: pp. 158–64).

58 "infamy": Representative DeFazio, speaking on H. Res. 27, Jan. 10, 1991, 102nd Cong., 1st Sess., *Congressional Record*, vol. 137, pt. 1, p. 549.

59 And all this: Consider, for instance, how the U.S. intelligence community warned the public of the Russian invasion of Ukraine, which helped the president prepare sanctions, rally an alliance, and win a decisive advantage in the information war (Julian E. Barnes and David E. Sanger, "Accurate U.S. Intelligence Did Not Stop Putin, But It Gave Biden Big Advantages," *New York Times*, Feb. 22, 2022).

2 THE BOMB: BORN SECRET

60 But starting with: To be sure, the government can find ways to threaten journalists with prosecution for publishing classified information even without using the Atomic Energy Act. As shown in the James Risen case, they can compel journalists to testify and threaten prison time if they do not give up their sources.

61 In 1998: Kyl-Lott Amendments to the Strom Thurmond National Defense Authorization Act for Fiscal Year 1999, Public Law 105-261, U.S. Statutes at Large 112 (1998).

61 In the first eight years: William Burr, "How Many and Where Were the Nukes?," ZNet, Aug. 21, 2006. Bible of 1,286 pages cost $4.9 million in 1996, so $3,810 per page; for the DOE program, $3,313 per page in 2006 (according to the Burr article) is $4,236 in 2020.

62 In the case of the "strike": NSC, *Function of the Special Committee of NSC on Atomic Energy to Advise the President on Use of Atomic Weapons*, 1952, U.S. DDO, doc. no. CK2349320976; White House, *Procedures to Be Followed in the Event the President Is Called Upon to Decide Whether or Not Atomic Weapons Should Be Used*, 1951, U.S. DDO, doc. no. CK2349137214; General Advisory Committee to the AEC, *Working Memorandum: Distinction Between the Atomic Bomb and the Super-Bomb*, 1949, U.S. DDO, doc. no. CK2349218994.

62 documents related to unidentified flying objects: Hannah Wallach, "Textual Analysis of Government Declassification Patterns," University of Massachusetts, 2013.

62 In an exception: Project 1794 Final Development Summary Report, 06/1956, and Program Planning Report, Project 1794 Extension Program, 04/1957, RG 342: Records of U.S. Air Force Commands, Activities, and Organizations, Entry UD-UP 138, Research and Development Project Files, USNA.

62 Scientists believed: A. J. Goodpaster, Memorandum of Con-

ference with the President, Feb. 13, 1959, U.S. DDO, doc. no. CK2349092480.

62 It will also reveal: See Advisory Committee on Human Radiation Experiments, "Staff Memoranda: Atomic Veterans," Sept. 8, 1994; "Recommendations for Remedies Pertaining to Experiments and Exposures During the Period 1944–1974," Sept. 22, 1995, OSTI.

63 In Hollywood movies: The best evidence that has emerged of a close encounter, a navy video of a UFO, was released after just thirteen years, more evidence that the government does not closely guard information about the possibility of extraterrestrial visitations—just the opposite (Helene Cooper, Ralph Blumenthal, and Leslie Kean, "Glowing Auras and 'Black Money': The Pentagon's Mysterious U.F.O. Program," *New York Times*, Dec. 16, 2017).

64 "ultimate weapon": For a typical example, see Graham Allison, *Nuclear Terrorism: The Ultimate Preventable Catastrophe* (New York: Times Books, 2004), p. 6. For the pervasiveness of this perception, see John E. Mueller, *Atomic Obsession: Nuclear Alarmism from Hiroshima to Al-Qaeda* (Oxford, U.K.: Oxford University Press, 2010), pp. 81–82.

65 This story begins: Barton J. Bernstein, "The Uneasy Alliance: Roosevelt, Churchill, and the Atomic Bomb, 1940–1945," *Western Political Quarterly*, vol. 29, no. 2 (1976): p. 205.

65 It started with: Bruce Cameron Reed, *The Manhattan Project: The Story of the Century* (Cham, Switzerland: Springer Nature, 2020), p. 91.

65 But to actually produce: Ibid., pp. 6–7.

65 Over the next few years: *Manhattan District History*, bk. 8, *Los Alamos Project*, vol. 1: *General* (Washington, D.C.: DOE, 1947).

65 But it was dwarfed: Kate Brown, *Plutopia: Nuclear Families, Atomic Cities, and the Great Soviet and American Plutonium Disasters* (New York: Oxford University Press, 2013), pp. 22, 27, 297; Reed, *Manhattan Project*, pp. 164–65, 168, 210–18.

66 "absolute secrecy": Manhattan District History, bk. 1, *General*, vol. 14: *Intelligence and Security* (Washington, D.C.: DOE, 1945), app. A-1, OSTI.

66 That was the main concern: Alex Wellerstein, *Restricted Data: The History of Nuclear Secrecy in the United States* (Chicago: University of Chicago Press, 2021), pp. 54–56.

66 Bush and George Marshall: Martin J. Sherwin, "The Atomic Bomb and the Origins of the Cold War: U.S. Atomic-Energy Policy and

Diplomacy, 1941–45," *American Historical Review*, vol. 78 (Oct. 1973): pp. 946–48.

66 But while the war: Bernstein, "Uneasy Alliance," pp. 206, 210; Barton J. Bernstein, "Roosevelt, Truman, and the Atomic Bomb, 1941–1945: A Reinterpretation," *Political Science Quarterly*, vol. 90, no. 1 (1975): p. 25.

66 "all other nations": Robert S. Norris, *Racing for the Bomb* (Hanover, N.H.: Steerforth Press, 2003), pp. 253–54.

67 Groves developed: Manhattan District History, *General*, vol. 14, p. 343.

67 In the three years: Ibid., p. 34.

67 the most senior: Alex Wellerstein, "Knowledge and the Bomb: Nuclear Secrecy in the United States, 1939–2008," Ph.D. diss., Harvard University, 2010, pp. 65–66.

68 Black women: Robert Bauman, "Jim Crow in the Tri-Cities, 1943–1950," *The Pacific Northwest Quarterly*, vol. 96, no. 3 (2005): pp. 124–31.

68 "careful checks": Brown, *Plutopia*, 27.

68 "Confidential": Exec. Order 10501, 3 C.F.R., pp. 979–86 (1953). Strangely, "Nation" was only capitalized in the definition of "Top Secret" information, but not for "Confidential" information.

69 "Compartmentalization of knowledge": Robert S. Norris, "Unprecedented Security Measures," in *The Manhattan Project: The Birth of the Atomic Bomb in the Words of Its Creators, Eyewitnesses, and Historians*, ed. Cynthia Kelly (New York: Black Dog & Leventhal, 2007), p. 235.

69 They pointed out: Richard Feynman, interview by Charles Weiner, *American Institute of Physics*, March 5, 1966.

69 "It was rare": Lt. Col. John Lansdale, Jr., "As If They Were Walking in the Woods," in *Manhattan Project*, ed. Kelly, p. 242. See also Alex Wellerstein, "What Did Bohr Do at Los Alamos?," *Restricted Data: The Nuclear Secrecy Blog*, May 11, 2015.

70 Other scientists, like Richard Feynman: Lawrence Badash, J. O. Hirschfelder, and H. P. Broida, *Reminiscences of Los Alamos 1943–1945* (Dordrecht: Springer Netherlands, 1980), pp. 115–16.

71 Feynman knew: Ibid., pp. 117–19.

71 The same system: Joseph Albright and Marcia Kunstel, *Bombshell: The Secret Story of America's Unknown Atomic Spy Conspiracy* (Darby, Pa.: Diane Publishing Company, 1997), p. 106.

72 Soviet agents: Gregg Herken, *Brotherhood of the Bomb: The Tangled Lives and Loyalties of Robert Oppenheimer, Ernest Lawrence, and Edward Teller* (New York: Henry Holt, 2013), p. 161.

72 As further proof: Wellerstein, *Restricted Data*, pp. 66–70.

72 Groves handled: Arvin Quist, *Security Classification of Information*, vol. 1 (Oak Ridge, Tenn.: Oak Ridge National Laboratories, 1989), p. 105; Wellerstein, "Knowledge and the Bomb," pp. 18, 134–36.

72 "Publicity day": Wellerstein, "Knowledge and the Bomb," p. 159.

73 With the creation: Wellerstein, *Restricted Data*, pp. 64, 130, 144, 152, 157.

74 It has been argued: Ibid., pp. 153–58.

74 "special access program": SAPs were only formally named and recognized as part of the government's information security system in 1972. For a good primer, see Tim McMillan and Tyler Rogoway, "Special Access Programs and the Pentagon's Ecosystem of Secrecy," *Drive*, July 22, 2019.

74 Groves finally got around: Wellerstein, "Knowledge and the Bomb," pp. 198, 207–8.

75 When a shortage of plutonium: Chuck Hansen, Eleanor Hansen, and Larry Hatfield, *The Swords of Armageddon* (Sunnyvale, Calif.: Chukelea Publications, 2007), vol. 2, pp. 116–17.

75 Groves therefore realized: Wellerstein, "Knowledge and the Bomb," pp. 195–205; Quist, *Security Classification*, p. 105.

75 The most sensitive information: DOE, *Report of Committee on Declassification*, 1945.

75 Decades later: David Pozen, "Deep Secrecy," *Stanford Law Review*, vol. 62, no. 2 (2010): p. 257.

76 "This revelation": Winston Churchill, "Statement by the Prime Minister," Aug. 6, 1945, in Manhattan District History, bk. 1, *General*, vol. 4, chap. 8.

76 "hunch": Wellerstein, "Knowledge and the Bomb," p. 224.

77 the theoretical possibility: Even Groves admitted that the most important secret of the Manhattan Project was simply "the fact that the thing went off" (Testimony of Gen. L. R. Groves, in House Committee on Military Affairs, *Atomic Energy: Hearings on H.R. 4280, An Act for the Development and Control of Atomic Energy, Oct. 9 and 18*, 79th Congress, 1st Sess., [1945]).

77 "utterly bizarre": David E. Lilienthal, *The Journals of David E. Lilienthal*, vol. 2, *The Atomic Energy Years, 1945–1950* (New York: Harper & Row, 1964), p. 16.

78 The published report: Henry Smyth, "The Work on the Atomic Bomb," in *Atomic Energy for Military Purposes: The Official Report on the Development of the Atomic Bomb Under the Auspices of the United States Government* (Princeton: Princeton University Press, 1945), p. 208.

78 But many of the specifics: John Coster-Mullen, *Atomic Bombs: The Top Secret Inside Story of Little Boy and Fat Man* (self-published, 2016), p. 27.

78 But even when you put: Ibid., p. 39.

78 But however clever: Alice L. Buck, *A History of the Atomic Energy Commission* (Washington, D.C.: DOE, 1983); "Summary of Declassified Nuclear Stockpile Information," DOE OpenNet. On Truman not being briefed, see David Alan Rosenberg, "U.S. Nuclear Stockpile, 1945–1950," *Bulletin of the Atomic Scientists*, vol. 38, no. 5 (1982): p. 27.

79 "hollow threat": Coster-Mullen, *Atomic Bombs*, p. 382.

79 Many of the planes: Harry R. Borowski, *A Hollow Threat: Strategic Air Power and Containment Before Korea* (Westport, Conn.: Greenwood Press, 1982), 103–5. See also Harry R. Borowski, "Air Force Atomic Capability from V-J Day to the Berlin Blockade—Potential or Real?," *Military Affairs*, vol. 44, no. 3 (1980): pp. 105–10.

79 When Curtis LeMay: Walton S. Moody, *Building a Strategic Air Force*, Air Force History and Museums Program (1995), p. 125.

79 In a simulated night attack: Borowski, "Air Force Atomic Capability," pp. 105–10.

80 At any given time: Moody, *Building a Strategic Air Force*, pp. 125, 168.

80 The AEC had custody: Hansen, Hansen, and Hatfield, *Swords of Armageddon*, pp. 146–49.

80 After your first strike: Ibid., p. 150.

80 After all, Roswell: Ibid., pp. 147–49.

80 Compounding the government's concern: Col. Richard L. Weaver and 1st Lt. James McAndrew, *The Roswell Report: Fact and Fiction in the New Mexico Desert* (Washington, D.C.: USAF, 1995), pp. 3–4; William J. Broad, "Wreckage in the Desert Was Odd but Not Alien," *New York Times*, Sept. 18, 1994.

82 "I'm glad": Wellerstein, "Knowledge and the Bomb," p. 289.

83 With the help: On Seborer, see Harvey Klehr and John Earl Haynes, "On the Trail of a Fourth Soviet Spy at Los Alamos," *Studies in Intelligence*, vol. 63, no. 3 (Sept. 2019), pp. 1–4.

83 But it was later confirmed: David Holloway, *Stalin and the Bomb: The Soviet Union and Atomic Energy, 1939–1956* (New Haven: Yale University Press, 1994), pp. 107–8.

83 All three did it: Joseph Albright and Marcia Kunstel, *Bombshell: The Secret Story of America's Unknown Atomic Spy Conspiracy* (New York: Diane Publishing Company, 1997), pp. 89–90.

84   "of the very atomic": Wellerstein, "Knowledge and the Bomb,"
      pp. 322–23.

85   top-secret intelligence estimate: CIA, "Special Estimate: Soviet
      Capabilities for a Surprise Attack on the Continental U.S. Before
      July 1952," SE-10, 1951, U.S. DDO, doc. no. CK2349034249.

86   President John F. Kennedy warned: Press Conference, March 21,
      1963, in *Public Papers of the Presidents of the United States: John
      F. Kennedy, 1963* (Washington, D.C.: GPO, 1964), p. 280. The
      top-secret briefing he was given considered Swedish, German,
      and Egyptian nukes to be plausible (Peter R. Lavoy, "Predict-
      ing Nuclear Proliferation: A Declassified Documentary Record,"
      Strategic Insights, vol. 3, no. 1 [Jan. 2004]: pp. 1–2).

86   In 1964: W. J. Frank, *Summary Report of the Nth Country Experi-
      ment* (Livermore, Calif.: Livermore Radiation Laboratory, 1967),
      pp. 40–43.

86   After newspapers reported: Wellerstein, "Knowledge and the
      Bomb," pp. 394–99.

87   "This is no bluff": Ibid., pp. 385–86. The leading theory for the
      lost uranium from Apollo is that it was purloined by Mossad and
      helped jump-start Israel's stockpile.

87   The hard part: Ibid., p. 108; Michael Levi, *On Nuclear Terrorism*
      (Cambridge, Mass.: Harvard University Press, 2007), pp. 40–41.

87   in 1986 the DOE: David Samuels, "Atomic John," *New Yorker*,
      Dec. 7, 2008.

88   There was no compelling: Peter Galison et al., "What We Have
      Learned About Limiting Knowledge in a Democracy," *Social
      Research*, vol. 77 (2010): p. 1034. For illustrations of Iraqi cen-
      trifuges, see *CIA Waffles on Alleged Nuclear Centrifuge*, Cryptome,
      July 2, 2003.

88   But the process: William Burr, "How Many and Where Were the
      Nukes?," ZNET, Aug. 21, 2006.

88   There are also: Matthew M. Aid, ed., "Declassification in Reverse:
      The U.S. Intelligence Community's Secret Historical Document
      Reclassification Program," National Security Archive, Feb. 26,
      2006.

89   Even in 1954: Wellerstein, "Knowledge and the Bomb," pp. 18,
      210–11.

91   document number 43: DOD, "Rolling Thunder: List of Unau-
      thorized Targets Recommended by the Joint Chiefs of Staff,"
      1968, U.S. DDO, doc. no. CK2349119281.

91   Richard Nixon would later: Jeffrey P. Kimball, *The Vietnam War*

Files: Uncovering the Secret History of Nixon-Era Strategy (Lawrence: University Press of Kansas, 2004), pp. 30–31, 214–18.

91 A more typical document: "Attachment: Description of Atomic Devices and Component Parts," n.d., U.S. DDO, doc. no. CK2349508376.

93 The most sensitive document: JCS, *Study on National Security Factors in a Comprehensive Test Ban Treaty*, 1966, U.S. DDO, doc. no. CK2349562865.

94 The next document: White House, "Disarmament Study: Task Forces Study of Inspection and Control Methods," Reports by the Task Force, vol. 2, 1955, U.S. DDO, doc. no. CK2349309553.

94 The third and final document: Joint Committee on Atomic Energy, *Study of U.S. and NATO Nuclear Weapons Arrangements*, 1961, U.S. DDO, doc. no. CK2349601635.

95 Here again: Peter Stein and Peter Feaver, *Assuring Control of Nuclear Weapons: The Evolution of Permissive Action Links* (Lanham, Md.: University Press of America, 1987), p. 32.

96 But government officials: In 2009, the director of National Intelligence replaced the "need to know" with the "responsibility to provide" principle, intended to push the intelligence community to more openly share intelligence information with other parts of the government. This could have been a fundamental reform. But insiders believe it is largely ignored within the intelligence community, and perhaps unknown in the rest of the government.

3 CODE MAKING AND CODE BREAKING: THE SECRET OF SECRETS

98 get at the heart of the matter: This experiment was done with the Declassified Documents Online database.

99 So, when U.S. soldiers: "Critique of Battle for Hill 1243," Dec. 27, 1951, RG457, Records of the National Security Agency, P/Entry 5, General Records, "Query on Security Matter," USNA.

99 When NASA began sending: The procedures can be found here: "Review of S2 Staff Study on Missiles, Satellites, and Special Projects," Dec. 26, 1961, RG457, Records of the National Security Agency, P/Entry 5, General Records, "Relationships on COMSEC R&D," USNA.

101 cryptologists would not share: "Minutes of the Sixth Meeting of the National Intelligence Authority," Aug. 21, 1946, *FRUS, 1945–1950, Emergence of the Intelligence Establishment*, p. 397; A. C. Peterson to Ennis, "Intelligence Liaison," Nov. 20, 1947, DNSA, doc. no. HN00237.

101   Amazingly, it appears: Hoover told Truman who was suspected of being a spy, but did not tell him how intercepted Soviet communications proved their guilt (J. Edgar Hoover to Harry Hawkins Vaughan, Nov. 8, 1945, in *Venona: Soviet Espionage and the American Response, 1939–1957*, eds. Robert Lewis Benson and Michael Warner [Washington, D.C.: NSA and CIA, 1996], p. 69).

101   But the person in charge: Daniel Patrick Moynihan, *Secrecy: The American Experience* (New Haven: Yale University Press, 1998), pp. 70–72.

102   In 1951: Disclosure of Classified Information, 18 U.S.C. § 798 (Oct. 31, 1951 & Supp. 1996). See also Stephen Budiansky, *Code Warriors: NSA's Codebreakers and the Secret Intelligence War Against the Soviet Union* (New York: Knopf, 2016), p. 160.

102   Those who try: Lauren Harper, "90-Year-Old Cryptanalytic Efforts Must Stay Secret, Says NSA," *Unredacted*, June 20, 2016.

102   In 2016: The CIA, not to be outdone, allowed someone to steal thirty-four terabytes' worth of computer viruses, malware, and zero-day exploits. They did not even realize it had happened until WikiLeaks started sharing the data. An internal report concluded that U.S. government hackers "prioritized building cyber weapons at the expense of securing their own systems." (Ellen Nakashima and Shane Harris, "Elite CIA Unit That Developed Hacking Tools Failed to Secure Its Own Systems, Allowing Massive Leak, an Internal Report Found," *Washington Post*, June 16, 2020; WikiLeaks Task Force to CIA Director, "WikiLeaks Task Force Final Report," Oct. 17, 2017).

103   "cocked weapon": David Alan Rosenberg, "The Origins of Overkill: Nuclear Weapons and American Strategy, 1945–1960," *International Security*, vol. 7, no. 4 (Spring 1983): p. 19.

103   "wargasm": Daniel Ellsberg, *The Doomsday Machine: Confessions of a Nuclear War Planner* (New York: Bloomsbury, 2017), p. 120.

103   This strategy: David Alan Rosenberg, "'A Smoking Radiating Ruin at the End of Two Hours': Documents on American Plans for Nuclear War with the Soviet Union, 1954–1955," *International Security*, vol. 6, no. 3 (Winter 1981–82), pp. 25, 31.

103   Air-force planners: Some air-force planners were inspired by the way Britain policed its colonies from the air, and proposed that coercive air power could be imposed on the USSR as an alternative to outright nuclear destruction (George R. Gagnon, *Air Control: Strategy for a Smaller United States Air Force* [Maxwell Air Force Base, Ala.: Air University Press, 1993], pp. 17–18).

104   Leading figures: "Project Solarium: Summary of Basic Concepts

of Task Forces," July 30, 1953, NSC Meeting Files, No. 157, Tab D, NSC Records, USNA; "Summaries Prepared by the NSC Staff of Project Solarium Presentations and Written Reports," July 22, 1953, *FRUS*, 1952–54, vol. 2, pp. 430–31.

104   "duty to future generations": Eisenhower to Dulles, Sept. 8, 1953, *FRUS*, 1952–54, vol. 2, p. 461.

104   He made clear: Dwight D. Eisenhower, "Statement to Senior Military Officers," June 19, 1954, James Hagerty Diary, James Hagerty Papers, box 1, DDEL.

104   But unless Moscow: Garrett M. Graff, *Raven Rock: The Story of the U.S. Government's Secret Plan to Save Itself—While the Rest of Us Die* (New York: Simon & Schuster, 2017), pp. 52–53.

104   "rougher road": Marc Trachtenberg, "A 'Wasting Asset': American Strategy and the Shifting Nuclear Balance, 1949–1954," *International Security*, vol. 13, no. 3 (Winter 1988–89), pp. 10, 42.

104   SAC sent a B-47 bomber: Harold R. Austin, "A Daytime Overflight of the Soviet Union," in *Early Cold War Overflight: Symposium Proceedings*, vol. 1, eds. R. Cargill Hall and Clayton D. Laurie (Washington, D.C.: National Reconnaissance Office, 2003), pp. 213–19.

104   By 1956: James Bamford, *Body of Secrets: Anatomy of the Ultra-Secret National Security Agency* (New York: Doubleday, 2001), pp. 35–36, citing R. Cargill Hall, "The Truth About Overflights," *MHQ: The Quarterly Journal of Military History*, vol. 9, no. 3 (Spring 1997): pp. 24–39.

104   In a further humiliation: Gregory W. Pedlow and Donald E. Welzenbach, "U-2 Operations in the Soviet Bloc and Middle East, 1956–1968," in *The CIA and the U-2 Program, 1954–1974* (Washington, D.C.: Center for the Study of Intelligence, 1998), pp. 102–8, FAS.

104   They had far fewer: Stephen J. Zaloga, *The Kremlin's Nuclear Sword: The Rise and Fall of Russia's Strategic Nuclear Forces, 1945–2000* (Washington, D.C.: Smithsonian Institution, 2002), p. 24.

105   Until the Soviets: NSA Scientific Advisory Board, *National Security Agency Historical Study* (Fort Meade, Md., 2010), pp. 10–11.

105   The KL-7: David G. Boak, "A History of U.S. Communications Security (the David Boak Lectures)," vols. 1 and 2 (Fort Meade, Md., 1973), pp. 36–37; NSA Center for Cryptologic History, *AFSAM-7*, in *Cryptologic Almanac 50th Anniversary Series* (Fort Meade, Md., 2003); NSA, "TEMPEST: A Signal Problem," pp. 26–27; NSA, *Plain Text Radiation Study of TSEC/KL-7 (AFSAM 7)*, UKUSA-344 (1955).

105   The NSA worked: Ed Fitzgerald, *History of U.S. Communica-

tions Security, Post–World War II (Fort Meade, Md.: NSA, 2011), pp. 8–9, 90–91; Boak, "History of U.S Communications Security," pp. 45–46.

106 But anyone they sent: NSA, *Study of the Security Division*, 1955, RG457, P/Entry 14, Security Policy, box 1, USNA; United States Communications Intelligence Board Special Committee to Study Communications Intelligence Personnel Security Standards and Practice, *Study of COMINT Personnel Security Standards and Practices* (Washington, D.C., 1955), DNSA, HN00942.

106 number of NSA personnel: Thomas R. Johnson, "The Move, or How NSA Came to Fort Meade," *Cryptologic History*, NSA doc. no. 3928654, pp. 93–95.

107 The new NSA headquarters: NSA, *Study of NSA Physical Security Program*, 1963, RG457, P/Entry 14, Security Policy, box 1, USNA.

107 At night: Ralph J. Canine to Commander of the Marine Corps, "Marine Guard Detachment for the National Security Agency at Fort George G. Meade, Maryland," July 28, 1955, RG457, P/Entry 14, Security Policy, box 1, USNA.

107 The marines: NSA, *Study of NSA Physical Security Program*.

107 And every day: James Bamford, *The Puzzle Palace: A Report on America's Most Secret Agency* (Boston: Houghton Mifflin, 1982), p. 118.

107 The new NSA building: Colin B. Burke, "It Wasn't All Magic: The Early Struggle to Automate Cryptanalysis, 1930s–1960s," *United States Cryptologic History*, special ser., vol. 6 (2002), p. 277.

108 They produced: Bamford, *Puzzle Palace*, p. 65.

108 It added up: AFSA to Commanding Officer, Military District of Washington, June 19, 1952, RG457.3, Records of the National Security Agency, P/Entry 5, General Records, container 2, USNA.

108 "a major riot": NSA, *Study of NSA Physical Security Program*.

108 "a continual conflict": Ibid.

108 Soviet Embassy staff: Carroll E. Williams, "Meade Work at Bid Stage," *Baltimore Sun*, March 14, 1954.

109 no polygraph exams: "The Role of Employer Practices in the Federal Industrial Personnel Security Program: A Field Study," *Stanford Law Review*, vol. 8, no. 2 (1956): pp. 240–41.

110 The national unemployment rate: "Booming Construction Industry Spurs Sharp Private Employment Rise," *Washington Post and Times Herald*, May 22, 1955.

110 This location: "Building Planning Service," May 17–19, 1953, NSA doc. no. 3978858.

112 "When the battery dies": Robert Wallace and H. Keith Melton,

Spycraft: The Secret History of the CIA's Spytechs from Communism to Al-Qaeda (New York: Plume, 2009), p. 188.

112 Luckily for the Soviets: Albert Glinsky, *Theremin: Ether Music and Espionage* (Urbana: University of Illinois Press, 2000), pp. 259–60.

112 new kind of wireless surveillance system: George F. Kennan, *Memoirs, 1950–1963* (New York: Pantheon, 1967), pp. 154–56.

113 Theremin realized: Glinsky, *Theremin*, pp. 260–61.

114 center for juvenile delinquents: "Man Is Held for Posing as Doctor," *Washington Post and Times Herald*, Aug. 30, 1957.

114 Once on staff: Eve Edstrom, "Counselor Suspended in Striking of Boy, 15," *Washington Post and Times Herald*, Nov. 8, 1957.

115 But KGB operatives: Alfred Hubest, "Audiosurveillance," *Studies in Intelligence*, vol. 4, no. 3 (Summer 1960): pp. 43–45; John P. Callahan, "Immigrants Fade in Building Field," *New York Times*, Oct. 13, 1957.

115 "It is now virtually": Hubest, "Audiosurveillance," pp. 40–41.

115 Simply dropping: Wallace and Melton, *Spycraft*, p. 173.

115 NSA was under such pressure: House Committee on Un-American Activities, *Security Practices in the National Security Agency (Defection of Bernon F. Mitchell and William H. Martin)*, 87th Cong., 2d Sess. (1962), 6, P/Entry 5, General Records, container 5, USNA.

116 "For Official Use Only": John J. Beiser to director of the National Security Agency, "Classifications of Investigations Conducted by the Army," Oct. 20th, 1958, RG457, P/Entry 5, General Records, container 4, USNA.

116 Each of these rooms: NSA, "TEMPEST," p. 28.

117 once-in-a-lifetime opportunity: Display ad 81, no title, *Washington Post and Times Herald*, March 21, 1954.

117 For the NSA's own move: "Ghosts," *Washington Post and Times Herald*, March 26, 1954.

117 It did fire: "ODM Fires Questionable Loyalty Risk," *Austin Statesman*, March 23, 1954.

118 But the plan itself: U.S. Army Corps of Engineers, "Operations Building 'A'—No. 401 and 'B'—No. 450, First Floor Plans," RG457, P/Entry-14, Security Policy, box 1, USNA.

118 As an enterprising journalist: Bamford, *The Puzzle Palace*, p. 124.

119 "Elements of NSA": "Interim Movement, 31 January 1955–24 June 1955," NSA doc. no. 3987308.

119 It took months: J. C. Bennett to DD/PROD, "Exceptions to NSA Regulation 121-7 Granted to NSA Elements at the Interim Site, Ft. Meade," Nov. 2, 1955, RG457, P/Entry 14, "Security Policy," box 1, USNA.

119 Finally, the Soviet Division: Thomas R. Johnson, "The Move," p. 97.

119 "a sense of false security": Leslie H. Wyman, "Designation of Areas," April 6, 1953, RG457, Records of the National Security Agency, P/Entry 14, Security Policy, box 1, "Physical Security," USNA.

119 Even at the new headquarters: NSA, *Study of NSA Physical Security Program*.

120 "If they are of": Ibid.

120 A 1963 report found: Ibid.

121 Security staff periodically: Ibid.

121 As the same 1963: Ibid.

121 "Their integrity": Ibid.

122 military personnel were exempt: Bamford, *The Puzzle Palace*, pp. 123–24.

122 Twenty years earlier: Christopher Andrew and Oleg Gordievsky, *KGB: The Inside Story of Its Foreign Operations from Lenin to Gorbachev* (London: Hodder & Stoughton, 1990), pp. 180–81.

123 when the CIA constructed: DDA to Agency/Office Division Directors, "Request for Thoughts on Reducing Bureaucracy," April 1, 1987, CIA-RDP91-00058R000200400010-4.

123 period of rapid growth: Steven Aftergood, "Proposed NSA Headquarters Expansion Under Review," March 15, 2017, FAS.

123 In 1957: David Easter, "Soviet Bloc and Western Bugging of Opponents' Diplomatic Premises during the Early Cold War," *Intelligence and National Security*, vol. 31, no. 1 (2016): p. 34.

123 Between 1953 and 1957: Andrew and Gordievsky, *KGB*, p. 375.

124 In the 1980s: Philip Shenon, "U.S. Drops Its Case Against a Marine in Embassy Spying," *New York Times*, June 13, 1987.

124 from the North Koreans: NSA, *Cryptographic Damage Assessment: USS Pueblo*, AGER-2, Jan. 23–Dec. 23 (1968), sect. V, 1969, pp. 1–2.

124 "For more than seventeen": Laura J. Heath, "An Analysis of the Systemic Security Weaknesses of the U.S. Navy Fleet Broadcasting System, 1967–1974, as Exploited by CWO John Walker," master's thesis, Georgia Institute of Technology, 2005, pp. 72–73, FAS; Bamford, *Body of Secrets*, pp. 276–77, 307–11.

124 In addition to giving: Heath, "Analysis of the Systemic Security Weaknesses," p. 29; Pete Early, *Family of Spies: Inside the John Walker Spy Ring* (New York: Bantam, 1988), p. 109.

125 "In its push": Scott Wilson, "NSA's Quest for Diversity Called Risky," *Baltimore Sun*, July 6, 1997.

126 "on full alert": Bamford, *Puzzle Palace*, pp. 133–50. See also David K. Johnson, *The Lavender Scare: The Cold War Persecution of Gays and Lesbians in the Federal Government* (Chicago: University of Chicago Press, 2009), pp. 145–46.

127 smashed their Great Seal: NSA, "TEMPEST," p. 26.

127 "They always had": "Report Prepared in the Department of State: Estimate of Damage to U.S. Foreign Policy Interests (from Net of Listening Devices in U.S. Embassy Moscow)," Oct. 2, 1969, *FRUS*, 1964–68, vol. 14, *Soviet Union*, no. 47.

128 Instead, between the embassy bugs: It was also recently revealed that in the 1970s and early 1980s the Soviets read the keystrokes from several IBM Selectric typewriters in the Moscow embassy (Sharon A. Maneki, NSA Center for Cryptologic History, *Learning from the Enemy: The GUNMAN Project* [2018]).

4 THE MILITARY-INDUSTRIAL COMPLEX: THE DIRTY SECRET OF CIVIL-MILITARY RELATIONS

129 "do something": Peter Stein and Peter Feaver, *Assuring Control of Nuclear Weapons: The Evolution of Permissive Action Links* (Lanham, Md.: University Press of America, 1987), p. 32.

129 The military resisted: Ibid., pp. 36–39; McGeorge Bundy, Memorandum of a Conversation, Oct. 4, 1961, U.S. DDO, doc. no. CK2349499904.

130 But in the 1970s: Bruce G. Blair, "Keeping Presidents in the Nuclear Dark: The SIOP Option that Wasn't," *Defense Monitor*, vol. 33, no. 2 (2004): p. 2. On Minuteman procedures, see also Bernard C. Nalty, *U.S. Air Force Ballistic Missile Programs, 1964–1966*, USAF Historical Division, 1967, p. 11, U.S. DDO, doc. no. CK2349654796.

131 "I am shocked": Blair, "Keeping Presidents," p. 2.

131 Consider what happened: Phil Stanford, "Who Pushes the Button?," *Parade* magazine, March 28, 1976; Ron Rosenbaum, *How the End Begins: The Road to Nuclear World War III* (New York: Simon & Schuster, 2011), p. 61; *First Use of Nuclear Weapons: Preserving Responsible Control: Hearings before the Subcommittee on International Security and Scientific Affairs of the Committee on International Relations*, 94th Cong., 2nd Sess. (1976), pp. 227–28.

131 "defective mental attitude": *First Use of Nuclear Weapons*, p. 228.

132 "Then we'd tell": "JCS Meeting," Memorandum for the Record, Sept. 13, 1971, National Security Archive.

132   "could lose two": Ibid.

132   "was not the end": "Command and Control Briefing Presented
      to DEPSECDEF," Memorandum for the Record, Sept. 3, 1971,
      National Security Archive.

132   Moorer went so far: Seymour Hersh, "Radford Says He Had
      Instructions to Pilfer Papers," *New York Times*, Feb. 9, 1974; James
      Rosen, "Nixon and the Chiefs," *Atlantic*, April 2002.

132   He remained chairman: John W. Finney, "Rockwell Names Penta-
      gon Guests," *New York Times*, March 18, 1976; Bernard Weinraub,
      "2 Officers Protest Plan to Strengthen Civilians in Pentagon,"
      New York Times, Feb. 6, 1978; Adam Bernstein, "Adm. Thomas
      Moorer Dies," *Washington Post*, Feb. 7, 2004.

132   It was not until 1977: Bruce G. Blair and Gary D. Brewer, "The
      Terrorist Threat to World Nuclear Programs," *Journal of Conflict
      Resolution*, vol. 21, no. 3 (Sept. 1977): pp. 386–89. Blair's experi-
      ence as a Minuteman launch-control officer so scarred him that he
      decided to devote the rest of his life to disarmament (Sam Roberts,
      "Bruce Blair, Crusader for Nuclear Arms Control, Dies at 72,"
      New York Times, July 24, 2020).

133   "dirty little secret": Andrew J. Bacevich, "Discord Still: Clinton
      and the Military," *Washington Post*, Jan. 3, 1999.

134   But in the 1940s: Samuel P. Huntington, *The Soldier and the State:
      The Theory and Politics of Civil-Military Relations* (Cambridge,
      Mass.: Harvard University Press, 1957), pp. 354–61.

135   For example, in 1949 Truman: Mark Perry, *Four Stars* (Boston:
      Houghton Mifflin, 1989), pp. 11–19.

135   "open rebellion": Barry M. Blechman et al., *The American Military
      in the 21st Century* (New York: Palgrave Macmillan, 1994), p. 14.

135   "Revolt of the Admirals": Huntington, *Soldier and State*,
      pp. 353–54.

136   The outbreak of the Korean War: Arthur Herman, *Douglas
      MacArthur: American Warrior* (New York: Random House, 2016),
      pp. 705–10.

136   how close MacArthur came: James E. Alexander, "Who's in Charge
      Here?," *Naval History*, vol. 11, no. 48 (1997): p. 48.

137   The planes buzzing: A veteran of this engagement recently noted
      the falsity of the ship's log—and the existence of other corrob-
      orating accounts of the engagement—in a post to the National
      Archives Web site (Lawson Winslow, "Seeking to Correct the
      Deck Log of the USS John A Bole," HistoryHub, Oct. 5, 2020).
      But the secrecy of the mission makes it unclear whether anyone

in the White House even knew about it. The official army history describes Truman as hastily making the announcement out of concern that the news of MacArthur's relief would leak. (Billy C. Mossman, *United States Army in the Korean War: Ebb and Flow, November 1950–July 1951* [Washington, D.C.: Center of Military History, 1988], pp. 364–65.)

137 "new and heretofore": M. B. Ridgway, "A Code of Loyalty," *New York Times*, May 2, 1973.

137 a secret came to light: Carol M. Petillo, "Douglas MacArthur and Manuel Quezon: A Note on an Imperial Bond," *Pacific Historical Review*, vol. 48, no. 1 (1979): pp. 108–15.

137 nine years later: Herman, *Douglas MacArthur*, p. 831.

138 Another popular general: Andrew J. Bacevich, "The Paradox of Professionalism: Eisenhower, Ridgway, and the Challenge to Civilian Control, 1953–1955," *Journal of Military History*, vol. 61 (1997): p. 307–8.

138 he expanded the nuclear arsenal: As Eisenhower told his NSC, "In a future nuclear war the chief task of the U.S. ground forces would be to preserve order in the United States. God only knew what the Navy would be doing in a nuclear attack." (Memorandum of Discussion at the 277th Meeting of the National Security Council, Feb. 27, 1956, *FRUS*, 1955–57, *National Security Policy*, vol. 19, p. 208.)

138 Army generals: Bacevich, "Paradox of Professionalism," pp. 315–19, 331.

139 "What would happen": S. Everett Gleason, "Discussion at the 229th Meeting of the National Security Council, Tuesday, December 21st, 1954," Dec. 22, 1954, U.S. DDO, doc. no. CK2349094730.

139 "I'd have to explain": Harold Austin, "A B-47 Overflight of Russia—1954," *Daedalus Flyer*, Spring 1995; also quoted in Robert S. Hopkins, "An Expanded Understanding of Eisenhower, American Policy and Overflights," *Intelligence and National Security*, vol. 11 (April 1996): p. 335.

140 "the exact manner": David Alan Rosenberg and W. B. Moore, "'Smoking Radiating Ruin at the End of Two Hours': Documents on American Plans for Nuclear War with the Soviet Union, 1954–55," *International Security*, vol. 6, no. 3 (Winter 1981–82): p. 25.

140 LeMay had shown: Warren Kozak, *LeMay: The Life and Wars of General Curtis LeMay* (Washington, D.C.: Regnery, 2009), pp. 216–27.

140 Now he would not: The navy's dogged resistance to letting SAC

develop a coordinated war plan was also a factor; see "Memorandum of Conference with President Eisenhower," Aug. 11, 1960, *FRUS*, 1958–60, vol. 3, p. 444.

140　share of the defense budget rose: Kevin N. Lewis, "The U.S. Air Force Budget and Posture Over Time," R-3807-AF (Santa Monica: RAND, 1990), pp. 12–14.

140　To fight back: Richard Aliano, *American Defense Policy from Eisenhower to Kennedy* (Athens: Ohio University Press, 1978), pp. 135–36.

140　"bomber gap": Memorandum of Discussion of the 172nd Meeting of the NSC, Nov. 24, 1953, NSC Series, box 6, AWF, DDEL.

141　"You could read": Memorandum of Discussion of the 223rd Meeting of the NSC, Nov. 9, 1954, NSC Series, box 6, AWF, DDEL.

141　By the mid-1950s: Huntington, *Soldier and State*, p. 366. See also James Fallows, *National Defense* (New York: Random House, 1981), p. 65, for more conservative estimates, and also figures for 1969 and 1979.

141　Unlike Truman: Glenn Fowler, "R. T. Ross, Ex-Congressman," *New York Times*, Oct. 3, 1981; Michael S. Mayer, *The Eisenhower Years* (New York: Facts on File, 2010), p. 485.

141　A lot of corruption: William M. Freeman, "Bradley Takes Over Tomorrow as Head of Bulova Research in $10,000,000 Plant," *New York Times*, Aug. 16, 1953; Huntington, *Soldier and State*, pp. 361–66; William Turner, "The Right Wing's Biggest Spender: Patrick J. Frawley," *Washington Post*, Aug. 30, 1970.

141　Eisenhower sought the help: John L. Sprague, *Sprague Electric: An Electronics Giant's Rise, Fall, and Life after Death* (North Charleston, S.C.: CreateSpace, 2015), pp. 32, 76–77; Joint Committee on Defense Production, *Deterrence and Survival in the Nuclear Age (The "Gaither Report" of 1957)*, 94th Cong., 2nd Sess. (1976), pp. 35–37.

142　"I'm going to knock": Interview with Robert Sprague, "*War and Peace in the Nuclear Age: A Bigger Bang for the Buck*," WGBH, March 5, 1986.

142　If Sprague was untroubled: Memorandum of a Conversation, Jan. 3, 1958, U.S. DDO, doc. no. CK2349061388.

142　Eisenhower declined: Interview with Robert Sprague, March 5, 1986; David Lindsey Snead, "Eisenhower and the Gaither Report: The Influence of a Committee of Experts on National Security Policy in the Late 1950s," Ph.D. diss., University of Virginia, 1997, pp. 218–19.

142　"This experience": Memorandum of a Conversation, Dec. 26, 1957, vol. 19, *FRUS*, 1955–57, National Security Policy, no. 174.

142 Thomas Power: Melvin G. Deaile, "The SAC Mentality: The Origins of Organizational Culture in Strategic Air Command, 1946–1962," Ph.D. diss., University of North Carolina at Chapel Hill, 2007, p. 259.

143 "Look. At the end": Fred Kaplan, *The Wizards of Armageddon* (Stanford: Stanford University Press, 1991), p. 246.

143 "I used to worry": Scott Sagan, *The Limits of Safety: Organizations, Accidents, and Nuclear Weapons* (Princeton: Princeton University Press, 1993), p. 150.

143 "to keep it out": Bruce G. Blair, *The Logic of Accidental Nuclear War* (Washington, D.C.: Brookings Institution Press, 1993), pp. 48–49.

143 "TYPICAL *First Strike*": Paul Edwards, *The Closed World: Computers and the Politics of Discourse in Cold War America* (Cambridge, Mass.: MIT Press, 1996), p. 112.

143 "disturbing evidence": Evan Thomas, *Ike's Bluff: President Eisenhower's Secret Battle to Save the World* (New York: Little, Brown, 2012), p. 250, citing Ann Whitman diary, July 31, 1958, and DDE to Neil McElroy, July 31, 1958, both in AWF, DDEL. For more about the program, see Steve Blank, "Balloon Wars," part 16 of his "Secret History of Silicon Valley."

144 "would take the man": Editorial Notes and Memorandum for the Record, July 29, 1958, *FRUS*, 1958–60, vol. 10, pp. 178–81. See Gregory W. Pedlow and Donald E. Welzenbach, *The Central Intelligence Agency and Overhead Reconnaissance: The U-2 and OXCART Programs, 1954–1974* (Washington, D.C.: CIA, 1992), p. 103.

144 "carried the danger": Editorial Note, *FRUS*, 1958–60, vol. 10, p. 155.

144 After all, from the Soviets': CIA, *Situation Estimate for Project Chalice: Fiscal Years 1961 and 1962*, 1960, CIA-RDP33-02415A000100380014-3.

144 If the USSR: Memorandum for the Record, Feb. 12, 1959, *FRUS*, 1958–60, vol. 10, p. 155. On Eisenhower's ambivalence regarding overflights, see Hopkins, "An Expanded Understanding," pp. 332–34.

144 "cocked weapon": David Alan Rosenberg, "The Origins of Overkill: Nuclear Weapons and American Strategy, 1945–1960," *International Security*, vol. 7, no. 4 (1983): p. 19.

144 In 1957: Interview with Robert Sprague.

144 But the next year: The civilian leadership of the Pentagon asked how the Soviets would react if, all of a sudden, many squadrons of American nuclear bombers began to approach their territory at

nearly supersonic speed. The generals drafted what they thought was a good answer: "For ten years we have been conducting exercises of similar nature and the only time we have ever had a Soviet reaction was when our airplanes inadvertently penetrated the Soviet early warning net." But the air-force chief of staff, General Thomas White, worried—with good reason—that this admission might cause alarm. He wanted to conceal the fact that SAC bombers had overflown the USSR. It was only at the insistence of the army that this was disclosed. Ironically, a promise not to repeat the "inadvertent" penetration helped secure for the SAC commander a new and expanded power. (Sagan, *Limits of Safety*, pp. 165–69.)

145 "Minimum Interval Takeoffs": Deaile, "SAC Mentality," pp. 261– 62.

146 Hitting the runway: DOD, "Narrative Summaries of Accidents Involving U.S. Nuclear Weapons 1950–1980," 1980.

146 secrecy was not an option: "'Dead' A-Bomb Hits U.S. Town," Universal-International News, 1955, in AIRBOYD, *B-47 Drops Atomic Bomb on Mars Bluff* (1958), YouTube video.

146 But in other cases: "Sidi Slimane Air Incident Involving Plane Loaded with Nuclear Weapon," Jan. 31, 1958, DNSA, NH00859; Eric Schlosser, *Command and Control: Nuclear Weapons, the Damascus Incident, and the Illusion of Safety* (New York: Penguin, 2013), p. 184.

146 near Goldsboro, North Carolina: Schlosser, *Command and Control*, pp. 450–52; Parker F. Jones, "Goldsboro Revisited: Account of Hydrogen Bomb Near-Disaster over North Carolina— Declassified Document," *Guardian*, Sept. 20, 2013.

147 The true gravity: The following account of the Thule incident is based on Sagan, *Limits of Safety*, chap. 4.

148 "enormously complex": Paul Bracken, "Delegation of Nuclear Command Authority," in *Managing Nuclear Operations*, eds. Ashton B. Carter et al. (Washington, D.C.: Brookings Institution Press, 1987), pp. 352–53.

148 Such a thing: Sagan, *The Limits of Safety*, p. 189.

149 Why would a pilot: Ibid., p. 254.

149 In a similar incident in 1962: Richard Hall, comment on "B-47 Losses," May 7, 2016, *B-47 Stratojet Historical Website*.

149 it was General Power: Gen. Horace M. Wade, interview by Hugh M. Ahmann, *United States Air Force Oral History Program*, Oct. 10– 12, 1978, Air Force Historical Research Agency, pp. 306–7.

149 How great was the danger: Sagan, *Limits of Safety*, p. 176.

150 But Sagan also found: Ibid., pp. 192–98.

150 In his last battle: John Prados, *The Soviet Estimate: U.S. Intelligence Analysis & Russian Military Strength* (New York: Dial, 1982), pp. 41–50.

151 Power even went public: Aliano, *American Defense Policy*, p. 136.

151 "legalized insubordination": *Public Papers of the Presidents of the United States: Dwight D. Eisenhower, 1958* (Washington, D.C.: GPO, 1959), p. 122.

151 "the potential": Dwight D. Eisenhower, "Military-Industrial Complex Speech," 1960, Public Papers of the Presidents, DDEL, Avalon Project, Yale Law School.

152 After his election: Kozak, *LeMay*, p. 335; Schlosser, *Command and Control*, pp. 429–32.

152 "We thought we could": Kozak, *LeMay*, p. 335.

152 But early on: Marc Trachtenberg, *A Constructed Peace: The Making of the European Settlement, 1945–1963* (Princeton: Princeton University Press, 1999), p. 224.

152 "why are we hitting": Carl Kaysen, interview by Vicki Daitch, Nov. 21, 2002, Oral History Program, transcript p. 18, JFKL. Emphasis added.

152 Kennedy was amazed: Daniel Ellsberg, *The Doomsday Machine: Confessions of a Nuclear War Planner* (New York: Bloomsbury, 2017), pp. 52–57, 107–11.

153 "It was very unpleasant": Carl Kaysen, interview with Marc Trachtenberg and David Rosenberg, Aug. 3, 1988, courtesy of Marc Trachtenberg.

154 his doubts about the competence: H. R. McMaster, *Dereliction of Duty: Johnson, McNamara, the Joint Chiefs of Staff, and the Lies that Led to Vietnam* (New York: Harper, 1997), pp. 15–17.

154 The Joint Chiefs came back: Joint Chiefs of Staff to Secretary of Defense, memorandum, "Justification for US Military Intervention in Cuba," March 13, 1962, National Security Archive. In fairness, after the United States discovered Soviet missiles in Cuba, the president's own brother asked "whether there is some other way we can get involved in this, through Guantanamo Bay or something . . . whether there's some ship that . . . you know, sink the Maine again or something" ("Off the Record Meeting on Cuba," Oct. 16, 1962, *FRUS*, accessed via FOIArchive).

154 "This is almost": Recording of conversation between JFK and JCS, Oct. 19, 1962, President's Office Files, Presidential Recordings Collection, tape 31.2, JFKL, in Jerry Goldman and Giel Stein, "The Cuban Missile Crisis, 1962," Wyzant.

155 "maximum readiness posture": Scott Sagan, "Nuclear Alerts and Crisis Management," *International Security*, vol. 9, no. 4 (1985): p. 109.

155 Taylor approved the plan: Martin J. Sherwin, *Gambling with Armageddon: Nuclear Roulette from Hiroshima to the Cuban Missile Crisis* (New York: Vintage, 2020), pp. 369–71. Michael E. Weaver, professor at the Air Command and Staff College, argues that there was nothing unusual about Power's decision to transmit the order in the clear. But there was nothing normal about this situation ("The Relationship Between Diplomacy and Military Force: An Example from the Cuban Missile Crisis," *Diplomatic History*, vol. 38, no. 1 [2014]: p. 162).

155 McNamara worried: Robert Dallek, *An Unfinished Life: John F. Kennedy, 1917–1963* (Boston: Little, Brown, 2003), p. 562.

156 "We thought": "Recollections of Vadim Orlov (USSR Submarine B-59), 'We Will Sink Them All, but We Will Not Disgrace Our Navy,'" in Alexander Mozgovoi, *The Cuban Samba of the Quartet of Foxtrots: Soviet Submarines in the Caribbean Crisis of 1962* (Moscow: Military Parade, 2002). Trans. Svetlana Savranskaya for the National Security Archive.

157 "could get out of control": Nikita Khrushchev, *Khrushchev Remembers*, trans. Strobe Talbott (New York: Bantam, 1971), p. 552.

157 "Anderson was absolutely": John F. Kennedy and Robert S. McNamara, "Meeting on Defense Contracts," Nov. 8, 1963, digitized audio recording, tape 120/A56, JFKL.

157 "definitely pink": Morris K. Udall, "The Dismissal of Maj. Gen. Edwin A. Walker: A Special Report," 1961, Special Collections, University of Arizona Libraries; Eric Pace, "Gen. Edwin Walker, 83, Is Dead; Promoted Rightist Causes in 60's," *New York Times*, Nov. 2, 1993.

157 "demand" . . . "immediately establish": *Military Cold War Education and Speech Review Policies: Hearings Before the Special Preparedness Subcommittee of the Committee on Armed Services*, pt. 3, 87th Cong., 2nd Sess. (1962), p. 1384. The extent of radical right influence in the military is difficult to assess, but for a nuanced treatment see Lori L. Bogle, *The Pentagon's Battle for the American Mind: The Early Cold War* (College Station: Texas A&M University Press, 2004), p. 147.

157 Walker was offered: Bogle, *Pentagon's Battle*, pp. 146–53; D. J. Mulloy, *The World of the John Birch Society: Conspiracy, Conservatism, and the Cold War* (Nashville: Vanderbilt University Press, 2014), pp. 8–9.

158 Pentagon-run: DOD, *Politico-Military Game Olympiad I-62: Draft (Decade After)* (1962), U.S. DDO, doc. no. CK2349262484, pp. 214–20. Kennedy went to his summer home in Hyannisport to make it easier for the film's director, John Frankenheimer, to shoot a riot scene outside the White House (Patrick Kiger, "The Movie That JFK Wanted Made, but Didn't Live to See," *Boundary Stones: WETA's Local History Blog*, May 13, 2013).

158 "watch the generals": Annie Jacobsen, *The Pentagon's Brain: An Uncensored History of DARPA, America's Top Secret Military Research Agency* (New York: Little, Brown, 2015), p. 138, and see also Benjamin Bradlee, *Conversations with Kennedy* (New York: Norton, 1975), p. 22.

158 "reconquest": Arthur M. Schlesinger, Jr., *A Thousand Days: John F. Kennedy in the White House* (Boston: Mariner Books, 2002), p. 315.

159 Mutual contempt: Robert Buzzanco, *Masters of War: Military Dissent and Politics in the Vietnam Era* (Cambridge, U.K.: Cambridge University Press, 1997); McMaster, *Dereliction of Duty*, pp. 143–54, 303–12.

159 It culminated: Scott D. Sagan and Jeremi Suri, "The Madman Nuclear Alert: Secrecy, Signaling, and Safety in October 1969," *International Security*, vol. 27, no. 4 (2003): pp. 150–83; Ellsberg, *Doomsday Machine*, pp. 309–12.

159 advised nuking North Vietnam: DOD, *SIGMA II-65 (U), 26 July 1955–5 August 1955: Final Report* (1965), F-23-24, U.S. DDO, doc. no. CK2349260286.

159 In 1968, LeMay ran: LeMay claimed to see no difference between killing with a nuke and killing with a rusty knife ("LeMay Favors Nuclear Arms in Viet If Needed to Win," *Lewiston Daily Sun*, Oct. 4, 1968).

160 many still claim: Memorandum of Discussion at the 333rd Meeting of the National Security Council, Aug. 1, 1957, U.S. DDO, unredacted version, doc. no. CK2349535825; redacted version, doc. no. CK2349102765; Memorandum on the Substance of Discussion at the Department of State-Joint Chiefs of Staff Meeting, Nov. 21, 1958, *FRUS*, 1958–60, vol. 8, Berlin Crisis, pp. 772–76; USCINCEUR to JCS, Dec. 8, 1958, RG 218, box 140, CCS 092 (4-20-50), sect. 8, USNA; Bromley Smith, Memorandum of Conference with the President, Jan. 13, 1964, U.S. DDO; unredacted version, doc. no. CK2349037513; redacted version, doc. no. CK2349243649; Maxwell Taylor to General LeMay, General Wheeler, Admiral McDonald, General Shoup, "Chinese

Nuclear Development," Nov. 18, 1963, RG 218, Records of the Joint Chiefs of Staff, Chairman's Files (Maxwell D. Taylor), box 1, CM-1963, USNA. See also Curtis LeMay to Secretary of Defense, "Study of Chinese Communist Vulnerability," April 29, 1963, RG 59, Records of Bureau of Far Eastern Affairs, Office of the Country Director for the Republic of China, Top Secret Files Relating to the Republic of China, 1954–65, box 4, 1963, USNA.

160 When polled: Frank Newport, "Americans Continue to Express Highest Confidence in Military," Gallup, June 17, 2016.

161 when Americans are surveyed: Frank Newport, "Memorial Day Finds Americans Very Positive About Military," Gallup, May 25, 2018.

161 When, as in the case: Donald P. Casler, "Credible to Whom? The Organizational Politics of Credibility in International Relations," Ph.D. diss., Columbia University, 2022, pp. 78, 155.

162 They can retire: In 2008, IRS data indicated that there were 2,435 former Pentagon officials—"generals, admirals, senior executives, program managers, contracting officers"—working for some fifty-two different defense contractors (GAO, *Defense Contracting: Post-Government Employment of Former DOD Officials Needs Greater Transparency* [2008], Executive Summary, GAO-08-485).

162 Colin Powell, for instance: Richard H. Kohn, "Out of Control: The Crisis in Civil-Military Relations," *National Interest*, no. 35, Spring 1994, pp. 9–15. See also John Lehman in: Colin Powell et al., "An Exchange on Civil-Military Relations," *National Interest*, no. 36, Summer 1994, pp. 23–25.

162 In a White House meeting: Josh Gerstein, "Clinton, Powell Talked Gays in Military," *Politico*, Oct. 10, 2014.

162 As for Powell: Christopher Marquis, "Powell's Wealth Now Over $28 Million," *New York Times*, Jan. 18, 2001.

162 Nevertheless, a steady stream: Kohn, "Out of Control," p. 3.

163 Even Donald Rumsfeld: Donald Rumsfeld, "DOD Acquisition and Logistics Excellence Week Kickoff—Bureaucracy to Battlefield," speech presented at the Pentagon, Sept. 10, 2001.

163 Rumsfeld, like Aspin: Donald Rumsfeld, *Known and Unknown: A Memoir* (New York: Sentinel, 2011), pp. 296–97.

163 "We failed the audit": Dave Lindorff, "Exclusive: The Pentagon's Massive Accounting Fraud Exposed," *Nation*, Nov. 27, 2018.

163 The growing resistance: Peter Feaver, *Guarding the Guardians: Civilian Control of Nuclear Weapons in the United States* (Ithaca, N.Y.: Cornell University Press, 1992), pp. 59–60.

164 managed to lose the "biscuit": Hugh Shelton, *Without Hesitation: The Odyssey of an American Warrior* (New York: St. Martin's, 2010), pp. 392–94.

164 Such a scenario: David Hoffman, "Cold-War Doctrines Refuse to Die," *Washington Post*, March 15, 1998.

164 Powell, for instance: Robert Parry and Norman Solomon, "Behind Colin Powell's Legend—My Lai," *Consortium*, 1996.

164 In his second memoir: Colin Powell, *It Worked for Me: In Life and Leadership* (New York: Harper, 2012), p. 109; Adam Sneed, "Powell Says He Doesn't Have Any of His State Emails," *Politico*, March 3, 2015.

164 He apparently encouraged: David Smith, "Colin Powell Told Clinton He Bypassed Official Servers to Email Foreign Leaders," *Guardian*, Sept. 8, 2016.

165 In 2010, crews: Bruce G. Blair, "Why Our Nuclear Weapons Can Be Hacked," *New York Times*, March 14, 2017.

165 In the summer of 2013: Robert Burns, "U.S. Air Force Flunked Defense of Nuclear Missile Silo Against Simulated Attack," *Consortium of Defense Analysts*, May 23, 2014.

165 Journalists found: Mark Thompson, "Are You Smarter than a Nuclear Launch Officer?," *Time*, Feb. 13, 2014.

165 The next year: Helene Cooper, "Air Force Fires 9 Officers in Scandal over Cheating on Proficiency Tests," *New York Times*, March 27, 2014.

165 Another captain: Kristen Davis, "AF: Missileer Who Ran 'Violent Street Gang' Gets 25 Years," *Air Force Times*, Feb. 2, 2015.

165 In 2016: Robert Burns, "Five Added to Drug Probe at Air Force Nuclear Base," Military.com, June 16, 2016.

165 "suspect" women: Mark Thompson, "Is This Any Way for a Nuclear-Armed U.S. Air Force General to Behave?," *Time*, Dec. 19, 2013.

165 Preventing public scrutiny: DOD, *Reducing the Backlog in Legally Required Historical Declassification Obligations of the Department of Defense* (2021). The report was released in October 2021, after Congress made it a legal requirement. But since Congress had set March 2021 as the deadline, the Pentagon backdated the report to March.

166 The military would never: Frank Newport, "The Military's Positive Image and the Defense Budget," Gallup, April 1, 2019.

166 "How can I": Rosenbaum, *How the End Begins*, p. 31.

166 In 2017, the commander: "General Heading Strategic Command

Says Illegal Nuclear Launch Order Can Be Refused," NBC News, Nov. 18, 2017. Hyten was later promoted to become the vice-chairman of the Joint Chiefs of Staff.

166 Even if a president: Dave Merrill, Nafeesa Syeed, and Brittany Harris, "To Launch a Nuclear Strike, President Trump Would Take These Steps," *Bloomberg*, Jan. 20, 2017.

5 SURVEILLANCE: OTHER PEOPLE'S SECRETS

168 In 1991, a retired: Ali Caron, "Margaret 'Daisy' Suckley," FDR Library & Museum.

168 "It is certainly": Gary Ginsberg, *First Friends: The Powerful, Unsung (and Unelected) People Who Shaped Our Presidents* (New York: Twelve, 2021), p. 189.

169 Roosevelt's friend kept his secrets: Geoffrey C. Ward, ed., *Closest Companion: The Unknown Story of the Intimate Friendship Between Franklin Roosevelt and Margaret Suckley* (New York: Simon & Schuster, 1995), p. xix; Ginsberg, *First Friends*, pp. 183–84, 190.

169 "honorable espionage": Matthew L. Jones, "The Spy Who Pwned Me," *Limn*, Feb. 2017.

169 "You need the haystack": J. D. Tuccille, "Why Spy on Everybody? Because 'You Need the Haystack To Find the Needle,' Says NSA Chief," *Reason*, July 19, 2013.

171 twenty people in the NSA: Rebecca J. Richards, "Review of U.S. Person Privacy Protections in the Production and Dissemination of Serialized Intelligence Reports Derived from Signals Intelligence Acquired Pursuant to Title I and Section 702 of the Foreign Intelligence Surveillance Act," NSA Civil Liberties and Privacy Office, 2017, pp. 7–8.

171 Officials with a clearance: Under new rules, issued in the last days of the Obama administration, any one of seventeen different intelligence agencies can now access NSA databases of intercepted communications, Charlie Savage, "N.S.A. Gets More Latitude to Share Intercepted Communications," *New York Times*, Jan. 12, 2017.

171 "dramatic, entertaining": David Easter, "Code Words, Euphemisms and What They Can Tell Us About Cold War Anglo-American Communications Intelligence," *Intelligence and National Security*, vol. 27 (2012): p. 880.

171 During the Cold War: James Bamford, *The Puzzle Palace* (Boston: Houghton Mifflin, 1982), p. 283.

172 No matter how: There is no public information about the number of secret informants run by the FBI, the CIA, the Defense Intelligence Agency, or more than a dozen other intelligence agencies. But the number of DEA informants is almost double the number of people in the DEA's own workforce, and it does not include the number of spies the DEA has recruited abroad. Altogether, these informants were paid some $237 million between 2010 and 2015. (DOJ Office of the Inspector General, *Audit of Drug Enforcement Administration's Management and Oversight of Its Confidential Source Program*, Audit Report 16-33 [Washington, D.C., 2016].)

173 "The special nature": "National Security Council Intelligence Directive No. 9 Revised," Dec. 29, 1952, *FRUS, 1950–1955, The Intelligence Community*, no. 257; "National Security Council Intelligence Directive No. 9," March 10, 1950, *FRUS, 1945–1950, Emergence of the Intelligence Establishment*, no. 435. See also Bamford, *Puzzle Palace* (Boston: Houghton Mifflin,1982), pp. 45–47.

173 "sensitive compartmented": CIA Center for the Study of Intelligence, *Critique of the Codeword Compartment in the CIA* (Washington, D.C., 1977), pp. 16–17, CIA-RDP83B00823R000900180001-6.

174 The oath not only committed them: NSA, "Oath for National Security Agency Employees," A40436.

174 "perpetual silence": "Security of AFSA COMINT Communications—AFSA Manual Changes," Jan. 28, 1952, NSA.

174 "so help me God": "Indoctrination for Navy Visitors," May 20, 1955, RG457, Records of the National Security Agency, P/Entry 14, Security Policy, box 1, "Sec-5," USNA.

174 The entire government agency: Bruce Berkowitz, *The National Reconnaissance Office at 50 Years: A Brief History* (Chantilly, Va.: Center for the Study of National Reconnaissance, 2011), p. 38.

174 Two years later: Memorandum for the Director of Central Intelligence, "BYEMAN Security Compromises," NRO, Oct. 30, 1973.

174 Until then: "Security Requirements of the NRO," March 28, 1974, NRO.

174 "special offices": Berkowitz, *National Reconnaissance Office*, p. 38.

175 It is a memo: Papers of Daniel Patrick Moynihan, Library of Congress, Washington, D.C. (hereafter Moynihan Papers), pt. II, box 39, folder 9.

175 Until 1999: Chief, Special Intelligence Staff, "Classification of talent and keyhole Information," Jan. 16, 1964, CIA-RDP67 R00587A000100140024-5.

175   Some of the code: For an inventory, see "Snowden Revelations,"
      Lawfare, March 25, 2019.

175   "The texts were placed": David Easter, "Code Words," p. 880.

175   "few would have the temerity": CIA Center for the Study of Intel-
      ligence, *Critique of the Codeword Department*, p. 18.

176   disproportionate number of prosecutions: This includes Ellsberg
      himself (the Pentagon Papers referenced communications intelli-
      gence methods); Samuel Loring Morison, satellite reconnaissance;
      Shamai Leibowitz, transcripts from wiretapped embassy commu-
      nications; Thomas Drake, NSA electronic surveillance methods;
      Edward Snowden, NSA electronic surveillance; Joshua Schulte,
      CIA hacking tools; Reality Winner, NSA intelligence on Russian
      hacking. For the authoritative list as of 2012, see Charlie Savage,
      "Nine Leak-Related Cases," *New York Times*, June 20, 2012. Since
      then, there have been ten more: including Snowden, Schulte, and
      Winner as well as Donald John Sachtleben, David Petraeus, James
      Cartwright, James Wolfe, Henry Kyle Frese, Daniel Everette
      Hale, and Terry Albury.

176   Conversely, even in: George Ellard, "NSA Inspector General's
      Letter to Senator Charles Grassley," 2013, release no. PA-023-18.

176   Even the best-informed: See, e.g., Jason Healey, "The U.S. Gov-
      ernment and Zero-Day Vulnerabilities," *Journal of International
      Affairs*, Nov. 2016, pp. 1–20. For good recent analyses of cyber-
      weapons, see David E. Sanger, *The Perfect Weapon: War, Sabotage,
      and Fear in the Cyber Age* (New York: Crown, 2018); Nicole Perl-
      roth, *They Tell Me This Is How the World Ends: The Cyber-Weapons
      Arms Race* (New York: Bloomsbury, 2021).

177   "Top Secret Dinar": Thomas R. Johnson, *American Cryptology
      During the Cold War, 1945–1989*, bk. II, *Centralization Wins, 1960–
      1972* (Washington, D.C.: NSA, 1995), p. 473. See also Easter,
      "Code Words," p. 885.

177   By 1972: Jeffrey T. Richelson, "Out of the Black: The Disclo-
      sure and Declassification of the National Reconnaissance Office,"
      International Journal of Intelligence and CounterIntelligence, vol. 11,
      no. 1 (1998): pp. 4–5.

177   Moreover, it was thought: Ibid.; Memorandum for the Record,
      "USIB Meeting on Release of 'Fact Of,'" NRO, July 12, 1974. On
      SIGINT and satellites more generally, see David B. Bradburn et
      al., *The SIGINT Satellite Story*, NRO, 1994.

178   "cryptographic naivete": Communications Intelligence Board Spe-
      cial Committee to Study Communications Intelligence Personnel

Security Standards, and Practice, *A Study of COMINT Personnel Security Standards and Practices*, 1955, HN00942, DSNA.

178 The same principle: "Questionable NPIC Projects," May 8, 1973, doc ID 1451843, NSA. See also Jeffrey T. Richelson, "U.S. Reconnaissance Satellites: Domestic Targets," in *National Security Archive Electronic Briefing Book No. 229* (2007).

178 "could lead to": "Security Requirements of the NRO."

178 The abnormally secret: *The National Reconnaissance Office at 50*, pp. 24–27; Richelson, "Out of the Black," pp. 16–17.

178 NRO had almost never: The Ford administration's response to the Church Committee did, however, create new oversight mechanisms that required the NRO to report any illegal activity. See Memorandum for Mr. Robert D. Murphy, Chairman, Intelligence Oversight Board, NRO, July 13, 1976.

179 "efficient and streamlined": "Security Requirements of the NRO."

179 "The best engineering": Dennis Fitzgerald, "Commentary on the 'Decline of the National Reconnaissance Office'—The NRO Leadership Replies," *Studies in Intelligence*, vol. 46, no. 2 (2002): p. 48.

179 internal study from the early 1990s: Matthew M. Aid, "The Times of Troubles: The US National Security Agency in the Twenty-First Century," *Intelligence and National Security*, vol. 15, no. 3 (2000): p. 7.

180 "The intelligence analyst": CIA Center for the Study of Intelligence, *Critique of the Codeword Compartment*, p. 25.

180 "I just had": Robert E. Newton, "The Capture of the USS Pueblo and Its Effect on SIGINT Operations," in *United States Cryptologic History*, Center for Cryptologic History, 1992, p. 68; NSA, *Cryptologic Damage Assessment: USS Pueblo*, vol. 1, sect. IV, 1968.

180 "The list": Center for the Study of Intelligence, *Critique of the Codeword Compartment*, p. 25.

180 And since the NSA prefers: Stephen Budiansky, *Code Warriors: NSA's Codebreakers and the Secret Intelligence War Against the Soviet Union* (New York: Knopf, 2016), p. 285.

181 "There was no filter": Jane Mayer, *The Dark Side: The Inside Story of How the War on Terror Turned Into a War on American Ideals* (New York: Doubleday, 2008), pp. 4–5. See also Jack Goldsmith, *The Terror Presidency: Law and Judgment Inside the Bush Administration* (New York: Norton, 2009), pp. 71–73.

182 J. Edgar Hoover: Tim Weiner, *Enemies: A History of the FBI* (New York: Random House, 2012), pp. 35, 44–45.

182 In 1939: William R. Rogers, "The Case for Wire Tapping,"

Yale Law Journal, vol. 63 (1954), pp. 792–93; Weiner, *Enemies*, pp. 76–77.

182 "We knew it was illegal": Steve Usdin, "We've Just Learned the Origins of Illegal Surveillance in the United States Go Back to the 1930s," *History News Network*, Oct. 18, 2015.

182 "the utmost degree": Weiner, *Enemies*, pp. 23, 80.

182 "engaged in espionage": Rogers, "The Case for Wire Tapping," pp. 794–97.

182 "it is almost bound": Weiner, *Enemies*, pp. 86–88.

183 Illegal surveillance unleashed: Frank J. Donner, *The Age of Surveillance: The Aims and Methods of America's Political Intelligence System* (New York: Knopf, 1980), pp. 23–24. This dynamic has been so frequently observed that it resembles a natural law, at least as far as U.S. surveillance is concerned. See, for instance, Richard A. Clarke et al., *The NSA Report: Liberty and Security in a Changing World* (Princeton: Princeton University Press, 2014), p. 15, which approvingly quotes the finding of the Church Committee "that there is a *natural* [emphasis added] 'tendency of intelligence activities to expand beyond their initial scope' and to 'generate ever-increasing demands for new data.'"

183 "Crime is contagious": *Olmstead v. United States*, 277 U.S. 438, 485 (June 4, 1928).

183 Black "messiah": FBI, "COINTEL Black Extremist," pt. 1 of 23.

183 Worried about the support: Beverly Gage, "What an Uncensored Letter to M.L.K. Reveals," *New York Times*, Nov. 11, 2014.

183 The president stayed up: Weiner, *Enemies*, p. 249.

183 Johnson also insisted: Budiansky, *Code Warriors*, p. 249.

183 As attorney general: David J. Garrow, "The FBI and Martin Luther King," *Atlantic*, July/Aug. 2002.

185 "Bobby Kennedy": Henry Kissinger, telephone conversation with Richard Nixon, June 1, 1973, National Security Archive.

185 Outside the Beltway: Hochman, *The Listeners*, pp. 181–94.

185 In 1968, the momentum: Ibid., pp. 195–96.

185 Conservative jurists: Alexander Charns, *Cloak and Gavel: FBI Wiretaps, Bugs, Informers, and the Supreme Court* (Urbana: University of Illinois Press, 1992), 87; "Georgia's Supreme Court Upholds Anti-trespass Act," *New York Times*, Jan. 1, 1964.

185 Of course, the FBI: Hochman, *The Listeners*, pp. 199–200.

187 Between 1965 and 1975: David E. Kaplan, "A Snooper's Guide," *Bill of Rights Journal*, vol. 17 (Dec. 1984): pp. 9–10.

187 The best summary: "About the Department of Defense Senior Intelligence Oversight Official," DOD.

188 "This is an area": "Evolution of Operation Chaos—Domestic Unrest in 1968," excerpt of CIA Paper 055/69, attached to Peter Rodman to Larry Eagleburger, "Restless Youth," June 10, 1975.

188 the Agency covered up: Henry Kissinger, "Colby Report," Dec. 25, 1974, U.S. DDO, doc. no. CK2349537645. Kissinger repeated CIA Director Colby's claim that there was no CIA surveillance of serving members of Congress when he informed President Ford. But when, for instance, the name of Congresswoman Bella Abzug appeared in the mailing list of an organization under Agency surveillance, the CIA shared that information with the FBI (Emma Best, "The Interagency CACTUS Program Served as the Conduit Between CIA's Operation CHAOS and FBI's COINTELPRO," *Muckrock*, Dec. 11, 2017).

188 targeted U.S. senators: Thomas R. Johnson, "Retrenchment and Reform, 1972–1980," in *American Cryptology During the Cold War, 1945–1989*, bk. III (Washington, D.C.: NSA, 1995), p. 85. See also Matthew M. Aid and William Burr, "Secret Cold War Documents Reveal NSA Spied on Senators," *Foreign Policy*, Sept. 25, 2013.

189 The NSA took care: Aid and Burr, "Secret Cold War Documents."

189 "disreputable if not": Matthew M. Aid and William Burr, "'Disreputable If Not Outright Illegal': The National Security Agency Versus Martin Luther King, Muhammad Ali, Art Buchwald, Frank Church, et al.," National Security Archive, Sept. 25, 2013.

189 In fact, Justice Department: DOJ, *Report on Inquiry into CIA Related Electronic Surveillance Activities*, 1976, pp. 171–72. Also in James Bamford, "The NSA and Me," *The Intercept*, Oct. 2, 2014.

190 "Once evidence is": The White House legal opinion has never been made public. Even the chair of the Senate Intelligence Committee, Diane Feinstein, was unable to obtain a copy. But it is quoted in a 2007 Justice Department memorandum authorizing the NSA overseas collection program (Kenneth L. Weinstein to the Attorney General, "Proposed Amendment to Department of Defense Procedures to Permit the National Security Agency to Conduct Analysis of Communications Metadata Associated with Persons in the United States," Nov. 20, 2007, https://www.aclu.org).

190 if the NSA "incidentally": Exec. Order No. 12333, 46 Fed. Reg. 59941, Dec. 4, 1981; Cyrus Farivasr, "Meet John Tye: The Kinder, Gentler, and By-the-Book Whistleblower," *Arstechnica*, Aug. 20, 2014.

190 the Star Chamber allowed: Daniel L. Vande Zande, "Coercive Power and the Demise of the Star Chamber," *American Journal of Legal History*, vol. 50 (2008): pp. 326–27, which takes issue

with Bamford's analogy (James Bamford, "Washington Bends the Rules," *New York Times*, Aug. 22, 2002).

191 "modified an order": William French Smith to the Director of the Administrative Office of the United States Courts, April 22, 1981, FAS (emphasis added). For overall statistics on FISA applications and approvals, see "Foreign Intelligence Surveillance Act Court Orders 1979–2017," Electronic Privacy Information Center.

191 "It is self evident": FISC, Memorandum Opinion, May 17, 2002, FAS.

191 It would be even more: Louis A. Chiarella and Michael A. Newton, "'So Judge, How Do I Get That FISA Warrant?': The Policy and Procedure for Conducting Electronic Surveillance," *Army Lawyer*, no. 10 (Oct. 1997), pp. 25–36, FAS.

191 FBI headquarters in 2000: M. E. Bowman to William Delahunt, Aug. 7, 2002, FAS; William Delahunt to Robert Mueller III, June 14, 2002, FAS.

192 One of the main purposes: FISC, Memorandum Opinion, May 17, 2002.

193 The FBI responded: Patrick G. Eddington, "Does the FBI Spy on FOIA Requesters?," *Cato Institute*, March 18, 2021.

193 The FBI already had: "PATRIOT Act," Electronic Privacy Information Center.

194 body of case law: Patrick Thibodeau, "Carnivore Controversy Aired Before Congress," *Computerworld*, Sept. 7, 2000.

194 "sophisticated attack": DOD Defense Science Board, *Protecting the Homeland: Report of the Defense Science Board Task Force on Defensive Information Operations, Summer 2000 Study*, vol. II (Washington, D.C., 2001). For an excellent introduction, see Matthew Jones, "Great Exploitations: Data Mining, Legal Modernization, and the NSA," lecture, University of California, Berkeley, Feb. 15, 2015.

194 one year later: "PATRIOT Act."

195 more than doubling: "Foreign Intelligence Surveillance Act Court Orders 1979–2017."

195 example of legal sophistry: Andrew E. Nieland, "National Security Letters and the Amended Patriot Act," *Cornell Law Review*, vol. 92, no. 6 (2007): pp. 1211–14.

195 In such a scenario: Dan Eggen, "FBI Found to Misuse Security Letters," *Washington Post*, March 14, 2008.

196 "because an unknown amount": DOJ Office of the Inspector General, *A Review of the Federal Bureau of Investigation's Use of National Security Letters* (Washington, D.C., 2007), p. xvii.

196   audits of these requests: DOJ Office of the Inspector General, *A Review of the FBI's Use of National Security Letters: Assessment of Corrective Actions and Examination of NSL Usage in 2006* (Washington, D.C., 2008), pp. 4, 78–89, FAS.

196   This rancor focused: James Risen and Eric Lichtblau, "Bush Lets U.S. Spy on Callers Without Courts," *New York Times*, Dec. 16, 2005. See also Elizabeth Bazan, *The Foreign Intelligence Surveillance Act: An Overview of Selected Issues*, CRS, RL34279 (2008), FAS.

197   The NSA had obtained: "FISC Order Approving the Government's Request for Authorization to Collect Bulk Telephony Metadata Under Section 501 of FISA, BR 06-05," May 24, 2006, FAS.

197   It was also collecting: Glenn Greenwald and Spencer Ackerman, "NSA Collected US Email Records in Bulk for More Than Two Years Under Obama," *Guardian*, June 27, 2013.

198   "daily violations": "FISC Order Approving the Government's Request to Continue Collecting Bulk Telephony Metadata Subject in Accordance with Order on December 8, 2008, BR 08-13," Electronic Frontier Foundation, March 2, 2009.

198   "deeply troubled": "FISC Order Regarding Further Compliance Incidents, BR 09-13," Office of the Director of National Intelligence, Sept. 25, 2009.

198   "The Government can": *United States v. Jones*, 565 U.S. 400, 3–4 (Jan. 23, 2012).

199   "in this age": *Halkin v. Helms*, 598 F.2d 1, D.C. Cir. (1978). I am grateful to my colleague Matthew L. Jones for pointing out this basic contradiction in how the government presents different mosaic dangers.

199   more than two hundred and thirty thousand: ODNI, *Annual Statistical Transparency Report: Regarding the Use of National Security Authorities, Calendar Year 2021* (2022).

199   according to its own rules: Jonathan Mayer and Patrick Mutchler, "MetaPhone: The NSA Three-Hop," *Web Policy*, Dec. 9, 2013. The NSA proved unable even to honor the limits the FISA Court had placed on this program, even after the agency was repeatedly caught, and repeatedly warned. In thousands of instances, it conducted "overly broad" searches, improperly surveilled people it was not supposed to spy on, and retained data it was not entitled to possess (John Solomon, "Newly Declassified Memos Detail Extent of Improper Obama-Era NSA Spying," *The Hill*, July 25, 2017).

199   gaining traction: Gabriel R. Schlabach, "Privacy in the Cloud: The

Mosaic Theory and the Stored Communications Act," *Stanford Law Review*, vol. 67 (March 2015): pp. 680–86.

200 The CIA could not: ODNI, *Statistical Transparency Report: Regarding Use of National Security Authorities, Calendar Year 2017* (2018).

200 A record of the numbers: Huiqi Zhang and Ram Dantu, "Discovery of Social Groups Using Call Detail Records," in *On the Move to Meaningful Internet Systems: OTM 2008 Workshops*, Lecture Notes in Computer Science, vol. 5333 (2008), p. 489.

200 There are many, many ways: Vincent Blondel, Adeline Decuyper, and Gautier Krings, "A Survey of Results on Mobile Phone Datasets Analysis," *EPJ Data Science*, vol. 4, no. 10 (2015): pp. 39–41.

200 The appeal of CDRs: Greene, "The Intel Community's Annual Report Raises . . . ," *Just Security*, 2018; ODNI, *Statistical Transparency Report . . . 2017*, pp. 34–35.

200 Congress did allow: Privacy and Civil Liberties Oversight Board, *Report on the Government's Use of the Call Detail Records Program Under the USA Freedom Act* (2020).

200 But the intelligence community: Andrew Crocker and Cindy Cohn, "Don't Worry, the Government Still Has Plenty of Surveillance Power If Section 215 Sunsets," Electronic Frontier Foundation, May 31, 2015.

200 Perhaps most striking: Arthur H. Michel, *Eyes in the Sky: The Secret Rise of Gorgon Stare and How It Will Watch Us All* (Boston: Houghton Mifflin Harcourt, 2019), pp. 44–50.

201 "Data Integration and Visualization System": Asha Rangappa, "Don't Fall for the Hype: How the FBI's Use of Section 702 Surveillance Data Really Works," *Just Security*, Nov. 29, 2017.

201 "Records may contain": "Notice of a New System of Records," CPCLO Order No. 012-2012, 77 Fed. Reg. 40631 (July 10, 2012).

201 "geospatial tools": Robert S. Mueller, III, "Statement Before the Senate Committee on Homeland Security and Government Affairs," FBI, Sept. 13, 2011; FBI, "New Database Search Tool Will Aid Bureau Investigations."

201 It was subsequently discovered: Rangappa, "Don't Fall for the Hype."

202 "technical irregularities": David Ruiz, "The NSA Continues to Blame Technology for Breaking the Law," Electronic Frontier Foundation, Sept. 5, 2018.

202 agents could have accessed NSA data: "Notice of a New System of Records."

203 "The rapid change": Jimmy Carter, "The President's News Conference," Jan. 17, 1979, in American Presidency Project.

203 when we analyzed: Matthew Connelly, Raymond Hicks, Robert Jervis, and Arthur Spirling, "New Evidence and New Methods for Analyzing the Iranian Revolution as an Intelligence Failure," *Intelligence and National Security*, vol. 36, no. 6 (2021): pp. 781–806.

204 To that end: Yuanjun Gao, Jack Goetz, Matthew Connelly, and Rahul Mazumder, "Mining Events with Declassified Diplomatic Documents," *Annals of Applied Statistics*, vol. 14, no. 4 (December 2020): pp. 1699–1723.

204 This radically inductive method: For an account of this experiment see history-lab.org/declassificationengine/man-versus-machine.

204 "Asmara" and "Amberley": "Prime Minister Whitlam's Interpretation of ALP Party Platform of 1971," March 9, 1973, CFPF.

206 "any Arab": Joe Stork and Rene Theberge, "'Any Arab or Others of a Suspicious Nature . . . ,'" *MERIP Reports*, no. 14, 1973, pp. 3–6, 13.

206 six months after 9/11: Andrew H. Card to Heads of Executive Departments and Agencies, "Action to Safeguard Information Regarding Weapons of Mass Destruction and Other Sensitive Documents Related to Homeland Security," March 19, 2002, FAS.

206 One striking fact: GAO, *Intelligence Agencies: Personnel Practices at NSA, CIA, NSA, and DIA Compared with Those of Other Agencies*, GAO/NSIAD-96-6 (1996), pp. 23–28, FAS; Scott Wilson, "NSA's Quest for Diversity Called Risky," *Baltimore Sun*, July 6, 1997.

208 In 2019: DOJ Office of the Inspector General, *Review of Four FISA Applications and Other Aspects of the FBI's Crossfire Hurricane Investigation*, 20-012 (2019).

208 ". . . that capability": James Bamford, "They Know Much More Than You Think," *New York Review* (Aug. 2013).

6 WEIRD SCIENCE: SECRETS THAT ARE STRANGER THAN FICTION

210 "continued protection": Exec. Order 11652, 37 Fed. Reg. 5209, March 8, 1972.

210 After the end: Steven Aftergood, "CIA Declassifies Documents from World War I," April 20, 2011, FAS.

210 "When historical information": "CIA Declassifies Oldest Documents in U.S. Government Collection," CIA.

210 recipes for making invisible ink: "Secret Writing," undated, CIA.

211 For Steven Aftergood: Toby Harnden, "Invisible Ink Used Dur-

ing First World War Among Declassified CIA Files," *Telegraph*, April 20, 2011.

211   the Jasons: Annie Jacobsen, *The Pentagon's Brain: An Uncensored History of DARPA, America's Top Secret Military Research Agency* (New York: Little, Brown, 2015), p. 87.

211   The cryptonym: David Kahn, *The Code-Breakers: The Story of Secret Writing* (New York: Macmillan, 1967), p. 79.

211   "If ever legends": Robert M. Gates, *From the Shadows: The Ultimate Insider's Story of Five Presidents and How They Won the Cold War* (New York: Simon & Schuster, 2007), p. 562. Gates originally made a slightly different version of this claim in 1999, "Dinner Remarks of Former DCI Robert Gates," Nov. 19, 1999, CIA.

211   "the pursuit of the magic weapon": James Fallows, *National Defense* (New York: Random House, 1985), p. 35. Fallows titles this chapter "The Magicians."

212   "Any sufficiently advanced": Arthur C. Clarke, "Hazards of Prophecy: The Failure of Imagination," in Clarke, *Profiles of the Future: An Inquiry into the Limits of the Possible* (New York: Harper & Row, 1973), pp. 30–39.

212   the Royal Navy: Katherine Epstein, *Torpedo: Inventing the Military-Industrial Complex in the United States and Great Britain* (Cambridge, Mass.: Harvard University Press, 2014), pp. 15–16, 39–40.

213   Leo Szilard: Richard Rhodes, *The Making of the Atomic Bomb* (New York: Simon & Schuster, 1986), pp. 224, 504–8.

213   The committee: Alex Wellerstein, "Knowledge and the Bomb: Nuclear Secrecy in the United States, 1939–2008," Ph.D. diss., Harvard University, 2010, chap. 6. On secrecy among scientists, see David B. Resnik, "Openness Versus Secrecy in Scientific Research," *Episteme*, vol. 2, no. 3 (2006): pp. 135–47.

213   After the Manhattan Project: Jacobsen, *Pentagon's Brain*, pp. 245–46.

213   Covert work continues: Pete J. Westwick, "Secret Science: A Classified Community in the National Laboratories," *Minerva*, vol. 38 (2000): pp. 363–91.

213   civilian spinoffs: John Collett, "The History of Electronics: From Vacuum Tubes to Transistors," in *Science in the Twentieth Century*, eds. John Krige and Dominique Pestre (New York: Routledge, 2013), pp. 269–72.

214   the most important innovation: For a nuanced discussion of the complex and distributed origins of the Internet, see Roy Rosen-

zweig, "Wizards, Bureaucrats, Warriors, and Hackers: Writing the History of the Internet," *American Historical Review*, vol. 103 (Dec. 1998): pp. 1530–52. On the culture of openness, see also Michael Hauben, "Behind the Net: The Untold History of the ARPANET and Computer Science," in Michael Hauben and Rhonda Hauben, *Netizens: On the History and Impact of Usenet and the Internet* (Los Alamitos, Calif.: IEEE Computer Society Press, 1997), chap. 7.

215 "Secrecy," he concluded: Robert W. Seidel, "Secret Scientific Communities: Classification and Scientific Communication in the DOE and DoD," in *Proceedings of the 1998 Conference on the History and Heritage of Science Information Systems*, eds. Mary Ellen Bowden, Trudi Bellardo Hahn, and Robert V. Williams (Medford, N.J.: Information Today, 1999), pp. 56–58.

215 Leo Szilard estimated: George E. Conklin, "Acquisition Systems Protection Planning," master's thesis, Army Command and General Staff College, Fort Leavenworth, Kans., 1994, p. 110, Moynihan Papers, pt. II, box 280, folder 4.

215 U.S. government devotes: This is clearly the case from 1980 to 2017. But starting in fiscal year 2017, the government began to claim that R&D did not include a lot of D—i.e., the costs of testing, evaluation, and late-stage development. Since these are mainly Pentagon programs, it artificially minimized the relative cost of military R&D, and made it harder to calculate. ("Historical Trends in Federal R&D," American Association for the Advancement of Science.)

215 This is proportionately: CRS, *Government Expenditures on Defense Research and Development by the United States and Other OECD Countries: Fact Sheet*, R45441 (2020), pp. 1–4. All this is based on the new, narrower definition of R&D. Under the previous definition, the United States accounted for 88 percent of military R&D among OECD countries.

215 "an improvement": Jack DeMent, "Method of Dispersing Materials in Water," U.S. Patent 2,637,536, filed Oct. 30, 1947, and issued May 5, 1953.

215 "capable of reducing": White House, Staff Notes no. 370, May 19, 1958, U.S. DDO; unredacted, doc. no. CK2349318759; redacted, doc. no. CK2349165310.

216 army radar: Joint Committee on the Investigation of the Pearl Harbor Attack, *Investigation of the Pearl Harbor Attack: Report of the Joint Committee on the Investigation of the Pearl Harbor Attack*, rep. no. 79-244, 1946, pp. 66, 242–43.

217 Aldrich Ames: John Deutch, "Statement of the Director of Central

Intelligence on the Clandestine Services and the Damage Caused by Aldrich Ames," Dec. 7, 1995, Moynihan Papers, pt. II, box 286.

217   The CIA admitted: The extent of the damage was difficult to esti-
       mate, since Pentagon officials "were often reluctant to state that
       this reporting had any significant impact" (Deutch, "Statement of
       the Director"; see also "Statement of Frederick P. Hitz, Inspector
       General, CIA," Nov. 9, 1995, Moynihan Papers, pt. II, box 286).

217   "transparent campaign": U.S. Navy, "War Gaming of Single Inte-
       grated Operational Plan," June 2, 1961, NH00321, DNSA.

217   "The money contest": U.S. Navy, "Atomic Strike Forces," April 12,
       1961, NH00314, p. 3, DNSA.

217   "maidens of extreme": Ed Mack Miller, "The Gutting of the
       Valkyrie," *Air Force Magazine*, Jan. 1, 1960.

218   grand total of two planes: Marcelle Size Knack, "Post World
       War II Bombers, 1945–1973," in *Encyclopedia of U.S. Air Force Air-
       craft and Missile Systems*, vol. 2 (Washington, D.C.: USAF, 1988),
       pp. 571–73.

219   the B-1: Stephen Walker, "B-1B Bombers Can No Longer Fly at
       Low-Level and Their Annual Flight Hours Have Been Restricted,"
       Drive, Feb. 14, 2020.

219   The B-2 stealth bomber: Scott Amey, "B-21 Comes with a Stealth
       Final Price Tag," April 7, 2016, Project on Government Oversight.

219   large-scale RAND study: Joseph G. Bolten et al., *Sources of Weapon
       System Cost Growth: Analysis of 35 Major Defense Acquisition Pro-
       grams* (Santa Monica: RAND, 2008), p. 41.

220   While the Pentagon: Scot Paltrow and Kelly Carr, "Special Report:
       How the Pentagon's Payroll Quagmire Traps America's Soldiers,"
       Reuters, July 9, 2013.

220   Out of total military spending: NATO Public Diplomacy Division,
       "Defence Expenditure of NATO Countries (2010–2017)," com-
       muniqué no. Pr/CP(2018)016, March 15, 2018, p. 3.

221   doubles the appropriations required: Arvin Quist, *Security Classifi-
       cation of Information*, vol. 1 (Oak Ridge, Tenn.: Oak Ridge National
       Laboratories, 1989), p. 152, FAS.

221   extreme cost of magic weapons: RAND researchers found that,
       along with errors in the original budget estimates, changing
       requirements for new weapons, such as improved performance or
       new capabilities, was a major contributor to the increasing cost
       of weapons during development (Bolten et al., *Sources of Weapon
       System Cost Growth*, pp. 31–32).

221   "General, I have fought": Matthew Connelly et al., "'General, I
       Have Fought Just as Many Nuclear Wars as You Have': Forecasts,

Future Scenarios, and the Politics of Armageddon," *The American Historical Review*, vol. 117, no. 5, 2012, pp. 1431–60.

221 Even in a blood-and-guts: Jacobsen, *Pentagon's Brain*, pp. 203–9.

222 Isidor Rabi revealed: Memorandum for the Record, Oct. 29, 1957, U.S. DDO; redacted, doc. no. CK2349443239; unredacted, doc. no. CK2349423695.

222 Andrew Marshall masterminded: Raymond L. Garthoff, "Polyakov's Run," *Bulletin of Atomic Scientists*, vol. 56, no. 7 (Sept./Oct. 2000): pp. 37–40; David Wise, *Cassidy's Run: The Secret Spy War over Nerve Gas* (New York: Random House, 2001), pp. 42–47; Steven Block, "The Growing Threat of Biological Weapons," *American Scientist*, vol. 89, no. 1 (Jan./Feb. 2001): p. 5.

222 When Reagan announced: Thomas Mahnken, *Technology and the American Way of War* (New York: Columbia University Press, 2008), pp. 124–25, 151.

223 The army finally decided: GAO, *Ballistic Missile Defense: Records Indicate Deception Program Did Not Affect 1984 Test Results*, GAO/NSIAD-94-219 (Washington, D.C., 1994), p. 25.

223 In press conferences: The GAO report is oddly titled. It shows how the program to deceive the Soviets had been discontinued before the test, making the concealment of the rigging to Congress even more difficult to defend. (GAO, *Ballistic Missile Defense*, pp. 26–30.)

223 "You're always trying": Tim Weiner, "Lies and Rigged 'Star Wars' Test Fooled the Kremlin, and Congress," *New York Times*, Aug. 18, 1993.

223 "air power is": *United States v. Reynolds*, 345 U.S. 1 (March 9, 1953).

224 more than 840 times: Todd Garvey and Edward C. Liu, "The State Secrets Privilege: Preventing the Disclosure of Sensitive National Security Information During Civil Litigation," CRS, R41741 (2011), p. 2.

224 the 1948 accident report: "Petition for a Writ of Error *Coram Nobis* to Remedy Fraud upon This Court," *United States v. Reynolds*, 345 U.S. 1 (March 9, 1953).

224 the widows had been forced: A federal judge declined to reopen the case in 2004 (*Herring v. United States*, 2004 WL 2040272 [September 10, 2004]). He ruled that the plaintiffs had not met the strenuous test for deliberate fraud. He credited the standard catch-all claim that the air force might have had a legitimate concern that the accident report would contribute to a "mosaic" revealing genuinely sensitive information. More interestingly, he

pointed out that the Soviets had reverse-engineered the B-29, and had the same problem with engines catching fire. But it should therefore have been no secret to Moscow that they needed to fix the problem: it was already a matter of public record in 1949. The real secret, itself a threat to national security, was that the air force had still failed to make their own planes airworthy. (B. K. Thorne, "'Bugs' in B-29's Date to War Tests," *New York Times*, Nov. 19, 1949.)

224   In the 1980s: Deutch, "Statement of the Director," and "Statement of Frederick P. Hitz." This kind of disinformation was also fed to the public. Pentagon publications like *Soviet Military Power* warned about how the USSR would soon deploy high-energy lasers on the battlefield and launch their own space shuttles (Kyle Mizokami, "What Ever Happened to the Russia's [*sic*] Cold War Super Weapons?," *National Interest*, Nov. 3, 2019).

224   truly villainous behavior: Committee on Energy and Commerce, *American Nuclear Guinea Pigs: Three Decades of Radiation Experiments on U.S. Citizens*, H.R. Rep. 65-0190 (1986), pp. 2, 9–11, 14–15.

225   "sinister doctrines": Dana Adams Schmidt, "Germans on Trial in 'Science' Crimes," *New York Times*, Dec. 10, 1946.

225   In April 1947: Jeffrey E. Stephenson and Arthur O. Anderson, "Ethical and Legal Dilemmas in Biodefense Research," in *Textbook of Military Medicine: Medical Aspects of Biological Warfare* (Houston: Borden Institute, 2007), pp. 565–67. On Nuremberg, see "Nuremberg Code," United States Holocaust Memorial Museum.

225   "might have adverse": O. G. Haywood to Dr. Fidler, "Medical Experiments on Humans," April 17, 1947, DOE.

226   But when defending: See chap. 8 in this book.

226   "a little of the Buchenwald touch": Keith Schneider, "1950 Note Warns About Radiation Test," *New York Times*, Dec. 28, 1993.

226   The AEC and the Pentagon: Michael R. Lehman, "Nuisance to Nemesis: Nuclear Fallout and Intelligence as Secrets, Problems, and Limitations on the Arms Race, 1940–1964," Ph.D. diss., University of Illinois at Urbana-Champaign, 2016, p. 10.

226   Officials also worried: Janet Farrell Brodie, "Radiation Secrecy and Censorship After Hiroshima and Nagasaki," *Journal of Social History*, vol. 48 (Summer 2015): pp. 842–64.

226   In 1953–54: Schneider, "1950 Note Warns About Radiation Test."

226   "to avoid any": Stuart Auerbach and Thomas O'Toole, "Pentagon Has Contract to Test Radiation Effect on Humans: Cancer

Patients Used in Radiation Testing," *Washington Post and Times Herald*, Oct. 8, 1971.

226 "nuclear calibration devices": Committee on Energy and Commerce, *American Nuclear Guinea Pigs*, pp. 1, 11–12, 15–16.

227 Having first irradiated: Alfred H. Hausrath et al., Operations Research Office, *Troop Performance on a Training Maneuver Involving the Use of Atomic Weapons*, ORO-T-170 (1952), pp. 8–10.

227 The army petitioned: See, e.g., Defense Nuclear Agency, *Exercise Desert Rock IV, April 11–June 1952*, ADA078565, 1952, p. 14; Joseph Trevithick, "During the 1950s, the Pentagon Played War Games with Troops and Nukes," *Medium*, April 20, 2015.

227 "might hurt other people": *United States v. Reynolds*; Barton C. Hacker, *Elements of Controversy: The Atomic Energy Commission and Radiation Safety in Nuclear Weapons Testing, 1947–1974* (Berkeley: University of California Press, 1994), p. 187.

227 two to three thousand: DOE Advisory Committee on Human Radiation Experiments, *Final Report of the Advisory Committee on Human Radiation Experiments* (Washington, D.C.: GPO, 1995).

227 They included paratroopers: Operations Research Office, *Troop Performance on a Training Maneuver*, pp. 20–21, 48.

227 "Nothing to get panicky about": Ibid., pp. 20, 24, 31, 33.

228 Decades later: D. Bross and N. S. Bross, "Do Atomic Veterans Have Excess Cancer? New Results Correcting for the Healthy Soldier Bias," *American Journal of Epidemiology*, vol. 126, no. 6 (Dec. 1987), pp. 1042–43.

229 scientists deliberately released: John M. Findlay and Bruce W. Hevly, *Atomic Frontier Days: Hanford and the American West* (Seattle: Center for the Study of the Pacific Northwest, 2011), p. 57; DOD, *Report on Search for Human Radiation Experiment Records, 1944–1994* (Washington, D.C., 1997), pp. 51–54.

229 The level in Walla Walla: Technical Steering Panel of the Hanford Environmental Dose Reconstruction Project, "The Green Run," fact sheet no. 12, March 1992, p. 3, http://library.state.or.us.

229 Even the 1949 incident: DOD, *Report on Search*, p. 54.

229 "Not all the residents": Findlay and Hevly, *Atomic Frontier Days*, p. 301.

231 Irving Langmuir: James Rodger Fleming, *Fixing the Sky: The Checkered History of Weather and Climate Control* (New York: Columbia University Press, 2010), pp. 151–54, 170–71. The scientist who actually achieved the breakthrough with silver iodide, Bernard

Vonnegut, thought Langmuir was "playing with fire," because it could have unpredictable effects thousands of miles away.

232   During the Vietnam War: Ibid., pp. 179–81.

232   covert and "experimental": James G. Lewis, "James G. Lewis on Smokey Bear in Vietnam," *Environmental History*, vol. 11 (2006): p. 598.

232   "experiments" and "tests": William A. Buckingham, Jr., *Operation Ranch Hand: The Air Force and Herbicides in Southeast Asia, 1961–1971* (Washington, D.C.: USAF, 1982), pp. 33, 43–44, 200.

232   But for the five years: National Academy of Sciences Committee to Review the Health Effects in Vietnam Veterans of Exposure to Herbicides, *Veterans and Agent Orange: Update 2014* (Washington, D.C.: National Academies Press, 2016), pp. 1–18. The health impact of Agent Orange exposure remains controversial. See Anh D. Ngo et al., "Association Between Agent Orange and Birth Defects: Systematic Review and Meta-Analysis," *International Journal of Epidemiology*, vol. 35 (Oct. 2006): pp. 1220–30; Arnold Schecter and John D. Constable, "Commentary: Agent Orange and Birth Defects in Vietnam," *International Journal of Epidemiology*, vol. 35 (Oct. 2006): pp. 1230–32.

232   continued to be shrouded: On the secrecy of the test program, doubts about safety, and calls for greater openness, see Lehman, "Nuisance to Nemesis," pp. 81–83; Hacker, *Elements of Controversy*, pp. 140–58; Thomas Kunkle and Byron Ristvet, *Castle Bravo: Fifty Years of Legend and Lore*, DTRIAC SR-12-001 (2013).

233   From August to September 1958: Defense Nuclear Agency, *Operation Argus 1958*, DNA 6039F (Washington, D.C., 1992), pp. 1–23.

233   The effect turned: Charles N. Vittitoe, *Did High Altitude EMP Cause the Hawaiian Streetlight Incident?*, System Design and Assessment Notes 31 (Albuquerque: Sandia National Laboratories, 1989), p. 22.

233   The first radiation testing: Buckingham, *Operation Ranch Hand*, p. 200.

234   "poorly-instrumented": Defense Atomic Support Agency, *Project Officer's Interim Report: Starfish Prime* (1962); Fleming, *Fixing the Sky*, p. 210.

234   As for Starfish Prime: Daniel G. DuPont, "Nuclear Explosions in Orbit," *Scientific American*, vol. 290, no. 6 (June 2004): pp. 100–102; Robert Ecoffet, "Overview of In-Orbit Radiation Induced Spacecraft Anomalies," *IEEE Transactions on Nuclear Science*, vol. 60 (June 2013): p. 1798.

235 "Far more progress": Quist, *Security Classification of Information*, p. 150.

235 "Some of the work": "Need for a Secrecy Commission," Moynihan Papers, pt. II, box 280, folder 10.

235 "remarkable scientific achievement": Memorandum, "Views on Trained Use of Cats," Sept. 1983, National Security Archive.

235 "A lot of money": John Ranelagh, *Agency: The Rise and Decline of the CIA* (New York: Simon & Schuster, 1986), p. 208. See also Jeffrey T. Richelson, *Wizards of Langley: Inside the CIA's Directorate of Science and Technology* (Boulder: Westview Press, 2001), p. 147.

236 "energy and imagination": Memorandum, "Views on Trained Use of Cats."

236 Solly Zuckerman: Robert G. W. Kirk, "In Dogs We Trust? Intersubjectivity, Response-able Relations, and the Making of Mine Detector Dogs," *Journal of the History of the Behavioral Sciences*, vol. 50, no.1 (2014): pp. 12–18.

236 J. B. Rhine: Kirk, "In Dogs We Trust," pp. 22–30; Annie Jacobsen, *Phenomena: The Secret History of the U.S. Government's Investigations into Extrasensory Perception and Psychokinesis* (New York: Little, Brown, 2017), pp. 42–44; J. G. Pratt, "Research on Animal Orientation, with Emphasis on the Phenomenon of Homing in Pigeons," DTIC-AD-24-294 (1954).

237 Rhine was a paragon: Jacobsen, *Phenomena*, pp. 61–64.

237 The CIA's Project MKUltra: These experiments were to be conducted with "the surreptitious oral application of drugs on unwilling subjects for speech inducement purposes." On the lack of controls, see John Marks, *The Search for the "Manchurian Candidate": The CIA and Mind Control* (New York: McGraw-Hill, 1980), p. 61.

237 Harold Blauer: *Barrett v. United States*, 660 F. Supp. 1291 (S.D.N.Y. 1987). According to the Agency's inspector general, "Dosage levels were set not by research on toxicity, but by guess" (Torsten Passie, "MDA, MDMA, and Other 'Mescaline-Like' Substances in the US Military's Search for a Truth Drug [1940s to 1960s]," *Drug Testing and Analysis*, vol. 10, no. 1 [Jan. 2018], p. 76).

237 "some unwitting testing": *Project MKULTRA, the CIA's Program of Research in Behavioral Modification: Joint Hearing Before the Select Committee on Intelligence and the Subcommittee on Health and Scientific Research of the Committee on Human Resources*, 95th Cong., 1st Sess., Aug, 3, 1997, p. 7. The experiment that killed Blauer was conducted by the Army Chemical Corps, but, as John Marks

has shown, the CIA organized, supplied, and funded mind-control research even when it was carried out by the services (Marks, *Search for the "Manchurian Candidate,"* pp. 67–68).

238 CIA also experimented: Marks, *Search for the "Manchurian Candidate,"* pp. 77–80.

238 Gottlieb was likely: Ibid., pp. 57, 86.

238 "professionally unethical": Select Committee to Study Government Operations with Respect to Intelligence Activities, Foreign and Military Intelligence, *Final Report of the Select Committee to Study Government Operations with Respect to Intelligence Activities,* bk. 1, S. Rep. 94-755 (1976), p. 390.

238 Gottlieb's deputy: Olson's distraught wife and children could not bring themselves to believe he had committed suicide. It took the CIA more than two decades to admit that Olson had been the subject of another government experiment, Marks, *Search for the "Manchurian Candidate,"* pp. 77–86. Marks suggests it was indeed a suicide, but the official CIA account strains credulity. See Sheffield Edwards, "Suicide of Frank Olsen [*sic*]," Memorandum for the Record, Nov. 28, 1953, in *CIA Documents Concerning the Death of Frank Olson,* National Security Archive.

238 "The most efficient accident": "A Study of Assassination," Jan. 5, 1954, CIA.

239 "were ready when called": Nicholas M. Horrock, "C.I.A. Documents Tell of 1954 Project to Create Involuntary Assassins," *New York Times,* Feb. 9, 1978.

239 Most of the MKUltra records: Marks, *Search for the "Manchurian Candidate,"* pp. 57, 197. Since the main period of MKUltra was 1953–64, the cost equivalent is adjusted for inflation since 1958.

239 "to determine whether": Edwin C. May to Office of Research Development, "Annotated Bibliography, Document Set from 1972 to Date," June 16, 1995, CIA-RDP96-00791R000200170016-2l. The money was distributed between 1972 and 1988, so this is adjusted for inflation since 1980.

239 Even escape artists: Jacobsen, *Phenomena,* pp. 145–46.

239 "no scientific warrant": John A. Swets and Robert A. Bjork, "Enhancing Human Performance: An Evaluation of 'New Age' Techniques Considered by the Army," *Psychological Science,* vol. 1, no. 2 (March 1990): pp. 85, 92.

240 In 1995: American Institutes for Research, "A Proposal to Review the Remote Viewing Research Program," May 25, 1995, CIA-RDP96-00791R000100080003-7.

240 "In no case": American Institutes for Research, "*An Evaluation of the Remote Viewing Program: Research and Operational Applications,*" draft report, 1995, CIA-RDP96-00791R000200180005-5, pp. E1–E4.

241 "In order to best inform": CIA Office of Medical Services, "OSM Guidelines on Medical and Psychological Support to Detainee Renditions, Interrogations, and Detentions," Dec. 2004, p. 20, CIA.

241 "was like an experiment": Jane Mayer, *The Dark Side: The Inside Story of How the War on Terror Turned Into a War on American Ideals* (New York: Doubleday, 2008), p. 156.

241 Waterboarding, "diapering": Mark Mazzetti, "Behind Clash Between C.I.A. and Congress, a Secret Report on Interrogations," *New York Times*, March 7, 2014. See also Senate Select Committee on Intelligence, *Committee Study of the Central Intelligence Agency's Detention and Interrogation Program: Findings and Conclusions* (2012), pp. 8–13.

241 experiments depended on deception: As the main sponsor of MKUltra, Richard Helms, argued to CIA Director Allen Dulles, there was no point in trying to test mind-control methods unless they used unwitting subjects (Marks, *Search for the "Manchurian Candidate,"* p. 87).

242 two concepts are fundamentally opposed: Peter Galison, "Removing Knowledge," *Critical Inquiry*, vol. 31 (2004): pp. 240–43.

242 This was already clear: Office of the Director of Defense Research and Engineering, *Report of the Defense Science Board Task Force on Secrecy* (1970), p. 11, FAS. See also Quist, *Security Classification of Information*, pp. 142–49. In recent years, a growing number of government research contracts prohibit collaboration with non-American scientists, and restrict the publication of the results. Export controls in electronics and biotechnology can discourage researchers from pursuing international collaboration even if the government is not paying for it. (Dirk Libaers, "Industry Relationships of DoD-funded Academics and Institutional Changes in the US University System," *Journal of Technology Transfer*, vol. 34 [2009], pp. 484–86.) On the earlier history of government efforts to restrict the free flow of scientific knowledge, see Harold Relyea, *Silencing Science: National Security Controls and Scientific Communication* (Norwood, N.J.: Ablex Publishing, 1994).

243 this history tarnished the reputation: DOE Advisory Committee, Final Report of the Advisory Committee on Human Radiation Experiments.

243 change by the 1970s: Debra D. Durocher, "Radiation Redux," *American Journalism Review*, vol. 16, no. 2 (1994): p. 34.

243 This did not change: Linda Turbyville, "Hazel O'Leary," interview, *Omni*, vol. 17, no. 5 (April 1995).

7 FOLLOWING THE MONEY: TRADE SECRETS

245 "The chief business": Ellen Terrell, "When a Quote Is Not (Exactly) a Quote: The Business of America Is Business Edition," Jan. 17, 2019, LOC.

246 Coolidge's successors: The classic text is William Appleman Williams, *The Tragedy of American Diplomacy* (Cleveland: World Publishing Co., 1959), pp. 145–47, where he identifies the foreign-policy elite as leaders of corporate America, and cites the pages of *Fortune* magazine as explicitly calling for expanded foreign trade and investment as essential for the U.S. economic system.

246 price list for each ambassadorship: Johannes Fedderke and Dennis Jett, "What Price the Court of St. James? Political Influences on Ambassadorial Postings of the United States of America," *Governance*, vol. 30 (July 2017): pp. 486, 506.

247 "US national security": Philip Agee, *Inside the Company: CIA Diary*, 2nd. ed. (New York: Farrar, Straus & Giroux, 1975), p. 485.

248 Weapons production: Louis Uchitelle, "The U.S. Still Leans on the Military-Industrial Complex," *New York Times*, Sept. 22, 2017.

248 During periods of growth: Doug Berenson, Chris Higgins, and Jim Tinsley, "The U.S. Defense Industry in a New Era," *War on the Rocks*, Jan. 13, 2021.

248 10 percent of manufacturing: Loren Thompson, "Defense Industry Profits Are Not Impressive," *Forbes*, July 24, 2013.

249 Arms manufacturers: Louis Uchitelle, "Arms Makers: Rather Fight than Switch," *New York Times*, Sept. 20, 1992.

249 these periods saw consolidation: Berenson, Higgins, and Tinsley, "U.S. Defense Industry."

249 The government often classifies: Paul Edwards, *The Closed World: Computers and the Politics of Discourse in Cold War America* (Cambridge, Mass.: MIT Press, 1996), pp. 62–64.

249 important exceptions: The economist Seymour Melman was one of the main proponents of the argument that the defense sector had a preponderant role in the American economy. But the inefficiency of Pentagon contractors (and contracting) undermined Melman's claim. I well remember that, when I took his "War Economy"

class at Columbia in 1989, he would not revise his thesis even as defense spending shrank as a share of overall output and dynamic new industries emerged. See, e.g., Seymour Melman, "Economic Consequences of the Arms Race: The Second-Rate Economy," *American Economic Review*, vol. 78, no. 2 (1988): pp. 55–59.

250   the government does not typically share: This prohibition against using signals or communications intelligence to help private businesses has been an explicit part of training those who work with SIGINT and COMINT. Some have argued otherwise, but the best evidence they offer is that the United States has "contemplated" industrial espionage on behalf of U.S. firms in future scenario exercises (Glenn Greenwald, "The U.S. Government's Secret Plans to Spy for American Corporations," *The Intercept*, Sept. 5, 2014).

250   generally been *bad* for business: Claire Miller, "Revelations of N.S.A. Spying Cost U.S. Tech Companies," *New York Times*, March 21, 2014; Daniel Castro and Alan McQuinn, "Beyond the USA Freedom Act: How U.S. Surveillance Still Subverts U.S. Competitiveness," Information Technology & Innovation Foundation, June 9, 2015.

250   "successfully completed our assignment": Refinitiv, "Q2 2021 Fluor Corp Earnings Call," Aug. 6, 2021; Isabel Debre, "Contractors Who Powered US War in Afghanistan Stuck in Dubai," *Military Times*, Aug. 9, 2021.

250   Building an Afghan military: William D. Hartung, "Profits of War: Corporate Beneficiaries of the Post-9/11 Pentagon Spending Surge," Watson Institute for International and Public Affairs, Sept. 13, 2021.

251   went to non-U.S. firms: Sandra Halperin, "The Political Economy of Anglo-American War: The Case of Iraq," *International Politics*, vol. 48, nos. 2–3 (March/May 2011): p. 213.

252   Lyndon Johnson: Doris Kearns Goodwin, *Lyndon Johnson and the American Dream* (New York: Harper & Row, 1976), p. 251.

252   Coolidge himself: Dennis R. Shaughnessy, "'The Business of America Is Business!,'" Social Enterprise Institute, Feb. 2, 2017. Coolidge never said that the government should only care about the private sector. But the phrase resonated at least in part because Coolidge himself was so pro-business, cutting taxes, opposing regulation, and using troops to back American business interests in Central America and the Caribbean.

252   "thorough, accurate": Joshua Botts, "'A Burden for the Depart-

ment'?: To the 1991 *FRUS* Statute," DOS Office of the Historian, Feb. 6, 2012.

252   But *FRUS* now totals: See ISOO annual reports, which provide annual figures for pages that have been declassified ("ISOO Annual Report Archive, Calendar Years 1979 Through 2019," NARA).

253   new and better methodology: Franco Moretti, *Distant Reading* (London: Verso, 2013), pp. 47–49.

253   topic modeling: For an accessible introduction by the pioneer of topic modeling, see David Blei, "Probabilistic Topic Models," *Communications of the ACM*, vol. 55, no. 4 (April 2012): pp. 77–84.

255   "Please guard": Ambassador in the United Kingdom to the Secretary of State, June 25, 1947, *FRUS*, accessed via FOIArchive.

255   not even classified: Gaston to Koo, Oct. 23, 1947, *FRUS*; Memorandum of Conversation by the Assistant Chief of the Division of European Affairs, March 28, 1941, *FRUS*, both accessed via FOIArchive.

256   One way to find: David Allen et al., "Topic Modeling Official Secrecy," paper presented at Knowledge Discovery and Data Mining, Bloomberg Headquarters, N.Y., Aug. 2014.

258   UFCO owned 42 percent: Stephen Schlesinger and Stephen Kinzer, *Bitter Fruit* (Cambridge, Mass.: David Rockefeller Center for Latin American Studies, 2005), pp. 70–74; Piero Gleijeses, *Shattered Hope: The Guatemalan Revolution and the United States, 1944–1954* (Princeton: Princeton University Press, 1999), p. 165.

258   recounted the true story: Gabriel García Márquez, *One Hundred Years of Solitude*, trans. Gregory Rabassa (New York: Avon Books, 1970).

259   "bloodthirsty flies": Pablo Neruda, "United Fruit Co.," in *Canto General* (1950), accessed via Brown University Library.

259   Historical research: Schlesinger and Kinzer, *Bitter Fruit*, p. 76.

259   many Guatemalan farmers: Gleijeses, *Shattered Hope*, pp. 149–51, 164–65.

259   usually downplayed: Ibid., pp. 143–47, 231–32.

260   Less than a year earlier: Mary Ann Heiss, "The United States, Great Britain, and the Creation of the Iranian Oil Consortium, 1953–1954," *International History Review*, vol. 16 (1994): pp. 515–16.

261   one of the top documents: Memorandum for the Record, New York, Nov. 20, 1953, *FRUS*, 1952–1954, *Guatemala*, no. 70.

262   Decades later: Gleijeses, *Shattered Hope*, p. 376. One or more oil companies did indeed comply with the CIA request. See Telegram

from the Central Intelligence Agency to Operation PBSUCCESS Headquarters in Florida, June 15, 1954, *FRUS*, 1952–1954, *Guatemala*, no. 187.

262 In fact, when more documents: See, e.g., Memorandum of Conversation, Washington, Sept. 15, 1953, *FRUS*, 1952–1954, *Guatemala*, no. 52. This document also references a memorandum in which King "explained that we were in need of the best business brains of the country for planning purposes and possibly subsequent action against Guatemala in the economic field; that we wished to explore all possible covert means of embarrassing the present Government by economic pressures."

262 "cut off our oil": Gleijeses, *Shattered Hope*, p. 322.

262 In June 1954: Ibid.

262 A week later: Chief of Station, Guatemala, to Lincoln, "Guatemala Government Interest in Local Gasoline Supply," June 11, 1954, CIA.

263 Others on the list: Matthew Connelly, *A Diplomatic Revolution: Algeria's Fight for Independence and the Origins of the Post–Cold War Era* (New York: Oxford University Press, 2002), pp. 149, 164.

265 case of the Saharan oil fields: 406th Meeting of the NSC, May 13, 1959, *FRUS*, 1958–60, vol. 13, pp. 729–30.

266 decades-long career: Message from William Pawley to President Nixon, March 25, 1959, *FRUS*, 1969–1976, vol. E-10, 1969–1972, *Documents on American Republics*, p. 584.

266 One discovers: Memorandum of Conference with the President, May 7, 1960, DDE Diaries, Staff Notes, May 1960 (2), box 32, AWF, DDEL; redacted, U.S. DDO, doc. no. CK2349426420; unredacted, doc. no. CK2349193456.

266 Pawley could be said: On Pawley's business career, see Anthony R. Carrozza, *William D. Pawley: The Extraordinary Life of the Adventurer, Entrepreneur, and Diplomat Who Cofounded the Flying Tigers* (Washington, D.C.: Potomac Books, 2012), pts. 1–2.

267 "war is a racket" and "a high class muscle man": Hans Schmidt, *Maverick Marine: General Smedley D. Butler and the Contradictions of American Military History* (Lexington: University Press of Kentucky, 1987), pp. 223–31.

267 But to Pawley: Max Holland, "Private Sources of U.S. Foreign Policy: William Pawley and the 1954 Coup d'État in Guatemala," *Journal of Cold War Studies*, vol. 7, no. 4 (2005): p. 42.

267 Truman decorated Pawley: Cheryl L. Miller, "Belvoir: A Colonial Revival Landmark in the Piedmont," prepared for the Garden Club of Virginia, 2014, p. 65.

267 Pawley took an office: Holland, "Private Sources of U.S. Foreign Policy," pp. 52–53, 57.

268 Despite Pawley's angry protestations: Ibid., p. 58.

268 source told the CIA: Telegram from the CIA Station in Guatemala to Operation PBSUCCESS Headquarters in Florida, June 23, 1954, *FRUS, 1952–1954, Guatemala,* no. 225.

268 "Bomb repeat Bomb": Telegram from the CIA Chief of Station in Guatemala to the Central Intelligence Agency, June 19, 1954, *FRUS, 1952–1954, Guatemala,* no. 208.

268 the insurgents' invasion stalled: This account of what happened on June 22 is based on Max Holland's excellent study, "Private Sources of U.S. Foreign Policy," pp. 58–62.

269 Holland, Dulles, and Pawley went: Max Holland notes that Pawley's account is corroborated by Eisenhower's own memoir as well as CIA documents from the time (ibid., p. 60).

269 Pawley told the Nicaraguan ambassador: Ibid., pp. 57, 61.

269 That same evening: Telegram from the Central Intelligence Agency to Operation PBSUCCESS Headquarters in Florida, June 22, 1954, *FRUS, 1952–1954, Guatemala,* no. 219; Telegram from CIA to Operation PBSUCCESS Headquarters, June 24, 1954, ibid., no. 233.

269 In the end: Telegram from the CIA Station in Guatemala to Operation PBSUCCESS Headquarters in Florida, June 27, 1954, *FRUS, 1952–1954, Guatemala,* no. 244; Telegram from Operation PBSUCCESS Headquarters in Florida to the Mission Broadcasting Station, June 28, 1954, *FRUS, 1952–1954, Guatemala,* no. 247; Gleijeses, *Shattered Hope,* pp. 338–52.

270 his name is missing: For a rare exception, see Holland, "Private Sources of U.S. Foreign Policy," pp. 52, 57–63.

270 The defeat of the Guatemalan Revolution: "Letter from President Eisenhower to General James H. Doolittle," July 26, 1954, *FRUS, 1950–1955, The Intelligence Community,* no. 185.

271 "There are no rules": James Doolittle et al., *Report on the Covert Activities of the Central Intelligence Agency,* CIA Special Study Group (1954).

271 "no better plan" . . . "must be prepared": A. J. Goodpaster, Memorandum of Conference with the President, March 17, 1960, U.S. DDO; redacted, doc. no. CK2349317538; unredacted, doc. no. CK2349098650.

272 Bay of Pigs: Max Holland, "A Luce Connection: Senator Keating, William Pawley, and the Cuban Missile Crisis," *Journal of Cold War Studies,* vol. 1, no. 3 (Fall 1999): pp. 163–65.

272   team of economists studied: Arindrajit Dube, Ethan Kaplan, and Suresh Naidu, "Coups, Corporations, and Classified Information," *Quarterly Journal of Economics*, vol. 126 (2011): 1380–81.

272   United Fruit's stock rose: Ibid., p. 1398.

273   Bedell Smith went on: "Elected to United Fruit Directorate," *New York Times*, April 21, 1955.

273   So one can easily: Dube, Kaplan, and Naidu, "Coups, Corporations," p. 1379, citing Tim Weiner, *Legacy of Ashes: A History of the CIA* (New York: Doubleday, 2007), p. 7.

273   "nothing more": Agee, *Inside the Company*, p. 575.

273   "serious foreign policy implications": Nick Cullather, *Secret History: The CIA's Classified Account of Its Operations in Guatemala, 1952–1954*, 2nd ed. (Stanford: Stanford University Press, 2006), p. 19.

273   "On balance": Editorial Note, *FRUS*, 1952–1954, *Guatemala*, no. 196.

274   Justice Department filed suit: Marcelo Bucheli, "Chronology," United Fruit Historical Society, 2001.

274   obvious quid pro quo: Heiss, "United States, Great Britain," pp. 515–16.

274   "prompt, adequate" . . . "nothing but words": Oliver Murphey, "A Bond That Will Permanently Endure: The Eisenhower Administration, the Bolivian Revolution and Latin American Leftist Nationalism," Ph.D. diss., Columbia University, 2017, chap. 6.

274   "change one iota": Murphey, "Bond That Will Permanently Endure," p. 213.

274   "grown no bananas": Gleijeses, *Shattered Hope*, pp. 3–4.

275   So, rather than: On this point, see also Cullather, *Secret History*, p. 19.

275   Fifty such operations: David Robarge, "The CIA and the Covert Cold War," presentation in Columbia University course "Cold War Power: Culture as a Weapon," New York, April 10, 2018. Robarge has not published this data, but for an analysis by an independent scholar, see John. G. Breen, "Covert Action and Unintended Consequences," *InterAgency Journal*, vol. 8, no. 3 (2017): pp. 106–22.

275   favorite partners: Connelly, *Diplomatic Revolution*, p. 165.

275   explicitly political interventions: Robarge, "CIA and the Covert Cold War."

276   "promote or protect": Ibid.

276   few cables involving Russia: On Assange's Russian ties, see Zack Beauchamp, "The WikiLeaks-Russia Connection Started Way Before the 2016 Election," *Vox*, Jan. 6, 2017.

276 collection includes the metadata: For an introduction, see "Frequently Asked Questions (FAQ), Record Group 59: General Records of the Department of State Central Foreign Policy File, 1973–1979," NARA.

277 37 percent . . . 21 percent: The total excludes records that are administrative in nature, or that relate to consular services like visas and passports. The economics and business categories also include military sales and assistance.

277 "a foreign policy": Jimmy Carter, "Human Rights and Foreign Policy," speech presented at Notre Dame University, South Bend, Ind., June 1977.

279 Nevertheless, exporters argued: Bradley Graham, "Trade Reorganization Urged," *Washington Post*, May 30, 1979; N. David Palmeter and Thomas Leonard Kossl, "Restructuring Executive Branch Trade Responsibilities: A Half-Step Forward," *Law and Policy in International Business*, vol. 12 (1980): pp. 636–37.

279 "jobs, jobs, jobs": Charley Reese, "Who's Better Off After the Persian Gulf War? Not the U.S. Public," *Orlando Sentinel*, Jan. 19, 1992.

280 First, we need: What follows is drawn from a paper I co-authored with Ray Hicks. For a summary, see Raymond Hicks and Matthew Connelly, "Underfunding the State Department Could Hurt U.S. Exports—and U.S. Companies," *Washington Post*, Feb. 14, 2018.

280 Hard-core capitalists: Andrew K. Rose, "The Foreign Service and Foreign Trade: Embassies as Export Promotion," *World Economy*, vol. 30, no. 1 (Jan. 2007): 23; Daniel Lederman, Marcelo Olarreaga, and Lucy Payton, *Export Promotion Agencies: What Works and What Doesn't*, World Bank Policy Research Working Paper 4044, 2006, p. 16.

281 Trans-Pacific Partnership: Patrice McDermott and Emily Manna, "Secrecy, Democracy and the TPP: Trade Transparency Is What the Public Wants—And Needs," *The Hill*, Sept. 12, 2016.

282 When they are surveyed: Bianca DiJulio, Mira Norton, and Mollyann Brodie, "Americans' Views on the U.S. Role in Global Health," Kaiser Family Foundation, Jan. 20, 2016.

282 $39.2 billion: George Ingram, "What Every American Should Know about US Foreign Aid," Brookings Institution, Oct. 15, 2019.

282 In fact, historically: Marian L. Lawson and Emily M. Morgenstern, *Foreign Aid: An Introduction to U.S. Programs and Policy*, CRS, R40213 (2019), FAS.

284   In June 1942: "Handbook of the Records Declassification Division," Office of the National Archives, Feb. 1975, Brownell Papers, box 184, DDEL; Arvin Quist, *Security Classification of Information*, vol. 1 (Oak Ridge, Tenn.: Oak Ridge National Laboratories, 2002), pp. 45–48, FAS.

284   That same month: W. H. Lawrence, "An 8,754 Mile Tour: Munitions Output Put at 94% of His Goals After Swing to West," *New York Times*, Oct. 2, 1942.

285   "You know": Betty Winfield, *FDR and the News Media* (New York: Columbia University Press, 1994), p. 181.

288   The *Tribune* claimed: Larry J. Frank, "The United States Navy v. the *Chicago Tribune*," *Historian*, vol. 42, no. 2 (1980): pp. 286–87, 295–96, 302.

288   But Roosevelt also: James Gregory Bradsher, " 'Fake News' 1942: President Roosevelt and the Chicago Tribune," *Text Message*, NARA, Feb. 1, 2018.

288   he resorted to public shaming: Richard W. Steele, "Franklin D. Roosevelt and His Foreign Policy Critics," *Political Science Quarterly*, vol. 94, no. 1 (1979): p. 29; Winfield, *FDR and the News Media*, pp. 68, 178.

289   the exception of nuclear secrets: Alex Wellerstein, *Restricted Data: The History of Nuclear Secrecy in the United States* (Chicago: University of Chicago Press, 2021), pp. 145–57.

289   "secrecy at the source": This was the original formulation of George Creel, who came up with the idea from the hard experience of trying to enforce press censorship during World War I (Commission on Government Security, *Report of the Commission on Government Security* [Washington, D.C.: GPO, 1957], p. 153).

289   "serious administrative embarrassment": Steelman to Irving Ives, Oct. 28, 1947, White House Official Files, box 1507, HSTL.

289   "some assistant secretary": Earl Richert, "Truman's Words Come Back to Haunt Him," *Washington Daily News*, Oct. 8, 1951; "Memorandum for the NSC Representative on Internal Security," Dec. 29, 1950, White House President's Secretary, box 182, HSTL. For Finney's original scoop, which also won a Pulitzer, see "U.S. Censorship Plan Revealed," *Minneapolis Sunday Tribune*, Oct. 19, 1947.

290   "prestige of the nation": "Prescribed Regulation Establishing Minimum Standards," Dec. 28, 1950, White House Official Files, box 2070, HSTL.

290 "a dangerous instrument": "Editors Assail Truman Curb on Civil News," *New York Herald Tribune*, Sept. 30, 1951.

290 proved self-defeating: Richard Hollander, "Under Capricious Classification Security Can Be Overdone," *Washington Daily News*, Sept. 27, 1951; U.S. Office of Censorship, *Code of Wartime Practices for the American Press* (Washington, D.C.: GPO, 1942).

290 "ridiculed": "Memorandum for Mr. Short," January 23, 1951, White House Official Files, box 2070, HSTL.

291 But Truman went on: Harry S. Truman, "The President's News Conference," address presented in Executive Office Building, Washington, D.C., Oct. 4, 1951, HSTL.

291 "The administration's approach": James Reston, "Suspicion of News Tinkering Overcasts Edict on Secrecy: Approach of the Administration to Public Information Likened to a Press Agent's Suppressions of Convenience," *New York Times*, Oct. 3, 1951.

292 "might prove embarrassing": "O.P.S. Bans 'Embarrassing' News, Truman Quickly Rescinds Order," *New York Times*, Sept. 28, 1951.

292 Federal Trade Commission: George M. Elsey to Irving Perlmeter, Nov. 23, 1951, Elsey Papers, box 89, HSTL.

292 The administration also claimed: Vaughan to Watson, Aug. 25, 1950, White House Official Files, box 1889, HSTL.

292 security professionals in the FBI: Murphy and Spingarn, Memorandum for Truman, May 16, 1950, White House Official Files, box 1888, HSTL.

292 judged to be sexually "deviant": David K. Johnson, *The Lavender Scare: The Cold War Persecution of Gays and Lesbians in the Federal Government* (Chicago: University of Chicago Press, 2009), p. 114. That is not to say no one tried. The Soviets attempted to blackmail Joseph Alsop, a highly influential columnist, after setting up a "honey trap" when he visited Moscow. But Alsop promptly informed the CIA, and benefited from an unspoken policy that protected well-connected people as long as they stayed in the closet. It likely helped that Alsop was a staunch anticommunist. (Greg Herken, *The Georgetown Set: Friends and Rivals in Cold War Washington* [New York: Knopf, 2014], pp. 205–8.)

293 overriding priority: Athan Theoharis, "The Soviet Espionage Threat," in *Chasing Spies: How the FBI Failed in Counter-Intelligence but Promoted the Politics of McCarthyism in the Cold War Years* (Chicago: Ivan R. Dee, 2002), p. 332.

293 "important only from": Summary of 96th Meeting of the NSC, July 12, 1951, White House President's Secretary, box 188, HSTL.

293 In his very first: Dwight Eisenhower, "1953 State of the Union Address," Feb. 2, 1953, DDEL.

293 In a press conference: White House Press Conference, June 17, 1953, Hagarty Papers, box 69, DDEL.

293 "dangerous policy": Brownell, "Free Flow of Information from the Government," Nov. 6, 1953, Brownell Papers, box 154, DDEL.

293 "the proposed order": Minutes of Cabinet Meeting, Oct. 30, 1953, White House Office of the Staff Secretary, Cabinet Minutes, box 1, DDEL.

293 Eisenhower believed: Discussion of the 172nd and 197th Meetings of the NSC, Nov. 23, 1953, and May 14, 1954, NSC Series, box 5, AWF, DDEL. Eisenhower also encouraged his postmaster general to deliberately "lose" mail that contained what was considered communist propaganda, even suggesting the Post Office be provided a secret budget to do so.

293 he was sure Moscow: Minutes of Cabinet Meeting, Oct. 30, 1953.

294 defense contractors reported: Morgan to Archibald, Nov. 9, 1956, Gerald D. Morgan Papers, box 22, DDEL.

294 When archivists: Handbook of the Records Declassification Division, Feb. 1975.

294 As for reducing: "Report to the Secretary of Defense by the Committee on Classified Information," Nov. 8, 1956, Gerald D. Morgan Papers, box 22, DDEL.

294 In just ten years: Rick Neustadt to Stu Eizenstadt, ca. July 1977, White House Staff Offices, Domestic Policy Staff, Richard Neustadt Files, box 29, "Declassification Project," JCPL.

295 "continuous staff supervision": "Department of Defense Reply to Questionnaire of Government Information Subcommittee," Sept. 30, 1955, Gerald D. Morgan Papers, box 23, DDEL.

295 Truman's 1951 order: Exec. Order 10290, 16 Fed. Reg. 9795, 1951; Exec. Order 10501, 18 Fed. Reg. 7049, 1953; Executive Order 10964, 26 Fed. Reg. 8932, 1961. Steven Aftergood has conveniently assembled all the executive orders relevant to state secrecy in one place: "Selected Executive Orders on National Security," FAS.

295 Kennedy left Eisenhower's order: Mansfield to Kennedy, June 14, 1962, White House Central Subject Files, box 632, JFKL.

296 "a time bomb": Bill Moyers to Lee White, Dec. 15, 1965, and Wilfred H. Rommel to LBJ, June 29, 1966, both in White House Central Files, LE/FE 14-1, box 44, LBJL.

296 "the fucking thing": Frederick A. O. Schwartz, *Democracy in the Dark: The Seduction of Government Secrecy* (New York: New Press,

2015), p. 198; Mary Graham, *Presidents' Secrets: The Use and Abuse of Hidden Power* (New Haven: Yale University Press, 2017), pp. 128–30. On LBJ's strategy, see Wilfred H. Rommel to LBJ, June 29, 1966.

296 "We've got the best": Lyndon Johnson and Cyrus Vance, Recording of a Conversation, June 24, 1965, Secret White House Tapes, University of Virginia, Charlottesville, Va.

296 "the Generals and the Admirals": Harry S. Truman, *Strictly Personal and Confidential: The Letters Harry Truman Never Mailed* (Columbia: University of Missouri Press, 1999), pp. 26–28; Arthur Krock, "Truman's Press Views Mystify the Capital," *New York Times*, Oct. 7, 1951.

297 Richard Nixon: William Rehnquist, "Department of Justice Submission Relating to Tightening Protection of Classified Documents," Aug. 5, 1971, RG59, Executive Secretariat Briefing Books, 1958–1976, lot 73D324, Advisory Panels, 2-1969 to Lin, USNA.

297 But the group: Report of the Justice Department Working Group, June 24, 1971, RG59, Executive Secretariat Briefing Books, 1958–1976, President Nixon's Letter, "Council on Classification Policy," USNA.

297 Nixon tried to devise: Transcript of July 24, 1971, Meeting, in *Statement of Information: Hearings Before the Committee of the Judiciary*, bk. VII, pt. 1, *White House Surveillance Activities and Campaign Activities*, 93rd Cong., 2nd. Sess. (1974), pp. 874–75.

298 "lift the veil": Richard Halloran, "President Orders Limit on Labeling of Data as Secret," *New York Times*, March 9, 1972.

298 The order reduced: Exec. Order No. 11652, 37 Fed. Reg. 5209, 1972.

298 "shall be held": Exec. Order 10290, 1951; Exec. Order No. 11652, 1972.

299 "We have reversed": Department of State Appropriations Authorization, Fiscal Year 1973, *Hearings Before the Committee on Foreign Relations*, 92nd Cong., 2nd sess., 1972, p. 528.

299 It seemed like sunlight: Nixon knew that, contrary to hagiographic accounts like Robert Kennedy's [just-published] *Thirteen Days*, JFK had been ready to withdraw American missiles in Turkey publicly to defuse the Cuban Missile Crisis. In 1970, when Nixon learned that the Soviets were building a submarine base in Cuba, he told Kissinger to look into whether the United States could deploy missiles or build its own submarine base on the Black Sea, "anything which will give us some trading stock." As Philip Nash notes, "Nixon had a fine sense of history" (Philip Nash, *The Other*

Missiles of October: Eisenhower, Kennedy, and the Jupiters, 1957–1963 [Chapel Hill: University of North Carolina Press, 1997], p. 172).

299 Just to make certain: Tom Latimer to General Haig, Oct. 8, 1971, folder 000076-011-0525, PQHV. Sure enough, as Cuban Missile Crisis documents were released during the 1970s, they showed that Kennedy was more willing to consider concessions to Khrushchev than had been acknowledged, though Nixon was out of office by this point (Barton J. Bernstein, "The Cuban Missile Crisis: Trading the Jupiters in Turkey?," *Political Science Quarterly*, vol. 95, no. 1 [1980]: pp. 97–125).

299 Nixon was actually "weaponizing": "A Conversation with the President about Foreign Policy," July 1, 1970, American Presidency Project.

299 "group of clowns": Transcript of July 24, 1971, Meeting, p. 877.

300 In the aftermath: David Greenberg, *Republic of Spin: An Inside History of the American Presidency* (New York: Norton, 2016), p. 402; Gerald R. Ford, "Remarks upon Taking the Oath of Office as President," Aug. 9, 1974, Gerald R. Ford Presidential Library, Ann Arbor, Mich.

300 "cover up dishonesty": Gerald R. Ford, "Mr. Ford's Early Views on Executive Privilege," *New York Times*, Nov. 4, 1973.

300 "open up": *Meet the Press*, July 11, 1976, White House Staff Offices, Domestic Policy Staff, Richard Neustadt Files, box 28, "Declassification—Jimmy Carter Statements," JCPL.

300 These promises seemed: Jimmy Carter, Robert Scheer, "The Playboy Interview with Jimmy Carter: A Candid Conversation with the Democratic Candidate for the Presidency," *Playboy*, Nov. 1, 1976.

300 "I was shocked": Q&A With State Department Employees, Feb. 29, 1977, White House Staff Offices, Domestic Policy Staff, Richard Neustadt Files, box 28, "Declassification—Jimmy Carter Statements," JCPL.

300 Just one "compartment": Memorandum for Robert Gates and 300 Neustadt, Presidential Review Memorandum (PRM)/NSC 29, "A Comprehensive Review of the Classification System," June 28, 1977, White House Staff Offices, Domestic Policy Staff, Richard Neustadt Files, box 28, "Declassification Project," JCPL.

301 "Does [the] President": Dan O'Neill to Rick Neustadt, June 29, 1977, White House Staff Offices, Domestic Policy Staff, Richard Neustadt Files, box 29, "Declassification Project," JCPL.

301 "time-consuming": Michael Hornblow, "Draft PRM on Classification," April 15, 1977, White House Staff Offices, Domestic Policy Staff, Richard Neustadt Files, box 28, "Declassification Project," JCPL.

301 One such reform: Exec. Order No. 12065, 43 Fed. Reg. 28949, June 29, 1978, FAS.

301 Carter insisted: "Statement by the President," June 29, 1978, White House Staff Offices, Domestic Policy Staff, Richard Neustadt Files, box 29, "Declassification—ISOO-GSA Relationship," JCPL.

301 "the American people": Jimmy Carter, "Human Rights and Foreign Policy," speech presented in Notre Dame University, South Bend, Ind., June 1977.

302 Critics argued: Jeane J. Kirkpatrick, "Dictatorships & Double Standards," *Commentary*, Nov. 1979.

302 some close Middle Eastern: Amnesty International, *Annual Report 1978* (London: Amnesty International Publications, 1978), pp. 253–55, 264–65.

303 Saudi Arabia: Roy Reed, "Saudis Provoke Outcry in Britain By Flogging 2 Who Brewed Beer," *New York Times*, June 15, 1978.

304 "People don't give": Recording of Conversation Between Rumsfeld and Nixon, 1971, "Rumsfeld and Nixon: Caught on Tape," *Frontline*, Oct. 26, 2004, PBS.

304 less risky in Latin America: "Telecon with FM Rabasa and Kissinger at 12:50 P.M.," Kissinger telecons, FOIArchive, doc. ID 0000C499.

304 All in all: ISOO, *Annual Report to the President: 1980–1981* (Washington, D.C., 1981), p. 12.

304 Another key element: Questions from Senator Huddleston and Senator Leahy, ca. February 1972, White House Staff, Peter Rusthoven Papers, box 3, "Executive Order on Classification," RRPL.

305 "rare" and "exceptional": David J. Anderson to Richard K. Willard, February 22, 1982, White House Staff, Edwin Meese Papers, box 24, "Executive Order on Classification," RRPL.

305 Government lawyers used: Edward P. Boland to William P. Clark, March 9, 1982, White House Staff, Edwin Meese Papers, box 24, "Executive Order on Classification," RRPL.

305 Carter did create: David Aaron and Stu Eizenstat to the President, Aug. 17, 1977, White House Staff Offices, Domestic Policy

Staff, Richard Neustadt Files, box 29, "Declassification Project," JCPL.

305 But no one wanted: Richard M. Neustadt, "Points for Classification Meeting," July 25, 1977, White House Staff Offices, Domestic Policy Staff, Richard Neustadt Files, box 28, JCPL.

305 50 percent more: ISOO, *Annual Report to the President: Fiscal Year 1979* (Washington, D.C., 1980), p. 41.

305 They blamed: Ibid., p. 16.

305 new designation: "royal": Pete Earley, "He Keeps Deepest Secrets," *Washington Post*, Dec. 14, 1983.

306 Reagan campaigned: Douglas Kneeland, "Reagan Assails Carter over Disclosure of Secret Plane," *New York Times*, Sept. 5, 1980.

306 "to reduce costly": Republican National Convention, "Republican Party Platform of 1980," Detroit, July 15, 1980.

306 Their primary concern: William P. Clark to Edwin Meese III, ca. Nov. 1981, White House Staff, Edwin Meese Papers, box 24, "Executive Order on Classification," RRPL.

306 So they crafted: Exec. Order 12356, 47 Fed. Reg. 14874, April 6, 1982.

306 But Reagan knew: Robert Parry, "News Media Opposes Reagan's Secrecy Plan," *Associated Press*, March 11, 1982.

306 "way too much classification": George Lardner Jr., "CIA Doublespeak Cloaks Proposals for Homespy and Datahide," *Washington Post*, Nov. 13, 1981.

306 "To minimize criticism": William P. Clark to Edwin Meese III, n.d. (ca. Feb. 1982), White House Staff, Edwin Meese Papers, box 24, RRPL.

307 White House source told Moynihan: The source was the deputy chief of staff, John Podesta (Memcon, March 3, 1998, Moynihan Papers, pt. II, box 39).

307 "a citizen-centered": "Gore Declares National Monuments in Pacific Northwest; Bush Touts Government Reform," CNN, June 9, 2000.

307 "drill through": George W. Bush, "Getting Results from Government," speech, Philadelphia, Pa., June 9, 2000.

307 Instead, Bush gave: Graham, *Presidents' Secrets*, pp. 163–65.

307 cited 9/11 as the reason: Mary Graham, "The Information Wars: Terrorism Has Become a Pretext for a New Culture of Secrecy," *Atlantic*, Sept. 2002.

307 Barack Obama promised: Exec. Order 13526, 75 Fed. Reg. 707, Jan. 5, 2010.

308 "If there is significant": Exec. Order 13526, 75 Fed. Reg. 707, Jan. 5, 2010, FAS.

308 exact same language: Exec. Order 12958, 60 Fed. Reg. 19825, April 20, 1995, FAS.

308 in Carter's: Exec. Order 12065, 43 Fed. Reg. 28949, June 29, 1978, FAS.

308 In all three cases: See "ISOO Annual Report Archive, Calendar Years 1979 Through 2019," NARA.

308 Obama really outdid: ISOO, *2012 Annual Report to the President* (Washington, D.C., 2013), p. 8.

308 At the same time: Tom Engelhardt, *Shadow Government: Surveillance, Secret Wars, and a Global Security State in a Single-Superpower World* (Chicago: Haymarket Books, 2014), p. 31.

308 Journalists reported: Committee to Protect Journalists, "The Obama Administration and the Press: Leak Investigations and Surveillance in Post-9/11 America," Oct. 10, 2013.

308 no better example: On the president's approval, see Cora Currier, "The Kill Chain: The Lethal Bureaucracy Behind Obama's Drone War," *The Intercept*, Oct. 15, 2015. On the CIA/Pentagon rivalry, see Gordon Lubold and Shane Harris, "Trump Broadens CIA Powers, Allows Deadly Drone Strikes," *Wall Street Journal*, March 13, 2017.

309 Agency quashed FOIA appeals: Memorandum Opinion, *American Civil Liberties Union et al. v. Department of Justice*, Civil Action No. 10-0436 (RMC).

309 "pleaks": Englehardt, *Shadow Government*, pp. 120–26; Lena Groeger and Cora Currier, "Stacking Up the Administration's Drone Claims," *ProPublica*, April 28, 2015.

309 Obama finally acknowledged: Ta-Nehisi Coates, " 'Better Is Good': Obama on Reparations, Civil Rights, and the Art of the Possible," *Atlantic*, Dec. 21, 2016.

309 between 64 and 116: Karen DeYoung, "White House Releases Its Count of Civilian Deaths in Counterterrorism Operations under Obama," *Washington Post*, July 1, 2016.

309 474 in total: Coates, " 'Better Is Good' "; Micah Zenko, "Do Not Believe the U.S. Government's Official Numbers on Drone Strike Civilian Casualties," *Foreign Policy*, July 5, 2016.

309 In a subsequent investigation: "What to Know About the Civilian Casualty Files," *New York Times*, Dec. 18, 2021.

310 Bush-Obama-era program: Lubold and Harris, "Trump Broadens CIA Powers."

310 He began his presidency: Ian Shapira, "Trump Delays Full Release of Some JFK Assassination Files Until 2021, Bowing to National Security Concerns," *Washington Post*, April 26, 2018.

310 In actual practice: Ashley Parker et al., "'He Never Stopped Ripping Things Up': Inside Trump's Relentless Document Destruction Habits," *Washington Post*, Feb. 5, 2022; Tom Porter, "Trump Warned John Bolton of 'Legal Consequences' If He Publishes His Tell-All Memoir, Claiming That All Conversations with Him Are Classified," *Business Insider*, June 16, 2020.

310 Even Ronald Reagan: David E. Pozen, "The Leaky Leviathan: Why the Government Condemns and Condones Unlawful Disclosures of Information," *Harvard Law Review*, vol. 127 (Dec. 2003): p. 550.

311 "a recommitment": Joseph R. Biden, Jr., "Memorandum on Revitalizing America's Foreign Policy and National Security Workforce, Institutions, and Partnerships," Feb. 4, 2021, FAS.

311 backlog of FOIA requests: GAO, "Freedom of Information Act: Selected Agencies Adapted to the COVID-19 Pandemic but Face Ongoing Challenges and Backlogs," GAO-22-105040, 2022, pp. 23–24.

311 But the Biden administration: C. J. Ciaramella, "FOIA Advocates Say Biden Administration Is Ignoring Transparency Issues," *Reason*, Feb. 4, 2022.

311 "The volume": Avril Haines to Sen. Ron Wyden and Jerry Moran, Jan. 5, 2022, https://www.wyden.senate.gov.

311 "The great secret": Pozen, "Leaky Leviathan," p. 635.

312 The cost of this system: Ibid., p. 516.

313 "excessive concern": Schwartz, *Democracy in the Dark*, p. 4.

314 "recognizes that it": Exec. Order 12356, 47 Fed. Reg. 14874, April 2, 1982, FAS.

314 Pentagon spent $159,010: For 1955 figures, see "Department of Defense Reply to Questionnaire," Sept. 30, 1955; Mordecai Lee, "When Congress Tried to Cut Pentagon Public Relations: A Lesson from History," *Public Relations Review*, vol. 26, no. 2 (2000): pp. 131–54.

314 By 2016, it was: GAO, *Public Relations Spending: Reported Data on Related Federal Activities*, GAO-16-877R (2016), p. 11.

314 "safes, locks": "Department of Defense Reply to Questionnaire," Sept. 30, 1955.

314 When Congress mandated: ISOO, *Classification Related Costs for FY 1995* (Washington, D.C., 1996), p. 2, FAS.

314 In 2017—the last time: ISOO, *2017 Report to the President* (Washington, D.C., 2018), p. 4.

314 "Every gun": Dwight D. Eisenhower, "Chance for Peace," speech, American Society of Newspaper Editors, Washington, D.C., April 16, 1953.

9 THERE IS NO THERE THERE: THE BEST-KEPT SECRET

316 Imagine you have: U.S. Office of Personnel Management, "Questionnaire for National Security Questions," Dec. 2020, 5 CFR pts. 731, 732, 736.

316 "It is imperative": Ibid.

317 reviewers have broad discretion: DOJ, "Judicial Review of Claims of Discrimination in Security Clearance Determinations," 1997.

317 Even seemingly objective criteria: Tepring Piquado et al., "Assessing the Potential for Racial Bias in the Security Clearance Process," 2021, RAND Corporation; "Title VII—Racial Discrimination in Employment—Employers Use of Record of Arrests Not Leading to Conviction," *Wayne Law Review*, vol. 17, no. 1 (Jan.–Feb. 1971): p. 233.

317 "unquestionable loyalty": "Personnel Security Investigative Standards and Procedures Governing Eligibility for Access to Sensitive Compartmented Information and Other Controlled Access Program Information," ICPG 701.1, 2008, p. 2.

319 George W. Bush, for instance: David Priess, *The President's Book of Secrets: The Untold Story of Intelligence Briefings to America's Presidents from Kennedy to Obama* (New York: PublicAffairs, 2016), p. 259.

319 "most tightly guarded": Aki Peritz, "Think U.S. Intel Is in Decline? These Declassified Memos May Change Your Mind," *Washington Post*, Feb. 19, 2016.

320 "I'm sure that": Priess, *President's Book of Secrets*, p. 261.

320 "The CIA tells": Richard Reeves, *President Nixon: Alone in the White House* (New York: Simon & Schuster, 2001), p. 350.

320 "slick magazines": Harry S. Truman, "The President's News Conference," address, Executive Office Building, Washington, D.C., Oct. 4, 1951, HSTL.

320 William Langer, came up with: Sherman Kent, *Miscellaneous Studies: Military Secrets in an Open Society: The Yale Report*, MS-10 (1973), CIA-RDP86M00886R002100140005-2; Robin W. Winks, *Cloak and Gown: Scholars in the Secret War, 1939–1961* (New York: Morrow, 1987), pp. 457–61.

321   who was chosen: Kent, *Miscellaneous Studies*, p. 6.

321   Ten weeks later: CIA, *Estimates of Capabilities of the United States Forces In-Being* (1951), CIA-RDP79R00971A000300020002-0.

321   Kent judged: CIA, Ibid., p. 368; Robert S. Norris and Hans M. Kristensen, "Global Nuclear Weapons Inventories, 1945–2010," *Bulletin of the Atomic Scientists*, vol. 66, no. 4 (July 2010): pp. 77–83.

322   When asked by reporters: Harry S. Truman, "President's News Conference," Oct. 4, 1951.

322   The president was wrong: Steven T. Usdin, *Bureau of Spies: The Secret Connections Between Espionage and Journalism in Washington* (Amherst, N.Y.: Prometheus Books, 2018), pp. 280, 289.

322   ultimate sources: Kent, *Miscellaneous Studies*, pp. 19, 30–32. When he wrote about this twenty years later, Kent pulled his punches, because friends in the Pentagon "didn't like the earlier drafts" (Kent to Editor of *Studies in Intelligence*, April 11, 1973, attached to *Miscellaneous Studies*).

322   All copies: Winks, *Cloak and Gown*, p. 460.

323   An intelligence agency: As of 1997, the CIA's own library subscribed to seventeen hundred serials, held 150,000 books, and stored millions of documents. "I think a lot of people have a deep misconception of what we do" at the CIA, one of the librarians explained. "We do research for people. We look for information for people. We don't all wear trench coats with large hats pulled over our heads. That is a very small part of what we are." (Susan L. Wright, "50 Years of Silent Service: Inside the CIA Library," *Information Outlook*, Feb. 1997.)

323   America's oldest intelligence agency: Ludwell Lee Montague, *General Walter Bedell Smith as Director of Central Intelligence, October 1950–February 1953* (University Park: Penn State University Press, 1992), pp. 131–36.

323   "a peculiar kind": AEC, *In the Matter of J. Robert Oppenheimer: Transcript of Hearing Before Personnel Security Board and Texts of Principal Documents and Letters* (Cambridge, Mass., 1970), p. 467.

323   This kind of psychology: Matthew Connelly et al., "'General, I Have Fought Just As Many Nuclear Wars As You Have': Forecasts, Future Scenarios, and the Politics of Armageddon," *American Historical Review*, vol. 117, no. 5 (Dec. 2012): 1438–39.

324   "The thing that rather": David E. Lilienthal, *The Journals of David E. Lilienthal*, vol. 2, *The Atomic Energy Years, 1945–1950* (New York: Harper & Row, 1964), p. 376.

324 "The Official Secrets Act": Antony Jay and Jonathan Lynn, "Jobs for the Boys," *Yes Minister*, BBC Two, April 7, 1980.

324 "fanatically defended": Max Weber, *From Max Weber: Essays in Sociology*, trans. H. H. Gerth and C. Wright Mills (Abingdon, U.K.: Routledge, 1948), p. 233.

325 "With great excitement": Robert Jervis, *Why Intelligence Fails: Lessons from the Iranian Revolution and the Iraq War* (Ithaca, N.Y.: Cornell University Press, 2010), p. 9.

325 "next morning's newspapers": Ibid., p. 11.

325 CIA seemed completely uninterested: Ibid., p. 10.

325 It is also possible: John Deutch, "Statement of the Director of Central Intelligence on the Clandestine Services and the Damage Caused by Aldrich Ames," Dec. 7, 1995, Moynihan Papers, pt. II, box 286. See also chap. 6 of this book.

325 "Iran is not": Gary Sick, *All Fall Down: America's Tragic Encounter with Iran* (New York: Random House, 1986), pp. 92–93.

326 "is expected to remain": James A. Bill, *The Eagle and the Lion: The Tragedy of American-Iranian Relations* (Berkeley: University of California Press, 2003), p. 258.

326 some obvious reasons: Jervis, *Why Intelligence Fails*, p. 23.

326 Perhaps it was no: Ibid., p. 22.

326 "Diplomatic telegrams": Edward G. Shirley, "Can't Anybody Here Play This Game?," *Atlantic*, Feb. 1998.

326 Psychologists have confirmed: Mark Travers et al., "The Secrecy Heuristic: Inferring Quality from Secrecy in Foreign Policy Contexts," *Political Psychology*, vol. 35, no. 1 (2014): pp. 101, 105–8.

327 in a follow-up study: Tore Pedersen and Pia Therese Jansen, "Seduced by Secrecy—Perplexed by Complexity: Effects of Secret vs Open-Source on Intelligence Credibility and Analytic Confidence," *Intelligence and National Security*, vol. 34, no. 6 (June 2019): p. 890.

327 "innocents": Kent, *Miscellaneous Studies*, p. 19.

327 "the first refuge": House Committee on Government Operations, *Availability of Information from Federal Departments and Agencies: The First Five Years and Progress of Study, August 1959–July 1960*, H.R. Rep. No. 86-2084, 1960, p. 36.

327 "In such a context": Ritchie P. Lowry, "Toward a Sociology of Secrecy and Security Systems," *Social Problems*, vol. 19, no. 4 (1972): p. 440.

328 ". . . the Government": Affidavit of Max Frankel, *New York Times Co. v. United States*, 403 U.S. 713 (1971).

328 no radical muckraker: Seymour M. Hersh, *Reporter: A Memoir* (New York: Random House, 2019), pp. 167–70.

328 Frankel's high-level access: Archconservative Senator Jesse Helms believed much the same thing: he and other members of Congress frequently found "national security" used to cover up information "which would be potentially politically embarrassing to officials in the Executive Branch or which would make known an illegal or indefensible policy" (Helms to Moynihan, July 15, 1996, Moynihan Papers, pt. II, box 284).

328 Pentagon Papers case: Ellsberg later revealed that he was also planning to release even more documents related to U.S. nuclear-war planning, but was thwarted when the documents were accidentally destroyed (Daniel Ellsberg, *The Doomsday Machine: Confessions of a Nuclear War Planner* [New York: Bloomsbury, 2017], pp. 5–10).

328 purpose of the leak: David Pozen, "The Leaky Leviathan: Why the Government Condemns and Condones Unlawful Disclosures of Information," *Harvard Law Review*, vol. 127 (2013): pp. 529–30. This has been true for a long time. See, e.g., "Report to the Secretary of Defense by the Committee on Classified Information," Nov. 8, 1956, Morgan Papers, Box 22, Security Order—Executive Order of November 3, 1953—Classification of Information #1, DDEL.

329 These officials: Spies and moles, on the other hand, happily deal in bulk. Aldrich Ames gave the Soviets fifteen to twenty *feet* of classified documents during just one assignment. Unlike most reporters, analysts can pore through seemingly arcane information for useful tidbits, and combine it with information they already have from other sources. (Deutch, "Statement of the Director," Dec. 7, 1995.)

329 "Cablegate": Julian Assange, *Julian Assange: The Unauthorised Autobiography*, ePub ed. (Edinburgh: Canongate Books, 2011), pp. 189–93.

329 Ironically, the State Department: On the effort to track the distribution list of the Pentagon Papers, see Egil Krogh and David Young to John Ehrlichman, Aug. 3, 1971, reprinted in "Memos Showing Concern Over Leaks," *New York Times*, July 19, 1974. On the implementation of the data-index recommendation, see Memorandum for the President from Interagency Classification Review Committee, ca. March 1973, and "Interagency Classification Review Committee Progress Report," March 31, 1973, both in *Documents of the National Security Council: Fourth Sup-*

plement (Frederick, Md.: University Publications of America, 1987).

329 Also ironically: David Langbart et al., "Appraisal of Records Covered by N1-59-07-3-P," June 4, 2007, on file with author.

329 Assange himself apparently meant: Assange blamed a *Guardian* editor, David Leigh, for publishing the password. But Leigh said that he was told the password was temporary, and he could not know that Assange inexplicably used the same password for other copies of the database, which Assange encouraged other Web sites to mirror. Moreover, one of Assange's associates had already been sharing unredacted cables with the pro-Putin government of Belarus. (Jerome Taylor, "Guardian Journalist Accused of Recklessly Disclosing Password," *Independent*, Sept. 2, 2011; "Wikileaks, Belarus and Israel Shamir," *Index on Censorship*, Feb. 5, 2011.)

329 The leak revealed: Mark MacKinnon, "Leaked Cables Spark Witch-Hunt for Chinese 'Rats,'" *Globe and Mail*, Sept. 14, 2011.

330 "We'll continue saying": Stephen A. Seche, "General Petraeus' Meeting with Saleh on Security Assistance, AQAP Strikes," Jan. 4, 2010; Scott Shane and Andrew W. Lehren, "Leaked Cables Offer Raw Look at U.S. Diplomacy," *New York Times*, Nov. 28, 2010.

330 already been reported: Thom Shanker and Mark Landler, "U.S. Aids Yemeni Raids on Al Qaeda, Officials Say," *New York Times*, Dec. 18, 2009.

331 One compilation: Herbert Mitgang, *Dangerous Dossiers: Exposing the Secret War Against America's Greatest Authors* (New York: Ballantine, 1988).

331 "Some war": Daniel Patrick Moynihan, *Secrecy: The American Experience* (New Haven: Yale University Press, 1998), pp. 42–43. On the number of employees, see William Webster, "FBI Proposals to Amend the Freedom of Information Act," June 19, 1979, Moynihan Papers, pt. II, box 1698.

331 "convince the public": "Oswald, Lee, Murder by Ruby," Nov. 24, 1973, John F. Kennedy Assassination Records, box 4, USNA.

331 "The public must": Nicholas Katzenbach to Bill Moyers, Nov. 25, 1963, FBI, https://www.maryferrell.org/showDoc.html?docId=62 268###relPageId=29&tab=page.

331 Did Katzenbach and Hoover: Select Committee on Assassinations, *Report of the Select Committee on Assassinations*, H.R. Rep. No. 95-1828, 1979, pp. 195–96. They only admitted destroying the note years later, when others came forward.

332 U.S. special forces: Brian Adam Jones, "The Majority of American

Combat Fatalities Since 2015 Have Been US Special Ops," *Business Insider*, May 26, 2017; Kyle Rempfer, "SOCOM: Bulk of War Casualties May Be Operators but SOF Readiness Is at All-Time High," *Military Times*, July 26, 2019.

332   Contrast this record: Remarks by Richard Stolz, May 31, 1988, CIA-RDP90G01353R002000070002-5; "The Stars on the Wall," April 30, 2013, CIA; Angus MacLean Theurmer to Deputy Director for Management and Services, "Memorial Stars in the Lobby," April 30, 1974, CIA-RDP87-01130R000200160011-0.

333   "We in intelligence": Proposed Remarks by William H. Webster, May 31, 1988, CIA-RDP90G01353R002000070002-5.

333   "Those of us here": Remarks by Stolz, May 31, 1988.

333   senior CIA leaders equate: Theurmer to Deputy Director, April 30, 1974; "Stars on the Wall."

333   "essence of the CIA": Paul D. Shinkman, "CIA Adds Names to Memorial Wall," *U.S. News & World Report*, May 24, 2016.

333   decision to build it: Director of Personnel to Director of Central Intelligence, "Memorial Plaque," Oct. 5, 1973, CIA-RDP87-01130R000200160016-5.

333   That was the year: On Watergate, see Tim Weiner, *Legacy of Ashes: The History of the CIA* (New York: Doubleday, 2007), pp. 327–29. For the dossier itself, see Howard J. Osborn to Executive Secretary of CIA Management Committee, "Family Jewels," May 16, 1973; Shinkman, "CIA Adds Names."

334   extremely safe career choice: Ian Shapira, "A CIA Suicide Sparks Hard Questions About the Agency's Memorial Wall," *Washington Post*, May 21, 2019. To be sure, some who died in accidents or during medical procedures were overseas doing dangerous work. See, e.g., "Remembering CIA's African American Heroes," CIA, July 10, 2014.

334   "gives us psychological problems": Donnalley provided some good reasons, such as the risk of losing a valued intelligence source. But Nixon's declassification order specifically exempted intelligence sources or methods, or anything that would endanger a specific individual. It is all the more striking, then, that Donnalley repeatedly emphasized how merely reviewing records for declassification "involves a considerable amount of trauma as a result of our previous history." (Gail F. Donnalley, "Declassification in an Open Society," *Studies in Intelligence*, vol. 18, no. 3 [1974]: pp. 11–18.)

334   what form this trauma took: For an insightful sociological analysis, see Fred M. Kaiser, "Secrecy, Intelligence, and Community: The

U.S. Intelligence Community," in *Secrecy, a Cross-Cultural Perspective*, ed. Stanton K. Tefft (New York: Human Sciences Press, 1980), pp. 273–96.

335 "we would have more": Office of the Director of Defense Research and Engineering, *Report of the Defense Science Board Task Force on Secrecy* (1970), p. 8, FAS.

335 George Kennan judged: Kennan to Daniel Patrick Moynihan, March 25, 1997, Moynihan Papers, pt. II, box 3014.

336 Howard Baker: James Q. Wilson, in relating this fact, wrote that he had had exactly the same experience while serving on the President's Foreign Intelligence Advisory Board—everything was revealed within days by the *Washington Post* or some other media outlet (Wilson to Moynihan, Oct. 25, 1996, Moynihan Papers, pt. II, box 284).

336 Reagan's secretary of state: Shultz, Memorandum of Conversation, Jan. 5, 1996, Moynihan Papers, pt. II, box 280.

336 "very narrow number": Jack Goldsmith, *Power and Constraint: The Accountable Presidency After 9/11* (New York: Norton, 2012), p. 68. "The very adjective 'covert' is a misnomer," Arthur Schlesinger observed. "Covert action is often easy to detect..." (Arthur Schlesinger, "A Democrat Looks at Foreign Policy," *Foreign Affairs*, vol. 66, no. 2 [1987]: p. 270.) The same is also true of "covert operatives." It is now illegal to deliberately reveal their identity. But back in 1975, the *Chicago Tribune* published a guide to unmasking CIA spies operating under diplomatic cover. They all worked in the same part of the embassy, stuck together when they went out, were listed as "Foreign Service Reserve" in the State Department's Foreign Service List, and had conspicuous gaps in their published biographies. The Agency would replace one officer with another ostensibly with the exact same cover title, same apartment, and even the same car. (John Marks, "How to Unmask CIA Spies Hidden in our Embassies," *Chicago Tribune*, Jan. 19, 1975.) See also Jonathan Haslam, "How to Explain the KGB's Amazing Success Identifying CIA Agents in the Field?," *Salon*, Sept. 25, 2015.

336 "The United States Government": Donald Rumsfeld, "U.S. Government Incapable of Keeping a Secret," Nov. 2, 2005, FAS.

336 CIA withholds 82 percent: The Information Security Oversight Office no longer provides this comparative breakdown of automatic declassification rates by department and agency. For the most recent data, see ISOO, *2014 Report to the President* (Washington, D.C., 2015).

336 after he was "read in": Jervis, *Why Intelligence Fails*, pp. 7–9.

336 "great stuff!": David A. Hatch, *Presidential Transition 2001: NSA Briefs a New Administration*, 4045841 (2004), p. 17, NSA.

337 "information overload": Barton Gellman and Greg Miller, "'Black Budget' Summary Details U.S. Spy Network's Successes, Failures and Objectives," *Washington Post*, Aug. 29, 2013. For a good introduction to the challenge information overload presents to intelligence agencies, see Robert Mandel, *Global Data Shock: Strategic Ambiguity, Deception, and Surprise in an Age of Information Overload* (Stanford: Stanford University Press, 2019).

337 "Conspiring against": CIA Center for the Study of Intelligence, *Critique of the Codeword Compartment in the CIA* (Washington, D.C., 1977), CIA-RDP83B00823R000900180001-6.

337 "uneven guidance": ODNI Community Technology Governance, *Intelligence Community Classification Guidance: Findings and Recommendations Report* (2008), p. iv, FAS.

337 In 1996: Commission on Protecting and Reducing Government Secrecy, "Possible Recommendations and Background Materials," June 28, 1996, Moynihan Papers, box 292.

338 There are even cases: For these and many more excellent examples, see "Redactions: The Declassified File," National Security Archive, April 22, 2019.

338 Academics have run: Samuel-Azran et al., "Jewish-Israeli Attitudes Towards the Iranian Football Team During the 2014 World Cup Tournament," *Media, War & Conflict*, vol. 9, no. 3 (2016): pp. 258–59; Jamie Boydstun, Jeralynn S. Cossman, and Denise Krause, "Oral Health Interventions in Appalachian States," *Journal of Appalachian Studies*, vol. 24, no. 1 (2018): pp. 74–76.

338 At a conference: "FOIA@ 50 Conference Day 2," video, YouTube, posted by Columbia Journalism School, June 3, 2016. Miriam Nisbet, founding director of the National Archives Office of Government Information Services, eventually agreed it would be a "fascinating study." None of the panelists could explain why it had never been done.

339 of the 30,490 e-mail chains: Note that the oft-cited figure of thirty thousand Clinton e-mails is actually the number of e-mail threads, many of which contain multiple messages. For more on this analysis, see Matthew Connelly and Rohan Shaw, "Here's What Data Science Tells Us About Hillary Clinton's Emails," *Washington Post*, Nov. 2, 2016.

340 "why the State Department": Michael S. Schmidt and Matt

Apuzzo, "Inquiry Sought in Hillary Clinton's Use of Email," *New York Times*, July 23, 2015.

340 "extremely careless": "Statement by FBI Director James B. Comey on the Investigation of Secretary Hillary Clinton's Use of a Personal E-Mail System," July 5, 2016, FBI.

340 "gross negligence": DOJ Office of the Inspector General, *A Review of Various Actions by the Federal Bureau of Investigation and Department of Justice in Advance of the 2016 Election*, Oversight and Review Division no. 18-04 (2018), pp. 29–34.

340 When he was later found: Kevin Schmidt and Thomas Kimbrell, "Records Show How Former FBI Director James Comey Misled the DOJ Inspector General About His Personal Email Use," Cause of Action Institute, Dec. 7, 2018.

341 secrecy is "random"?: Abbe David Lowell, "The Broken System of Classifying Government Documents," *New York Times*, Feb. 29, 2016.

341 "practically everything": Affidavit of Max Frankel, *New York Times Co. v. United States*, 403 U.S. 713 (1971).

341 We devised our own experiment: For a fuller description than is given in the text, see Renato Rocha Souza et al., "Using Artificial Intelligence to Identify State Secrets," draft, https://arxiv.org/pdf /1611.00356.pdf.

342 resulting from technical problems: "Central Foreign Policy File (CFPF), 1973–1979," NARA.

343 "a subject which is": Philip P. Alston to Richard Holbrooke, "Information on Indian Ocean; Information on 1977 Meat," Dec. 1, 1977, https://search.wikileaks.org.

343 Lebanese Christian leaders: "South Lebanon Situation—Phalange View," July 6, 1977, CFPF.

343 Japanese government's sensitivity: "USG Safeguards Review at Tokai Mura," Sept. 7, 1977, CFPF.

344 president of Cyprus: "Rumored Kidnapping of President Kyprianou's Son," Dec. 15, 1977, CFPF.

344 almost certainly overclassified: "Earth Station," April 23, 1977, CFPF.

345 category has different names: Peter Galison, "Secrecy in Three Acts," *Social Research*, vol. 77 (Fall 2010): p. 966.

345 Unlike "top secret": Daniel J. Metcalfe, "The Nature of Government Secrecy," *Government Information Quarterly*, vol. 26 (2009): p. 308.

347 The documents are displayed: Mary Lynn Ritzenthaler and Catherine Nicholson, "The Declaration of Independence and the Hand of Time," *Prologue*, Fall 2016.

349 "to penetrate": John Acton, *Lectures on Modern History* (London: Macmillan, 1906), p. 10.

349 "Power tends": John Acton, *Historical Essays & Studies* (London: Macmillan, 1907), p. 504.

350 To see fully: Terry Cook, "Archival Science and Postmodernism: New Formulations for Old Concepts," *Archival Science*, vol. 1, no. 1 (March 2001), p. 8, citing Jacques Le Goff.

350 When power shifts: Patricia Kennedy Grimsted, "Twice Plundered or 'Twice Saved'? Identifying Russia's 'Trophy' Archives and the Loot of the Reichssicherheitshauptamt," *Holocaust and Genocide Studies*, vol. 15, no. 2 (Fall 2001): pp. 192–93; Grimsted, "'Trophy' Archives and Non-Restitution: Russia's Cultural 'Cold War' with the European Community," *Problems of Post-Communism*, vol. 45, no. 3 (1998): 6.

350 "The Archivist's career": Terry Cook, "What Is Past Is Prologue: A History of Archival Ideas Since 1898, and the Future Paradigm Shift," *Archivaria*, vol. 43 (Spring 1997): 23.

351 But, however selfless: Historians have long understood archives as institutions of state power, typically citing the French theorist Jacques Derrida. But they rarely delve deeper into the rich intellectual history produced by archivists themselves. For an excellent introduction, see Cook, "What Is Past Is Prologue," pp. 17–58.

351 When the U.S. government: Ibid., p. 26.

351 "The struggle of man": Milan Kundera, *The Book of Laughter and Forgetting* (New York: Penguin, 1980), p. 3.

351 in 1890, abolitionists: Amy Chazkel, "History Out of the Ashes: Remembering Brazilian Slavery After Rui Barbosa's Burning of the Documents," in *From the Ashes of History: Loss and Recovery of Archives and Libraries in Modern Latin America*, eds. Carlos Aguirre and Javier Villa-Flores (Raleigh, N.C.: Editorial A Contracorriente, 2015), pp. 70–72.

352 Conversely, archives: See, for example, Elidor Mëhilli, "Documents as Weapons: The Uses of a Dictatorship's Archives," *Contemporary European History*, vol. 28, no. 1 (2019): pp. 88–89.

352 In India: Ashis Nandy, "History's Forgotten Doubles," *History and Theory*, vol. 34, no. 2 (1995): p. 60.

352 "That place was like": Manuela Adreoni and Ernesto Londoño,

"Loss of Indigenous Works in Brazil Museum Fire Felt 'like a New Genocide,'" *New York Times*, Sept. 13, 2018.

353 Firefighters arrived: "The 1973 Fire, National Personnel Records Center," NARA.

353 we will never know: Ibid.; Walter W. Stender and Evans Walker, "The National Personnel Records Center Fire: A Study in Disaster," *American Archivist*, vol. 37, no. 4 (Oct. 1974): pp. 521–22.

353 The State Department had already: "Administrative History of the Department of State," vol. 1, chap. 13, Administrative Histories, State, box 4, LBJL; "Airgram Distribution Analysis," March 15, 1967, RG59, CFPF, 1967–1969, Administration CR to CR4, box 47, USNA.

355 This particular record: Jakarta Embassy to Secretary of State, "Ford-Sukarno Meeting," Dec. 6, 1975, National Security Archive.

355 "That will leak": Mark Hertsgaard, "The Secret Life of Henry Kissinger: Minutes of a 1975 Meeting with Lawrence Eagleburger," *Nation*, Oct. 29, 1990.

355 Other notable gaps: Bruce P. Montgomery, "'Source Material'— Sequestered from the Court of History: The Kissinger Transcripts," *Presidential Studies Quarterly*, vol. 34 (2004): p. 870.

357 "culture of destruction": Tim Weiner, "CIA Destroyed Files on 1953 Iran Coup," *New York Times*, May 29, 1997. See also "Opening Up CIA History," *New York Times*, May 30, 1997.

357 "Since the program": "1973: Richard Helms and Sid Gottlieb Ordered All Records Re: Mind-Control Projects Destroyed," Alliance for Human Research Protection, Jan. 18, 2015.

357 "innocuous information": *Halkin v. Helms*, 598 F.2d 1 (D.C. Cir. 1978).

357 if documents are destroyed: David A. Wallace, "Preserving the U.S. Government's White House Electronic Mail: Archival Challenges and Policy Implications," paper, Sixth DELOS Workshop: Preserving Digital Information, Lisbon, June 19, 1998, p. 2.

358 Nevertheless, on the last: Ibid., pp. 3–6; *Armstrong v. Executive Office of the President*, 810 F. Supp. 335 (D.D.C. 1993).

358 Dedicated National Archives staff: Wallace, "Preserving Electronic Mail," pp. 11–13.

358 By the year 2000: The figures for declassification costs were included in the annual reports of the Information Security Oversight Office, which are available here: "ISOO Annual Report Archive, Calendar Years 1979 through 2019," NARA. After 2012, the declassification costs of the intelligence community were also included, complicating comparisons over time. But in 2017—the

last year ISOO tried to estimate these costs—the total for the entire government was $103 million.

359   Agency established a "factory": Carla Anne Robbin, "Psst, Want to Hear Some CIA Secrets?," *Wall Street Journal*, March 19, 1998.

359   CIA factory shut down: ISOO, *2012 Annual Report to the President* (Washington, D.C., 2013), p. 26.

359   The overall budget: These figures, for the NARA operating budget, are published online each year for NARA's "Performance Budget."

359   absorbed by Lockheed Martin: GAO, "Electronic Records Archive: National Archives Needs to Strengthen Its Capacity to Use Earned Value Techniques to Manage and Oversee Development," GAO-11-86 (2011), p. 22.

360   National Archives now cannot: Minutes of the Advisory Committee on Historical Diplomatic Documentation, June 17–18, 2019, and March 2–3, 2020, both at https://history.state.gov/about/hac.

360   Year after year: "NARA Challenges Regarding Staffing and Responsibilities," Dec. 20, 2019, on file with author.

361   In 2013, the Archives': See NARA, Office of the Inspector General, *Audit of the Electronic Records Archives System's Ability to Preserve Records*, audit report no. 13-03, 2013, pp. 24–25.

361   management continues to use: NARA, Office of the Inspector General, *Audit of NARA's Legacy Systems*, 18-AUD-06 (2018), pp. 7–8.

361   Nevertheless, all federal: Jeffery Zeints to David Ferriero, Aug. 24, 2012; NARA, *FY 2020 Congressional Justification* (2019), p. 3.

361   supposed to be more efficient: Michael Moss, in Moss and Barbara Endicott-Popovsky, *Is Digital Different?: How Information Creation, Capture, Preservation and Discovery Are Being Transformed* (London: Facet Publishing, 2015), pp. 6–7.

361   In 2007, archivists: David Langbart et al., "Appraisal of Records Covered by N1-59-07-3-P," June 4, 2007, on file with author.

362   Solon Buck: James Gregory Bradsher, "An Administrative History of the Disposal of Federal Records, 1789–1949," *Provenance, Journal of the Society of Georgia Archivists*, vol. 3, no. 2 (Jan. 1985): p. 13.

362   in December 1940: Peter M. Rutkoff, William B. Scott, and Marc Bloch, "Letters to America: The Correspondence of Marc Bloch, 1940–41," *French Historical Studies*, vol. 12, no. 2 (1981): p. 278.

364   fewer than 15 percent: The data is available at "Wars/International Relations: Diplomatic Records," NARA.

364   One from 1975: Emma North-Best, "State Department Cable Shows Exposure of Lockheed Bribes Threatened NATO's Stabil-

ity," *MuckRock*, Nov. 7, 2018. The subject of the scandal, Prince Bernhard, happened to be a founding member of the Bilderberg Group. Like many such bribes, it was apparently given with the full knowledge of the CIA and the Pentagon.

365 "thorough, accurate": William B. McAllister et al., *Toward Thorough, Accurate, and Reliable: A History of the Foreign Relations of the United States Series* (Washington, D.C.: DOS Office of the Historian, 2015), p. 2.

366 Other statistics: Compare "Status of the Foreign Relations of the United States Series," available here (https://history.state.gov/historicaldocuments/status-of-the-series) with the archived versions of the same Web page available through the Wayback Machine.

367 In 2021, the National Archives: See "Unauthorized Disposition of Federal Records," NARA.

367 Colin Powell: Adam Sneed, "Powell Says He Doesn't Have Any of His State emails," *Politico*, March 8, 2015.

367 Some twenty-two million: "Millions of Bush Administration E-Mails Recovered," CNN, Dec. 14, 2009.

367 "the real issues": Hillary Clinton, *What Happened* (New York: Simon & Schuster, 2017), p. 309.

367 "never been used": DOJ Office of the Inspector General, *A Review of Various Actions by the Federal Bureau of Investigation and Department of Justice in Advance of the 2016 Election*, no. 18-04 (2018), pp. 36, 257.

368 "the situation": Personal communication, on file with author.

368 "involvement on major decisions": "Request for Records Disposition Authority: Records Schedule Number DAA-0059-2019-0002," Dec. 7, 2018, DOS. The request was subsequently withdrawn, and taken down from government Web sites. It is not clear what the department will propose in its place.

369 "health, safety": The Department of the Interior and the National Archives had already decided they should delete files on endangered species, offshore-drilling inspections, and the safety of drinking water. They even claimed that papers from a case in which the department mismanaged Native American land and assets—resulting in a multibillion-dollar settlement—would be of no interest to researchers. (Megan Black, "Appetite for Destruction? Making Sense of the Interior Department's Request to Destroy Files," *Cambridge Core Blog*, Nov. 5, 2018.)

369 The last inspector-general report: "At the current pace NARA may never get through the processing backlog if no changes are made

to the presidential libraries processing program" (NARA Office of the Inspector General, *Audit of Processing of Textual Records*, report no. 13-14 [2013], pp. 12–16).

369   After Obama left: "NARA Challenges Regarding Staffing and Responsibilities," Dec. 20, 2019.

370   Years ago, much of: Personal communication with the author.

370   The IRS: Michael Wyland, "IRS Lois Lerner Emails Impossible to Find or Save," *Nonprofit Quarterly*, June 25, 2015.

370   Immigration and Customs Enforcement: Department of Homeland Security Office of the Inspector General, *ICE Needs to Improve Its Oversight of Segregation Use in Detention Facilities*, OIG-22-01 (Washington, D.C., 2021), pp. 5–7.

371   Gina Haspel: Glenn Kessler, "CIA Director Nominee Haspel and the Destruction of Interrogation Tapes: Contradictions and Questions," *Washington Post*, May 11, 2018.

371   "I don't think": Karoun Demirjan and Shane Harris, "Gina Haspel, Trump's Pick to Lead CIA, Pledges She Won't Restart Interrogation Program," *Washington Post*, May 9, 2018.

371   Thanks to Haspel's decision: Matthew Connelly, "State Secrecy, Archival Negligence, and the End of History As We Know It," Knight First Amendment Institute, Sept. 13, 2018.

371   "historical monuments": Laila Hussein Moustafa, "Cultural Heritage and Preservation: Lessons from World War II and the Contemporary Conflict in the Middle East," *American Archivist*, vol. 79 (Fall/Winter 2016): p. 325.

371   April 9, 2003: Robert Fisk, "Americans Defend Two Untouchable Ministries from the Hordes of Looters," *Independent*, April 14, 2003.

371   Baath Party: Mary-Jane Deeb, Michael Albin, and Alan Haley, *Report on the National Library and the House of Manuscripts, October 27–November 3, 2003*, LOC and DOS Mission to Baghdad, 2003.

371   "Stuff happens": Nabil Al-Tikriti, "'Stuff Happens': A Brief Overview of the 2003 Destruction of Iraqi Manuscript Collections, Archives, and Libraries," *Library Trends*, vol. 55 (Winter 2007): p. 743.

372   "boggles the mind": William A. Mayer, "Session 1 Panel—2014 CRL Leviathan Forum: Conference on Leviathan: Libraries and Government Information in the Age of Big Data," YouTube video, April 24, 2014.

372   "monitoring role": This initiative was not publicly confirmed until I published an op-ed in *The New York Times* warning about the

pitfalls, as well as the problems with the ICE and State Department records schedules, prompting an angry rebuttal from the archivist of the United States, David Ferriero (Matthew Connelly, "Why You May Never Learn the Truth About ICE," *New York Times*, Feb. 4, 2020; David S. Ferriero, "The National Archives Responds," *New York Times*, Feb. 7, 2020).

373 "The owl": Georg Wilhelm Fredrich Hegel, preface, *Elements of the Philosophy of Right*, trans. Allen W. Wood and H. B. Nisbet (Cambridge, U.K.: Cambridge University Press, 1991), p. 23.

373 In our experiment: Joseph Risi et al., "Predicting History," *Nature Human Behaviour*, vol. 3 (Sept. 2019): pp. 906–12.

374 Inspiring stories: Margot Lee Shetterly, *Hidden Figures: The American Dream and the Untold Story of the Black Women Mathematicians Who Helped Win the Space Race* (New York: HarperCollins, 2016).

375 NASA seems to have: Zoë Jackson, "Archiving the Final Frontier: Preserving Space History for the Future," *Perspectives on History*, vol. 56, no. 5 (May 1, 2018).

CONCLUSION: THE END OF HISTORY AS WE KNOW IT

378 The biggest worry: Abbe David Lowell, "The Broken System of Classifying Government Documents," *New York Times*, Feb. 29, 2016.

378 White House had specifically: "Presidential Memorandum— Implementation of the Executive Order, 'Classified National Security Information,'" December 29, 2009.

380 "The government must": PIDB, *Setting Priorities: An Essential Step in Transforming Declassification* (2014), p. 4.

381 "The heritage of the past": Jessie Kratz, "The National Archives' Larger-Than-Life Statues," NARA, *Pieces of History*, May 22, 2018.

381 *Guardianship:* Ibid.

386 "redaction integrity": Personal communication with the author.

386 fifty-eight pages long: ISOO, *2017 Report to the President* (Washington, D.C., 2018).

386 "many of the same": ISOO, *2018 Report to the President* (Washington, D.C., 2019). As this book goes to bed, the PIDB is showing signs of life, with a flurry of appointments and public meetings. But the ISOO is still not reporting any data on declassification.

387 "reflect how agencies": Ibid.

387 "We're ringing": Steven Aftergood, "Modernization of Secrecy System Is Stalled," Aug. 21, 2019, FAS.

390 They included a large facility: James Mann, *Rise of the Vulcans:*

The History of Bush's War Cabinet (New York: Penguin, 2004), pp. 139–43.

390 Long before, large-scale shelters: Erica X. Eisen, "Blackness and the Bomb," *Boston Review*, June 29, 2021.

390 At the CIA, not one woman: Walter Pincus, "CIA and the 'Glass Ceiling' Secret," *Washington Post*, Sept. 9, 1994.

391 "cultural imperative": *Glass Ceiling Study Summary* (1992), CIA.

391 1991 Pentagon study: Theodore R. Sarbin, *Homosexuality and Personnel Security* (Defense Personnel Security Research and Education Center, 1991), p. 30.

391 When new leaders: *Director's Diversity in Leadership Study* (2015), Homeland Security Digital Library.

392 the same troubling legacy: National Geospatial-Intelligence Agency, *State of Black Promotions at the National Geospatial-Intelligence Agency* (2018).

392 Historians are still surveying: For an excellent introduction, see Paul A. Kramer, "Shades of Sovereignty: Racialized Power, the United States and the World," in *Explaining the History of American Foreign Relations*, 3rd edition, eds. Frank Costigliola and Michael Hogan (New York: Cambridge University Press, 2016), pp. 245–70.

392 Even well-studied topics: Robert D. Dean, *Imperial Brotherhood: Gender and the Making of Cold War Foreign Policy* (Amherst: University of Massachusetts Press, 2003); Amy J. Rutenberg, *Rough Draft: Cold War Military Manpower Policy and the Origins of Vietnam-Era Draft Resistance* (Ithaca, N.Y.: Cornell University Press, 2019).

393 "brown people": Gary R. Hess, *Vietnam and the United States: Origins and Legacy of a War* (Boston: Twayne, 1990), p. 29.

393 "the one and a half billion" and "a constant worry": NSC Meetings, May 28 and Aug. 18, 1959, NSC Series, AWF, DDEL.

393 "strong men": Ebere Nwaubani, *The United States and Decolonization in West Africa, 1950–1960* (Rochester, N.Y.: University of Rochester Press, 2001), p. 50.

393 For John F. Kennedy: Walter LaFeber, *America, Russia, and the Cold War, 1945–1992* (New York: McGraw-Hill, 1993), p. 232.

393 "There are 3 billion": Remarks to American and Korean Servicemen at Camp Stanley, Nov. 1966, in *Public Papers of the Presidents of the United States: Lyndon B. Johnson* (Washington, D.C.: GPO, 1966), bk. II, p. 1287.

394 You can see the difference: Cameron Averill, Ye Seul Byeon, and Matthew Connelly, "What Can Computational Methods Reveal

about Diplomatic History and the Future of the Historical Profession?" Society for Historians of American Foreign Relations
annual conference, June 17, 2022.

395 even the 1970s: Niall Ferguson, *The Shock of the Global: The 1970s
in Perspective* (Cambridge, Mass.: Belknap Press of Harvard University Press, 2010), introduction.

395 And might not: For a sterling example of how a determined historian can pursue every avenue to uncover more recent and extremely
relevant history, see Mary Sarotte, *Not One Inch: America, Russia, and the Making of Post–Cold War Stalemate* (New Haven: Yale
University Press, 2021). This study required dozens of requests
to the Interagency Security Classification Appeals Panel, which
produced a trove of previously denied documents on U.S.-Russian
meetings in the 1990s. But such a strategy would be fruitless
now. In the most recent report, for 2020, ISCAP reported having
received only forty-five new requests. This is far fewer than were
recorded in previous years, likely because most people have given
up. Of these, they resolved exactly two, leaving a backlog of 1,313
appeals. (ISOO, *2020 Report to the President* [Washington, D.C.,
2021].)

396 "proceeded upon": Thucydides, *The History of the Peloponnesian
War*, trans. Richard Crawley (Project Gutenberg, 2003), p. 20.

396 a profound change: Tim Hitchcock, "Confronting the Digital: Or
How Academic History Writing Lost the Plot," *Cultural and Social
History*, vol. 10, no. 1 (2013): pp. 14–18. Studies have shown that,
though digital sources are more likely to be consulted, scholars are
less likely to cite them, instead preferring to footnote a manuscript
source for the very same information (Donghee Sinn and Nicholas Soares, "Historians' Use of Digital Archival Collections: The
Web, Historical Scholarship, and Archival Research," *Journal of
the Association for Information Science and Technology*, vol. 65, no. 9
[2014]: pp. 1794–1809).

396 scholars are actually becoming: Lara Putnam, "The Trans-
national and the Text-Searchable: Digitized Sources and the
Shadows They Cast," *American Historical Review*, vol. 121 (2016):
pp. 377–402.

396 how the algorithms actually work: Hitchcock, "Confronting the
Digital," p. 13. One of the most common problems is that optical-
character-recognition software cannot clearly "see" many of the
words in the original books and documents. They are garbled or
missing.

397   Too many scholars: The reductio ad absurdum of this way of work-
      ing is the increasingly common practice of citing the results of key-
      word searches as if they can sustain some claim about the content
      of archives or trends in scholarship. For a fuller discussion of the
      pitfalls of this practice, and the possibility of more rigorous analy-
      sis, see Cameron Averill, Ye Seul Byeon, and Matthew Connelly,
      "History Versus the Archive: What Do Historians Write About
      When They Write About the History of American Foreign Rela-
      tions?," seminar, Data for Good, Nov. 11, 2020.

397   the most revolutionary advance: As Anthony Grafton, then presi-
      dent of the American Historical Association, has observed, "The
      Future Is Here: Pioneers Discuss the Future of Digital Humani-
      ties," presentation, 126th annual meeting of the AHA, Chicago,
      Ill., Jan. 6, 2012.

397   realization of Ranke's dream: The data for all the experiments
      described in this book is available both at History-lab.org and
      through an Application Programming Interface (see History-lab
      .org).

Archives and Online Databases

The American Presidency Project, University of California, Santa Barbara (https://www.presidency.ucsb.edu).

The Avalon Project, Yale University (http://www.avalon.law.yale.edu).

R.D.W. Connor Papers, Louis Round Wilson Special Collections Library, University of North Carolina at Chapel Hill.

The Digital National Security Archive, ProQuest.

Dwight D. Eisenhower Presidential Library, Abilene, Kans.

Federation of American Scientists (https://fas.org/issues/government -secrecy).

The Foreign Relations of the United States (Washington, D.C.: GPO) (https://history.state.gov/historicaldocuments).

Founders Online, U.S. National Archives (https://founders.archives .gov).

Gerald R. Ford Presidential Library, Ann Arbor, Mich.

Jimmy Carter Presidential Library, Atlanta, Ga.

John F. Kennedy Presidential Library, Boston, Mass.

Lyndon B. Johnson Presidential Library, Austin, Tex.

Papers of Daniel Patrick Moynihan, Library of Congress, Washington, D.C.

The National Security Archive (https://www.nsarchive2.gwu.edu).

ProQuest History Vault (https://hv.proquest.com).

Ronald Reagan Presidential Library, Simi Valley, Calif.

U.S. Declassified Documents Online, Gale Cengage (https://www.gale .com/c/us-declassified-documents-online).

U.S. National Archives, College Park, Md.

Index

Page numbers in *italics* refer to figures and illustrations.

Illustration Credits

278 Courtesy of the author
285 Newscom, used with permission
291 Associated Press, used with permission
303 Courtesy of the author
348 National Archives
349 National Archives
354 National Archives
356 Courtesy of the author
359 Library of Congress
360 Courtesy of the author
363 Public Interest Declassification Board
365 William B. McAllister et al., *Toward "Thorough, Accurate, and Reliable": A History of the Foreign Relations of the United States Series*
366 Courtesy of the author
381 Courtesy of the author

A NOTE ABOUT THE AUTHOR

Matthew Connelly is a professor of international and global history at Columbia University, co-director of its social science institute, and the principal investigator at History Lab, a project to apply data science to the problem of preserving the public record and accelerating its release. He received his B.A. from Columbia and his Ph.D. from Yale. His previous publications include *A Diplomatic Revolution: Algeria's Fight for Independence and the Origins of the Post–Cold War Era* and *Fatal Misconception: The Struggle to Control World Population.*

A NOTE ON THE TYPE

This book was set in Janson, a typeface long thought to have been made by the Dutchman Anton Janson, who was a practicing typefounder in Leipzig during the years 1668–1687. However, it has been conclusively demonstrated that these types are actually the work of Nicholas Kis (1650–1702), a Hungarian, who most probably learned his trade from the master Dutch typefounder Dirk Voskens. The type is an excellent example of the influential and sturdy Dutch types that prevailed in England up to the time William Caslon (1692–1766) developed his own incomparable designs from them.

Composed by North Market Street Graphics,
Lancaster, Pennsylvania

Printed and bound by Lakeside Book Company,
Harrisonburg, Virginia

Designed by Soonyoung Kwon